The Matter of
WALES

JAN MORRIS

THE MATTER OF
WALES

EPIC VIEWS OF A
SMALL COUNTRY

Photographs by Paul Wakefield

OXFORD UNIVERSITY PRESS
New York

Text © Jan Morris 1984
Photographs © Paul Wakefield 1984

First published in 1984 in the United States by Oxford University Press, Inc.,
200 Madison Avenue, New York, New York 10016
First issued as an Oxford University Press paperback, 1986

Oxford is a registered trademark of Oxford University Press

British Library Cataloguing in Publication Data

Morris, Jan
The matter of Wales.
1. Civilization, Welsh
I. Title
942.9 DA711.5
ISBN 0-19-215846-5
ISBN 0-19-504221-2 (pbk.)

Printing (last digit): 9 8 7 6 5 4 3 2 1
Printed in the United States of America

Contents

Prologue   1

Map *by Denys Baker*   7

A Note about Language   8

  1. The Nature of Things   9

  2. A Long History   45

  3. Holy Country   75

  4. In the Mind   125

  5. Towards a National Character   163

Interlude   205

  6. The Order of Things   213

  7. Earning a Living   247

  8. Building Wales   289

  9. Wales and the World   317

  10. The Neighbour   347

  11. The Resistance   385

Epilogue   421

Further Reading   427

Index of Names   431

Cyflwynir y llyfr hwn
gyda chariad a diolchgarwch
i'w destun

This book is dedicated
with love and gratitude
to its subject

Prologue

BROODED over by mist, more often than swirled about by cloud, drizzled rather than storm-swept, on the western perimeter of Europe lies the damp, demanding and obsessively interesting country called by its own people Cymru, signifying it is thought a comradeship, and known to the rest of the world, if it is known at all, as Wales. It is a small country, in many ways the archetype of a small country, but its smallness is not petty: on the contrary, it is profound. Intense and unaccommodating continuity is the essence of the place, and if its frontiers were ever to be extended, or its nature somehow eased, its personality would lose stature, not gain it.

You must look hard to find Wales in an atlas, for it is a peninsula not much larger than Swaziland, rather smaller than Massachusetts, inhabited by a mere 2.75 million people. Also it is so obscurely tucked away there, in the heart of the British archipelago, that many maps fail to name it at all, and as often as not people elsewhere have never heard of it, or at best assume it to be a municipality somewhere, or a lake in Florida. Its image is habitually blurred: partly by this geographical unfamiliarity, partly by the opaque and moody climate, partly by its own somewhat obfuscatory character, which is entrammelled in a dizzy repertoire of folklore, but most of all by historical circumstance.

For though Wales is a country, it is not a State. It has a capital city, but not a Government; its own postage stamps, but not its own currency; a flag, but no embassies; an indigenous language, but not indigenous laws. All this is because, though it is surrounded on three sides by sea, on the fourth its border marches with the powerful kingdom of England, and for some 700 years it has been absorbed into the political entity of Great Britain, with its seat of power in London. The King or Queen of England is willy-nilly the sovereign of Wales, and the heir to the British throne is formally entitled Prince of Wales. England's Government is Wales's too, and that is why Cymru is marked so unobtrusively, in English, upon the smaller-scale maps, and why you will not find it listed among its peers, the Guianas and the

I

Bechuanalands, the Icelands and the Timors of the international rosters.

Yet Wales remains not only a separate nation, but a distinctly separate and often vehement idea. It lies there uneasily between England and Ireland, nurturing its individual culture, defending its own ancient and creative language, in the shadow always of its tremendous suzerain. It is an anomaly and an anachronism: like an ember glowing always at the back of an old grate, when the household has long since turned to central heating. Often hated and generally scorned by the English, the Welsh have fluctuated down the centuries from arrogance to self-doubt, from quiescence to rebellion, and today only a minority of them actively fight for their national identity, or even speak their native language; yet despite the overwhelming proximity of the English presence, a force which has affected the manners, thoughts and systems of half the world, for better or for worse Wales has not lost its Welshness.

For better or for worse, because this abstraction is certainly not to all tastes—not all Welsh tastes, even. In some senses Wales may be an epitome of the small country, but it is certainly not all traditional charm and cowbells. Its activists have long believed themselves to be of a special breed, and they have some of the exhausting resilience of Afrikaners, Jews and other chosen races, seldom behaving as passive provincials, on the edge of things, but rather as campaigners in the very eye of history. The ideal Wales, Welsh patriots feel, is the ideal nation, and from the dignity of their 8,000 square miles they often talk of all that the Welsh way of life has to offer the world at large.

It is not mere braggadocio. Their history really *is* special, and their communal memories are as old as any on earth. Nobody knows who were the original inhabitants of Wales, the people of the Stone and Bronze Ages, but the first historically identified settlers in the country were Celts from the European continent. In the centuries before the rise of the Roman Empire the Celtic peoples dominated wide regions of Europe, in a shifting and centrifugal kind of way, from Turkey in the east to the British islands in the west. Warlike, artistic, quarrelsome, ill-organized, showy, flighty, witty, headstrong, over many generations they were subdued by the expanding Roman imperium, and mostly assimilated into the Roman civilization. Gradually they abandoned their manners, their methods, their languages, until when the Romans themselves lost their supremacy, and the various tribes of Goths,

Angles, Saxons and Teutons in their turn seized the hegemony of Europe, recognizable Celtic societies survived only in the far west, in those territories of the Atlantic seaboard which are known to this day as the Celtic fringe.

And of those territories, only one emerged from the experience of Rome with its Celticity more or less intact. The Romans never reached Ireland, the westernmost Celtic territory. They did however occupy Wales, not it seems much disrupting the ancient social arrangements of the place, but introducing the Welsh people to their own well-ordered style of life and government, and to the first glimmerings of Christianity. The triple heritage that resulted, of Celticness, of Rome, of the Christian faith, the Welsh were to honour for centuries to come. Among all the Roman possessions of the western Empire, only Wales was never overrun by its heathen successors, and Welsh literature was the first in all Europe to emerge from the debacle. England fell to the Angles, the Saxons, the Jutes and the Franks: Wales never did, and the Welsh accordingly came to see themselves as inheritors of Roman urbanity and Christian devotion, and as trustees of a lost Celtic civilization which was to become ever more marvellous in the imagination, peopled by ever more heroic heroes, inspired by saintlier saints, until the very dream of it became part of the whole world's consciousness in the legendary paragon of King Arthur. Wales was the folk-memory of Europe!

Its people shared the fissiparous tendencies of the Celts, and were generally divided among themselves into several rival kingdoms; but as the Saxon power spread across England, obliterating the Celtic culture there even in its last strongholds of the north and the south-west, the people of Wales also came to see themselves as the last of the true Britons. Only they, in the end, spoke the ancient British language, presently evolved into Cymraeg, Welsh: only they honoured the customs and traditions which had flourished all over the British Isles before the Romans came. They considered themselves the only natives of the soil, of the spirit too, and this conviction made a nation of them. The Saxons never did succeed in subduing them, and the boundaries of Wales established in the Dark Ages remain its boundaries today.

Presently the Normans came, though, moving swiftly into Wales after their conquest of England in the eleventh century, and after the freebooting barons came the Anglo-Norman kings to clamp the little country once and for all beneath their vast authority, and half-smother its culture with their all-conquering English language. So it was that the Welsh, one of the first of the nations, in the age of the Nation-States never did become a State, but were to remain ever after a kind of subject people, displaying all the characteristics of their condition —torn between cultures, languages and loyalties, uncertain of their true identity, divided even among themselves by conflicting notions of patriotism or national interest.

But so it was too, by the laws of challenge and response, that they never lost their sense of separateness and specialness, never allowed their language to die, and never altogether abandoned their perennial vision of a golden age, an age at once lost and still to come—a vision of another country almost, somewhere beyond time or even geography, which has remained ever since a distillation of history and imagination, poetry and hard fact, landscape and aspiration, and which we may call, in the absence of any more exact definition, the Matter of Wales.

Once, once only, this old intuition was translated for a few years into political reality. These were the years of Owain Glyndŵr—Owen Glendower to the English—the most compelling of the emblematic heroes of the Welsh resistance. Rather more than a century after the English conquest of Wales Owain, a prominent North Wales land-owner, rose against the Crown, and between the years 1400 and 1410 united almost all the Welsh behind him in a desperate guerrilla war of independence. Others had made a political unity of Wales before him, but none had inspired the ordinary people so, or given that unity a meaning not just political, but intellectual or mystical too. For those few years it seemed that the nation, small enough to feel itself a tribe or even a family, might yet fulfil itself, so late in the day, in its own style and to its own traditions.

The rebellion was defeated in the end, of course—geopolitics made it inevitable—and the Welsh were bound more firmly than ever beneath the English dominion, but Owain's wild and romantic explosion of resentment was to be remembered by Welsh people ever after as a glimpse of that other age, that other state of being, which was embedded so deeply in their fancy. 'Not even in his darkest hour', wrote Professor J. E. Lloyd, Owain's chief biographer, five centuries later, 'was any one found to betray him to his foes . . . for the Welshman of all subsequent ages, Glyndŵr has been a national hero.' He is honoured still today, and his rising is idealized as the one grand moment of Welsh national completeness.

Hard-headed historians see it in a different light, disparage its motives, deplore its effects, and present it as just another regional disruption in a period of distress and disaffection all over Europe. They are too late, though. Legend is far stronger than academic analysis, and Owain was long ago transmuted into a figure of myth. We see him to this day larger than life, the very image of the Welsh identity, slaughtering the English on bloody battlefields, undertaking adventures of picaresque effrontery, ranging the country north and south with his unconquerable Welsh guerrillas, *Plant Owain*, Owain's Children. We see him treating on equal terms with French kings and English earls, and stamping his Great Seal upon the decrees of his own Welsh Princedom. We see him advised by seers and heralded by comets. Above all we see him followed to the end by the mass of the Welsh people, united in loyalty, triumphant in their own ways, refulgent, far back there in the popular memory amidst their own music, poetry and holiness.

Such is the power of historical suggestion. What became of Owain Glyndŵr nobody quite knows. In the best legendary way he disappeared from history, to be confused in after-years with Arthur himself as the once-and-to-be saviour of the nation. By now he is more than a man, but an instinct. He is the Welshness in all Welshmen, whether they consciously acknowledge it or not. He is the spirit of their origins. That he achieved nothing material in the end is only apposite, for if there is one constant to the Welsh feel of things it is a sense of might-have-been, tinged sometimes with despair. When Welsh patriots think of Owain Glyndŵr, they tend to feel a mixture of pride, sadness, defiance, hope and longing: and when they speak of him to Englishmen, even now into those cool Saxon eyes there often enters just the same sceptical half-amused irritation that Shakespeare's Hotspur expressed, when he spoke of Owain Glyndŵr's skimble-skamble talk, and declared him more tedious than a smoky house.

So this old champion's misty figure, and his brief years of achievement, have come to represent some crystallization of Welshness. His vision of the country, at least as I interpret it in artistic hindsight, was a vision of the place as a human entity, not just a country but a nation, not just a State but a fellowship, and a culture, and a heritage, and a sense of home, and a reconciliation of time, in which the affairs of the remotest past might overlap the present and embrace the future. This is my conception too of the Matter of Wales. I see it not as a continuum, but timeless, one kind of Welshness blurred into another, one influence absorbed into the next, the whole bound together, often unconsciously, by the age, strength and fascination of the Welsh tradition, and the spell of the Welsh landscape.

In this book I have accordingly used as a symbolical index the story and the purpose of Glyndŵr, looking at the country always not so much through his eyes as in his company. He is present throughout the work, even when I do not mention him, and if he is hardly an unbiased monitor, he is certainly a mighty guide. A folk story from Llŷn, the north-western peninsula of Wales, tells of a householder who has made the acquaintance of one of the *Tylwyth Teg*, the Fair People, the Other Ones of Welsh lore. When the Welshman expresses a desire to see the homeland of the *Tylwyth*, normally invisible to mortals, he is invited to place his foot on top of the fairy's: immediately, by virtue of the contact, an altogether unsuspected world is revealed in a chasm in the ground before him, with all its crowded streets and fertile fields, its smoking chimneys and its gleaming rivers twisting to the sea.

I would hesitate before stepping upon one of Owain's buskins—he was a hot-tempered man, besides having, so his enemies swore, supernatural powers—but perhaps we may acquire some similar insights just by standing at his side, and sharing his perspectives. Perhaps then we may glimpse for ourselves, through those lowering skies and drifting rains, the organic force of Wales that he so briefly liberated long ago, time, place and people all conjoined: and by putting the whole of it between covers, mark the country more distinctly upon the map of our minds—a small country, but seen in such circumstances, in such epic company, bigger than it seems.

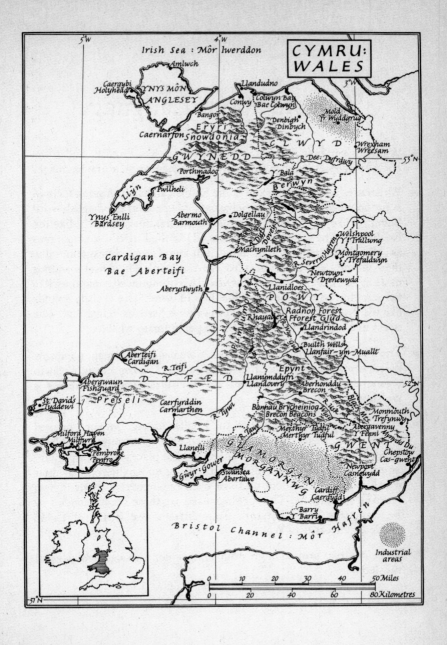

A Note about Language

- Wales is a bilingual country. Everybody speaks English, and some 500,000 people also speak Welsh, most of them as their first language.

- Welsh uses several letters not in the English alphabet. Among them *ch* is pronounced as in Johann Sebastian, *dd* like *th* in the English word 'them', *ff* like the English *f,* and *ll* something, but not much, like the English *thl.* The vowel *w* is pronounced like the English *oo,* sometimes as in 'book', sometimes as in 'loom'. The vowel *i* sometimes sounds like the *e* in 'me', and sometimes like the *i* in 'win'. The vowel *u* sounds more or less like the vowel *i.* The vowel *y* is pronounced sometimes like the *u* in 'but', and sometimes like the *i* in 'slim'. The Welsh *f* sounds like the English *v,* and the Welsh *g* is always hard, as in 'garden'. The stress in a word generally falls on the penultimate syllable.

- The Welsh word for Wales is *Cymru. Cymro* is a Welshman, *Cymraes* a Welshwoman, *Y Cymry* are the Welsh people, *Cymreig* means Welsh in a general sense, *Cymraeg* means the Welsh language, *Cymreictod* is Welshness.

- Many Welsh places have Welsh and English names. Both are indexed in this book. In the text both are used at first mention of a place: thereafter the Welsh is preferred, except for places which are internationally known by their English names, or so Anglicized that their Welsh names are seldom used, or even remembered, by their own deprived inhabitants. The spellings used are those recommended by the Language and Literature Committee of the Board of Celtic Studies, University of Wales.

- Welsh poetry is printed in the original, together with a generally literal translation.

1. The Nature of Things

We stand first with Owain Glyndŵr upon his own particular ground, at Sycharth in Powys near the English border. It is hardly more than a grassy tump now, with a moat around it, and some fine old trees, but it is full of suggestion. Here the hero spent the easy years, a Welsh landowner rooted in his own acres. Here he was chieftain of the countryside. Here were his farms and water-meadows, his rabbit warrens and his fishponds, and here he entertained friends and strangers, so the poets tell us, as generously as a Welsh gentleman should. Owain's rising against the English began as a squabble over land rights, and even when it erupted into political insurrection it remained a strongly territorial struggle, impelled by a powerful sense of place. In time Owain himself came to embody that sense, his personality mystically confused with the personality of the landscape that nurtured and remembered him: and so as we stand in his presence on the mound at Sycharth, in the heart of the physical estate that was to grow into an imaginative kingdom, before we see what man has made of Wales, we will first consider the nature of things.

To look at, the nature of Wales is deceptive. Within its small expanse the style of terrain changes so often, the mountainous countryside is so constantly corrugated, this way and that, by ridges, valleys, lakes and passes, the sea appears so often, and so unexpectedly, at the ends of vistas or around the flanks of hills—the scene in short is so cunningly variegated that it sometimes seems not natural at all, but like some elegantly conceived parkland or domain.

It is not all of equal beauty, of course, and large parts of Wales have been mutated by tourism and industrialization, but in natural terms it is a wonderfully well-proportioned country. Nothing is too big, nothing lasts too long, and there is perpetual variety. It is only some 130 miles from the northern coast of Wales to the southern, only 40 miles from east to west at the narrowest point—a day's drive one way, a couple of hours the other. Yet within this narrow compass there are places that feel rather like India, and places not at all unlike Australia, and places that remind one of Wyoming or northern Spain, and many places that are, with their especial piquant blend of age, damp, intricacy and surprise, altogether and unmistakably Welsh. Let us survey, for an opening look at organic Wales, three or four textbook specimens from this cheek-by-jowl variety of the rural landscape.

The most famous first: the view of Yr Wyddfa, Snowdon, the highest mountain in Wales, from the waters of Porthmadog Bay, looking over the artificial embankment which there crosses the estuary of the Glaslyn river. This grand prospect is like an ideal landscape, its central feature exquisitely framed, its balance exact, its horizontals and perpendiculars in splendid counterpoint. Cloud generally drifts obligingly around the crags of the mountain, and lies vaporously in its grey gulleys; in the green-and-blue foreground swans swim, cormorants dive, cattle really do stand up to their hocks in the shallows of the estuary, as in old water-colours, and the hussocked grass of the saltings is overlooked by gentle green woods on either side.

It is the classic illumination of Wales, being not much like anywhere else on earth. The bare Welsh mountains have few peers, and the illusory scale of them is peculiarly indigenous. That noble peak before us, one of the most celebrated of mountain forms, is only 3,500 feet high, and you could easily fit the whole landscape, its rocky eminences, its winding river, its woods and its salt-flats, into one of the lesser Alpine glaciers. It is a dream-view. It is as though everything is refracted by the pale, moist quality of the air, so that we see the mountain through a lens, heightened or dramatized. 'There is no corner of Europe that I know', wrote Hilaire Belloc, wondering at it from the deck of his yacht, 'which so moves me with the awe and majesty of great things as does this mass of the northern Welsh mountains seen from this corner of their silent sea.'

Next to the south, to Pont ar Fynach, Devil's Bridge to the English, a favourite among lovers of the picturesque since Victorian times, and still to be approached, if you arrange things properly, by the antique steam train which puffs in summer up the sinuous valley of the Ystwyth from the coast. We are still within 75 miles of Yr Wyddfa, but we might be in a different continent—might indeed easily be visiting a lesser-known summer station of the British Raj, high in the Punjab hills perhaps, or among the tea gardens of Sri Lanka, so lush and tumbled is the environment about us now, and so neo-tropical the ambience.

It is true that the Hafod Arms Hotel, with its flamboyantly overhanging eaves, consciously contributes to this effect, and that the refreshment pavilions and picnic sites dotted here and there, though jammed with cars and coaches in the tourist season, would be perfectly compatible with mem-sahibs. The exotic suggestion, though, comes from the site itself, the precipitously wooded slopes of the valley that falls away below, the rich, thick, humid-looking foliage, the smell of pine and damp moss, the brownish hill-ridges protruding above the woods, and far away beyond the rustic fencing and woodland walks, the distant white froth of waterfalls slashing through the forest, so excitingly violent, so apparently remote, that upon their rocks one can almost make out the slender poised figures of aboriginals with fishing-spears.

Only another twenty or thirty miles, and we are in the hinterland they used to call The Great Welsh Desert. There can be a terrific solitude to the bleak and featureless slabs of highland which form the inner massif of this country. Up you climb, from coast or valley, up through the foothill pasture-land, fenced with barbed wire and speckled with sheep, crossing cattle-grids now and then (resonant rattle of wheels, disconcerting vibration of steering wheel) until you reach the crest of the ridge; and there, stopping your car on the stubby beast-nibbled grass at the side of the road, you see before you the gaunt heart of Wales sweeping away ridge after ridge from Gwynedd down to Glamorgan.

It looks immense, and there are dark rectangles of conifer forest here and there, and vast cloud-shadows swing slowly across the counties. No towns show, no villages even, only a few white farmhouses tucked away with their outbuildings in the flanks of hills, and the only sound is the steady drone of a tractor somewhere out of sight. It feels uninhabited, more or less, and it looks roadless, and the mountains to the north, snow-capped very likely if it is winter, look like the inaccessible peaks of some other country altogether: yet nothing is far away really, every valley down there is snugly farmed, and almost nowhere in that whole wide wilderness would you be out of reach of a cup of tea.

Hallucinatory grandeur, romantic exoticism, Outback emptiness —and finally, away to the south we may find lowland landscapes of a Loire-like gentleness: where the Tywi river loiters among its dairy farms towards the sea, say, or the meadows shelter in the lee of the Epynt moors. These are hardly dramatic prospects, but rather wistful —landscapes for impressionist painters, and summer evening reveries, and picnics, and country race meetings, and market days.

There are castles about, in such a pastoral Welsh setting—probably not spectacular castles, but modest ones, crumbling on bluffs above rivers, protruding apologetically above car parks. There are thickets of beech or sessile oak, and neat fir plantations, and hedges meticulously layered. Gentlemanly streams sprawl through the countryside between shingly flats or wooded banks, small grey towns stand beside bridges, and the meadows all around are grazed by plump and genial Herefords. It is milk and salmon country, serene, constant: the heroines, monsters and fairy animals of Welsh lore frequent those river reaches, and are portrayed on jugs in road-side workshops by ecologically-minded potters.

Wales is no Arcadia, though, and the corners of the natural landscape that are most insidiously Welsh often come upon the traveller more unexpectedly, not as lustrous set pieces or sweet idylls, but slyly, and sometimes shabbily.

For instance, you may come across Wales absolute, Wales undiluted, in the very middle of the crowded industrial settlements of the south, when taking a side-lane among the terrace houses of some deep-sunk mining town on the valley floor, abruptly, in a few moments, you find yourself climbing a treeless moorland high above the pit-gears and the factory chimneys. Its rocks are a little blackened by so many years of smoke from the works below, but its bald contours, interrupted here and there by stony outcrops that might be volcanic, but might just as well be the constructions of Neolithic priests, are blurred by the damp mist with a true Welsh opacity, and scented by the authentic Welsh mountain smells of turf and bracken, water and wind: and a couple of half-wild ponies, as likely as not, their long manes tangled and unkempt, expectantly watch your approach up the winding pot-holed lane, hoping you will deposit some edible litter.

Or you may stray into some unregarded corner of the *cefn gwlad*, the back country of Wales, where the land seems so full of echoes, allusions and half-memories as to be almost metaphysical itself. At first sight such places seldom seem anything special—a glade up a green lane, perhaps, a thicket behind a farm—but they can be heady of sensation. Small twisted and lichened oaks may stand about, boulders are fuzzed with moss, crooked old iron fences are patched with wire mesh against the sheep, and the grass edges away into sedgy ditch or dewpond at the side of the track. Everything seems knobbly, bent, split or complicated: and even as you stand there, intrigued and perhaps a little disturbed by the sudden still of it, *caw, caw*, all at once like testy *genii loci* the rooks swarm tumbling and quarrelling around the high beech trees, and make you feel you are intruding upon something old, strange and confidential.

Or most elliptically, most microcosmically of all, the whole sensation of rural Wales can be concentrated into one small patch of ground, a foot or two square, if that ground is Welsh enough: if it is tufted and ferned and mossed enough, that is, if its slab of stone is sufficiently mottled, if the earth is properly peaty and the air slightly mushroomy, and if even as you stare at it, it is plunged into shade by the movement of the clouds above, while a great blob of Welsh rain falls quivering upon its boulder, and a sudden gusty wind swishes the reeds around its edges.

*

The substance of Welsh nature is largely rock, for some four-fifths of the surface of Wales is hard upland, where the soil is so thin that stones seem always to be forcing their way restlessly through, and it feels as though a really heavy rain-storm would wash all the turf away. The softness of the valleys, the calm of the low farmlands are only subsidiary to the character of the country: the real thing, the dominant, is hard, bare, grey and stony.

This means that the truest Welsh places offer experiences as much tactile as visual, for everywhere there are stones that seem to invite your stroking, your rolling, your sitting upon or, if you happen to be a Druid or a survivor from the Stone Age, your worshipping. There are thrilling clumps of jagged stones on hilltops, and stark solitary stones beside moorland roads, and stones gleaming perpetually with the splash of earth-dark streams, and stone walls which seem less like walls than masonry contour-lines, snaking away across the mountain elevations mile after mile as far as the eye can see.

Often the stones are warm to the touch—or if they are not actually warm, in the distracting atmosphere of a Welsh hillside curiously seem so—unguent, yielding objects, tinted often with green lichen: and sometimes they are hollowed out into caverns, immense underground chambers of the southern hills, with frigid lakes and pavilions of crystal stalagmite, or dark little half-caves, formed by the toppling of boulders in the sides of hills, within which the sheltering sheep, over the centuries, have worn themselves declivities in the black damp earth, and are to be discovered half in sunshine or drizzle, half in shade and dry, chewing the cud like complacent householders.

Watch how a Welsh farmer picks up one of those boulders! It is as though the two of them are flesh and blood. A preliminary flexing of the shoulders, a bending of tough stocky legs, a bit of a grunt, and the thing is up in his arms like a baby. The ancient constancy of the stones provides a permanent consolation to Welsh people. Whether they are suffering from political grievance or economic distress, whether they are homesick far away or lonely at their own firesides, the great old shapes provide a kind of reassurance. Read almost any work of Welsh literature and you will feel the hills shadowing its pages, sometimes more live than the characters, and it is no surprise that probably the best-loved of all Welsh poems, by the nineteenth-century railwayman John Ceiriog Hughes, celebrates in a mixture of triumph and elegy the comforting eternity of the stones:

Aros mae'r mynyddau mawr,
Rhuo trostynt mae y gwynt;
Clywir eto gyda'r wawr
Gân bugeiliaid megis cynt . . .

The mighty hills unchanging stand,
Tireless the winds across them blow;
The shepherds' song across the land
Sounds with the dawn as long ago . . .

But the stones can be eerie too. Set in a niche in the churchyard wall at Llanllyfni in Gwynedd a rather froward-looking slab peers out across the windswept graves. If you get down on your hands and knees you can just make out an inscription on it, but it will not make you much the wiser, only perhaps a little uncomfortable. Y GARREG A LEFA O'R MUR, it simply says—THE STONE CRIES FROM THE WALL.

Beneath the Welsh stones treasures lie. Most of the wealth of this country is streaked and layered among its rocky subsoil—gold, lead, tin, manganese, iron ore, copper, coal—and much of its character too is dictated by the presence of the underground. The Celts used to sink deep shafts to reach the earth-gods, and Welsh lore is full of the life of the nether-world, in the most ancient of the folk-tales as in the superstitions of modern miners. Tunnels run everywhere in Wales, if we are to believe the local fabulists. Hidden hoards are all over the place—even in 1975 a man who was pitchforked and burnt alive on a pile of straw in Llanrwst, Gwynedd, was generally supposed to have cherished the secret of a buried treasure. Countless figures of Welsh mythology stumble into hidden labyrinths, are lured down pot-holes, or spend long years in subterranean states of being.

Hearing a knock on the kitchen door one night (for example) Twm the farmer finds there a strange little man in green, and obliges him by giving him a bowl of milk. As a reward for his kindness, the stranger tells him, if he goes to the ash grove on the mountainside he will find a secret cavern full of treasure. 'Take your fill!' says the fairy, 'but pay only one visit, never go back again!' Twm goes where he is told, finds the great pile of gold within the cave and staggers back to the farm with as much as he can carry. Very soon, however, he fritters it all away in reckless living, and disregarding the fairy's warning returns to the wood for more. Hunt though he may, he cannot find that treasure-cave, and while he is away up there looking for it, lo, his house down the hill and all he possesses are consumed by a raging fire, and he is left far poorer than ever he was in the first place.

For they are often bitter gods below, and illusory heaps of gold: the sleeping heroes never wake, Twm is left weeping on the hillside. Nor are these allegories unjust, for all those minerals in the rocks have not made many Welshmen rich. A totem all too true was the pit frame which, in the heyday of King Coal, dominated every community in the mining valleys of the Welsh south. It stood there beckoning but unlovely among the rooftops, and night and day, with a whirring of its spoked wheel and a chuffing of its steam gears, it sent its cage-loads of Welshmen plummeting towards the earth-gods, like so many cheerful propitiations at five bob a day.

As for the water of Wales, it is ubiquitous. Millions of tons of it pour out of the heavens. This is one of the wettest corners of Europe, and the rainfall annals are full of proud statistics: at Llyn Glaslyn in Gwynedd 246 inches fell in 1922, ten times the London rate, while at Cowbridge, Pontfaen, in Glamorgan, in 1880, the heavens opened one day to deposit 2.9 inches in 30 minutes, the greatest half-hour load of rain ever recorded in Britain. Wales is soaked in rain, and its uplands spout with a myriad springs, and squelch with numberless morasses.

Out of these high sources the water seeps and pours its way down the valleys to the sea, assembling its energies as it runs, and transforming itself out of the soggy squash of the moors into the sparkling streams, the dizzy waterfalls, the rivers rich in salmon, trout and sewin, which bring a rich freshness to every part of this country. You can hardly move a mile in Wales without coming across rivers. Sometimes they travel only a dozen miles or so in their headlong descent from mountain spring to ocean: sometimes they move more stately towards their estuaries, gathering majesty as they go, and nurture towns along their banks, and are crossed by venerable bridges, until they debouch all mud, docks and eel-traps into Bristol Channel or Liverpool Bay.

They are the life-bringers of Wales—'rivers', wrote the lyrical Edward Thomas in 1911, 'that cut across my childhood with silver bars, and cloud it with their apple flowers and their mountain ash trees, and make it musical with the curlew's despair and the sound of the blackbird'—rivers, reported the practical John Leland in the 1530s, which 'oftentimes dronith in Winter divers Menne for lakke of a Bridge'—rivers so dominant that whole regions of Wales are known as *Rhwng Gwy a Hafren*, 'Between Wye and Severn', or *Rhwng Dwyfor a Dwyfach*, 'Between Dwyfor and Dwyfach'—rivers so essential to the identity of this country that almost all are still known by their ancient indigenous names (the one great exception being the Severn, which relatively early in its course deserts Wales for England, and whose Welsh name, Hafren, means 'trollop').

The main river system is simple enough. Five major rivers flow southward, two northward, two westward, and all the lesser rushing or meandering streams are hardly more than spill-overs from their watersheds. The Welsh lakes are much harder to grasp, for they are strewn at random over the whole country, 500 of them at least, and range from dark reed-fringed tarns of the high mountains to ceremonial Victorian reservoirs with castellated pump-houses, or the lily-fronded pleasure-ponds of country houses. There are lakes as unrewarding as Llyn Terfyn, 2,000 feet up in the Eryri mountains, of which even the greatest Welsh lake enthusiast, Frank Ward, can only say that 'it runs dry sometimes and does not contain fish'; but there are also lakes of sparkling charm, and no Maggiore, no Annecy is livelier than the spectacle of Llyn Tegid, Bala Lake to the English, on a bright summer afternoon. At one end of this long oval lake rise the wild summits of the Aran mountains: at the other stands the market town of Y Bala, a straggly group of grey houses around its shopping street. Between the two the lake, when the day is right, is Dufy-like in its innocent vivacity, the water so greeny-blue, the meadows around so comfortably wooded, the harsh uplands at the southern end so severe by contrast, while the bright sails of yachts flicker all over the mere, flags fly and oars splash, and along the eastern shore a little steam train of *Rheilffordd Llyn Tegid*, the Bala Lake Railway Company, trundles its complement of two boxy coaches from Y Bala to Llanuwchllyn.

Often all you can see of a Welsh lake is a distant inaccessible glint in the hills, when the sun catches its surface: often the first you know of a Welsh waterfall is an apparently static white streak, high on a vertical cliff, which does not at first look like water at all, but more like a tall white rock, until as you approach it more closely you can just make out a curious rocking motion to it. The waterfalls of Wales are small enough in scale, but they can be strangely splendid in character. The most famous of them all (and there are thousands) is called Pistyll Rhaeadr, which means in effect Waterfall Cataract, so powerfully did it affect the ancients: it manages to be at once quaint and dramatic, for though it rushes over the lip of its plateau with a grand plume, to fall some 240 feet to a foaming pool below, part way down its white course it disappears for a moment behind a natural rock bridge, for all the world as though its descent has been planned by the same nineteenth-century landscape improver who built the rustic refreshment room among the trees below.

There are bogs in Wales, of course. Half the country is waterlogged really, for much of the time. Sometimes on a mountain you hear the boom and gurgle of unseen water deep beneath your boots, and everywhere there are sedgy expanses of ground, half earth and turf, half water, in which the bog-plants blossom and the marsh insects proliferate. In satellite photographs of Wales the biggest of them, Cors Fochno on the western coast, Cors Goch near Tregaron inland, show as great patches of rot or mould upon the surface of the land, and at ground level too they sometimes look, when you come across them unexpectedly out of the hills, as though some catastrophe has blighted them. Marsh gases occasionally emerge from such Welsh wetlands, giving rise to popular rumours and commotions. In 1694, we are told, a vapour 'resembling a weak blue flame' rose from a marsh near Harlech, in Gwynedd, and roaming at night time pestilentially over the countryside, set fire to barns and hayricks, and infected the grass with noxious vapours: on the other hand in 1908 a group of German scientists working at Cors Goch were able to illuminate their entire laboratory with the gases they captured from the ooze.

Legends have attached themselves over the ages to almost every body of water in Wales. The Englishman Daniel Defoe, touring the country early in the eighteenth century, soon learnt to discount most of them: of Llyn Syfaddan, for instance, Llangorse Lake in Powys, he simply reported that 'they have a great many Welsh fables, not worth relating'. Ancient reputations linger all the same, and tales weird and disturbing attach themselves still to many Welsh waters. Several lakes are claimed to be bottomless (though the most celebratedly unfathomable, Llyn Glaslyn, turned out when it was finally plumbed to be only 127 feet deep, while the deepest of them all, Llyn Cowlyd, has been sounded to

229 feet). Many another is said to be without any form of life, or alternatively to be inhabited by monstrous eels, or one-eyed fish. Some are said to bewitch passing travellers, and drown them, and we are assured that over the dark waters of Llyn Idwal in Gwynedd no bird will ever fly.

The most persistent theme of all the tales is that of inundation. Glittering cities, say the fables, lie beneath Welsh waters, bells are heard hauntingly from the deep, towers are glimpsed by fishermen far down among the waterweeds. There can be substance to the fancy. The remains of a prehistoric stilted village at Llyn Syfaddan give a frail confirmation to one of Defoe's rejected legends, and now and then our own times have ironically turned tradition into prophecy: for in several parts of Wales modern reservoirs have drowned entire communities, and when their water levels are low sometimes you really can see the rotting shells of houses and chapels jutting from the mud.

Here is the best-known of all the drowning tales. Long ago, in the days of the Independence, Robyn the harper went to play at a princely banquet, in a magnificent palace in Gwynedd. The occasion was splendid, the company grand, and Robyn sang and played to perfection. As the hours passed, though, he felt something ominous in the air. The prince was not a good prince, being dissolute, cruel to his subjects and vicious to his neighbours, and there surrounded his palace that night some sense of impending retribution. As he played Robyn gradually became aware of a voice sounding in his ear. It was the voice of a small bird that hovered about his harp. 'Be gone', said the bird, over and over again, 'be gone, vengeance is coming, vengeance is coming.' The harper played on none the less, and the evening grew gayer and more tumultuous, more depraved too, and again and again the bird whispered the warning in his ear—'be gone, be gone . . .'.

So when the revellers began to sink into drunken sleep or orgy, Robyn took his harp and went out into the dark. A terrific gale was blowing out there, the night was black and wild, and before long he lay down beneath a hedge and went to sleep, with the voice echoing still in his ear—'vengeance comes, vengeance comes . . .'. All that night the great storm blew, but Robyn slept through it huddled in his cloak; and when he awoke in the morning it had all died away, and a strange calm lay over Gwynedd. He looked down the hill towards the palace, whose lights had burnt so brightly the night before, but there was no sign of it. All was gone. The waters of the mountains had burst their bounds, and all those splendours, all those flags and luxuries, were covered by the still waters of Llyn Tegid—around whose shores on stormy nights the sounds of gaiety may still be heard, and in whose green depths, by moonlight only, you may sometimes glimpse the golden baubles of the palace towers.

Then there is the sea. You are never more than 50 miles from the sea in Wales, yet even so it is often a surprise to find it there. Strangers entering Wales from England, and driving through the close-packed highlands of mid-Wales, may feel themselves to be in an almost continental setting, so dense is the terrain of the mountain centre. Range after range they seem to cross, valley after valley they traverse, every horizon blocked by lofty ridges: until at last, though they know all the time that the sea awaits them, still it comes as a queer shock when, passing through a last defile, they find it lying there before them. The sea! And not just generic sea, but specifically Welsh or at least Celtic sea, for its colour is likely to be green or gun-metal, over it a fitful western light is shining, beside it the stone walls of the sheep-runs descend mesh-like to the edge of the cliff, and above it, if they have chosen their route scrupulously, there stands one of the grey castles of the Welsh sea-shore, derelict but still watchful across the bay.

The coast of Wales is dramatically varied. In some places it is rocky and romantic, with high bird-swarmed cliffs and spindrifts of spray flying helter-skelter over the heather. In others wide and level sands run away from river estuaries, or there are pebble beaches with rims of seaweed and plastic flotsam, or the immense stretches of mud that line the Severn estuary, where the rise and fall of the tide, as much as 45 feet sometimes, is exceeded only by tides in the Bay of Fundy. And in the north-west the mountains of Eryri, Rhinog and Llŷn come superbly down almost to the sea's edge, so that late on a summer evening, when they stand there deep blue against the sky, and the lights of the farms and seaside towns speckle their mass above the darkening water, it all looks incongruously like some very different landfall, beach of Lebanon, olive-shore of Cyprus . . .

Aesthetically the great merit of the Welsh sea itself is that land generally shows across it. On the west coast the great indentation of Bae Aberteifi, Cardigan Bay, a half-moon cutting so deeply into the land that it nearly bisects the country, ensures that every seascape is visibly shore-bounded—by the peninsula of Llŷn to the far north, by Penmaendewi, St David's Head, to the south, by the long sweeping foreshore of Dyfed and Gwynedd. In the north you can look over the estuary of the Dee, the Dyfrdwy, to the Lancashire coast of England; in the south, where the Severn estuary opens into the Bristol Channel, you can see the undulating shores of Somerset and Devon; and up in the far north-west, if the weather is fine, magically across St David's Strait show the hills of Ireland, a dim compelling streak along the western horizon.

Islands always appear out there, too, for the coast of Wales is strewn with them, from vicious little rocks with lighthouses on them, like the Bishop and Seven Clerks off Dyfed ('they preach deadly doctrine', George Owen wrote wittily of them in the seventeenth century, 'to their winter audience'), to the great green isle of Môn or Anglesey, so productive that it has traditionally been called Mam Cymru, Mother of Wales, and still announces itself thus on road signs. Most of these islands are uninhabited, except for birdwatchers, occasional lighthouse keepers and a handful of monks, but since they are usually close to the shore their outlines are an everyday part of life to the people of the mainland: and most of them look quite quintessentially insular, the black tide-swept lump of Enlli in the north-west, the ominous chain of the Bishop and his acolytes, or Caldy, Ynys Bŷr off the Dyfed coast, with the tower and roofs of its Trappist monastery.

But they can be misleading. Among the most familiar of them is Flat Holm, a mile long by half a mile wide, which lies only four miles off the Glamorgan shore. Everyone knows the shape of Flat Holm. In spring it looks through binoculars like one lovely sheen of bluebells, with its white lighthouse perky at its southern point, and the boats of the weekend fishermen looking for cod and conger in its lee. Try visiting it, however, when a winter fog is coming in from the Atlantic. Then a peculiar shine surrounds its outline as you approach it, created partly by the gathering mist, but partly by the oily reflection of the water out there, which is thick with the alluvial mud of the river, and blotched with viscous eddies. Every half-minute the island fog-horn sounds, colossally reverberating through the mist, and answered by gloomy echoes far, far away down the Channel: and when you beach your boat upon the rocky foreshore this terrible noise blasts at you ever louder from the cliffs above, until the very ground seems to shake with it.

Flat Holm is not an island of happy memories. The murderers of

Thomas à Becket are supposed to be buried upon it, a force of marauding Danes was once left to starve upon it, it has been a fortress and a cholera hospital. On the spot, in the fog, all these morose allusions stir. The ruins of the cholera station stand there skeletonically, a couple of muzzle-loading guns are still toppled on their emplacements. Over everything a thick tangled scrub has grown, and amongst it lie in their scores the shattered and stinking corpses of seabirds. Boom, boom, like a torture that fog-horn sounds, as you retreat to the boat-landing, and get away while the ferocious tide allows: but as likely as not, by the time you get back to the mainland the fog will have lifted, and when you look back again the island lies there green and blithe amidst the dancing sea.

The presence of the sea deeply affects the nature of Wales. Far inland you may often smell the tang of salt, and see the trees bent with the long push of the sea-wind, 'soe that a straunger maye travell', as George Owen wrote, 'by the bendinge of the trees, as the Mariner dothe by his compasse'. Out of the sea have come ideas, peoples, treasures and disasters—war-bands, travelling saints, visiting giants, orange trees from wrecked galleons, wines from torpedoed freighters, Irishmen, pirates, even it is said the entire clan of Morgans, whose name means Born of the Sea, and who are sometimes said to be descended from mermaids.

And conversely into the sea, at one time or another, have gone sizeable chunks of Wales, for along this harsh western coast sea and land are constantly in tussle. Tales of catastrophic sea-floods, real or imaginary, haunt the Welsh folk-memory, and so many lives have been lost to the water that for centuries people in Gŵyr, the Gower Peninsula of Glamorgan, would never eat flat fish, those well-known scavengers of the drowned. Everywhere there are signs of the endless struggle. Sea-shore churches are wave-washed or choked with sand, like the unhappy church of Llandrwg in Dyfed, which is desperately boarded up against the dunes, or the church at Cwm-yr-Eglwys in the same county, most of which fell into the sea during a Sunday evening service in 1859. Even towns and villages are threatened. On the southern coast huge sand-dunes have already obliterated the medieval borough of Kenfyg, with its church and castle, loom ominously through the woods outside the hamlet of Merthyr Mawr, and look poised to continue their advance over the M4 motorway towards the settlements of the interior.

A small metal plaque near the altar of Goldcliffe church, in the lowlands of Gwent, laconically records the most disastrous of historically recorded floods. At nine o'clock on a January morning in 1606 the sea came suddenly storming over the flatlands there, running 'with a swiftnesse so incredible, as that no greyhound could have escaped by running before them'—'huge and mighty hills of water', as the contemporary chronicler adds, 'tumbling over one another'. The whole coastal plain of Gwent was flooded, entire villages were swept away and 2,000 people were drowned, but this is how that plaque records the event:

> 1606. On the XX day of January
> even as it came to pass the flud
> did flow to the edge of this same
> brus and in this parish theare was
> lost 5000 and od pownds besides,
> XXII people was in this parish
> drown.

Today the Gwent flatlands shelter behind a long sea-wall, and the villages are safe (though even now their old buildings often have a washed-through, dried-out feel to them). Elsewhere around the coasts of Wales, however, are reminders of lands lost permanently to the sea—stumps of blackened trees revealed at low tide, islets where cattle used to graze, legends still current in guidebooks and pub talk about broken sea defences or inundated towns. In 1864 Mr C. H. Hall of Liverpool reported to the Liverpool Geological Society the finding of a round tower, huge walls and a garden two miles out at sea off Dwygyfylchi, on the north coast, and innumerable less scholarly anecdotes tell of the Cantref Gwaelod the Bottom Hundred, a lost Atlantean province of the Welsh heritage which was drowned long ago by the Irish Sea—'cleene eatin away', Leland said, 'wher now the wild se is'.

The name of Cynfelin, Cunobelinus, Shakespeare's Cymbeline, is obscurely linked with this once fertile territory, which lay in what is now Cardigan Bay, and perhaps the legends look back to the days when a bridge of land really did unite Wales and Ireland. Of all the mementoes of the long sea-struggle, none are more suggestive than the *Sarnau*, the

Causeways, five strange ridges of rock which extend some miles out to sea from the coast, and which, though geologists claim them to be perfectly natural, have always been indulged in the tradition as constructions of the Cantref Gwaelod. They all have ancient names. Sarn Gynfelin remembers old Cymbeline, Sarn Badrig commemorates Ireland's patron saint; and when the tide is low, and the long black outlines of the *Sarnau* are half-revealed above the water's surface, they really do look like boundary walls of a lost land, or highways leading through the shallows to Ireland—clattered across long ago by gold-harnessed horses, and paraded by kings with great flags.

In the waters of Wales, around the rocks, life has probably existed as long as it has anywhere on earth. Certainly it was here, in 1964, that the oldest surviving life-form was identified—the organism *Kakabekia barghoorniana*, which was found near Harlech in Gwynedd, which looks like a microscopic orange slice, and which Harvard scientists declared to have been in existence for 2,000 million years.

The trees feel quite old enough. Much of the country is bare of them, but much is richly wooded, and several kinds of tree always had special meanings for the Welsh. The oak was the symbol of divinity, the rowan and the gorse would protect you against demons, the birch was the image of love, the alder the badge of kingship, the ivy stood for permanence, the honeysuckle for fidelity. In some parts a walnut tree was considered a prerequisite of domestic bliss, which is why, if you look hard enough around any old Gwent cottage, you are likely to find one somewhere.

They say that Wales was once covered all over with stout oaks, denuded down the generations first by house-builders, then by contractors for the British navy's warships. When Lord Nelson visited Gwent in 1802, he came to inspect the state of the fleet's raw materials, and as a result the famous oak tree at the village of Basaleg, said to be the biggest tree in Britain, was converted into 2,426 cubic feet of timber for the shipyards, then the most ever recorded from a single tree. Today the battleship oaks have almost disappeared. The wild oaks that remain, in small twisted thickets all over the country, are the stunted sessile oaks, with crinkled leaves and cracked-looking barks, and these are the most Welsh of Welsh trees now: they have a dogged but mysterious air, crouching there in the lee of the hills, or standing in contorted sentinel up farm lanes, their shapes are often cranky or goblinesque, and they have a look of wizened age that makes them proper partners to the caves and boulders.

The yews of Wales are suggestive too, and rich in allusion, like the twelve lugubrious yews of Llanelli in Gwent, which form a supposedly magic circle around the village church, or the bleeding yew of Nevern in Dyfed, which oozes a sticky sap immemorially supposed to be blood, or the old yew in the churchyard of Guilsfield, Cegidfa, in Powys, under which Richard Jones, Gent., when he died in 1707, caused to be placed this epitaph:

> Under this yew tree
> Buried would he bee
> For his father and hee
> Planted this yew tree.

In parts of the south there are grand forests of beech, and piquantly isolated here and there all over the country remain the stands of ornamental trees, redwoods and Japanese willows, hornbeams and exotic limes, planted by proud squires long ago, now all too often strangled by creepers, tangled undergrowth and rhododendron uncontrolled.

And marching inexorably upon them all, or so it often seems, come the armies of the conifer forests, whose geometrical splodges we saw from our high vantage point in the Desert of Wales. In half a century, hardly more, they have transformed the look of Wales, for they have sprung up suddenly, massed rows of larch, spruce and fir, wherever land can be acquired by the foresters—high on moorlands or in valley pockets, appearing abruptly, growing so fast, that in a few years huge areas can be made all but unrecognizable to the returning native. They are like invaders from some alien sensibility, for generally their woodlands take no account of the contour of the land or the style of the setting, but are planted in stern disciplined ranks of profit—the very opposite of the wrinkled coppices of little oaks whose place they have often usurped, or the lonely magic rowans of the Welsh memory.

There are moments among the landscapes of Wales, especially in the spring, when the whole country, sea-shore to mountain crest, seems to burst with animal life. Then even its quietest corners, so sparse in human population, acquire a tumultuous air. All over the mountain faces, their outlines so clear that they seem to stand two-dimensionally against the sky, the countless white blobs of sheep are disposed as in a naïve painting. Multitudes more graze the fields below, ewes meditatively munching, lambs hilariously butting each other, and long trains of cattle meander down lanes, and herds of ponies stand pictorially on ridges, and there are goats tethered at the road's edge, and flocks of geese in muddy fields, and cats pouncing in long grasses, and a solitary black and white sheep-dog, perhaps, hastens importantly home to his farmyard.

Around these domestic creatures, too, a host of wilder beasts gobbles, flaps, preens or pullulates. Buzzards soar high above the oak woods, ravens croak, rooks raucously congregate, kingfishers flash, house-martins flutter about cottage eaves, herons stand tense on river banks, hares spring from thickets—a woodpecker raps a tree somewhere, a flock of choughs wheels beneath a sea-cliff, herring gulls quarrel on garbage-dumps, porpoises leap in sheltered bays, salmon jump at weirs, thousands of flickering oyster-catchers swing in unison, like spindly little soldiers on the foreshore, to face the wind or escape the incoming tide. You may glimpse a badger waddling between the hedgerows after dark; you may watch the bats flitting over deep green river pools; you may catch sight of a fox streaking across a field towards his lair in the wood beyond. Seals lounge on many a rocky shore. Pine martens rustle the conifer woods. Generations of poor hedgehogs lie squashed in the tracks of cars, or are trapped in the pits of cattle-grids. And for every creature you see, hear or smell about you, think what millions more are hidden, stirring or sleeping, in lake or burrow, dingle or coppice in every square foot of this teeming little country!

There used to be more still. Beavers lingered here long after their appointed time: Defoe was told of their existence in the eighteenth century, but that was probably no more than folk-memory—their nibblings and gnawings are supposed to be at the root of more than one of those inundatory legends. Wolves are remembered in many place-names, like Bedd y Blaidd, Wolf's Grave, or Bleddfa, Wolf's Place: the last of the wild wolves of Britain are said to have roamed the Powys hills in the seventeenth century, and perhaps the last of all was the lonely survivor which, in the 1680s, kept watch in the dry moat of Chirk

Castle, Y Waun in Clwyd. Donkeys were ubiquitous not so long ago, hard at work on farms, in mines, on country roads, and in the nineteenth century people often went hunting on them. The last Welsh wild cat is thought to have lived near Usk, Brynbuga in Gwent, in the eighteenth century: but in rougher country parts to this day there are cats of the hedgerow which look, especially when their ears are back and their yellow eyes afire, of sufficiently direct descent.

And there have been other creatures not visible to all eyes, or heard by everyone, for this has always been a land of chimerae. Sometimes they are probably just distortions of memory or perception. The awful *afanc*, which ravaged the countryside around Betws-y-Coed in Gwynedd, until it was dragged over the mountain by oxen and deposited in Llyn Glaslyn—the *afanc* may be no more than a gigantic apotheosis of the beaver. The howls of the monstrous dogs still to be heard on winter nights may merely be last echoes of the wolf-packs, and the mermaids frequently glimpsed ('making a strange sneezing noise', reported a farmer of Llanychaiarn, Dyfed, in 1826) are almost certainly seals.

Others are harder to account for. What was the dread creature which, in the eighteenth century, allegedly seized a young swimmer in the high mountain lake called Llyn y Cau? What was the thing like a lizard which, at the turn of the present century, entered the mouth of a man of Clwyd, while he sat on a stile, and gave him hallucinatory visions? And Who, rather than What, was the Great Toad of Cors Fochno, the bog north of Aberystwyth, which was known to be the oldest living creature on the face of the earth, and which was consulted as the oracular repository of all knowledge—a misshapen hermit perhaps, a pock-marked witch, some grotesque green-clad ecstatic?

There is no questioning the identity of the Red Dragon, the ultimate chimera, for he is the national creature of Wales. Not only does he bestride the national flag of green and white, but he supports innumerable coats of arms, embellishes a host of logos, ennobles beer-bottles, dominates posters, is sold to tourists in a thousand guises, ash-trays to door-knockers, and has been emblazoned on the uniforms of Welsh soldiers for hundreds of years. Dragons twisted in ironwork, rampant on gateposts, give many a civic building of Wales its authoritative air: a musical apotheosis of the dragon is afforded by the organ at Usk Church, for every one of its pipes is moulded into a dragon's head, from the mighty monsters of the great diapasons to the squeaky infant creatures of the treble. Comical Welshmen dress up as the Red Dragon sometimes, and prance on to rugby football pitches, and the dragon welcomes every visitor to Wales on the road signs along the border—*Croeso i Gymru!* it says, sticking out its forked tongue and raising an admonitory claw—'Welcome to Wales!'

There have always been dragons in this country. Dragons, we learn from the medieval mnemonics called the Triads, were among the Three Things One Does Well to Hide, and the last live one was reported to have spent his nights in the church tower of Llandeilo Graban, in Powys, which does have a dragon-chamber near the top of it. Sometimes the dragons of Wales have been vile, sometimes very beautiful. The dragon called the *carrog* which gave its name to the village of Dol-y-Garrog in Gwynedd was so malicious that when at last it was hunted down and killed, even in death one of its teeth fatally poisoned a man who kicked its carcass. On the other hand the winged serpents of Llancarfan in Glamorgan, though they were as pestilential as foxes, were said to have crests that shone with all the colours of the rainbow, and wings like feathers of a peacock's tail, and when they were disturbed they 'glided swiftly, sparkling all over, to their hiding places'.

This is how the Red Dragon became the national beast of Wales. In the heart of Eryri in Gwynedd, a few miles north of Beddgelert, a hillock beside the road marks the traditional site of Dinas Emrys, an ancient seat of Welsh power. Here the king Gwrtheyrn, Vortigern, laid the foundations of a new capital, but hardly had his builders started work on it than all its stones disappeared. Repeatedly they tried, repeatedly their materials vanished, until the young Myrddin, Merlin the magician, disclosed the reason why. Dig beneath the ground, he said, and they would find a pool, and in the pool there would be a tent, and in the tent two sleeping dragons, one white, one red. They did as they were told, and there were the two dragons, and they awoke, and they fought each other, writhing in the tent and in the pool, until they disappeared from the hill. 'The white dragon is the Saxon,' pronounced Merlin, 'the red dragon is Cymrû, and so they will fight, the red against the white, until at last the dragon of Wales is triumphant over the dragon of the Saxons.' The king, he said, must build his city somewhere else: and so it is that while Dinas Emrys is only a wooded tump, with a public footpath up its flank, the Red Dragon lives on as Myrddin prophesied, still the champion of the Welsh, and still squabbling with its ancient enemy.

But others say that the Welsh Dragon is descended directly from the purple griffin of the Roman imperial banners, and that the Welsh national flag is therefore the oldest on earth.

First among the living beasts of Wales stands the horse, *ceffyl*, haunting, teasing and sometimes disturbing the Welsh imagination from the earliest times. What lovely grey stallions storm through the mysteries of the tradition! What spirited mares are spurred into the night by the eloping couples of the folk-tales! And what poignant partnerships were established, in life as in literature, between pit-man and pony in the deep Welsh mines!

There have been horses in Wales at least since the days of the Celtic chieftains, who went to the land of the dead on horseback: the greatest hoard of horse-trappings ever found in Britain, a marvel of buckles, bits and decorations from the Bronze Age, was found in Clwyd in the nineteenth century on a site that had always been called Parc-y-Meirch, the Horse Park. In the Triads the Three Chief Steeds of the Isle of Britain are listed as Tall Black-Tinted, Eager Long Fore-Legs and Red Wolf-Tread; in the thirteenth-century Book of Taliesin we hear of other great Welsh horses, Grey Tawny-Colour, Lively Full-Nostril, and most famous of them all, Black Moroedd, 'horse of Brwyn Wily-Breast'.

By the tenth century the place of the horse in Welsh life was codified by law. Five kinds of horse were officially recognized—chargers, hunters, hacks, pack-horses and draught-horses. A horse was not to be put to the plough—that was oxen's work—and if it was borrowed without the owner's permission the culprit might be fined fourpence for mounting it, and fourpence for every league he rode. Pedigrees were cherished. The poet Guto'r Glyn wrote of his Welsh cob in the fifteenth century that he was the son of Du o Brydyn ('Black of Britain'), that his mother was daughter to a stallion of Môn which had carried eight people, and that he was of the stock of Ffwg Warin's stallion, 'and that stock grinds its fodder small with its strong jaws . . .'. The nicer points of horseflesh were carefully analysed, too. A good stallion, wrote another horse-loving poet, Tudur Aled, in the following century, should have the poise and temperament of a stag, nostrils like a gun-muzzle, eyes like ripe pears, dancing in his head, small fine restless ears, wide forehead and a coat like new silk.

By the eighteenth century two specifically Welsh breeds of horse had evolved: the spruce, deft and lively Mountain Pony, the strong and stocky Cob. The pony carried the farmer around his business, conveyed the suitor to his girl, pulled the coal-wagons down the pits, rushed the results of the Irish lottery helter-skelter into England, and sometimes went between the shafts of gentlemanly phaetons—where he often neighed as he trotted along, quaintly enhancing the effect. The cob went to London, pulling so many milk-vans around the streets of the capital that he became known as 'the vanner', or put down miners' riots as the cavalry of the mounted police, or was crossed with Hackneys to produce ostentatious carriage horses for the aristocracy. Pony and cob alike were essential to Wales. The gorse which blossoms yellow everywhere was grown as a crop specifically to feed them; there were gorse-fields, gorse-stacks, and gorse-mills to crush the prickles into nourishment.

And by then of course the horse was stabled too in the folklore of the country. The wooden hobby-horse called Mari Lwyd, which means both Grey Mare and Holy Mary, stumped mischievously around the streets at Christmas time; witches turned themselves, or sometimes their victims, into black stallions; the mythology was full of horses magical or illusory, strong as Wolf-Tread, grand as Black Moroedd, learned as the well-attested nineteenth-century horse of Derwenlas in Powys, which reproved its own driver in purest chapel rhetoric for his drunken habits, heroic as the legendary pit-pony which, by leaning against a falling mine-wall, saved the lives of several miners in Glamorgan. Far away in Patagonia, in the nineteenth century, the Welsh explorer John Evans erected a monument to his indomitable mare Malacara, which had seen him safely through many perils: high on the Blorenge hill at home in Gwent, a century later, the Olympic show-jumper Harry Llewelyn buried his famous horse Foxhunter beneath a slab of stone on a windy ridge, with a plaque to mark the spot.

There are many places still where the tough Welsh ponies, with their sweeping tails and cocky ears, roam unattended over the moorlands, and give to the scene a haunting sense of constancy. Far across an empty bog you may see them, tossing their heads testily against the flies, or grazing in herds of five or six, like zebras, in the lusher grass beside the road. They are scattered across the wide saltings of Penclawdd in the south, distant silhouettes against the shining sea; they haunt the lonely crests of the Black Mountains, Mynydd Du, up to their hocks in heather and bilberry bush.

An aristocratic bearing often distinguishes them: this is because they were long ago cross-bred with Arabs, perhaps even in Roman times. Your properly native animal, nevertheless, is sturdily down-to-earth, bred out of hard work by harsh climate, and in many parts of Wales you may find the ponies labouring still. Even in the days of four-wheel drive it is common enough to see farmers herding their cattle on pony-back, or trotting the heather moors to check their sheep, their dogs streaking exuberantly around them, their shouts and whistles echoing across the stillness. And in the mountains of mid-Wales you may often discern strings of work-weary ponies, twenty or thirty at a time, looking for all the world like medieval pack-trains, but actually carrying tourists on pony-trekking holidays.

On the last Thursday in every month a horse-fair, said to be the biggest in Europe, is held at Llanybydder in Dyfed, several hundred animals changing hands at every meeting (and several score of them, it is sadly safe to assume, going straight to the slaughterers). Here you may see the association of horse and Welshman at its most intense, for on fair day the whole little market town thinks, plans, bargains and argues horse. There are horses parading around rings or exercise yards, there are horses jammed wild-eyed and hugger-mugger in stalls, there are horses ridden hilariously by urchins through the crowded streets, there are splendid hunters stalking out of Rover-drawn horse-boxes and there are doomed carcasses of cat-food being herded into trucks. 'This very strong fine animal', says the auctioneer, his amplified and distorted voice reverberating all over town, 'was working only yesterday up on the mountain', or 'Very very sweet natural pony, very easy to catch', or 'This animal comes from the very well-known breeder, you all know him ladies and gentlemen, Mr Tom Williams Pentwyn . . .'. Everyone does know him, too, for the horse-fair at Llanybydder is a recondite kind of club. Affectedly accented English-women in head-scarves, solemn Belgian breeders in raincoats, rubi-cund hill farmers, gypsy traders in speckled kerchiefs, rapscallion urchins, auctioneers, all seem to be old acquaintances, fellow-members: and even the horse, chained, haltered and beaten though it be, seems complicit to the goings-on.

*

The horse holds its own most heroically in the valleys of the extreme south, the coal valleys of Gwent and Glamorgan. Fifty years ago thousands of ponies were working deep beneath those valleys, living all their lives in underground stables: today there are no pit-ponies left below, though sometimes you may see a venerable survivor cherished in its retirement by some old colleague of the mine. Up above, however, the pony occupies a familiar and inescapable place in society still, and you find it all over the place, grazing in back yards, or in pockets of grassland among the factories, or on the very verge of trunk roads.

In the heart of the coalfield a hamlet called Llanwynno, a church, a pub and a couple of houses, stands curiously isolated in a forest glade above the blackened community of Mountain Ash. It is a shabby enough sort of place, its churchyard untidily toppled by subsidence, sheep scavenging fecklessly all around, but it is a favourite resort of valley families at Sunday lunchtimes, when the inn yard is full of cars and motor-bikes, and the air rich in beer, potato crisps and exhaust smoke.

Hang about there one Sunday until the pub closes for the afternoon, the crowd has gone, and all is silent on the hill, and you may experience an unexpected glory. From the jumble of outbuildings behind the inn there comes the sound of horse's hoofs, and perhaps a gentle whinny: and into the yard there emerges a young Welshman and his pony. The man is a lean, dark kind of Welshman, common in the valleys, Italianate of style like a huntsman in an old painting: the pony is like a thing of air, tense, eager, stag-like in balance as Tudur Aled would wish it; and out of the yard the two of them come, treading elegantly among the discarded crisp packets and the last uncollected beer mugs—until suddenly, almost silently, like the wind they fly away from the Brynfynnon Inn—figures straight from the old tales, light-footed over the sedgy grassland along the edge of the wood, above the coal-pits of Glamorgan.

If the horse flaunts and prances a way through the imagination of Wales, the dog, *ci*, runs always at its heels. The dog has been important here at least since the beginning of recorded history, and probably long before that too. Place-names everywhere recall the place of the hound in ancient Welsh society—Carnedd y Filiast, the Cairn of the Greyhound, Twll y Filiast, the Greyhound's Kennel—and of all Welsh legends the best-known is probably the story of the hound who sacrificed its life for its master's child, and whose sad fate is allegedly remembered in the name of Beddgelert in Gwynedd, Gelert's Grave. In the anthology commonly called the Mabinogion, the principal collection of medieval Welsh stories, we see the princes of the Independence with their dogs always at their sides, and sometimes too the Cŵn Arawn, the hunting-dogs of the Underworld, come baying and yapping through the forests. From these ancient breeds is doubtless descended the white Welsh hound of today, a gaunt patrician animal, high-rumped, crinkle-haired, who looks now more like a beast in an old tapestry than a real living creature, but still takes to the field with several of the Welsh fox-hunts (and perhaps dimly related to Cŵn Arawn, too, are the whippets of the South Wales miners, so assiduously exercised on Sunday afternoons that their owners used to be called *pobl y cŵn*, people of the dogs, as against *pobl y capel* . . .).

The dog has not only herded the cattle of Wales, and gathered its sheep, and rounded up its horses, and hunted its foxes, and retrieved its game-birds, and scrabbled away its badger-warrens; we also find it giving motive power to the churns of old farmhouses, diligently turning the spits of mansions and regularly accompanying its owners to morning service (whence it was sometimes ejected, if inattentive, with the long iron dog-tongs still preserved here and there in Welsh churches). The dog is an absolute essential of Welsh country life, no farm being complete, or indeed viable, without one, and even the towns of Wales sometimes seem to have almost as many dogs as humans: Haverfordwest, 'the doggiest town in the kingdom', really was alleged in the 1920s to have issued 6,000 dog licences for its 6,000 inhabitants.

There is a Welsh Springer Spaniel, a cheerful sporting dog, and a Welsh Terrier, which is used to hunt foxes in North Wales; and there is the low-slung Corgi, 'Dwarf-Dog', which was bred originally close to the ground for cattle-herding, nipping its way around the ankles of cows rather than leaping at their flanks, and wonderfully dextrous at avoiding kicks. Some visionaries claim this to be a Neolithic animal, bred in Wales since the beginning of all things, others believe that it was first brought by Vikings—there are similar dogs in Sweden: certainly for centuries it was the work-dog of every Welsh farm, herding, guarding and going to market with the drovers. There are two kinds of Corgi. The Cardigan Corgi has a long tail, and a belly that almost touches the ground: but it has long since been replaced in the public mind by the Pembrokeshire, which has slightly longer legs and hardly a tail at all, but which has been a favourite of the British royal family since King George VI acquired one in 1936, so that its ubiquitous presence at royal occasions, being gingerly lifted into aircraft by apprehensive aides, waddling on communal leads in royal parks, has given it a cachet far removed from the cow-muck and puddle-sloshes of its origins.

Everybody's idea of a Welsh dog, however, is that sheep-dog we saw pacing about his business down a country lane some pages back. He is a Border Collie really, originating on the border between England and Scotland, and is to be found in England and Scotland too, and in places like Australia and New Zealand where sheep-farmers have imported him. Welsh people nevertheless think of him as their own, and there is hardly a Welsh farm without him, and never a Welsh journey when you do not see him. There he sits outside the barn now awaiting new arrivals, tongue out, eyes fixed, crouching watchfully over his paws: and at the approach of your car his hindquarters wiggle a little, his ears prick forward, his weight shifts gradually to his front legs, and whoosh! there he is barking wildly, kicking the dust up and biting at your tyres as you drive into the farmyard.

He is a dog of excitable extremes. If he charges your car as though he wants to eat it, when you step out of its door, offering him a tentative hand and a word of ingratiation, instantly he is sitting there on his haunches with his tail wildly wagging, all a-quiver with goodwill. Your Welsh sheep-dog is often neurotic, and sometimes distinctly queer: though a particular blazing quality of the eye, which may put the imaginative visitor in mind of rabies injections, is often prized by shepherds as a sign of intelligent zeal, and used to be thought to mean that a dog could see the wind.

Anyway, out comes the farmer to greet you, and in a trice Mot, or Toss, or Sam, returns to his proper place in the yard, shaking himself a bit to get rid of the dust, and casting a baleful or perhaps reproachful glance at your car. If he looks a little foolish then, do not judge him hastily: wait until the afternoon, when he will be up on the mountain-side with his master, and when the slightest wispy whistle will trigger him magnificently into his real *métier*—whirling around the edges of the sheep-flock, chivvying the wanderers in the long grass, patiently squeezing the whole bewildered crew through a half-open gate or streaking far, far away up the craggy hill to marshal the last wayward stragglers towards the fold.

Cattle were sacred to the Celts—white cattle they appear to have been, whose descendants are still to be seen, long-horned between the oaks, in the parks of Dinefwr Castle in Dyfed, and Vaynol in Gwynedd. Like African tribespeople, the old Welsh numbered their wealth in such beasts, and paid their debts and taxes in them: in medieval writings we find a hawk worth twelve cows, a hunting-dog worth three, and a Golden Apple in a legend, a hundred cattle flat. The Welsh noun *da*, which means goods, or money, or for that matter goodness, also means cattle, and in some parts of west Wales even now they sum up a farm by the cattle it can support—*lle pum buwch*, for instance, 'a place of five cows'.

Later the powerful Welsh Blacks became the prime stock-beasts of Welsh farmers, and though these animals are outnumbered now by Herefords from England, Friesians and Charolais from the continent of Europe, still they above all other kine are the emblematic cattle of Wales. Until this century the Welsh raised huge herds of Welsh Blacks for the English market, driving them hundreds of miles out of the mountains to the fattening plains and the stock yards. They ploughed with Welsh Blacks, too, until the end of the nineteenth century, and pulled wagons with them sometimes, and there is still no creature more indomitably organic to the Welsh scene than a tough and stocky black bull, impervious it seems to rain or cold, broad-shouldered and straight-backed, four-square on his soggy pasture and looking more like a fighting beast of the corrida than any domesticated ox (the fierceness of Welsh Blacks used to be attributed to the prevalence in some parts of the aphrodisiac herb centaury, but at Trelystan in Powys they preserve the memory of a particularly terrible bull which was exorcized by a priest, reduced to the size of a fly and shut up in a bottle).

The pig too, *mochyn* in Welsh, is an old inhabitant. 'We claim,' bragged the first President of the National Welsh Pig Society, founded in the 1930s 'that there is no breed of swine older and purer than ours.' In Celtic mythology the pig was an important creature of the underworld, and a famous Welsh legend concerns the magician Gwydion who drove a stolen herd of pigs from South Wales to North: all the way across

Wales place-names preserve the memory of this celebrated exploit—Nant-y-Moch, Mochdref, Llanrhaeadr-ym-Mochnant, Mochras, and far up in the mountains of the north, Creuwyrion, the Sties, where the resourceful wizard finally housed his porkers.

The first of all Welsh pigs are supposed to have emerged out of the underworld, but they became homely companions of the Welsh household. In the southern coal valleys, well into our own times, many mining families raised their own pig in a backyard sty, and the annual occasion of its killing, when the butcher was called in to do the deed, was a moment of mixed tears and celebration; for though the salted pork and bacon was fine for the diet, the kind-hearted mining people often mourned the loss of a friend as the last sad squeal came from the bottom of the garden.

The Welsh sheep, *dafad*, is generally less sentimentally regarded, if only because there is no avoiding it: in quarry towns as in moorland pasture, statuesque on crags or degradedly fawning upon tourists at beauty spots, infuriating suburban gardeners, wriggling line ahead through infinitesimal gaps in fences, filling country highways in a solid woolly heaving mass or deafening the streets of market towns with bleats and baas on market day, wherever you go in Wales the sheep is there. Some 15 per cent of all the sheep in the entire European Common Market live in Wales (but only 1 per cent of the people). There are far more sheep here than there are human beings, and there is almost no Welsh environment to which they cannot adapt. Noble-looking or scraggly with burrs and torn wool, enchanting in lambhood or sly as Satan in old age, the sheep is the true familiar of the place, and even the passing of the seasons is illustrated most tellingly, in the Welsh countryside, by the old sequences of lambing, dipping, shearing and sale.

Sheep began to take over Wales in the Middle Ages, when monks introduced sheep farming on a big scale, but until recently they were even less socially disciplined than they are today, and roamed the sheep-runs altogether scrawny and disreputable. The eighteenth-century agriculturist Arthur Young could dismiss the average Welsh sheep simply as 'the most despicable of all types', while a judge at the Devynock Agricultural Show as late as the 1880s described the Welsh Mountain entry as 'a diminutive ill-shapen animal with its shaggy coat more reminiscent of hair than of wool'. Sheep of extremely primitive characteristics flourished all over Wales until the present century, generally horned, sometimes almost black, and behaving very like wild goats.

Tamed by selective breeding and agricultural education, your modern Welsh sheep is genetically most respectable, and has sent its relatives indeed all over the world. Plenty of breeds and sub-breeds survive, all the same—the archaic Dafad Rhiw, for instance, which lives only in the Rhiw area of Llŷn, and the Dafad Torddu, the Black-Bellied or Badger-Faced, and the half-breed Welsh Mule, and the Beulah Speckle-Faced, and the ornamental all-black sheep, and the Llanwenog, which has a prominent woolly tuft on top of its black face, like the last remnant of a unicorn's horn, and the Clun Forest which has black bare legs and big ears, and the Kerry Hill, which has emigrated in its millions from the hills of Powys to America, South Africa, Australia and New Zealand.

The still wayward master of them all is the Welsh Mountain Sheep, the Welsh sheep *in excelsis*, so adapted to the particular terrain and climate of this country that no misery of damp, no depth of snow, no treachery of marsh or cliff-side seems able to disconcert it. Often it is descended from many generations grazing the same mountainside, for the farmers try to breed their herds *cynefin*, 'familiar', to keep them manageable: and though the Mountain Sheep can certainly be infuriating sometimes, still this profound sense of association, coupled with its sometimes melancholy eye and disarming gentleness of expression, means that Wales could never be Wales without it.

Once upon a time, in the hills above Tregaron, Cadwaladr the goatherd noticed that the loveliest of all his animals, a nanny-goat most dear to his heart, was straying far along the mountainside. When he followed her she ran away, bounding mischievously before him, until as dusk fell he grew tired of the game and threw a stone at her in annoyance. It hit her in the head. She crumpled to the ground at once, but when in a misery of remorse he reached her, and cradled her head in his arms, she turned before his eyes into a beautiful woman.

'Cadwaladr,' this delectable creature breathed, 'I have found you at last'—and rising gracefully to her feet she led him once more up the mountain. It was dark now, a great moon was rising, and presently as he climbed he heard an astonishing sound in the distance high above—the bleating of thousands of goats in the night. Up the two of them went, over a ridge, into a gulley, and there sure enough was massed the greatest of all goat herds, bleating deafeningly and powerfully odorous.

A terrific he-goat stood at their head. 'Our king', whispered the girl, and she curtsied before him. The great goat stamped his hoof and looked sternly at Cadwaladr. 'So you are here at last', he brayed. 'Well, do you take this nanny-goat to be your lawful wedded wife?'—and even as he spoke, the woman seemed to turn almost imperceptibly back to goathood. 'I do not,' cried the appalled Cadwaladr, 'and after tonight I never want to see another goat again.' The listening herd seemed stunned. A fearful silence descended upon the mountainside, the girl-goat recoiled in horror, the clouds scudded over the moon, and the goat-king, lowering his immense horned head, launched himself at Cadwaladr in a mighty charge and knocked him head over heels down the mountainside. When he got home nobody recognized him, for he had been lost for fifty years.

Such is the Welsh reputation of *gafr*, the goat: formidable and a little sinister. The animal has always been symbolically associated with the country, in legends, in cartoons, decorating the covers of Victorian travel books or holding up armorial bearings in partnership with dragons. David Lloyd George, Prime Minister of Great Britain in the second decade of the twentieth century, was nicknamed The Goat not merely because of his virile habits, but also because he was Welsh, and since 1844 the mascot of the Royal Welch Fusiliers has always been a bruiser of a Kashmir billy, his horns tipped with silver, descended from a pair given to Queen Victoria by the Shah of Persia. It was an alcoholic goat whose example brought to his senses the hitherto besotted Rees Prichard, vicar of Llanymddyfri, Llandovery, in the sixteenth century and thereafter the author of a seminally spiritual manual. In the eighteenth century a peremptory noblewoman seized the goat of Evan Thomas the poet, and he responded with a properly outraged apostrophe to the lady:

> Black-maned, horse-haired unworthy one,
> What did you do to the goat, your sister?
> She had your father's horns, your mother's head—
> Why did you falsely put her in prison?

Goats were once very common in Wales. Thousands of them ran more or less wild all over the place—when in 1774 Mr Henry Thrale offered his daughter a penny for every goat she could spot on Yr

Wyddfa, his friend Dr Johnson kept the score, and recorded 149 in his notebook. In those days the goat was economically important, too, and the goats of Abergavenny, Y Fenni in Gwent, were especially valuable: their hair was used for wigs, their milk was dispatched by messenger to invalids and valetudinarians all over the place, and even their smell was cherished, for it was thought to be healthy for horses.

Today half the domestic goats of Wales seem to be kept by organically self-sufficient communes of English immigrants, but the honest-to-goodness Welsh farm goat has lately been enjoying a revival, while in several mountain parts there are feral herds, most of them released deliberately generations ago to nibble the grass from ledges dangerous to sheep: so that even now, in the highlands of Eryri, the remoter reaches of the Rhinog hills, or even on the headland immediately above the holiday resort of Llandudno, you may still come face to face, as you cross a crest or round a boulder, with the very same great-horned King of Capricorn that butted poor Cadwaladr out of his time.

Often enough, in the mountain country between Aberystwyth and Llanidloes, in mid-Wales, there circles above the highway, serene but distinctly predatory, the great droop-tail form of a red kite, *barcut* in Welsh, *Milvus milvus* in the ornithological textbooks. Its appearance there is a little miracle, for eighty years ago its kind was all but extinct in the islands of Britain, persecuted almost out of existence by farmers and gamekeepers. In 1905 only five birds were known to survive, in one remote corner of the Welsh hills. Gradually though, *barcut* fought back and modestly proliferated, some think by maintaining contact with kites on the European continent—in 1972 a kite ringed in Germany was found dead in Wales—and by now there are stretches of Welsh road where it is almost a surprise *not* to see one, gliding lordly above the heather, and totally unafraid it seems of the human species which so nearly obliterated it.

The red kite is the most spectacular of the Welsh birds (the golden eagle having disappeared in the 1930s). Several other species, though, have particular meanings for Wales. The owl is a leading character of Welsh art and literature, the buzzard an inescapable component of any any proper Welsh sky, and the Welsh cuckoo has always been more than just a bird: in the old poetry the orthography of his plaintive cry, *cw-cw*, *cw-cw*, also meant 'whither? whither?', and one hears the bird singing its own enquiring elegy when a bard laments the death of a kinsman or the loss of a hero in war. Welsh falcons were celebrated among medieval hawkers, especially those of Ynys Dewi, Ramsey Island off the Dyfed coast, which were discovered by King Henry II of England when he was *en route* to Ireland one day, and in consequence, like the corgis later, were in fashionable demand ever after.

The puffin has been used by the Welsh at one time or another as a supplier of feather-filled cushions, as an admissible diet during Lent and as bait for lobster pots. The huge kind of sea-goose called the gannet, often six feet in wing-span, has given fame to the island of Grassholm, eight miles out from the Dyfed coast, where its numbers have increased in just a century from twelve pairs to more than 15,000, making the bare and lonely rock the chief gannetry of Europe. The cormorant's only inland British nesting-place is the strange slab called Craig Aderyn, Bird's Rock, six miles up the valley of the Dysynni from the Gwynedd coast. This tall crag stood by the sea in ancient times, and the forty pairs of cormorants which habitually nest upon its face look rather like pterodactyls up there, so far from the ocean: while on a nearby creek sometimes two or three hundred visiting colleagues sit with wings outstretched in prehistoric attitudes, staring towards Craig Aderyn as though they are trying to figure out what on earth has happened.

But as the horse is to the beasts of Wales, *brân* the crow is to the birds, in all his variations. Not only are rooks, crows, jackdaws, ravens and choughs ubiquitous in Wales, even on the sea-shores, but the family is inextricably involved in the earliest myths of the Welsh origin. Bendigeidfran, Brân the Blessed (whose sister was Branwen, White Crow), was the most potent of all the heroes of antiquity, too big for any house, strong enough to make himself a bridge for his army to cross a river, so forceful that when he was decapitated his head assumed all its body's vigour, and was carried around loyally by his followers, providing excellent company. In the end it was taken to London, as the king himself instructed, and buried beneath the White Hill beside the Thames: and there, through convoluted declensions of tradition, allusion, symbolism and perhaps misinterpretation, Brân remains today personified in the black ravens of the Tower of London, which are fed there at the expense of the English Crown, and jealously guarded by Beefeaters.

*

The flora and fauna of Wales are nothing prodigious really. A few rare Alpine plants grow on inaccessible ledges of Eryri. An otherwise unknown vole inhabits the island of Skomer, and the rabbits of Ynys Dewi are flealess. The trout called the *gwyniad* is found nowhere except in Llyn Tegid and one or two smaller Gwynedd lakes (it has never been caught on rod and line, but you may inspect one pickled in a jar in a bar-room of the White Lion inn at Y Bala). The British black adder is confined to the great bog of Tregaron. The polecat, which thrives in the new conifer forests, used to be a rarity, but is rare no longer. The Atlantic salmon, whose Welsh name *eog* is a very synonym of virility, and which leaps up so many Welsh rivers to its mountain spawning grounds, is not a rarity yet, but may be one day, so relentlessly is it hunted along its migratory routes. Do not laugh at a Welsh toad—it will count your teeth as you do so, and they will fall out one by one!

But anyway it is not the rarity of natural life that is remarkable in Wales. It is the profusion of it still, its closeness and its constancy. It sings to you out of the morning, and wriggles with the toad-flax through rotting window-frames. When the landscape is enduring one of its periodical spells of depression, when the rain seems unlikely ever to stop, it is easy to feel that out there the whole of creation is sharing your gloom, a fellow-suffering confederacy of bedraggled sheep, huddled cows, dogs crouched in kennels, mice in holes, birds forlorn on telegraph wires and spiders clenched in dejection in the crannies of their webs. And conversely when the sun shines over Wales, the mountains are brilliant with heather and the sea glistens, then how gloriously the sap runs in humans as in little oaks!

The comradeship of man and beast has always been the subject of Welsh legend. Many an old Welsh holy person depended upon the friendship of the animals, for company as for evidence of miracles—St Beuno shared quarters with a curlew, for instance, St Melangell was the intimate of hares. Leland tells us of a miner in a Dyfed lead-mine who befriended a crow: one day the bird inexplicably stole his benefactor's purse, making off with it across the moors, but while the infuriated Welshman gave chase the walls of the pit fell in and all his colleagues died. It is said of Irddw, an otherwise forgotten prince of Llŷn, that when he was taken prisoner during a Crusade his friends the wild birds rescued him from the Saracens and carried him safely over the seas to Aberdaron.

Many communities of rural Wales still live intimately close to nature—among the central uplands, and more unexpectedly in farmlands along the English border, there are people leading lives that have not changed in fundamentals since the nineteenth century. The advent of electricity, the car and the telephone has hardly frayed their unbroken attachment to their own particular patch of soil, or their loyalty to the unwritten rural traditions, good or bad, that govern their affairs. Their ring of mountains, their few acres of valley floor, their *bro* and all the creatures in it constitute a world for them. One sometimes meets citizens who have never been further than their nearest market town: and when the snows come, and countless Welsh farms and hamlets are cut off from everywhere else, such people are not much put out, finding the truth of their own cosmology only confirmed by the turn of events.

The devotion of the Welsh to their land is proverbial, and homesickness is much the best-publicized of their national emotions—*hiraeth*, that sense of longing which has been sentimentalized in so many treacly songs, and has even given its name to a range of hills, the Hiraethog mountains of the north. There are few more rooted peoples than the country Cymry, many of whose families have doubtless lived in the same district, pursuing the same callings, for a thousand years and more.

Instinctively, then, Welshmen have striven towards a happy relationship with the earth itself, *daear* in the Welsh, emotionally, architecturally, professionally. The Welsh miner used to develop an uncanny rapport with the walls and tunnels of his pit, learning to recognize almost with affection its every creak or rumble. The Welsh farmer has traditionally built his farm in such organic conformity with the rocks around that it often looks hardly more than an outcrop itself, altered and expanded over the years just as a boulder sinks deeper into its soil, is layered with moss or lichen, or is cracked by the power of the frost. The Welsh poet has been inspired by a strong streak of animism, the conviction that God resides equally in all living things: beasts, birds and fishes figure in Welsh literature not simply as picturesque details or metaphors, but as principals, or at least accessories. In one of the earliest of all Welsh poems, indeed, a lyricist goes further than mere coexistence with the state of nature, but actually claims to have experienced animal-ness, bird-ness, fish-ness for himself—he was

43

born of a salmon he says, he jumped like a hare, he had been in his time toad and horse and cat . . .

Today half the people of Wales live in big towns and cities, but even so everything about them, even their urban politics or their industrial diseases, should be seen against this profound affinity with the nature of the place, which is something very different from mere patriotism, but is more akin to the territorial instincts of the beasts themselves, or the migratory urges of the birds. When the historian Gwyn Williams distilled his interpretation of Wales into a single book, he called it *The Land Remembers*. When the poet David Jones tried to express the meaning of Wales in verse, he saw it embodied in the substance of the landscape, as in the person of some slumbering hero:

> Does the land wait the sleeping lord
> > or is the wasted land
> that very lord who sleeps?

For there are moments, bitter moments of historical despair, when the Welsh patriot feels that the nature of Wales is all he can really call his own, his only true allegiance.

2. A Long History

Even in Owain Glyndŵr's day, nearly six centuries ago, the history of Wales was long, and the people were intensely conscious of it. Mankind by then had made many a mark upon that wild countryside, and an obsession with the past, real or imaginary, was already one of the characteristics of the Welshman. When he urged his followers into battle against the English, Owain offered himself as a reincarnation of the oldest Welsh glories, reaching far back into the half-truths of the Dark Ages, and even further still, back to the times before the Romans came, to the misty priests and chieftains of pre-history. His campaigns took his raggle-taggle armies through all the monuments of the Welsh story, hill-fort to monastery—seizing the past itself consciously or unconsciously into his cause. Then Owain was recognized as the embodiment of ancient prophecies, foretelling the emergence of a liberator for Wales: today Welsh patriots cling to the idea of him as a historical compensation, or a pledge of fulfilments yet to come.

WALES is enormously old, old in geology, old in humanity, but its history is unusually explicit. The detritus of the ages is all around, from mysterious litter of the primitives to the abandoned mining gear of yesterday. The hill-forts are still there to camp in, the castles to occupy or deface, and the geography of the country, complex but compact, makes the past particularly easy to understand. One can see precisely why a castle was built where it was, or how an industry was linked with its markets, and local events of remote antiquity are often recalled with an easy familiarity. Many a Welsh legend, having taken its hero on adventures romantic or exotic, brings him back like Cadwaladr the goatherd to a time that is not his own: and so it is often in the Wales of everyday, where the old often seems contemporary, and the new is streaked with immemorial suggestion.

Here is an example. In a flank of the mountain called Yr Eifl, above the sea in Gwynedd, a grey cluster of ruined stone huts shelters unsuccessfully from the wind. They seem to be crowded together for comfort, and they are protected too by a long stone wall undulating over the hillside. Some of the buildings are mere piles of stones, some are recognizably houses, and there is a track leading up the mountain to the site, with the grass-covered remains of a gateway. High on the summit above a great stone cairn marks the spot.

This was a settlement of the prehistoric Welsh. It is called Tre'r Ceiri, generally interpreted as Town of Giants, because as the centuries passed, and people forgot who really lived up there, imagination peopled it with beings larger than ordinary life. Yet wandering around it is not at all an eerie experience. It feels rather homely, actually, despite that wind down the gully, and one can quite comfortably fancy the comings and goings up the track, the shouts of the watchmen at the gate, the cattle grazing in their stony enclosures, the kitchen fires smoking into the sky, the squabbling Neolithic children and the barking aboriginal dogs. The climate of Wales is anything but preservative in a physical sense, but it is marvellously retentive metaphysically, and the *mana* of such old Welsh sites, their sense of life and movement, magically survives the ages.

This is partly because the Welsh people have, as a people, never moved. Their conquerors have never shifted them, and the line of their possession is as direct and unbroken as any nation's on the face of the earth. The inhabitants of Tre'r Ceiri came from stocks so ancient that nobody can swear to their genesis, yet even in our own century anthropologists have claimed to identify their descendants, in Welshmen of a particular gait, build and cranium: the long heads of the western moorland people, a prevalence of blood group B along the Tywi valley—these are said to be tell-tale traces of the original Cymry, come to this country from Heaven knows where.

The Stone Age, the Bronze Age, the early Iron Age, pass through the Welsh memory like a blurred dream. We know nothing of the people really. We do not know what they looked like, what they believed, how they lived, what they wanted of life. Yet we feel their presence constantly, for all over Wales they have their monuments: crumbled stone villages and turf-covered hill-forts—queer circles of boulders on isolated moors, astronomically aligned perhaps, or ritually conceived —burial chambers, cromlechs, whose great stone uprights and massive capstones make them look like gigantic fungi—spectral field systems, still to be discerned when the light is right—and most haunting of all, the single enigmatic boulders, brutal or elegant, which stand here and there all alone on empty landscapes, as markers, as memorials, or perhaps as warnings.

One such stands near the head of a shallow pass in the hills above Ystradfellte in Powys. The country there is treeless, and the road winds slowly out of the farmlands towards the high massif of Bannau Brycheiniog, the Brecon Beacons. At first sight Maen Llia, Llia's Stone, looks like an illusion, something on the windscreen possibly, or even a flaw in your eye—a thin black vertical line apparently incised on a deserted moor. As you get nearer, however, it becomes almost too real, and grows both in size and significance, until when you draw alongside it, and see it finally in silhouette against the sky, like the huge blade of a buried dagger, it seems to draw your attention off the road ahead with a deliberate fascination, as though its erectors had charged it with some mesmeric energy of its own.

But it was perhaps just a memorial really, or a guide-stone for the wandering herdsmen and war-bands of the ancients. In modern times cattle-drovers have used the megaliths as marker-signs and meeting-points, and walkers and exercising soldiers often align their compasses upon them, but nobody really knows why the people of the stones put them up in the first place. If anything the immanent mysteries of those forgotten peoples, the slow passage of their ages, the laborious development of one culture out of another, can be glimpsed more revealingly in the myths of Wales. Sometimes the old races are thought of there as giants, sometimes as Irishmen, come from the misty shoreline we sighted from the coast of Gwynedd: and we may recognize vague memories of them no doubt in the persons of the *Tylwyth Teg*, the Fair People—the *Bendith y Mamau* or Mothers' Blessing, the subjects of King Gwyn ap Nudd, Gwyn son of Mist, whose homes were generally accessible only through caves or holes in the ground, or under lake-surfaces.

Perhaps the last of those Neolithic peoples hid themselves in caverns or lake-dwellings; perhaps they had their own shadowy kings, and revealed themselves only on dark nights, or in fleeting glimpses, terrified by the technology of later immigrants, but themselves supposed, as primitives often are, to possess arcane wisdoms of their own. All these ideas, anyway, are detectable in stories like the legend of Llyn y Fan Fach, a small lake in the foothills of Mynydd Du, the Black Mountain of Dyfed. The lake has now been converted into a reservoir, with a small dam, and a keeper's cottage below; but it is still a long rough trudge up the track to the edge of the water, and the lake itself, enclosed within a huge curving wall of precipitous shale, is still suggestive enough of unseen beings and immemorial happenings.

The story, which is a long one, concerns a farmer, a lady of the lake and a herd of magic cattle. The farmer falls in love with the lake-person, and she is permitted by her father, an indistinct amphibian, to leave the lake and marry him, taking all her cattle with her. Only one condition is imposed by the patriarch, namely that if the young man strikes her three times with iron, he will lose her for ever. For years all goes well, and the bride teaches her husband much of the lore of the lake, which is mostly medical, and he becomes a well-known doctor in those parts. However, three times he does deal his wife an iron blow: once when he flings a horseshoe at her in a temper, once when he makes her trip over a pot, once when he slams an iron gate in her face: and at the third time, though they have been married for years and years, silently she leaves the house, and summoning her lovely white cattle to follow her, returns to the water and is seen no more.

Surely she is a figure of the enigmatic Neolithics, still opaquely remembered, as through a veil, by the story-tellers of later generations. The metal which sent her home is a recollection, perhaps, of the technique by which one people, having leapt the gap from the Bronze Age to the Iron, overcame another. The cattle may be rumours of some extinct and fecund breed. The grim father-figure is an image of ancient chieftains. And that body of medical wisdom, brought by the lady from the green depths of the lake, is a suggestion of the secret powers, holy or satanic, superstitiously attributed always to the people of the circles and the standing stones.

Such are our dim memories of the first Welsh. We see far more clearly the Celts who are thought to have moved into the peninsula during the third and fourth centuries before Christ: not because they left more revealing structures—they left almost nothing but hill-forts—but because the Romans knew them, and described them for us.

Ethnically they were the same people as the Gauls, having crossed into the British islands, it seems, in two separate migrations—one from northern Europe, which has supposedly left its blood-stream in the tall, big-limbed Welsh type of the north, the other from the Iberian peninsula, whose descendants are said to be your stocky, dark South Walians, all verve and sudden passion. Four principal tribes settled in what is now Wales: Demetae and Silures in the south, Deceangli and Ordovices in the north, and by the time the Romans arrived these people had become, so to speak, the metropolitan Celts. The religious and cultural focus of the Celtic race, subdued on the continent of Europe by Roman power, had retreated into Wales, and particularly into the far north-western island of Môn, 'the Isle of the Glory of the Powerful Ones'.

This remote place thus became a centre of resistance to which Celtic partisans might look from all over Roman-occupied Europe. In its sacred oak groves the Celtic identity was concentrated, and the champions of a great civilization stood at bay in the heart of their remaining territories. In Môn lived, worked, schemed and taught the Druids, the necromantic priests of Celticism, with their marvellous store of memorized knowledge, their command of ritual and animist dogma, their mystic hold over the public will and their alleged altars of human sacrifice. There sang the bards, the propagandists of the culture, who could inflame the people into frenzied excesses of pride. There were the warriors with their tall crested helmets and their chased shields, woad-painted, their hair grotesquely thickened with lime-wash, attended by tall dogs, riding in chariots.

The Romans entered Wales in about the year AD 50 and fought their way with difficulty towards this Celtic Berchtesgaden: not until AD 59 did they stand at last upon the Menai Strait, the narrow stretch of water which divides Môn from the mainland of Gwynedd. We do not know exactly where they made their crossing of the strait, which is nowhere more than a mile wide, but we do know just how they felt when, arriving upon its flat green shore and looking apprehensively over the water to the island beyond, they saw the Druids, their captains and their followers lined up on the opposite bank. 'At this sight', says the historian Tacitus frankly, 'our soldiers were gripped by fear.'

The setting has hardly changed since then. Behind the Romans rose the noble range of Eryri, the most dramatic mountain mass they had set eyes on since they left the Alps. Around them the moist meadows ran gently to the foreshore, with shoals and mudbanks jutting into the strait when the tide was low. The opposite shore lay placid and tantalizingly close, with shingle beaches here and there, thickets of oak and beech almost at the water's edge, and occasional small creeks spilling into the strait: and the scene is likely to have been bathed in a flat, dead, unwavering sort of light which is particular to the Menai, and which gives the place even now an air of constant expectancy.

Over the water it really was a fearful spectacle. The warriors were ranged along the water's edge 'like a forest of weapons'; the Druids stood with their heads raised to the sky, howling curses; and all around ran shrieking women, 'like furies', all in black, with hair wildly dishevelled and lighted torches in their hands. Even the Roman commanders, Tacitus tells us, hesitated before crossing the strait into such an apparent madhouse: but they were not the masters of Europe for nothing, and paddling across on rafts, swimming their horses, wading where it was shallow enough, the legionaries fell upon the Celts of Môn, slaughtering or capturing every one. All the holy altars of the Druids, all the magic groves of their culture were destroyed.

So at a stroke the authority of Druidism, with its wealth of inherited lore and wisdom, was expunged from history. Its culture was essentially oral, transmitted by memory, and it was rapidly dispersed, or confused hopelessly in the folk-consciousness with the Giants of Tre'r Ceiri or the kings of the standing stones. Only in much later years, when its truths had long been obscured in myth, was it to catch the imagination of the Romantics, and inspire the Welsh to lofty reinterpretations of their origins.

From time to time, when they are draining a lake, building an airfield or repairing a road, Welsh workmen unearth marvellous Celtic objects: shields, cauldrons, gold necklets, embossed plaques of beaten bronze, iron fire-dogs with bulls' heads, tankards and elaborate harness-fittings. Whenever this happens it is like a transmutation, the sudden turning of one element into another, and when the artefacts go on display in glass cases they shine there like things plucked out of the imagination. The Celtic legacy in Wales has mostly been insubstantial, if not actually fictional. The gleam of bronze in the lake-bottom is more often the glimmer of fantasy in a fairy tale, or a poetical flash: what the Victorians used to call the Celtic Mist drifts fitfully over Wales as it drifts over Ireland, obscuring the truth in a veil of uncertainty.

Undoubtedly the wonderful body of Welsh folk-tale, though mostly written down in medieval times, is descended from the oral tradition of the Celts, and Welsh poetry, too, often seems Celtic in its sensibilities. For centuries the Welsh retained a strongly Celtic dislike for town life, preferring to live not even in villages, but in dispersed homesteads, and they retain still a Celtic kind of centrifugal instinct, a suspicion of centralism or formal control: just as the Celts never did coalesce into a nation, but remained in coagulations of separate tribes, so the University of Wales is scattered through five widely separated campuses, while the festival called the Eisteddfod Genedlaethol, the National Eisteddfod, the supreme exhibition of the Welsh culture, has no permanent home, but moves from year to year, alternately in South Wales and in North, from site to site across the countryside.

It is a hazy heritage perhaps, and over successive centuries many another culture has been superimposed upon the Celtic, many another strain introduced into the blood-stream. Yet the Welsh still like to think of themselves as Celts, and often attribute their own merits, and sometimes even their own faults, to their Celtic temperament. The pageantry of that National Eisteddfod is enthusiastically modelled, if only in fantasy, upon Druidical ritual: its president is called the Archdruid, its governing council is the Gorsedd or Assembly of Bards, members assemble for its ceremonies in robes and hoods, maidens dance with flowers and mistletoe as in the sacrificial woods of Môn.

There are cultural links too with the other Celtic peoples, the western Scots, the Irish, the Bretons. A Celtic film festival is held in Caerdydd, Cardiff, and every year in the Gwynedd town of Dolgellau you may hear the assorted bagpipes, harps, flutes and poetic declamations of the Gŵyl Werin Geltaidd, the Celtic Folk Festival. The Celtic language has long been split into two streams, the Brythonic and the Goedelic; but though Cymraeg, Welsh, no longer has much in common with the Irish and Scots Gaelic languages, the Goedelic branches, Welsh-speakers find it relatively easy to understand their fellow-Brythonians, the Bretons of western France (and easier still to converse with the last survivors, or rather revivers, of the lost Cornish vernacular).

Even ethnological cynics must detect among the Welsh attitudes and responses different from those of other European peoples, which can be attributed partly of course to the accumulated effects of history, but partly too to the ineradicable Celtic strain. The notorious deviousness of Welsh people, for example, finds its exact imagery in the convoluted art forms of the Celts, which depended upon illusory circles, disturbing knots and bafflingly inconclusive squiggles. There is a sort of Celtic fluidity to the outlook of the Welsh: for example an often free-and-easy attitude to names, which allows people to spell their names in an English or a Welsh way, almost indiscriminately, to call anyone by a nickname, or virtually to abandon their own names in favour of poetic pseudonyms—in Welsh papers poets are often referred to simply by their lofty bardic names, and only initiates can identify them as plain Mr Jones or Tom Evans the schoolmaster. We can recognize in the modern Welsh just the same volatile mixture of flamboyance, wild courage and easy discouragement that the Roman writers reported among the Gallic tribes. The love of music, poetry and provocative conversation, still headily apparent among Welsh people of all kinds, was well known among the ancient Celts, and from their day until our own the learned man and the artist have been honoured in Welsh society as among few other peoples of the West.

Another detectably Celtic trait is a certain sense of the dream of things, a conviction that some other state of being exists, invisible but sensible, outside our own windows. To patriots of mystic tendency this is the truest manifestation of the Welsh identity: and though outsiders frequently scoff at the fancy, and believe it to be compounded of sentimentality, religiosity, purple prose and too much alcohol, it can be traced soberly enough to the animism of Celtic thought, which found the divine in every leaf and tree, which knew the spirits of the running streams, and believed the next world, like the last, to be with us all the time.

The Romans would have no truck with such enigmas: they brought to Wales not only their own robust pantheon of gods, lusty Venus to fighting Mithras, but also the first speculations of monotheism, the very antithesis of Celtic belief. Nothing could be much less Druid-like than the Roman Army.

The conquest of Wales was difficult, and was never complete—most of Wales remained a military zone throughout the Roman occupation. For years the great Celtic leader Caradog, Caractacus, led a fiery Welsh resistance, until he was captured and sent to Rome, and in AD 78, Tacitus reports, it was necessary to exterminate 'almost the entire race' of the Ordovices. When the Romans withdrew from Britain, three centuries later, two of their four legions in the islands were still engaged in keeping the Welsh down. They had one legionary headquarters in Wales, at Caerleon, Caerllion, in Gwent (and another just outside, at Chester). They founded two substantial towns, at Caerfyrddin, Carmarthen, in Dyfed, at Caerwent in Gwent, complete with the usual amenities of Roman provincial urbanism, its baths, its temples, its amphitheatres, its forums, its shops—'novelties of civilization', as Tacitus drily observed, 'which were really a form of slavery'. They maintained forts and transit camps at strategic points, from Caernarfon in the far north to Cardiff in the south. They worked lead and gold mines in the hinterland. They built a network of roads.

For the rest, it seems, they generally left well alone, avoiding the dangerous highlands when they could, and seldom interfering, if they could help it, with the scattered Celtic tribespeople under their local chiefs—the aboriginal hill-village on Yr Eifl lived its own windswept life throughout the Roman era, and its distant bumps and smoke-columns must have given a curious *frisson* to the soldiers from Spain or Tuscany patrolling the lowlands beneath.

The Romans are entrenched, all the same, in the landscapes of modern Wales. They have left their masonry relics all over the country, and here and there their stalwart shades as well. One place where their presence lingers with an earthy immediacy is the little amphitheatre they built on the edge of Trawsfynydd moor, in Gwynedd, near the sea. No Welsh site could be much Welsher than this. The moor is dank, sedgy and mostly treeless, the mountains that rim it are stark, the weather is habitually awful, and over everything, especially in the rain, there hangs a dank but sweetish smell of bracken, moss and sheep-droppings. Even now there are few buildings about, and usually the only living things to be seen are the moorland birds and the inescapable ewes.

A long straight road, part of a north–south Roman highway, still runs across the moor, and beside it the Roman Army built itself a very small fort. There can surely have been few less popular stations in the whole imperial service—five days' march from a city, in territory almost uninhabited except by marauding tribesmen and their harridan wives. The Romans built the station with their usual textbook precision, to regulation pattern and authorized dimension: and beside it they dug out a small sunken amphitheatre, hardly fifty feet across, which archaeologists suggest was intended for the demonstration of weapons or instruction in elementary tactics.

Poor soldiers! To anyone familiar with the Naming of Parts or the Demonstration of Use by Numbers, the little hollow at Trawsfynydd, now all covered with turf and nibbled by wandering sheep, offers all too poignant evocations. One can almost hear the rasping voice of the centurion, and the clash of weaponry in the pit; one can almost see and smell the garlic rank-and-file, packed tight and breathing heavily on the bank around, wrapped in cloaks against the raw Welsh wind, and dreaming no doubt of taverns far away, or warm Castilian suns.

Sometimes in more tangible ways, too, the Roman occupation seems astonishingly close. That military highway north to south, though in some places it has disappeared, and in others is covered by modern tarmac, is often still recognizable. It ran originally from Caernarfon to Caerfyrddin, perhaps to give access and protection to the mines of mid-Wales, and long ago its various stretches became collectively known as Sarnau Elen. This may really be no more than a corruption of *Sarn y Lleng*, Causeway of the Legion, but legend has always preferred to translate it as Helen's Causeway, confusedly attributing the road's construction to the Welsh wife of a Roman commander in Britain (a lady also remembered, in North Wales especially, by the continuing popularity of her name).

At one place in particular, not far from Ystradfellte, Sarn Elen remains very much as it was in Roman times, and you can actually drive a car, if a little bumpily, over the very paving-slabs laid down by the Romans 2,000 years ago. Down this highway in Roman times travelled not only military traffic, but wagon-trains of lead and gold on their way to the southern ports, and the feel of the stones beneath you, the steady line of the road ahead, illustrates the system with a wonderful clarity: best of all when you discover erect and commanding beside the highway the immemorially misnamed Madog's Stone, a landmark which is, in the Roman way, as practical as it is impressive, and which is still faintly marked, in letters running down one flank, with the name of the man it commemorates—Darvacius, son of Justus. Madog's Stone indeed!

The style of things Roman seems all the more Roman, in this land of the blurred edge. The big amphitheatre at the military station of Caerleon, which old antiquarians stoutly maintained to be King Arthur's Round Table, looks startlingly clear and mathematical in its muddled purlieus of meadows, playing-fields and suburbia; the military station of Segontium, outside Caernarfon, looks almost ostentatiously rational, against the jumbled heights of Eryri. And one of the most peculiar of all Welsh sensations is the feel of the village of Caerwent, which was the Roman provincial capital of Venta Silurum, and is still in many respects a Roman town: substantial Roman walls surround it still, glaring over the pasture-lands, its streets still follow the pattern of the imperial grid, the church of St Stephen stands where the temple stood, and in its porch is an altar to the god Mars Ocelus erected by an officer of the Augusta Legion. The little village square occupies the site of the Roman forum, more or less, and behind the Northgate pub, on the main road between Newport, Casnewydd, and Chepstow, Cas-gwent, the arch of the Roman north gate still stands, clambered about by roses, in a corner of the little garden.

What is more, be it fact or fancy, some of the farms in the green valley all around seem to have a distinctly Roman look to their lay-out, some nagging hint of the Campagna. Down here, in the fertile and easy lowlands of the south-east, the Romans became in the end well assimilated into local society, or vice versa. The Silurians of these parts had fiercely resisted the Roman invasion, but when once they had capitulated they evidently became willing collaborators. Lured from the hills by Roman policy, many Silurians built themselves farms and villas under the protection of the Caerleon fortress; and over the years they became more and more like Romans themselves, providing the imperial Power with functionaries, wives and eventually soldiers, until the line between occupiers and occupied must have been distinctly tenuous, and there were Celts living the lives of proper Roman gentlemen, and thousands of people of mixed race.

Elsewhere in Wales the same thing happened, and when the Romans abandoned Britain in the fifth century they left behind them in Wales a fertile Romano-Celtic legacy, sown already with the first seeds of Christianity. Long before their final retreat from the British Isles the legions had withdrawn from Wales. In the chaotic decline of central control their Spanish-born commander at Caernarfon, the Christian Magnus Maximus, allegedly husband to Helen of the Causeways and known to the Welsh as Macsen Wledig, was proclaimed an anti-Emperor by his soldiers. In 381 he left for the Continent to claim the purple, accompanied by a Welsh bodyguard and handing over authority in Wales to Romanized indigenes. Welsh patriots accordingly like to claim that theirs was the first of all Roman territories to achieve peaceful self-government, and Macsen Wledig, who was killed at Aquileia in 388, has ever since been celebrated as an honorary hero of Wales.

By then educated Welshmen evidently considered themselves Welsh Romans. They wrote their lapidary texts in Latin—HERE LIES PAULINUS, says one noble sixth-century example, at Caio in Dyfed, UPHOLDER OF THE FAITH AND LOVER OF HIS COUNTRY ALWAYS. They freely absorbed Latin words into their language—*porth, pont, ffenestr, mur.* They sometimes adopted Latin names for themselves—for example Sextilius, presently mutated to Seisyllt, and eventually to Cecil. They thought of their leaders as successors to the proconsuls, of their social arrangements as extensions of the Roman *civitates,* of their values as the grandly ordered values of the Empire in its prime. And so, bracing themselves to defend all this against the coming of the barbarians, little by little the Celts of western Britain, all alone in their mountainous peninsula, evolved into the Cymry: or as the pagan peoples who presently ruled England were to call them, the Welsh (a name which is thought to have implied Roman connections, and which they share with the Wallachians of Rumania, the Walachians of Greece, the Walloons of Belgium, the Galicians, the Galatians and the vanished Gauls).

There is a little museum, housed in a former school, at the bottom of the churchyard at Margam, in Glamorgan, which offers a haunting first impression of the Wales of the Independence, the Age of the Saints and the Princes. It is often closed, but if you make your way round to the side of it, among the gravestones, you can see through the windows anyway. Your view may be complicated by the reflections of the churchyard yews, rippling on the window panes, but that is all to the good, for the gentle movement of their leaves casts a properly mysterious screen upon the scene inside. It is rather dark in there, except where shafts of sunshine cast sudden patches of light; and strangely all over the whitewashed room, dimly to be discerned by pressing your eyes very close to the glass, there stand the silent shapes of old stone crosses.

Some are white and slender, some squat and grey, some have faces carved on them, some are curiously patterned, and some seem to have been hewn just as they are from the living rock: but they all look, there among the shadows, through the dancing filigree of the leaves, immensely holy and enormously old. They are an age petrified. They are like princes and saints themselves, turned to granite and limestone.

The years after the Roman withdrawal were confused years for Wales, as for every other country of western Europe: but whereas almost everywhere else they were to be known as the Dark Ages, the Welsh were always to remember them, or idealize them perhaps, as years of golden glory. These were the years when the Christians, setting up their austere hermitages and monasteries all over Wales, made it a passionate enclave of their faith at a time when almost all Europe was pagan. These were the years of the *tywysogion*, the princes, and the *uchelwyr*, the noblemen, whose glittering figures were to beguile the Welsh memory ever after—aristocrats who lived in the collective consciousness as aristocrats always should, with poetry and music all around them, with wine and fine meats, with beautiful horses and beautiful women, with friends who would follow them to the ends of the earth, and bards who would sing their praises to the end of time.

These were the years when the Cymry lived heroically, beating off the assaults of Saxons from the east, Irish from the west, marauding Vikings from almost everywhere. These were the years of Arthur, whoever he was, the ultimate prince, the Once-and-Future King, whom the Welsh were to claim always as their own, and whose name was to erupt from this small country to inspire the chivalries of half the world—'Who is there who does not speak of Arthur?', as Alain de Lille was to cry in the twelfth century. 'The eastern peoples speak of him as do the western, though the whole earth stands between them. Egypt speaks of him, the Bosphorus is not silent, Rome, the queen of cities, sings of his deeds . . .'

All this holy glory you may see in your imagination, glowing in the half-light around the stones of the Margam schoolroom.

Perhaps it was not much like that really, during the centuries in which the tribes of Wales became princedoms and kingdoms, and then fitfully emerged as a Welsh nation. It was doubtless squalid enough in many ways, and was certainly so confused that by now all is inextricably tangled in myth, historical theory, misreporting and propaganda. The few annals and chronicles of the day are a bewilderment of recondite claims and genealogies, and modern Welsh historians, when they get into the thick of their medievalism, are hardly more intelligible. Like phantoms and dream-objects the mysteries pass before us, the icons and totems, the strange names and the veiled allusions—the Pillar of Eliseg, the Cross of Grutne, the Host of Catraeth—CATAMANUS REX SAPIENTISSIMUS OPINATISSIMUS—'Concenn, son of Catteli, Catteli son of Brochmail'—the Royal Tribes, the Old North, the Black Gentiles, Urien—the shades of old shades, the echoes of echoes, dimly perceivable out of the smoky past.

In the early years there were as many as eighteen separate princedoms within the 8,000 square miles of Wales, largely because the Welsh law of portion, gavelkind, divided inheritances equally among all a man's sons, and so fragmented kingdoms as it fragmented farms. They often fought against each other, besides being engaged in interminable warfare with their enemies from without. Between 949 and 1045, according to the thirteenth-century *Brut y Tywysogyon*, the Chronicle of the Princes, thirty-five of their rulers died by violence and four more were forcibly blinded. Roman systems may have been admired, and Roman pedigrees claimed, but Roman roads were allowed to decay, Roman towns were overgrown, and the country remained comfortless and inaccessible, clothed in thick forests where brigands lurked, while pirates, Irishmen and Vikings infested the shores and plagued the coastal traffic.

And yet, it *was* a golden age. The story is told of the holy man Beuno hearing, across the Severn river, a man calling to his dogs in an incomprehensible tongue, and so realizing with a shudder that the heathens had reached the frontier of Wales. There they were held, however, establishing only precarious and temporary footholds west of the river, and inspiring an implacable loathing when they did. Behind the barricades, in this far corner of the old Empire, a culture unique to itself was brought tentatively into being. It was all alone. England was gradually Saxonized, and its Celtic language lapsed into patois or died. Ireland was alien and often hostile. The Celts of Scotland were remote and increasingly unintelligible. Even the Christianity of the rest of Europe, gradually reviving, was a different kind of Christianity: the Welsh recognized no allegiance to Rome, and held to their own particularly Celtic forms of sanctity. 'Listen!' the saint had cried upon the river bank, 'I hear the heathen coming!': but by the eighth century a frontier dyke, built by King Offa of the Mercians, acknowledged the particular separateness of Wales.

The dyke is still there, a bumpy ditch and earthwork which still marks, in many places, the border between England and Wales. It is not a very fearsome barrier, in many stretches hardly more than a gentle heave at the edge of a meadow, and it seems to have been made by agreement between the parties, not as a fortification but as a demarcation line (though its more puzzling gaps may have been left deliberately as killing grounds). Its construction however was to have a profoundly allegorical meaning: on the eastern side of it the English rose to world supremacy, on the west the Welsh survived.

Gradually those multitudinous little princedoms were consolidated into greater wholes, and four major Welsh kingdoms emerged: Gwynedd in the north, Powys in the east, Deheubarth and Morgannwg in the south. They generally came into being peacefully, by policy and marriage, and though they were often at odds with each other, they seldom went to war. Several great rulers indeed, Rhodri Mawr of Powys, Hywel Dda of Deheubarth, the two Llywelyns of Gwynedd, each briefly succeeded in uniting almost all Wales under one aegis, and slowly the country coalesced into nationhood of a kind. A single written language united it—Cymraeg, Welsh, forged out of the ancient Celtic and the Latin. A single body of customary law was diffused through all the princedoms. A single social system prevailed, based essentially upon kinship: beneath their rulers the people were divided into tribes, some big, some small, each supposedly descended from a single forebear. As for the rulers themselves, they nearly all acknowledged common ancestry, giving to the whole gallimaufry a constant sense of family.

So the characteristics of the modern Welsh were crystallized out of the confusion. The tales of the oral tradition, written down at last, became in time that resplendent body of folklore which delights Welsh people still, and distracts their every chronicler. The simplicities of the early Christians were to be translated in the end into the austere discipline of the Welsh chapels. The princely heritage of merriment and high spirits survives to cheer us still. The bond of family is strong still in Wales, fanciful pedigrees continue to be cherished. And above all the tradition of Welsh literature, the greatest glory of Wales, has flourished without a break from those times to our own—written in the same language, practising the same techniques, honouring the same spirit, part festive, part melancholy, part mystical, and shot through still with a humour that is sometimes medievally black.

It lasted, one might say, a thousand years. There were still free Welsh princes, living in the Welsh way, sounding the last echoes of the Independence, until the closing years of the thirteenth century. They never did succeed in creating one Welsh nation for long, but the shine of them has never faded, and their high freedom of spirit has played through the Welsh memory ever since, and resolved itself into the sense of indefinable loss which is part of the Welsh condition.

But long before the last of the princes had lost his sovereignty, the Normans had come. 'Woe to the English!' wrote Winston Churchill of these formidable predators, 900 years later: and it was woe to the Welsh too, for within half a century of the Norman landings in England, a quarter of Wales was in fief to alien barons.

Nobody indeed could be much *more* alien than the swaggering freebooters who now appeared with such ferocity among the border princedoms. Societies which had resisted the Saxons for 500 years collapsed in the face of these formidable newcomers, and a deep swathe of eastern and southern Wales, extending almost into the heart of the country, was assigned by the new Norman kings of England as booty to their generals. Three great earldoms, just within England, dominated the Marches, as the border country now became known —Hereford, Shrewsbury and Chester. Lesser baronies were established up and down Offa's Dyke, along the southern coast and in boldly isolated outposts elsewhere. These were semi-independent lordships, ruled by quasi-regal lords, standing between England proper on the one side, the territory of the kings in London, and Wales proper on the other, the territory of the independent princes.

The Normans began as they meant to continue, dominant. In no time at all they had built a mesh of castles—twenty-five in Gwent alone, three just to defend the town of Monmouth, Trefynwy, supported by a host of waspish country fortresses, high on their tumps at the entrances to valleys, the crests of passes or the junctions of roads. The castle of Gilbert de Clare at Caerphilly, Caerffili in Glamorgan, was one of the most powerful ever built in Europe, surrounded by unprecedently elaborate water-works: the castle of Pembroke, Penfro in Dyfed, was capped by a weird and sinister tower, round, immensely strong and roofed with a vaulted dome, which remains to this day the most frightening thing in Wales. And after the soldiers came the monks and friars of the great Continental Orders, holy men very different from the anchorites and nomadic preachers of Celtic Christianity, whose great monasteries along the eastern borderlands, with their hugely soaring naves, their gorgeous rituals and their efficient apparatus, must have seemed to the wondering Welsh almost as overwhelming in their strength and strangeness as the terrible castles themselves.

To this day Wales remains half-Norman, at least in superficials, for the Normans gave much of the country a new and durable pattern. In particular they established within their occupied territories a system of market towns—the first towns to be built in Wales since the departure of the Romans—which radically changed the social system. The Welsh were generally allowed to keep the rough high ground: the Normans seized the lowlands for themselves—in Gwent and Glamorgan, for instance, they seldom went higher than the 300-foot contour—and it was in the new towns that they concentrated their presence, with a castle nearly always, very often a priory church, and around these nuclei a subservient huddle of shops and houses.

Often the stance of such old Norman settlements remains symbolically cap-à-pie. At Manorbier, Maenorbŷr in Dyfed, the Norman castle stands splendidly on a hilltop on one side of a river valley, the Norman church faces it staunchly from the other, and a properly inchoate tumble of Welshness, all scattered cottages and car parks, lies hangdog in between. At Painscastle, Castell-paen in the Powys hills, the remains of the Norman castle stand lordly above the cluster of farmhouses that skulks in its eastern flank, while away to the west a green empty valley leads into the wild Welsh heartland. At Presteigne, Llanandras, further to the north, though the castle demesne is now a pretty park with bluebells and picnic tables, still it offers an ordered contrast to the brooding Welsh mountains to be seen between its trees, and still the curfew rings, each night except Sunday, from the church the Normans built near by. Subtle social or historical nuances even now distinguish the inhabitants of these settlements from their upland neighbours, and sometimes, through all their own long histories, the Norman towns have never really been reconciled to the Welshness of the country all about.

Take the minute town of Montgomery, Trefaldwyn, near the English border in Powys. In appearance it is very English, and predominantly Georgian. It has a neat little market hall in a pretty sloping square, lots of nice square-windowed houses, a couple of pubs, a church rich in handsome family tombs. On the hill above the town a ruined castle stands, and there is a Town Hall, a Court House and a former County Gaol. This place is pure Norman. Its eponymous founder was Roger de Montgomery, from Saint-Fol-de-Montgommerie in Calvados, who built his first castle here within a decade of the Battle of Hastings. Even its Welsh name commemorates a later Marcher lord, Baldwin de Boller. The first purpose of the settlement was purely colonial—it was the key to the great gap that runs through the central Welsh highlands to the western sea.

Five hundred years later, when Montgomery became the capital of a county under English rule, all that gap to the sea fell beneath its authority, as if to confirm the old Norman writ, and almost everything you see in the town now falls into the same line of descent. The castle on the hill directly succeeded Roger's original fortress. The court house and the gaol faithfully fulfilled Norman functions. The tall towered church above the square stands in classic exposition of the Norman system, deliberately balancing, the Priest beside the Baron, the stronghold on the hill. The grandest tombs inside it are all of families descended directly from the conquerors, and there have probably never been, all through the history of Montgomery, more than a handful of Welsh-speaking Welsh people living in the town.

Well into the twentieth century the Lords Marcher of Cemaes, in Dyfed, retained the hereditary right of appointing the local mayor, and in some parts of Wales the descendants of the barons are still in possession of the lands they seized, long since transmuted into the estates of country gentlemen. An inner frontier was established in Wales, between Norman Welshness and Welsh Welshness, which was to have a permanently disruptive effect upon the psychology of the people: the regions of *Walia Pura*, where the barons did not go, remain to this day the Welshest parts of the country, and the heartland of Gwynedd in the north, the bunker of Welsh defiance then, is still the undefeated bastion of Welsh nationalism.

The Normans turned thousands of free Welshmen into serfs, and drove thousands more out of their fertile flatlands into the mountains. They introduced feudalism to Wales. They humiliated many an ancient house, and implanted arrogant dynasties of their own—Carews and Corbets, Turbervilles and Laceys, Cliffords and Mortimers and Baskervilles. They brutalized the landscape with their fortresses and savaged the people with their campaigns: William de Breos was popularly known as 'The Ogre', and it was said of Robert of Rhuddlan that he spent fifteen full years harrying the Welsh—'some he slaughtered mercilessly on the spot like cattle, others he kept for years in fetters, or forced into a harsh and unlawful slavery'.

Yet the Welsh attitude to these violent swells was always to be ambivalent. The Normans were at least Christians, they were magnificent soldiers, and they lived in a manner not altogether foreign to the stylized festivity of the Welsh patricians. They made many Welsh people feel part of a greater whole, a world beyond the Dyke. The Welsh never despised them, as they despised the coarse and Godless Saxons: to this day *Sais*, Saxon, though it means an Englishman now, remains a term of abuse in Welsh—'bloody Sais', says the Welshman under his breath, when affronted by some boorish visitor from across the border—but only a handful of individual Normans entered the demonology of the people. (Some indeed became folk-heroes: Sir John

Salusbury, known as Siôn y Bodiau, John of the Thumbs, because he had two thumbs on each hand, was popularly supposed to have rescued the inhabitants of the Vale of Clwyd from a winged dragon—single-handedly, or at least four-thumbedly.)

Many a politic alliance was struck up, between Welsh prince and Norman lord. Many Norman barons married Welshwomen, and many turned into Welshmen themselves, founding lines honoured in later years as archetypically of the country. Even the most Welsh of the Welsh princes adopted some Norman ways, enthusiastically taking up, for instance, the art of heraldry. 'I am sprung from the Princes of Wales and from the Barons of the Marches', declared the twelfth-century scholar Giraldus Cambrensis, Gerallt Gymro, Gerald the Welshman, who grew up in that castle above the car parks at Manorbier—'when I see an injustice in either race, I hate it': for it was possible to be loyal to both sides, another dichotomy which has complicated the attitudes of Welsh people ever since.

On the other hand resistance to the Normans never ended—they were never able permanently to seize much more than their originally conquered territory, and even there guerrilla fighting was incessant. Successive kings of England brought expeditions into Wales, in support of the Marcher Lords, and bold tales were told by the Welsh of the long conflict—the snatching of princesses from duress in Norman castles, the kidnapping of extortionate barons, and sometimes a smashing set-piece victory, like the one in the Berwyn hills in 1167 when the princes of Gwynedd, Powys and Deheubarth combined to beat an army drawn from Normandy, Scotland, France and England, supported by a Danish fleet and financed by the merchants of London. Heroic leaders with heroic names—Rhys ap Tudur, Owain Gwynedd, the great Lord Rhys of Dinefwr—burnt their reputations for ever into the Welsh memory, and there are many places still hallowed, or haunted, by legends of the Norman wars.

High in the Black Mountains, for example, on the borders of Gwent and Powys, stands Crug Dial, the Cairn of Revenge. This remembers an episode in 1135 when the Norman Lord Richard de Clare was returning home after a visit to his colleague Brian de Wallingford at his castle in Abergavenny. De Clare was a member of one of the most powerful of the Norman Marcher families, related to William the Conqueror himself and extremely rich, and he seems to have behaved that day with a rash confidence: for according to the tradition he dismissed de Wallingford's escort as he approached the mountains, and entered the dark valley of the Grwyne Fawr, thick with beech forests, accompanied only by a few attendants (or as Giraldus fancifully suggested, by a fiddler and a singer).

There, in that remote and dangerous place, a band of Welsh partisans, commanded by Iorwerth ap Owain of Caerleon, ambushed the party. None of the Normans, we are told, escaped—even the poor musicians died. On the bare mountain ridge above the forest the Welsh erected that cairn to commemorate the day: around it still, and in the Wood of Revenge that spills darkly down the hillside below, those susceptible to such things profess to feel a lingering air of tragedy, or of triumph.

Terrible as a battleship, strong as a cliff-face, imperially magnificent, arrogantly overbearing, at the point where the river Seiont joins the Menai Strait, opposite the south-western tip of Môn, stands the castle of Caernarfon, one of the supreme military monuments of Europe. Thirteen polygonal towers rise above its walls, and its ramparts are banded with layers of red sandstone, giving it an air of bullying flamboyance. Dr Johnson, looking at it in 1760, said he never knew buildings of such size existed. Thomas Pennant, writing in 1773, called it the most magnificent badge of Welsh subjection.

From a distance Caernarfon Castle looks like part of the landscape, a great heap of rocks perhaps, a blur against the blue mass of Eryri beyond. From a nearer vantage-point, especially when the castle is floodlit late on a summer night, its resplendent bulk beside the water there, looming over the yachts and fishing-boats moored at the quay below, and all but obliterating the darkened town behind, seems anything but organic. It looks then deliberately planted for despotic effect: and so it was, for this was the chief of the new fortresses, more formidable even than Pembroke or Caerphilly, by which the Crown of England, in the last decades of the thirteenth century, proclaimed its final conquest of the Welsh.

By then the Normans had become the English, and the dynasty of the Conqueror had given way to the house of Plantagenet. England had been intervening in the affairs of Wales for 200 years, but outside the territories of the Marcher Lords, who acted as viceroys in those regions, it had never established its supremacy for long. The confrontation was not black and white. It was entrammelled in deals and arrangements, marriages across the border, treacheries, subtleties of suzerainty or medieval protocol. Nevertheless out of the Welsh heartland leader after leader sprang to defy the English power, culminating in the two Llewelyns of Gwynedd, the Great and the Last, who made a virtual federation of independent Wales, and were to personify for ever the spirit of the resistance. A running war that had lasted, on and off, through eight English reigns had never achieved serenity for the English in Wales—'we dwell here', wrote one unhappy soldier of the thirteenth century, 'in watchings and fastings, in prayer, in cold and nakedness . . .'. Two Williams, three Henrys, a Stephen, a Richard and a John all failed to impose the peace of the English upon their nearest neighbours: it was only in the reign of the first of the Edwards that a soldier in the royal service killed Llywelyn ap Gruffydd of Gwynedd, and so symbolically ended the Independence of the Welsh.

Actually resistance continued even after the death of this charismatic prince, but it is the killing of Llywelyn Olaf, Llywelyn the Last, near the hamlet of Cilmeri in Powys, that has remained in Welsh minds the fatal fact. A big stone of rough-hewn granite beside the road marks the place where he is said to have died, on a bitter snowy day in the winter of 1282. When Henry III was on the throne of England Llywelyn was recognized even in London as Prince of Wales, and in return he acknowledged the suzerainty of the English Crown. Under Edward I matters changed. First Llywelyn refused to pay tribute, then he insisted on building a new castle and town, Dolforwyn in Powys, which the king forbade. Edward declared the prince a rebel and invaded his territories with a powerful army, and by the winter of 1282, after several years of shifting fortunes, the Welsh resistance was cracked. In the north the armies of Gwynedd were dispersed; in mid-Wales the Welsh were shatteringly defeated in a battle near Builth, Llanfair-ym-Muallt, in Powys. On 11 December Llywelyn himself, travelling away from that battlefield with a small group of followers, was ambushed and mortally wounded.

Time has blurred the truth about his death. Some accounts say he was betrayed by the townspeople of Builth, who turned him away from their gates. Others have him hiding in a cave at Aberedw, five miles away, and riding through the snow that morning with his horses' shoes reversed to baffle pursuers. Somewhere near Cilmeri, anyway, it is thought on a bridge over the Irfon river, the English caught him. When they discovered that they had killed the Prince of Wales, they cut his head off, washed it in the well of a nearby cottage, and sent it to Conwy in Gwynedd, where King Edward was, together with a message from the English commander in Powys: 'Know, sire, that the force that you placed under my command fought with Llywelyn ap Gruffydd in the land of Builth on Friday after the feast of St Nicholas, and that Llywelyn ap Gruffydd is dead, his army broken and all the flower of his men killed . . .' The head of the prince was then conveyed to London, like the head of Brân before it, paraded through the streets with a crown of ivy on it, and finally stuck up on the Tower of London.

The anguish of the Welsh was terrible, and was expressed in one of the most tremendous of all Welsh laments, by Gruffydd ab yr Ynad Coch, Gruffydd Son of the Red Judge:

> *Och hyd atat-ti, Dduw, na ddaw—môr dros dir!*
> *Pa beth y'n gedir i ohiriaw?*
>
> O God, why does not the sea cover the land?
> Why are we left to linger?

Even into our own century a popular nickname for the people of Builth was *bradwyr Buallt*, 'Builth traitors', but in 1966, six and a half centuries after the event, the stone of Cilmeri was erected on its mound. Two plaques, one in Welsh, one in English, pointedly announce its meaning. The English sign describes Llywelyn merely as 'our prince', but the Welsh one has a subtler inference. *Llywelyn ein Llyw Olaf*, it says—'Llywelyn Our Last Leader'.

This was conquest: not infiltration, not suzerainty or sphere of influence, but the seizure of one country by the armed forces of another, and its suppression by an army of occupation. Llywelyn's dynasty was obliterated. His only child, his daughter Gwenllian, was condemned to live the rest of her life in English nunneries. His nephew Owain was imprisoned in Bristol Castle, and twenty years later we hear of Edward ordering its Constable to make 'a wooden cage bound with iron, in which Owain may be enclosed at night'. His brother Dafydd was dragged by horses through the streets of Shrewsbury, before being hanged, drawn and quartered: the several parts of his corpse were distributed throughout England, the cities of York and Winchester disputing possession of the right shoulder. English rule was now to be direct, and absolute, over all those parts of Wales not already within the Marcher Lordships. As a symbolic spit in the eye of Welshness the King appointed his own heir, the future Edward II, to be Prince of Wales, and by the Statute of Rhuddlan, in 1284, he formally declared all Welshmen to be subjects of the English Crown.

To clinch their victory, all around the mountain mass of Eryri, the innermost fastness of Welsh nationality, the English built a colossal series of fortresses: Rhuddlan, Flint (Y Fflint), Beaumaris (Biwmares), Conwy, Harlech, Aberystwyth, Caernarfon, ringing Gwynedd like so many fearful guard-houses. This was one of the greatest of medieval building operations. Labour was impressed from all over England, and hundreds of ships brought building materials from France, Ireland, East Anglia and the English south coast ports. Dykers came from the fen country, castle masons from France, huge quantities of lead, iron, timber, lime and freestone were assembled. The records show that 400 masons, 2,000 quarrymen, 2,000 unskilled labourers and thirty smiths were employed in the building of Beaumaris in Môn—the equivalent, it is said, of 13 per cent of the entire London labour force: from the site of this castle an entire Welsh community was expelled, to be resettled in the new town of Newborough, while the monastery of Aberconwy was moved stone by stone to make way for the castle of Conwy.

The castles are all there still, in varying states of decay and magnificence, and supreme among them is Caernarfon. The symbolism of this building was carefully calculated. The Welsh had always associated the town with the Roman Empire, and particularly with their adopted hero Macsen Wledig, and owing to a confusion of names they wrongly linked it too with the Emperor Constantine, who was said to have been born there to Macsen's Welsh wife. There was a tradition that Macsen had somehow come back there to die—the English themselves claimed to have found his body during the building of their castle—and one of the best-known of all the medieval Welsh stories, *The Dream of Macsen Wledig*, had the Emperor of Rome dreaming about a fair fortress at the mouth of a river, in a land of high mountains, opposite an island, and a tower of many colours at the fort, and golden eagles on its ramparts—where else, thought the Welsh, but Caernarfon?

To exploit all this body of myth and half-history, Edward's Savoyard military architect, Master James of Saint-Georges-d'Espéranche, built into Caernarfon Castle references both to the legends and to the imperial city which Constantine had founded on the other side of the Roman Empire. The castle was built within sight of Segontium, the old Roman fortress on the foothills above, three gigantic imperial eagles were raised above its tallest tower, and those reddish layers in its walls were direct copies of the sandstone inlay in the city walls of Constantinople. By these means the King of England appropriated the Welsh heritage to his own conquering propaganda.

In other ways too Caernarfon was a kind of masonry decree, explicitly illustrating the authority of England in Wales. Behind the castle a town was built, enclosed with tough walls, with four gates and a harbour in the lee of the fortress. This was not merely an English garrison town, but an English colony too. English merchants were encouraged to settle there by exclusive trading rights, while Welshmen were forbidden to live within the city gates. Caernarfon was clearly a steely place from the start, and Welsh people approaching it from the higher ground above, and seeing it down there at the water's edge with its flags flying and its smoke rising, the sentries patrolling its castle walls, the warships lying in its harbour, the methodical English bustle of its streets—Welsh people going to town in those days surely approached it with a shudder.

Once more, once only, the Welsh rose to arms in a last concerted convulsion of liberty—during the years of Owain Glyndŵr's rebellion, at the start of the fifteenth century, which was thereafter to be remembered as the allegorical climax of their history, the one moment when all the old prides, resentments, despairs and defiances found a brief satisfaction. It failed, the glory receded into myth and longing, and in the course of the next 500 years the English established a hold over almost every aspect of Welsh life. There were periods when the two nations seemed destined to total assimilation, and in 1485 the accession to the English throne of the part-Welsh, and Welsh-born, Henry VII, Henry Tudor, persuaded many Welsh people that the best hope for Wales lay in London after all.

They thought the advent of the Tudors would make the Welsh, the Original Britons, supreme in Britain once again: even the Venetian Ambassador in London reported to his Signory that the Welsh 'may now be said to have recovered their former independence . . .'. The royal family's Welsh origins were cherished and assiduously propagated—Henry's eldest son was christened Arthur—and Welshmen flocked to London in the hope of preferences. At home the Welsh landowning class precipitately Anglicized itself (the Tudors themselves having long since tactfully substituted three empty helmets for the heads of three decapitated Englishmen that used to grace their coats of arms).

But in the event Tudor England, not Tudor Wales, prevailed. The Welshified Prince Arthur died young, and the next on the throne was Henry VIII, whose ancestral loyalties were demonstrated in different ways. In 1536 he declared that henceforth there would be, in effect, no Wales. An Act of Union abolished the Marcher Lordships at last, and made England and all Wales one indissoluble kingdom—'albeit the Dominion, Principality and Country of Wales justly and righteously is, and ever hath been, incorporated, annexed, united and subject to and under the imperial Crown of this Realm, as a very member and joint of the same'. Wales was to be administered throughout on English lines, divided into counties on the English pattern, and represented in Parliament by knights and burgesses: and 'from henceforth no Person or Persons that use the Welsh Speech or Language shall have or enjoy any Manner of Office or Fees within this Realm . . .'.

To the English, and to many of the Welsh too, there was an end to it. Wales as a nation was dead and gone. There were no more Glyndŵrs. The Welsh gentry threw themselves enthusiastically into their new roles as English country squires: 'I rejoice', cried William Vaughan of Llangyndeyrn in Dyfed, 'that the memorial of Offa's Dyke is extinguished with love and charity; that our green leeks, somewhat offensive to your dainty nostril, are now tempered with your fragrant roses.' Among his kind Welsh ways gradually fell into disrepute, and even the language itself seemed doomed, as the gentry neglected it, and an opportunist new bourgeoisie denied it altogether. When the Welsh Tudors gave way to the Scottish Stuarts, and then to the German Hanovers, it was too late to go back.

Anyway, as Britain rose to world pre-eminence, through the eighteenth and nineteenth centuries, many Welshmen came to feel that the advantages of Britishness far outweighed the claims of Welshness: a never-ceasing migration took the ambitious over the border to England, or over the seas to the British Empire. At the same time more and more Englishmen came to live in Wales, nibbling away at the Welshness of society, and the mighty industrialization of South

Wales, which made it one of the power-houses of the whole world (and which we shall experience for ourselves in a later chapter), explosively accelerated the process. By 1914 ordinary Welshmen in their hundreds of thousands were flocking to fight for the English Crown in the Great War. By the second half of the twentieth century only one inhabitant in five spoke the Welsh language, and all too many of the Cymry seemed, with their pride of material possession, their socially aspiring English accents, their careful conformities and their fulsome devotion to the monarchy in London, as English as the English themselves.

But it was never altogether so.

In the village of Pencader, near Llandysul in Dyfed, a large modern memorial commemorates a well-loved Welsh patriot known to history, thanks to Giraldus Cambrensis, simply as An Old Man of Pencader. It seems that Henry II of England, marching through this village in the twelfth century, asked the Old Man if he thought Welsh opposition to England likely to last. The sage's reply has never been forgotten, and is chiselled in its entirety (perhaps rather *more* than its entirety) upon the stone.

This nation, O King, may now as in former times, be harassed, and in a great measure weakened and destroyed by your and other Powers . . . but it can never be totally subdued through the wrath of man, unless the wrath of God shall concur. Nor do I think that any other nation than this of Wales, or any other language, whatever may hereafter come to pass, shall, on the day of severe examination before the Supreme Judge, answer for this corner of the earth.

Innumerable other saws and prophecies have assured the Welsh, throughout the history of their subjection, of liberation to come. We hear again and again of champions yet to be born, or alternatively to be resurrected. We hear of the magic birds of Llyn Syfaddan, who would obey only the rightful owner of the land, flatly ignoring the Norman Earl Milo, diligently obeying the Welsh Gruffydd ap Rhys. For centuries the bards of Wales, clinging to their patrimony, assured the people of future fulfilments, and though all the prophecies proved untrue, and all the legends meaningless, and though every rebellion came to nothing in the end, still there were Welsh patriots always to keep the hope alive.

So far the Old Man has proved right, and the Welsh identity has survived. Among all the minority peoples of Europe, swallowed willynilly into the authority of the great Nation-States, none have remained more distinctly themselves than the Welsh. Over the years they were to find themselves leaders of a new sort, out of the common people, the *gwerin*. If the gentry abandoned their old Welsh loyalties, the *gwerin* hung on to them; the old traditions, forgotten in the manor house, were cherished on the farm; the tales were told from one kitchen to another, the poems were written no longer by courtly bards, but by a multitude of peasant poets. The culture of the nation, which had been a patrician culture, became above all populist, and the new leaders of the people, coming to the fore in the nineteenth century, were no longer Welsh aristocrats, but teachers, writers, ministers of religion. The arrival of industry, far from obliterating the Welsh identity, paradoxically fortified it after all, so that by the mid-twentieth century, when foreigners thought of a Welshman they generally thought not of a country person, speaking a locally dialected Welsh, rooted in the earth of his own *bro*, but of a miner or steelworker, speaking a Welshy sort of English and hot in loyalty to pit, town and rugby team.

Not that Wales was ever to achieve historical serenity. This remains a nation crippled by its past, by the inescapable facts of *realpolitik*, and the tide of Welshness has flowed, and ebbed, and flowed again, in successive waves of enthusiasm and disillusionment. But the struggle continues still—not just for a Welsh nationality, but for the abstraction of *Cymreictod*, the consciousness of being and feeling Welsh. Though English is spoken everywhere in Wales today, though there is virtually nobody who does not understand it, though the links with England grow stronger every year, though English money, English management, English settlers, English examples of every kind pour incessantly over the border, 46 million souls against 2.75 million—though the odds are greater now than they have ever been, and the particular nuances and subtleties of Welshness are threatened not only by Englishness itself, but by the unimaginable power of Western material civilization as a whole—still, despite it all, somehow the idea of the nation survives, the language is spoken, the poems are written, and the sense of specialness, or otherness, stubbornly perseveres. Not all Welshmen admit its compulsion—many prefer to ignore it, or even denigrate it—but there are probably few of the Cymry, whether or not they speak the language of their ancestors, whether or not they honour their own *Cymreictod*, who are not subtly affected by its influence, and attracted by its immemorial pull as a compass needle swings to the magnetism of the pole.

3. Holy Country

In the early spring of 1402, at the moment when Owain Glyndŵr's rising developed into full-scale rebellion against the English, a comet blazed its way across the skies, confirming the popular belief that he was in league with supernatural powers. Seers advised him, bards proclaimed the prophecies fulfilled in his mission. Many thought him a wizard: he had a palace he could sink at will below the waters of a lake, he had a stone which could make him invisible, such virtue was embodied in his very banners that his followers tore them up as talismans. Yet he was a devout Christian, with priests in attendance, with an archdeacon as his chancellor, so that in his person were concentrated many lines of faith and superstition. In this too his presence may serve us as a national example: for Wales has generally been an intensely holy country, and its spirituality has been confused—the occult crossed with the intellectual, dogma reacting against ritual, and a rumour of mystery often hovering, as it hovered around the reputation of Owain, over its affairs and territories.

THE holiest Welsh place is Dewisland, Pebidiog, a stony protrusion from the coast of Dyfed which was once a spiritual hub of the whole Celtic world. Not only does the countryside there seem holy by its very nature, so ascetic but so exciting, all bare rock and heather headland falling to the wild Atlantic sea, but its associations too are intensely sanctified. Here the Celtic missionaries came and went, on their journeys through the western seas, and here the itinerant Irish preachers landed on their way to evangelize a pagan Europe. Everywhere there are the remains of shrines and chapels—neither the Welsh nor the Normans ever fortified the peninsula, in respect for its sacred meaning: and in the middle of it stands the most venerated structure of all, the cathedral of Dewi Sant, St David, not only the mother-church of Welsh Christianity, but the vortex of all that is holy in Wales.

From the sea-shore path that skirts the peninsula, a marvellous windswept track of bilberries and whirling seabirds, one first sees this building as a group of four grey pinnacles apparently embedded in the rocks. It was built for safety's sake in a deep hollow known in medieval times as Mynyw, four miles from the sea, out of reach of storms, out of sight of heathen warships. A little town has grown up around the rim of the declivity, with a few hotels for the tourists, a handful of shops and a war memorial, but even from its main street the cathedral hardly shows. It is reached through a towered gateway, down a long steep flight of steps, and around it there stands a cluster of old buildings, a ruined palace of the bishops, a derelict medieval college, comfortable Georgian houses for the cathedral functionaries, with the little river Alun running through.

Above them the great square tower of the cathedral rises tall and chaste, crowned with those four grey pinnacles, and fluttered all about by rooks. It is the fourth holy building to stand upon the site, since Dewi Sant founded his original church in the sixth century, and it was mostly built by the Normans. It has been altered, extended and repeatedly rebuilt down the ages, and has fine things to show the sightseer: a gorgeous roof of Irish oak, monumental pillars, quaintly carved misericords, memorials to long-dead bishops, bequests of forgotten grandees.

Visitors sensitive to numen, though, will hardly notice these things, for much the most compelling element of the building is something much more ethereal, a tremulous combination of light, hush and muted colour. The light is the sea-light that comes through the windows, pale, watery and unclear; the colour is a purplish, drifting kind of colour, almost tangible, emanating perhaps from the stone of the walls; and the hush is the unmistakable pause of holiness, which catches the breath for a moment, and awes one suddenly with the power of old conviction.

Up through that hush one passes, among the colossal slightly leaning pillars, past the reredos, into the small chapel behind the high altar: and there within a gilded grille lies the studded oak reliquary that contains, so the trustful believe, the bones of Dewi Sant himself. Through this grille, and through a slit-window immediately above the casket, one may see as in a vision the great golden cross upon the altar, and beyond it the blue-grey luminous mist that suffuses the place so strangely.

Far older still, of course, are other holy places of Wales. Some of the cromlechs and standing stones are as old as the Great Pyramid at least—their huge boulders were being raised in ritual zeal four millennia before David went to Dewisland. Yet often some holiness still attends these eerie constructions too, surrounded as they are liable to be by accretions of awestruck tradition, and standing as they so frequently do triumphantly on ridges or secretive in scrubby dells. There are megaliths forbidding and endearing, lovable and malignant, but hardly one of them fails to impress the visitor with some tingle of ancient sanctity.

Some it is true have been scoured of atmosphere, like the great Tinkinswood cromlech in Glamorgan, which is thought to have been the burial place of several hundred people, but whose magic was long ago atrophied by archaeologists. Some are fouled by tourism, like the terrific Arthur's Stone upon a ridge above the sea in Gŵyr, to whose once-unearthly presence a well-beaten track leads from the nearby car park, signed in season by a trail of chocolate wrappers and cigarette butts. But no cathedral, mosque or temple could be much more wistfully moving than the cromlech of Pentre Ifan, say, which stands in the foothills of Mynydd Preseli, the Preseli hills of Dyfed. The Preselis are said to have been of such innate holiness to the ancients that huge pieces of them were dragged and floated to Wiltshire to form the bluestone megaliths of Stonehenge itself, and Pentre Ifan possesses an unmistakably soothing or reconciliatory air. It is not one of the largest of the cromlechs, and stands in not especially striking countryside: but it looks down a green hillside to the sea, and if you visit it on the right day, when the breeze is soft off Cardigan Bay, and the water down there is flecked with white, its grand but gentle presence makes you feel that it can only commemorate some kind and useful life, and a calm and hopeful end to it.

Most of these monuments have their local legends, of hidden treasure or heroic association, and often enough research confirms some old truth to them. The magic cauldron children have known about for several hundred years turns out, when the site is excavated, to be a copper cooking pot; the fairy dogs heard baying at midnight down the ages resolve themselves into a buried box of animal bones. In the past, folklorists say, interference with the megaliths raised terrible thunderstorms, or horrible noises, or swarms of vicious bees. Modern farmers too are sometimes reluctant to shift standing stones, however awkwardly they interrupt the ploughing, and mystics claim to experience the electric vitality, the earth force, which is said to be trapped within them. Three of the most potent stones are alleged to be the group which gives its name to the village of Trelleck—Trelech, Place of Stones, in Gwent. These stand in witch-like postures in a field outside the village, crooked in their sockets and leaning conspiratorially towards one another, and they are highly regarded by contemporary occultists. In the 1960s two diviners examined them, and so violent was the energy embodied in their material, so they reported, that the mere touch of a finger upon their lichenous mass knocked one investigator flat on his back, and sent the other reeling across the meadow.

The old Celts loved mystery. They loved riddles and gnomic rhymes. They loved the number three. They loved transformations, shape-changes. This Sufi-like taste for the opaque and the enigmatic, cherished no doubt by the Druids, was always to colour the spirituality of the Welsh, and give an arcane inference to many ordinary matters.

Eerie receptacles, for instance, were a perpetual fascination—the Cauldron of Ceridwen, which possessed the power of poetic inspiration, the Stew-pot of Tyrnog, which would not cook for a coward, the oak chest in which the young bride of Nant Gwrtheyrn, in Gwynedd, immured herself on her wedding night, or the hollow oak in which the corpse of Owain Glyndŵr's enemy Hywel Sele was hidden, to be found as a skeleton centuries later. Puzzles and spells abounded. On a rock near Llanfairfechan, on the Gwynedd coast, are inscribed the squares of a riddle-game scratched there by Welsh shepherds long ago—they liked to cut mazes in the mountain turf, too, and called them mysteriously Caerau Droia, Cities of Troy. And if you drive up the long narrow road, through a forested valley, that leads to the medieval church of Casgob in Powys, dark with ancient yews and besieged by bracken from the mountain, on a wall inside you will find the Charm of Casgob, frayed at the edges, with a hole in it; it has signs of the zodiac all around its margins, and the formula ABRACADABRA many times repeated, and safely framed though it is up there, with an explanation beside it in a fastidious clerical hand, still looks gloomily effective.

Some people thought the souls of the Druids, or even later the Romans, had been transmuted into the *Tylwyth Teg*. Whether those Others were some such historical epilogue, or a folk-memory of the Neolithic people, or projections of some profounder insight altogether, from another time-scale, another plane of existence—whatever their origins, they were to acquire over the generations transcendental truths of their own, and for many centuries most Welsh people believed in their existence as a matter of course.

They were powerful beings. Though they were generally small of stature, they were not winged or dainty in the nursery kind. Usually invisible, they manifested themselves especially at scenes of ritual or festivity—dances, weddings, funerals, when unsuspecting mortals, very often drunk, were liable to be snatched into their spell. They were unpredictable and often vindictive, and they were able to change a man's character, so that under their influence thrifty citizens became spendthrifts, modest youths were turned into braggarts. More alarming still, they could play around with time—cross the path of the *Tylwyth Teg*, and chronology could lose all meaning for you, yesterday and tomorrow might be confused, age would either abruptly ignore you, or shrink you into abrupt senescence. The *Tylwyth Teg* were Einsteinians: either they were beyond Time, or they had acquired the skills to travel through it as they would.

The idea that some of these creatures might enter your own life was obviously disturbing, and if we are to go by the folklore Welsh people were prepared to pay handsome protection dues to keep them at a distance—regular supplies of milk, for example, left outside the dairy door. Perhaps the most disconcerting of all the Welsh folk-tales concerns the baby substituted by the *Tylwyth Teg* for the beloved child of a farmer's wife. The changeling, sweet enough at first, gradually assumes another personality: week by week his temper worsens, month by month his greed and viciousness grow, and he is only expelled in the end, on the advice of a local wizard, by the baking of a black hen before a wood fire, a process so distasteful to the *Tylwyth Teg* that in a trice the little monster disappears through the door, and is replaced once more by the lost darling of the house.

Such ideas come down to us from the earliest days of Welsh coherence, transformed by the successive gifts of generations of story-tellers, but never quite seeming pure fiction. It is less than a century since a Roman pavement, uncovered at Painscastle in Powys, was covered up again for fear of upsetting the *Tylwyth Teg*, and hardly longer since the miller of Rhos-goch, in the same valley, claimed to have stayed up all night beside his mill-stone to watch the fairies dance. For that matter to this day you may be able to see for yourself, if your temperament is congenial, a lost territory of the *Tylwyth Teg* off the coast of Dyfed. It appears to mortals, now and then, who stand upon a particular patch of ground in the village of Llanon, on the gently sloping hillside a mile or two above the sea: and if you wait outside the post office on a suitable morning, one of those grey-green, patchy, illusory Welsh mornings when nothing is quite distinct, even your own perceptions—if you wait there on such a day in the right frame of mind, presently you may just make out, not far off shore, the dim green form of some other country, half awash in the tide, and rippled with white waves. Some people claim to hear bells and music, when the wind is right: others can see and hear nothing at all.

The Welsh mind has not lost its taste for enigma, and it is hardly surprising that unidentified flying objects, whose mythology has much in common with that of the *Tylwyth Teg*, should commonly be sighted in Wales, and attested by people of undoubted integrity, or absolute innocence. They are nothing new. Strange lights in the sky are a familiar phenomenon of Welsh lore, and the apparition called the Tanwedd, the Fiery One, was very like a flying saucer—it appeared from nowhere, moved about in level flight, shooting here and there, travelled generally three or four miles and then as suddenly disappeared. In the eighteenth century a farmer of Peibio, Môn, three times saw, at ten year intervals to the day, a ketch-rigged ship flying out of the Eryri mountains, surrounded by inquisitive birds: his wife and farmhand saw it too, and scholarly research at the time could not shake any of them in their evidence. Some 140 years later a well-respected family at Rhoslan, in Gwynedd, also watched a mechanism of some kind hover and wheel, brightly illuminated, against the majestic backdrop of Eryri, while in 1977 an entire class of primary school children claimed to have seen a UFO land in a field at Broad Haven, in Dyfed, the most rigorous interrogation, from that day to this, failing to reveal any discrepancies in their separate stories—the pictures they drew of the phenomenon hang in the school hall.

Policemen, clergymen, schoolteachers, farmers have all in recent years testified to peculiar happenings in the skies of Wales. Is it some inherited sensibility, that enables them to witness these mysteries? Are they sublimating the collective unconsciousness of their race? Are the flying-saucer men the very same beings that the folk-tellers have described down the centuries, the prancing fiddlers, the grimacing changelings, the beautiful lake-maidens, manifesting themselves again in another swoop out of their command of time?

Wizards and Wales have always gone together. The cloudy remoteness of the country, the foreignness of the people and their language, itself like some impenetrable code—all these have traditionally raised magical images in the minds of strangers.

The wizard of all wizards was a Welshman—Myrddin Emrys, Merlin, who has supposedly given his name to his birthplace, Caerfyrddin, Anglicized to Carmarthen. Until the 1980s there stood in one of its streets an ancient leafless oak, clamped together with iron struts and infusions of concrete, which was known as Merlin's Oak, and of which it was said that if ever it was removed, calamity would befall the town (they removed it anyway for traffic improvements, but perhaps the effect was retroactive, for Carmarthen had already been fatally vandalized by developers). Myrddin is commemorated in North Wales by sundry sites and legends, and in Monmouth they will fondly, if altogether fallaciously, show you the window in which the monk Geoffrey sat to write his *History of the Kings of Britain*, and so give the great seer's name to the world at large. Myrddin is said to be buried on the island of Enlli, off the remotest tip of Llŷn; there his shade guards to this day the Thirteen Precious Curiosities of Britain, including the Hamper of Gwyddno, which will turn meat for one person into meat for a hundred, the Chair of Morgan Mwynfawr, which will carry a person wherever he wishes to go, and the ominous Knife of the Hand of Havoc.

In historical times too men of magic have been eminent in Wales. The truly mysterious Siôn Cent, for instance, whom some scholars identify with Owain Glyndŵr himself, was widely regarded as a wizard during his lifetime. A poet and a scholar, he was vicar of Grosmont, Y Grysmwnt in Gwent, but he lived the life of a secretive recluse, and all kinds of supernatural feats were attributed to him. He could cast spells on men or animals, he could leap enormous distances, he could summon up spirits, and the fact that he was buried (aged at least 120) beneath the wall of his own church, half in the chancel half in the graveyard outside, is explained by the fact that in one of his several compacts with Satan he undertook to be buried neither in, nor out, of a consecrated building. His grave really is there: so is the bridge over the river Monnow which has always been named for him, and which he is said to have built by the exertion of his demonic powers.

A powerful dynasty of magicians, the Harrieses, lived for many generations at Cwrt y Cadno near Llanpumsaint in Dyfed. In the sixteenth century one Harries magically split a megalith in half, leaving its remains still on a hill above the hamlet. In the eighteenth century another possessed so powerful a magic book that even he was terrified of it, and kept it chained and padlocked: once a year he and a brother-practitioner took the book into a wood, unchained it and consulted its dread wisdoms, and then thunder reverberated all down the Cothi valley, and people said to each other *O! mae'r meddygon wedi agor y Llyfr Du*—'the Doctors have opened the Black Book . . .'.

Almost into our own times the Conjuror, the *consuriwr* or *dyn hysbys*, was an important figure in Welsh country society, and people of all kinds would resort to him if they were sick, they had lost something, or they wanted advice about an investment. In the 1870s an innkeeper at

Abermo, Barmouth, in Gwynedd, distressed that his mother had run away with a man called Solomon, was told by a wizard to stick pins in a toad, put it in a mug and bury it at midnight on the grave of some member of the Solomon family: if he left it there for five weeks Mr Solomon would go mad and his mother would leave him (alas, the publican failed to bury the cup at midnight exactly, and went mad himself). In the 1890s Isaac Jones and his family at Ebbw Vale in Gwent were terribly troubled by the ghost of a crippled shoe repairer who, we are told, 'haunted the drawers of the furniture': they called in Mr Peter Phillips, 'and as soon as his hand had touched the door', the closet racket ceased. Even in the present century the cultivated Miss Clara Thomas, chatelaine of Llwyn Madoc in Powys, encouraged her tenants to shave powder off the *Llaeth Faen*, the Milk Stone, a mysterious lump of chalky stone held by her family for generations, in order to drink it with milk and cure themselves of ailments.

A prince among these varied sorcerers was Huw Llwyd of Cynfal Fawr near Ffestiniog in Gwynedd, not far from the amphitheatre of the Roman soldiers at Trawsfynydd. He was a man of learning, a soldier and a poet of marvellous gifts, but like many another country scholar he was best known as a wizard. He was supposed to have regular assignations with the Devil on a rock in the middle of the Cynfal river, running through a gorge half a mile from his house, and this has been remembered ironically ever since as Huw Llwyd's Pulpit. It is one of the strangest places in all Wales, enough to make the severest rationalist think again about the paranormal. Deep in its gulley the river rushes there, green and brown and swirling leaf, and the thick woods above cast it all into dappled shadow. Everything smells of moss and water, tinged with rot. Tangled shrubs and branches obscure the view, but a muddy track along the high bank, trodden no doubt by generations of half-terrified peasants, leads to the place where one may spy upon the Pulpit.

There it stands, more a pillar than a rock, like some living being petrified in an old legend of its own, with a gently sloping summit that reflects almost phosphorescently the sunshine through the trees. The river rushes madly by—the branches flicker with the wind—the musty smell is like an incense—look! the magician is there for all to see, kneeling on his high rock, shrieking incantations and brandishing his Bible defiant above his head!

*

It was all part of a wider magic, *hud* in Welsh, which is really a key to life and matter itself—the sense that the divine resides in everything around us. This has powerfully affected the Welsh view of creation at least since the days of the Druids. The sacred oak-groves of the Celts, the intimate nature-poems of medieval lyricists, the imagery of the folklore, all attest to this ancient instinct, which gave sanctity to the land itself, and made the days full of wonder. The tales of the Mabinogion, which are really the collected imaginations of countless generations, are alive with a constant sense of astonishment: dazzling effects of fantasy and delusion are achieved on every page, and the whole *mise-en-scène* is illuminated with a strange bright supernatural light. Here, in one of the most famous passages of the collection (translated by Gwyn Jones and Thomas Jones), the curious stillness of a dream-world is so exactly evoked that it does not seem like fiction at all, but more like a hallucinatory kind of reportage:

And he came his way towards a river valley, and the bounds of the valley were forest, and on either side of the river, level meadows. And one side of the river he could see a flock of white sheep, and on the other side he could see a flock of black sheep. And as one of the white sheep bleated, one of the black sheep would come across and would be white; and as one of the black sheep bleated one of the white sheep would come across and would be black.

And he could see a tall tree on the river bank, and one half of it was burning from its roots to its tip, and the other half with green leaves on it. And beyond that he could see a squire seated on top of a mound, and two greyhounds, white-breasted, brindled, on a leash, lying beside him. And he felt certain that he had never seen a squire of such princely mien as he. And in the forest fronting him he could hear staghounds raising a herd of stags. And he greeted the squire; and the squire greeted Peredur . . .

Into this land of magical allure the Christians came, but they never altogether traduced it. In many an old Welsh parish church, beyond the notice-board warning Mrs Evans and Miss Wyn-Thomas that they are responsible for the Michaelmas flower arrangements, you may still feel the presence of Peredur, the princely squire and the brindled white-breasted greyhounds. For many centuries Cross and Magic cohabited in Wales, and the faith of the people was a rich palimpsest, one belief layered upon another, reaching back to the earliest atavistic convictions of the Neoliths.

Embedded in the porch of Corwen church, in Gwynedd, is a large crooked stone. The church itself is mostly Victorian, but the stone is probably the immemorial boulder known to ancient legend as Carreg y Big yn y Fach Rewlyd, the Pointed Stone in the Icy Nook. It plays no structural part in the building. It has never been dressed or apparently shaped. But so terribly old is it, so brawny, so queerly crooked, that it seems to attract all the spirituality of the structure into its own peculiar form. It is one of innumerable boulders, holy to far older religions, which the early Christian builders of Wales incorporated into their churches in ecumenical synthesis. Often they had no choice. For one thing the people insisted upon it, and for another, the fables say, disconcerting things happened when they declined: churches repeatedly fell down during construction, or removed themselves during the night to the site of the nearest sacred megalith.

Sometimes the church went up, in the end, side by side with a holy stone, or actually in the middle of a megalithic circle, now metamorphosed into a churchyard. At Ysbyty Cynfyn, in Dyfed, four great stones of the ancients form part of the churchyard wall, a grandly pagan portal to the house of Christ. At Maentwrog, in Gwynedd, Twrog's Stone, the boulder which originally gave its name to the place, stands like a gigantic pebble beside the church porch, while at Welshpool, Trallwng in Powys, the stone called Maen Llog stands more pointedly still immediately outside the main door, where every congregationalist must pass it. In the church of Old Radnor, in Powys, a marvellous old hulk of a sacred stone now does proud service as a font: on the other hand at the riverside church of Llanawden in Dyfed the resident megalith is hidden shamefaced at the back of the building—only a muddy anglers' track leads around there, and the queer old object stands at the base of the tower, a foot or two from the edge of the water, like a parish secret.

There are churches in Wales where burials are confined to the south side, the north being Devil's territory. There are churches adorned with pagan images, like the church of Llanbadarn Fawr in Powys, whose tympanum above the south door displays a cat's face, a tree of life, a sun, a couple of unidentified animals and assorted grinning imps. The image of a skeleton in Partrishow (Patrisio) church in Powys was allegedly painted with human blood, and the most pagan of pagans would be satisfied by the church of Llanidan in Môn, ruined and yew-shaded above the Menai Strait, whose half-derelict chancel contains a woman's skull in a reliquary, whose walls are embedded with human remains, whose masonry somewhere includes the legendary Stone of the Thigh, whose holy-water stoup miraculously fills itself, and which had in recent years its own resident familiar in the form of General Sir Otway Herbert, Royal Artillery, who lived next door, and who often materialized like a thoughtful ghost himself with dog and stick beside the gate.

For even in modern times the arcanum of these places has not been disregarded. General Herbert was on guard against scientific zealots, ready to destory the fabric of the church to discover the secret of that holy stoup, but elsewhere darker secrets sometimes reveal themselves in Welsh holy places. The ruined church of St Mary on the hillside above Tintern in Gwent was said in the 1970s to be a resort of necromancers, and there were whispers of cabbalistic rites and decapitated rams. And in the most frequently reproduced of all Welsh paintings, a picture by the Edwardian artist Sydney Curnow Vosper of the congregation of Salem Chapel above Llanbedr in Gwynedd, some people profess to see a demoniac influence betrayed: the high-hatted old lady who dominates the scene, reverently clutching her Bible, may look innocent enough at a casual glance, but hidden away within her Paisley shawl, it is said, a devilish face, a face from the remotest heathen past, can sometimes be discerned.

From time to time the authorities of the Church tried to suppress all these remnants of the old religions, threatening stone-worshippers or oak-devotees with the awful penalties of sacrilege. They were never entirely successful, and especially they failed to stamp out the most persistent pagan practice of them all, the reverencing of sacred springs, translated over the centuries into holy wells. There is hardly a parish in Wales without its holy well, sometimes filled in and forgotten, sometimes still littered with coins and pins by surreptitious votaries. They stand boldly beside high roads, with stone enclosures around them, and finely stone-flagged pools: they are hidden away and ivy-covered in woods behind churches, or in damp corners of unfrequented fields.

Failing to discredit these springs of paganism, the Church Christianized them instead, and gave them the names of holy persons. Some were famous throughout Wales, and beyond, for their miraculous powers of cure or divination—the relief of eye diseases, arthritis, the pox or melancholia, the thwarting of witchcraft, the detection of thieves, the casting of spells. There were wells which specialized in the cure of sick animals (like the one near Llanbadarn Fynydd in Powys, now hardly more than an ooze from a meadow, but in living memory crowded every Sunday afternoon by farmers with their scrofulous heifers, lame dogs or inexplicably sickened ewes). There were wells containing divinatory fish or eels, whose movements foretold the future (like the one at Llanberis in Gwynedd, whose trout survived at least until the 1970s, but whose resident eel once so startled a pilgrim that she died of fright on the spot).

The most famous of them has always been the well of St Winifred, Gwenfrewi in Welsh, at Holywell or Treffynnon in Clwyd, which has been in uninterrupted use as a place of healing since the Middle Ages. Here the holy man Beuno restored to its neck the head of his niece Winifred, decapitated by a thwarted seducer: she herself came instantly back to life, her spilled blood turned into a fountain of health-giving water and has been curing people ever since. In its prime Holywell was one of the great shrines of Britain, pilgrims frequenting it night and day, and bedecking it with rich gifts. Not even the Reformation disrupted its miraculous activities, and since 1873 it has been administered by resident Jesuits.

It is a monumental well, for over the holy spring there was built in the fifteenth century an elaborate Renaissance canopy, one of the most sophisticated structures in all Wales, with fan-vaulting and delicate pillars, and over that again stands a now disused but once opulent chapel which was a reliquary for Winifred's remains. The water flows into a rectangular pool, into which twice a day the sick and the maimed are still assisted. Until recently, in the universal tradition of curative shrines, piles of discarded crutches were left lying about in gratitude: and though all is more hygienically ordered these days, and there are nicely tended lawns about, and a souvenir shop, still the hundreds of graffiti scratched upon the old walls, the secret signs and primitive initials, preserve some of the well's ancient mystery, and remind you of the saint, the seducer and the holy blood.

At another extreme is the well of Mair Sant, Holy Mary, at Penrhys in the heart of the South Wales coalfield. For many centuries this was almost as famous as Holywell, and its site is much more dramatic, for it stands on a steep hillside at the point where the two valleys of the

Rhondda, the most congested of all the industrial regions of Glamorgan, unite below the town of Tonypandy. On both sides the valley floors are thick with terraced houses, and there are still pit wheels here and there, and shunting trains of coal wagons, and buses climbing the steep hill over to Aberdare. On a bare patch of land above the valley junction stands the well of Mair, broken up in the Reformation, rebuilt in 1953. Above it the local Roman Catholics have erected a modern figure of the Virgin, but if you scramble down the scrubby slope to the well itself you will find all trace of its sanctity gone. A dingy concrete structure covers it, littered with old beer cans and smelling of urine, and there are no medieval graffiti scratched upon its walls, only rude contemporary slogans. If anybody goes down there now, it is only small boys to play in and out of its stinking doors, or smoke forbidden cigarettes in the darkness.

Sometimes the magic water was malevolent. There were several well-known cursing wells in Wales, and of these the most notorious was the well of Elian near Llanelian-yn-Rhos in Clwyd. How this once saintly place acquired its evil nobody knows, but from the Middle Ages until the nineteenth century, perhaps later, it remained a centre of malediction. It stood in a corner of a field above a ditch, well away from the parish church on the higher ground above, and you can still see the faint track across the grass left by suppliants moving from the place of God to the place of mumbo-jumbo. The rivalry was direct. The well had its own self-ordained priest, and its forms, rituals and not least charges, like those of the church above, were established by centuries of usage.

If you wished to cast a curse a guardian would write it on a piece of paper and throw it into the well, and generations of rogues made a living from the practice. In the end the church authorities desperately arranged for the well to be filled in, and it was stoppered like a genie's bottle in 1929: but though it certainly seems sufficiently blocked now, and is surrounded too by a barbed-wire fence, hung with shreds of sheep's wool, still an unmistakably baleful sensation surrounds the place, as though evil effluences may still be escaping from it, and seeping into the muddy ground around.

We should not leave the holy wells on a Satanic note, though, for their presence everywhere in this little country is really full of grace. Instead let us visit, last of all, the spring of Patrisio, Father Isio, in the Black Mountains of the south-east—within sight of the place where

Richard de Clare was killed by Iorwerth of Caerleon. Isio was a Celtic holy man, otherwise unknown either to history or to legend, who is said to have been martyred here by marauding Saxons. It is a remote and beautiful spot, approached by a winding lane above the Grwyne, and today a small church stands above the site. In Isio's day, when he lived as a hermit beside his spring, it must have been formidably inaccessible, hidden in a deep forest of beech and oak, in country virtually uninhabited.

His well is still there, in a dingle below the church, and is the frondiest, mossiest and shadowiest place imaginable. A path of stone flags leads down to it, and a trickling stream runs away through the woods to join the Grwyne below. Small ornate ferns sprout in the darkness of its grotto, and spiders sometimes spin their webs among the stones, but no insects ever seem to disturb the calmness of the water. Now and then you may find a bunch of wild flowers, primroses, bluebells or wayside celandines, carefully laid upon the ledge inside.

Gradually the palimpsest resolved itself, and the paganism of the old Wales was absorbed into the innocent Christianity of the Celtic evangelists. Any one of a hundred Welsh country churches will illustrate this osmosis, but we will choose the little white church of St David's, Rhulen, high up the valley of the Edw in Powys. It is one of half a dozen such holy buildings in these still sparsely populated hills, and though it has been rebuilt in parts since its foundation in the eighth century, it has never lost its sense of simple wonder. Whitewashed and belfried, it stands quaintly in the middle of the circular churchyard it inherited from the pagans, and is small, and plain, and surprising. On its font (scooped out of a single stone) there are habitually displayed small objects made by young parishioners, and offered there as gifts to visitors—pin-cushions, book-marks, pots of jam, sometimes pictures of the church itself: as though the *Tylwyth Teg* themselves, transmuted now into angels, have crept into the church at dead of night to leave those presents there.

The first news of Christianity reached Wales in Roman times—with the wandering Joseph of Arimathaea, tradition was later to insist, or even with St Paul. Two Christian martyrs, Julian and Aaron, are said to have been put to death at Caerleon—there is a church dedicated to them at Newport, and a pub named for Julian—and the founder of the

princedom of Gwynedd, the Romanized Celt Cunedda, is thought to have been a Christian. By the fifth or sixth centuries the faith had reached every last Rhulen of the place, implanted by the wandering Celtic missionaries who had sailed to these shores, in their fragile boats of tar and wicker, from Ireland and from Brittany. These ascetics often set up their cells in sites already accepted as holy, easing the people into monotheism, and around such a settlement there frequently arose a *llan* or enclosure, where the guru and a couple of proselytes, perhaps, lived lives of endless work, vigil and prostration. The word *llan* thus acquired a sacred connotation, and when it appears on a Welsh map now it nearly always signifies a sacred place, and is generally coupled with the name of a Celtic saint.

Well, Wales calls them saints, but nobody else does. Most of them are utterly forgotten, except as a component in a place-name or a church dedication, and very few are historically verifiable. Some are honoured still in Welsh Christian names unknown elsewhere, like Tysilio, Illtyd or Tegwyn. Some are inextricably entangled in fable—St Govan, for instance, whose hermitage is embedded in a Dyfed cliff-face above the sea, is identified with the Arthurian Sir Gawain, while the Five Saints of the village called Llanpumsaint have been claimed as the earliest recorded quins.

A single locality remembers some of these pioneer Christians, but others were evidently the leaders or objects of widespread cults. Thus St Derbyn gave his name to only two churches, and St Ursula only to one (but Ursula was to triumph in a wider sphere, for she it was who was martyred by Huns with all her company of virgins, to be commemorated by Carpaccio the Venetian and thus made the most familiar Welsh saint of them all). On the other hand saints like Dewi, Padarn, Teilo, Beuno, Illtyd and Cadoc are all honoured in scores of dedications, and sometimes their *llannau* developed into monastic settlements, called in Welsh *clasau*. These probably began as mere huddles of thatched huts, not unlike African villages, grouped around a mud and wattle church and surrounded by a protective ditch, but some of them grew into impressive seats of learning: the *clas* that St Illtyd founded in the Glamorgan village still called in Welsh Llanilltyd Fawr, but comically Anglicized as Llantwit Major, became one of the great international centres of Celtic Christianity, and one of the chief instruments by which Roman and European traditions were cherished in Welsh Wales.

Pre-eminent among the evangelists stands the figure of Dewi Sant, who is now the patron saint of Wales, and is the only one of them to have been canonized by the Church in Rome—Dewi Sant, barefoot, clad in skins, holding a stick he has cut from the woods and a bell of miraculous powers. His legend, like his cult, has left traces of varying historical reliability all over Wales. By the sea in Dewisland is a ruined chapel on the site where, we are told, in about the year 500 his mother St Non gave birth to him, all on the gull-shrieked windy moor. In the valley of the Honddu in the Black Mountains, on the other side of Wales, is the site of his own first hermitage, now occupied by an ancient church of his dedication: here he lived the simplest of lives, drinking only water from the stream (he is known as Dyfrwr, the Water Man) and eating those wild leeks which were to become in consequence the national emblem of Wales. At Llanddewi Brefi, in inland Dyfed, is the churchyard where, during an address to a great gathering of priests and people, the ground rose in a mound beneath his feet, elevating him above the crowd, and set into the wall of the church are two fragments of a stone, dated to the sixth century, which contain the earliest written reference to his existence.

And at Tyddewi itself, where he established his own *clas* after a lifetime of wandering, the saint ended his days. Supernatural signs foretold his death, his twelfth-century biographer tells us, and sorrowing crowds assembled in the little town to hear his last sermon, the most famous of all the famous sermons ever preached in Wales. 'Lords, brethren and sisters', cried the old man, 'rejoice, and hold fast your faith and belief; and do the little things that you have heard from and seen in me.' And a great host of angels filled the town, and all manner of delectable music was heard, and the sun shone brightly, 'and Jesu Christ took unto himself the soul of David the Saint with great pomp and honour'. The date was 1 March, and on that day patriotic Welshmen still wear Dewi Sant's leek in their buttonhole to commemorate the national day of Wales (while the church at Llanthony, the site of his first ministry and original onion, is oriented to the place where the sun rises above the mountain ridge on that sad but blessed date).

The Celtic Church was part of Wales by the time, in 597, St Augustine came from Rome to Dover to reintroduce the Christian faith to pagan

England. The Welsh clergy were understandably reluctant to place themselves under the authority of Canterbury, when the metropolitan see of England was established there, or to adopt its Roman usages (they rejected the rule of priestly celibacy, and they disagreed with Roman manners of dating Easter, conducting baptisms and cutting tonsures). Celtic Christianity was different in kind, rooted not only in the faith of the early saints, but in all those ideas and symbols inherited from older religions altogether: the Celtic monk Pelagius, whose doctrine of human self-determination racked the Christian world in the fifth century, is thought by some theorists to have been harking back to Druid philosophies. The battle which accordingly began between the Welsh people's choice of religion and the religion of those seeking to impose their authority on them was to recur down the centuries, in one form or another, and do much to mould the matter of Wales.

In about 604, we are told, Augustine invited the Welsh bishops to meet him somewhere in England. The Venerable Bede says that before they went the Welshmen took counsel of a holy hermit as to their best course of action, and were advised to observe closely how Augustine received them. If upon their entrance he rose in courteous greeting, they should enter into discussions. If he remained seated proudly on his throne, they should withdraw. Augustine, seldom having met Welshmen before, declined to rise: the bishops, concluding as the hermit suggested that if he failed in small condescensions he would fail in greater matters too, left the conference.

As a result, long after Augustine's mission in England had succeeded, the Celtic Christians of Wales would have nothing to do with the Romanized Christians of England. St Aldhelm of Wessex complained in the eighth century that they would never celebrate Mass with Saxons, or even for that matter sit at the same dining-table with them, while Bede said it was the Welsh fashion 'to reckon the faith and religion of Englishmen as naught, and to hold no more converse with them than with the heathen'. The Celtic Church was not formally united with the Catholic Church for another two centuries after that abortive conference, and did not accept all its practices for another six.

By then Christianity had become an instrument of temporal power in Wales. The Norman barons first, the English kings after them, frankly used the authority of the Catholic Church as an adjunct to their own.

The old country churches of the missionaries found themselves, all too often, rededicated to more universal saints, and rebuilt in grander style—out went the thatched roof and the rush floor, in came the arch, the misericord, the gargoyles and the vestments of medieval Catholicism. Beside every castle a church arose, and foreign priests were imported to minister them: as early as 1115 even the cathedral of St David's, temporarily rededicated to St Andrew, had a Norman bishop and a moiety of Norman canons.

Claiming to find the Welsh Church horribly corrupt, the Normans broke up the *clasau*, seized their lands and endowments, and invited monks, friars and nuns of the great Continental orders to settle in Wales. Fifty monastic houses arose: the Benedictines, the Augustinians, the White Canons, the Cistercians, the Black Friars, the Grey Friars, the Austin Friars and the Carmelites were all represented in this spectacular display of muscular Christianity. But while in the beginning all were clients of the Norman power, implanted in safe places and loyal to their local lords, the monks of one order in particular, the Cistercians, eventually identified themselves with Welsh ways, found patrons among the Welsh princes too, and so became the most powerful surviving link between the Celtic and the Catholic sensibilities.

The Cistercians were ascetics, like the old saints of the *llannau*. They believed in extreme simplicity and hard practical work, and chose to settle in the harshest and loneliest parts of Wales, in search not of wild beauty, but of sheer discomfort. In 1140 they established a monastery far in the west, at Whitland, Hendy Gwyn, in Dyfed. Only a few tumbled stones, all among an apple orchard, remain to mark its site today: but from this forward headquarters in the valley of the Gronw the White Monks went out to establish eight more houses under the patronage of Welsh noblemen, all of them powerful in their time, and many of them still to be seen, in quiet ruin, among their former farms, sheep-runs and water-meadows.

The Cistercian Order in Wales was not only a spiritual force, but an economic power too. In country far from the modern techniques of the Marches, the monks introduced new means of production, new ways of marketing, to a Welsh society still in a primitive pastoral state. The Cistercians were the first big sheep-farmers in Wales. They worked coal, silver, lead and iron ore mines, smelting the ore themselves. They had their own ships. They built roads to their isolated properties, they threw bridges over inconvenient streams, they made fish-traps on the Dyfed coast and stocked the Teifi pools with trout.

They were also scholars, and patrons of the arts: Dafydd ap Gwilym, the supreme Welsh lyricist, was befriended by the Order, and the *Brut y Tywysogyon* was compiled by Cistercian researchers. Welsh patriots still remember the White Monks with affection, for though they were, as it happens, notoriously greedy agriculturists, they became trustees of the Welsh meaning. When Llywelyn ap Gruffydd was killed at Cilmeri, his head was sent to the King of England, but his body went to the Cistercians at Abaty Cwm Hir, the Abbey of the Long Valley, deep in a lonely countryside beside the Clywedog river in Powys. Eight centuries later a memorial stone was placed there in gratitude, a plain slab of slate with the prince's name upon it: generally a bunch of flowers is fixed to the oak tree above, among the few truncated columns and scattered paving stones which are all that is left of the monastery itself.

The Cistercian ruins of Ystrad Fflur, Strata Florida, Valley of Flowers, stand in a wilder site still, near the Dyfed village of Pontrhyd-fendigaid—the Bridge of the Blessed Ford. Once this monastery possessed huge sheep-runs, grew wheat and oats, bred trout and eels in valley pools, caught herring in sea fisheries, produced peat from Cors Goch, ran a lead-mine, several corn mills and several fulling mills. Now it is only an arch or two of masonry and a few foundations embedded in the turf, to which a modern cemetery has been gloomily appended. It can be a cruel raw place on a wet day in winter, when the rain slants down the valley and there is not a living soul to be seen, but for a solitary huddled mourner, perhaps, weeding her husband's grave.

For Welsh people, though, Ystrad Fflur is full of grand significance. For one thing, suggestively marshalled in a small enclosure behind a shed is a line of battered, crooked but distinctly consequential graves —the graves of Welsh chieftains, their names now forgotten, who were buried here in their pride beneath the Cistercian blessing. For another, under a yew tree in the middle of the cemetery Dafydd ap Gwilym himself is supposed to lie, with a slate slab propped against the trunk to mark the spot, and a nobler plaque upon a nearby wall.

But for a third and subtler token, you must look closely at the tall pointed arch which, now standing all by itself, is the last relic of Ystrad Fflur's once-lofty chancel. It speaks at first sight entirely of the Renaissance, in its high and masterful elegance against the sky: but all around it, you will discover, the Cistercian architect has incorporated a maze-like device of stone altogether at odds with the haughty style of the construction. It is a sly, perhaps wistful declaration of affinity with the Celtic past, before Normans, monks or even Christians ever came to Wales at all.

In the Middle Ages several pilgrim routes led the Christian faithful into Wales, for its holy places were acknowledged throughout Europe. The shrine of St David's, Tyddewi, was so famous that in the twelfth century Pope Calixtus II decreed two Tyddewi pilgrimages, 'in search of David', the equal of one to Rome 'in search of the Apostles'. The little Welsh town was thus placed on an equal standing with that epitome of pilgrim shrines, Santiago de Compostela in Spain, and there were many less celebrated Welsh sites, too, which the indefatigable palmer might visit on the same pilgrimage.

The most curious of these was Llandderfel, a small tucked-away village in Gwynedd which had in ages long gone been the home of a holy man called Derfel. The reputation of this ambiguous anchorite was dark but compelling, and made him widely famous. Some believed him to have been one of Arthur's knights, withdrawn from the world of chivalry, while many thought him more a wizard than a saint, and linked his name with Satanic cults. For centuries he was remembered by a magical effigy of himself, a huge wooden figure which was mounted on the rood screen, and which moved its eyes and its arms when pilgrims appealed to it. Thousands did, for this object had the power to transfer spirits from hell to heaven, and with it was another wooden figure, of Derfel's horse, upon which pilgrims were ritually jogged up the neighbouring hillock of Bryn Derfel. The image of Derfel himself was destroyed at the Reformation, being used as firewood, it is said, for the burning of a heretic monk in London, but the horse is still there, brown and dusty in the church porch, and looking less like a holy relic than a long-cherished rocking-horse from a medieval play-room.

A pilgrimage more properly in the grand tradition was the journey to Ynys Enlli, Bardsey. The holiness of this remotest Welsh island was not only perfectly obvious, from its magnificent stance among the racing tides and furious blusters of the west, but had long been attested by legend too—did not Myrddin himself lie there, surrounded by those potent Curiosities? A Celtic *clas* was founded on the island in the sixth century, an Augustinian monastery in the thirteenth, and many holy persons (including Derfel) chose to be interred with Myrddin in its soil. When the Vatican promised special indulgences to pilgrims making the difficult journey there, so many responded, some in an advanced state of age or disease, some actually dead already, that to this day 20,000 saints are popularly claimed to be buried on the island.

Little remains of the Enlli monasteries, except for the myriad bones still emerging from time to time out of their unmarked graves—so numerous that in the 1850s they were used for fencing. The island is a bird sanctuary, the last farmer having left it after the Second World War, and in the 1980s the only living reminder of its holy past was a solitary hermitess roughing it still in one of the old monastic outbuildings. Along the way there, though, the pilgrim churches still stand, sometimes with the remains of their hostels beside them—St Tanwg at Llandanwg, which was a chapel of rest for corpses on their way to holy burial, St Beuno's at Pistyll, with the fishpond for its hostelry still near by, and finally, on the very shore of Enlli Sound, the tall church of Aberdaron in its churchyard above the sea, looking down to the boat-landings and the hulk of the island beyond.

Aberdaron is a thriving little resort now, jam-packed in summer with cars, its beach studded with portable windbreaks, its bay alive with wind-surfers and inflatable boats. It has two prosperous pubs, and several car parks. There is one small building in the village, nevertheless, which more or less fulfils its original pious function. It is called Y Gegin Fawr, the Big Kitchen, and it is made of enormously heavy stones, whitewashed, with a low roof that was doubtless thatched once, and is now of heavy slate. It was built in the Middle Ages as a place of refreshment for the pilgrims, nervously awaiting their perilous passage across the Sound, or complacently eating a fish stew before the long trail home. Today it is a tourist café, and its customers in their sticky congestion, some all jolliness, some tired, testy and flushed with too much sea air, are doubtless much as they always were.

On his way to this shrine or that, the pilgrim in Wales could offer his devotion to one of the country's sacred relics, which were many. The ear of Malchus was preserved at Bangor in Gwynedd, and thousands of visitors paid a measure of corn, a grote of cheese, or IVd for the privilege of kissing it. The skull of St Teilo was in the hereditary possession of the Melchior family, who lived near Llandeilo in Dyfed, and until the 1930s offered pilgrims curative draughts of water out of it. Most famous of all, at Ystrad Fflur the monks kept a cup of healing first identified as being made from the wood of the True Cross, and later claimed to be that mysterious Holy Grail, perhaps the very chalice of the Last Supper, which was the ultimate object of quest for King Arthur and his knights.

This strange relic could cure many diseases, especially women's ailments, and long after Ystrad Fflur was just a ruin, pilgrims still pursued it to the nearby mansion of Nanteos, where the Powell family had become its custodians, and where it remained until after the Second World War, by then hardly more than a blackened fragment. In 1887 a celebrated gypsy harper, John Roberts, 'Telynor Cymru, Harpist of Wales', went to play at Nanteos, and at supper in the butler's pantry made some disrespectful jokes about the power of the cup. That night he regretted his levity, and was troubled by misgivings, so next day he was allowed to spend a little time alone with the relic in the library. There we may imagine him among the country-house book-cases, dressed all in black, a tall white-bearded gypsy man, with a long straight nose and a fine high brow, hunched over that fragment of old wood to seek its reassurance. When his seance was over he left a note beside the relic. 'This cup was handled', it said, 'by John Roberts, Telynor Cymru, on the morning of the 4th May 1887. Mind completely at ease.'

Now let us travel east, on wings perhaps as those old magicians did, over the quiet hills where Rhulen shelters, past the wilder Black Mountains where Isio the eremite hid himself, to the cracked and jagged summit of the hill called Ysgyryd Fawr, The Skirrid to the English, which reaches a height of 1,500 feet almost on the English border in Gwent. The chasm which splits this hill is said by folklorists to have been caused by a leap of Siôn Cent, and by geologists to have been caused by an earthquake: but the old Welsh Christians maintained that the rock was sundered when the veil of the temple of Jerusalem was rent in twain, at the moment of Christ's death. The mountain has been considered holy for centuries. Soil taken from its cleft used to be sprinkled on coffins at burials, and like many another isolated high place it has been especially associated with St Michael the

Archangel, who is supposed to have appeared there once. The village with a church at the foot of the hill is called Llanfihangel Crucornau, the Holy Place of Michael at the Corner of the Rock, and on the flat bare turf of the summit itself, where swifts scurry about like mad things on summer evenings, and swarms of butterflies meander, there are the vestigial remains of another sacred building. Here it was, high in this legend-haunted place, that during the days of their persecution the Roman Catholics of Gwent celebrated their Masses, huddled groups of people up there in the sky among the whirling birds.

The Protestant Reformation, which outlawed the Roman Catholic Church throughout the King of England's realm, fell upon Wales even more dramatically than it fell upon England, for only four years separated Henry VIII's rupture with Rome from the forcible incorporation of Wales into his United Kingdom. Suddenly *everything* changed! By then the Church in Wales was stagnant, its bishops often absent, its monasteries long past their prime, its resident priests so few that the homilies of wandering friars, selling holy images and indulgences, were the only sermons many people ever heard. Still, the Welsh had long been reconciled to the Catholic kind of Christianity. Their holy places had been thoroughly Catholicized, and their Celtic saints had been joined by a host of more orthodox sanctities: many a well of Teilo, Cadman or Illtyd was a Well of St Mary now, and St Michael had alighted on countless Welsh hilltops. There is even said to have been a Welsh Pope, the dim and tantalizing Kyric.

Welsh people at large seem to have been more baffled than antagonized by the Reformation, objecting only so far as to cling to the beliefs in signs, wonders and holy relics that the new Establishment so despised, or to cross themselves and tell their beads in church. Sophisticated traditionalists protested more actively, though, and several Welsh priests fled abroad to continue a resistance in exile. Morris Clynnog, who wanted to overthrow the new order by force, became head of the English College in Rome; Gruffydd Robert became confessor to the great Cardinal Carlo Borromeo of Milan, and in his homesickness also compiled a famous Welsh grammar; Owen Lewis became Bishop of Cassano, Naples, and if the Spanish Armada had succeeded in reuniting Britain to Catholicism, would have come home triumphantly as Bishop of St David's.

Others again honoured their faith secretly, and sometimes not so secretly, in Wales. Pilgrimages never ceased to the well of St Winifred at Holywell, where Catholic recusants acquired both the Star Inn and the Cross Keys as thinly disguised hostels for the faithful. Celia Fiennes the diarist, who went there in 1698, saw many papists openly at the pool, 'poor people . . . deluded into an ignorant blind zeale and to be pity'd by us that have the advantage of knowing better'. Twenty-five years later Daniel Defoe, who thought the story of the well's sanctity 'smells too much of the legend to take up any of my time', reported that Catholic priests abounded there, pretending to be physicians, surgeons and sometimes patients, 'or any thing as occasion presents', and holding Masses at secret oratories in the neighbourhood: and though St Winifred's relics had been scattered, one finger had been smuggled safely away to Rome—in 1852 half of it went back to Holywell, where they keep it now.

The monasteries of Wales were all abolished by the Reformation, their buildings falling into ruin, their estates as often as not acquired by opportunist local landowners, but here and there recusants carried on their traditions. In Powys they revived the charcoal iron industry of the monks of Ystrad Marchell, Strata Marcella, and became some of the first of the modern Welsh industrialists. And perilously in a cave above the sea in the Little Orme, a headland at Llandudno in Gwynedd, Jesuits operating a secret press printed in 1585 the exiled Gruffydd Robert's *Y Drych Cristianogawl*, 'The Christian Mirror' (though the title-page says, no doubt for safety's sake, that it was printed in Rouen).

Some parts of Wales were especially loyal to the forbidden faith. Llŷn was always staunch, the gentry there, on the pilgrim road to Enlli, sticking firm to the old ways for many years. And the most Catholic district of all Wales, probably of all Britain, was that corner of Gwent, over there by the English border, which looked towards the holy mountain of Ysgyryd Fawr. The Gwent recusants enjoyed several advantages. Their part of the country had a long tradition of sanctuary, started by the Templars who had been great landowners there four centuries before, and they enjoyed the protection of one of the most powerful families of the Welsh borders, the strongly Catholic Somersets of Raglan Castle, Rhaglan to the Welsh. Also near at hand to help them was a formidable cell of Jesuit resistance in a house called Cwm, The Valley, at Llanrothall, just over the English border in Herefordshire.

Cwm has long been rebuilt, and is now a pleasant Georgian house tucked away down a steep winding lane, at the bottom of which an old humped bridge crosses the river Monnow into Wales. In recusant days it was far more inaccessible, and a veil of mystery surrounded it. 'A great many doors to go in and go out', it was said darkly of the house in 1679, 'and likewise many passages from one room to the other . . .' From this place, then the clandestine College of St Francis Xavier, at a time when the penalty for being a Catholic priest was a traitor's death, for nearly half a century Jesuits were sent across the border into Wales, keeping the faith alive in private houses and secret meeting places. Sometimes there were as many as twenty-seven priests at the Cwm, sometimes no more than half a dozen, and they were often visited by the formidable Father Robert Jones, Superior of the Jesuits throughout Britain, and 'the Fyerbrande of all'.

Sometimes, probably because of Somerset influence, authority turned a blind eye to their activities, and carts from Cwm, we are told, openly showed themselves at Monmouth market. At other times the persecution was intense, and local Catholics were obliged to meet in utmost secrecy: in the Robin Hood Inn near the Monnow bridge in Monmouth, above a shop in Abergavenny High Street, or at that ruined chapel on the mountain-top—in 1676 Pope Clement X provocatively promised plenary indulgences to those who went up there on the feast day of St Michael.

Of all the persecutors of the Catholics in Wales, the most ferocious lived, as it happened, at the very foot of Ysgyryd Fawr, in the manor house of Llanfihangel Crucornau. John Arnold, a Member of Parliament and a magistrate, was a fanatical Protestant and an old enemy of the Somersets, who liked to search out Jesuits with an armed posse of his own servants. At Westminster in 1678 he raised the subject of Cwm and its influence on the neighbourhood—'he hath seen a Hundred Papists meet on the top of the Skyrrid for Mass'—and the house was raided. The seven priests in residence, five of them probably Welsh, had fled the place already, but they were hunted meticulously down, and Arnold's own posse caught the most important of them, David Lewis the Rector of Cwm.

Nobody can be quite sure who Lewis was—his name may have been an alias—but he seems to have been a local man, and for thirty years he had carried out his mission among the Catholics of South Wales, who called him *Tad y Tlodion*, Father of the Poor. He could expect no mercy from John Arnold. Arnold's men had arrested him; Arnold conducted his first interrogation in Abergavenny; he was held at Arnold's house at

Llanfihangel; he was charged in Monmouth court before a jury approved by Arnold, Arnold being not only his chief prosecutor, but also a kinsman of the judge. Inevitably he was found guilty, and was condemned to be hanged, cut down alive, disembowelled, dismembered and beheaded. They took him in a cart to Usk, and there, on 27 August 1679, the sentence was carried out.

Three centuries later Lewis was canonized by Pope Paul VI. At the place where he was executed, beside the Abergavenny road in Usk, there now stands a Catholic church, dedicated jointly to St David Lewis and St Francis Xavier, and every August sees a pilgrimage there. The grave of the martyr is harder to find. It lies ironically in the graveyard of Usk Parish Church, the Established Protestant church of the town, but is no more than a flat broken slab near the west door of the church, grassy and mossy: only recently has a small plaque been added, with the date of the saint's death, and a little metal crucifix. You need not go far up the road, past the castle, to see the gaunt outline of Ysgyryd Fawr on the horizon, with its deep suggestive cleft.

There are not many Catholics in Wales now—some 130,000 in the 1980s. Probably not more than five hundred are Welsh-speaking Welsh people, Cymry Cymraeg, and the statistical maps show them scattered in small communities, like recusants still, sometimes in places where the Irish have settled, sometimes where old families have kept the faith throughout. Roman habits died hard in Wales—even now, in parts of Powys, they still use the word *bicafio*, to cringe, in direct derivation from the confessional's *peccavi*—but in time the Welsh became as a whole severely anti-Catholic. Even when Catholics were allowed to practise their religion openly again, discretion was advisable. Two centuries after the raiding of Cwm they built their first post-Reformation church in Monmouth, but they were told it must be invisible from the high road: and so it is still, tucked away behind a row of cottages in St Mary Street, not far from the Robin Hood.

Yet in this century the old Church has gradually made its presence more apparent. Modest little churches have sprung up here and there, converted from barns sometimes, sometimes built from scratch, and old associations have been gently revived. The Cistercian monastery on the island of Caldy, off the Dyfed coast, claims to possess the oldest British church now in Roman Catholic hands, the fourteenth-century priory church of St Illtyd, which has been in its time a brewery, a laundry and an Anglican chapel. One of the two Welsh Catholic dioceses, Menevia, pointedly takes its name from the ancient sanctuary of Mynyw, upon which Dewi Sant himself built his monastery. The provincial cathedral in Cardiff, Caerdydd, is dedicated to St David. And in 1982, in a gesture unthinkable fifty years ago, the Pope himself, John Paul II, made an ecumenical visit to Wales, and kissed the Welsh soil in full papist canonicals!

Is there something familiar to this tentative revival? Perhaps it may remind us of the first missions of the Celtic saints, quietly building their hermitages beside the sacred stones. Some Welsh patriots have certainly felt the pull of its internationalism, offering a return to the unity of medieval Christendom, and to an older, less Anglicized Welsh style of things—to what the poet Raymond Garlick once called 'a Wales cast in the mould of Europe'. The Catholics in return have consciously courted *Cymreictod*, Welshness—hoping to 'insert themselves', as their Archbishop said cautiously in 1983, into the Welsh language and the Welsh culture. In many of their churches you see the Stations of the Cross explained in Welsh: in Llŷn, the old stronghold, they recently printed the order of Mass in the old language, for the first time ever.

At the Capuchin friary of Pantasaph, Pantasa in Clwyd, which was founded in 1852, one feels a distinct sense of populist crusade. Three times every Sunday a friar drives out from its grand but gloomy buildings to celebrate Mass with the scattered Catholics of the Clwyd hills, the driver acting as celebrant and confessor; and at functions up and down Wales, cultural festivals to agricultural shows, you may come across Brother Francis the Singing Friar of Pantasaph, strumming a song to his guitar ('Is he real then?' passing countrymen sometimes ask, eyeing his monkish robes. 'Perfectly real', the Singing Friar interrupts his lyric to retort). On a hill above the monastery, above the Lourdes Grotto and the Stations of the Cross, there stands a tall bronze Calvary, which looks with a poignant splendour across the still mostly heretical countryside of Wales, but bears upon its plinth a message almost as sharp as the inscription at Cilmeri. 'Special indulgences', it says, 'are granted by the Holy See to all who shall devoutly visit this Calvary or make the stations or who looking from a distance to this cross shall say a Hail Mary! for the conversion of England.'

*

Not that the rule of Anglican Protestantism in Wales was all wicked in the eyes of God, or in the eyes of Welshmen either. If it fell heavily on many an old native custom, stamping out beloved superstitions, breaking up miraculous effigies, in its early years it did much to restore a more rational Welshness to the Christian faith. Welshmen were appointed to Welsh sees again. Jesus College, Oxford, was founded specifically for the education of Welsh clerics. The first book printed in the Welsh language, in 1546, was done under Anglican auspices: a compendium of the Lord's Prayer, the Ten Commandments and the Creed, it had no title, but has always been splendidly known by its opening words—*Yny lhyvyr hwnn*, 'In this book'. Much more importantly, hardly had the new Church of England banished from its liturgies the Latin which Welsh people knew at least by rote, substituting the English of which very few understood a word—hardly had it Anglicized the forms of worship than Queen Elizabeth I, Defender of the Faith, more in policy than in piety ordered the translation of the Holy Bible into Welsh.

Its purpose was to get the people into church, and forestall their disaffection, but it was a noble enterprise for all that. Four Welsh scholars took twenty-five years to complete the work, and it goes usually by the name of William Morgan's Bible, after the farmer's son who did much of the translation while rector of Llanrhaeadr-ym-Mochnant in the back-country of Clwyd, and whose humble birthplace among the forests of Penmachno, in Gwynedd, is now a national shrine. It was not only a work of religious devotion, religious expediency too: it was a miracle of literary revival. It created a standard Welsh prose, a literary prose, which drew upon the best traditions of Welsh writing, and permanently affected the manners and standards of the language. This is how the opening words of Genesis appear, in Bishop Morgan's version:

Yn y dechreuad y creodd Duw y nefoedd a'r ddaear. A'r ddaear oedd afluniaidd a gwag, a thywyllwch oedd ar wyneb y dyfnder, ac Ysbryd Duw yn ymsymmud ar wyneb y dyfroedd . . .

And this is what Christ cried to his Father in Heaven, in his last anguish upon the Cross:

O Dad, i'th ddywlaw di y gorchymynnaf fy yspryd . . .

*

To some it seemed that Protestantism was only reviving the old struggle of the Celtic Church against the supremacy of Rome—the defiance of the bishops in the presence of Augustine. Certainly many remarkable men brought life and distinction to the Anglican Church during the 300 years in which it was the official church of Wales. There were several martyrs, during the brief return of Catholicism under Queen Mary—a bishop, a fisherman, a gentleman of Haverfordwest, all burnt at the stake for their obduracy. There were clergymen of radical theology, like the many who eventually left the church for Nonconformism, or the several who tried to convert Wales to Tractarianism, introducing congregations of bewildered bucolics to all the high-flown Oxford rituals of incense and chasuble. There were innumerable religious writers, some with a genius for the memorable title: Ellis Wynne (1670–1734), author of *Gweledigaethau y Bardd Cwsg*, 'The Visions of the Sleeping Bard', or Theophilus Evans (1693–1767), author of *Drych y Prif Oesoedd*, 'The Mirror of the First Ages'. There were hymnists, indefatigable Bible glossers, lexicographers. There were poets of wayward genius—Evan Evans for instance, Ieuan Brydydd Hir, 'Evan the Tall Poet', described by Dr Johnson as 'a drunken Welsh curate', who rediscovered some of the great early poetry of Wales, or Goronwy Owen, who was seen in his lifetime as an eighteenth-century Welsh Milton, but ended up as a tobacco planter in Virginia, too fond of drink, too difficult and too Welsh for clerical promotion. There were men of heroic public service: the Revd James Williams of Llanfair-yng-Nghornwy in Môn, and his son the Revd Owen Lloyd Williams, were both famous lifeboatmen—when in 1835 the smack *Active* of Belfast went ashore near Cemais, and no boat could get near her, the Revd James swam his horse into the sea, threw a grapnel into her bowsprit shrouds, and so rescued the crew of five.

Many priests designed, and sometimes built, their own churches. The damp and gloomy church of Whitebrook, above the Wye Valley in Gwent, was decorated single-handedly by an early twentieth-century wood-working incumbent, the Revd Joshua Stanfield: ornamental tablets and desks everywhere, chiselled vestry doors, and above it all a mighty reredos, standing there to this day in glory amidst the mildew. On the other side of Wales the contumacious Revd W. E. Jelf, objecting to the fact that the parish church of Llanaber in Dyfed held its services only in Welsh, decided in the 1850s to build a church where everything would be *un*-Welsh: not only was his church of St Philip to be entirely English in liturgy, it was to be absolutely alien in architecture too, and so it stands there on its wooded slope above the Mawddach estuary, looking towards the summit of Cader Idris across one of the grandest of Welsh prospects, exactly like an importation from the Basque country, with a veranda on stout square pillars, and an open belfry with four bells in purest Pyrenean.

The Revd Thomas Price, vicar of Cwmdu in Powys in the early nineteenth century, was not only a poet (his bardic name was Carn-huanawg), an artist, a naturalist, a musician (he made his own harps), an antiquarian and a historian, but he also translated much of the New Testament into Breton. Also in Powys lived the Revd J. Y. W. Hinde, who began his career as an Anglican curate, but became a Catholic, served as a Zouave of the Pontifical troops, and was made a Knight of St Gregory by Pope Pius IX: on inheriting the estate of Clochfaen near Llangurig this enterprising cleric returned to the Church of England, changed his name to Lloyd, spent his later years decorating the local church with stained glass windows commemorating Welsh saints and princely heroes, together with the heraldry of the Clochfaen family between 1200 and 1748, and is honoured today as The Chevalier Lloyd on an admiring obelisk in the village.

Flowers are still reverently placed upon the grave of 'The Solitary', the Revd John Price, vicar of Llanbedr, Painscastle, in Powys, who is buried on the south side (the Godly side, that is) of his little church in the hills. A worker-priest of the most utter kind, Price lived variously in an old shack, a group of disused bathing-huts and a former hen-house. Every Sunday he held a service exclusively for tramps, who cooked meals for themselves on the oil-stoves in their pews during the sermon, adjourning afterwards, with the vicar, to eat them in a neighbouring barn. The Solitary died in 1895, aged 85, the inventor of two shorthand systems, and profoundly respected by his parishioners, said a colleague from a neighbouring parish, as 'a very holy man'.

And that colleague was Francis Kilvert, rector of Clyro in Powys between 1865 and 1872, the happiest exemplar of them all, and almost the only one whose name is remembered in the wider world. His diaries, rediscovered only in the 1920s, have attracted a devoted cult, and all around the Clyro country, the Black Mountains to the south, the gentler hills to the north, the magnificently rolling country of the Wye between, *aficionados* spend Sunday afternoons following his tracks. He describes with tender tolerance the life of a country parson in Wales in late Victorian times—high Anglican times, when the Bishop in Hereford was a power to be feared, when rural deans progressed grandly about in first-class railway compartments, when squires entertained suitable curates to dinners, or took them for rides with young ladies in jaunting-traps.

Kilvert was an Englishman, but he found himself profoundly sympathetic to the Welsh—who even then, in that Anglicized corner of Wales, appear in his pages like survivors from some all-but-extinct culture. Over the mountains he tramped to meet them, sensitive to every nuance of light and landscape; and in their cottages he listened to their tales of the old Wales, heard the words of their magnificent language, and wondered like so many rationalists before him at their quaint and atavistic convictions. He did not stay long in Clyro, moving to a living near Rhayader to the west, then to Herefordshire in England, and dying at the age of 39: but among all the priests of the Church of England who came to work in Wales, from the first storming iconoclasts of the Reformation to the last apologetic advocates of Establishmentarianism, he is the least likely to be forgotten.

Kilvert's curate world was altogether innocent, and of course there were many like him in the parishes of Wales, working for the good of their people, devoted to the Welsh tradition, and trying to achieve continuity between the profoundest instincts of Welshness and the 38 Articles of the Established Faith. Often they lived in poverty, the stipends of many parishes being no more than pittances, and had to tramp miles in all weathers to visit their scattered flocks—the saintly Rice Price of Llanwrthwl, Powys, in the last years of the eighteenth century, walked sixteen miles every Sunday to minister his three churches, and gave an extempore sermon in each.

But over the years the hierarchy at large grew more distant from the people, and bore itself, as well it might, as part of a governing élite. The Welsh language was heard less and less in the country churches, and between 1714 and 1870 not a single Welsh-speaking bishop was appointed to a Welsh see. Richard Watson, Bishop of Llandaff in the 1780s, lived in the Lake District of England; Benjamin Hoadly, Bishop of Bangor earlier in the same century, is said never to have set foot in Wales at all. Trollopian trappings incongruously surrounded little churches of the back-country, and the old Norman duality, castle beside priory church, was translated into a more subtle but strictly analogous partnership, the squire beside the parson.

The tithes indeed, the agricultural taxes which were supposed to finance the Church, had very often been appropriated by members of the local gentry, and turned into properties like any other. The tithes of fifteen parishes in Dyfed went to a family in Devon: they got an income of £6,000 a year from them, while the fifteen parish priests earned less than £2,000 between them. Other ecclesiastical prerogatives were just as freely bought and sold. In 1839 the advowson of Maenclochog in Dyfed was advertised as a 'safe investment', excellent for any gentlemen wanting to put his son into the Church, while in 1842 there went on the market proprietorship of the north chancel of St Peter's Church, Caerfyrddin, together with exclusive rights to fees for burials within it.

All too often now the worldlier clergymen conducted themselves as spokesmen of the status quo. Discontent with one's allotted place in society, the Revd James Francis of Newport, Gwent, assured his congregation in 1839, was resistance to the divine will—to be poor and lowly was to experience God's mysterious ways, like being deaf and dumb. Many a priest in Wales saw his own allotted place in society as that of ally or agent to the landed classes. We read of hunting vicars, shooting rectors, archdeacons living in plush consequence among the stony simplicities of the land. The Revd Hugh Bold, who was vicar of Llanfihangel Tal-y-Llyn in Powys for more than sixty years of the nineteenth century, lived all that time in the splendour of Boughrood Castle, a very stately pile eight miles away. The Revd John Jones, who was incumbent of Llaneilian in Môn for fifty-three years in the eighteenth century, kept a private harpist and a pack of hounds. A parishioner of Llangynllo in Dyfed, at the turn of the twentieth century, reported entering the church one afternoon and finding the Revd Rhys Jones Lloyd flat on his face in the chancel, praying aloud, with his gloves and riding crop on one side of him, and his silk hat on the other—home from hunting, and offering thanks for a good run.

More fatefully, the clergy became identified over the years with political authority, and so with Englishness, and Toryness, and reaction. They were often magistrates too, and thus called upon not only to counsel, but to judge and to punish. The Revd William Powell, vicar of Abergavenny in the 1800s, maintained a system of private spies to keep him informed on political activities among the local ironworkers, and during a strike in 1822 put the fear of God into the populace by assuming command of a troop of Scots Greys. So year by year the inheritors of Welsh holiness, standing direct in line from Dewi Sant and the wandering saints, became more alienated from the ordinary people of Wales, socially aloof to them, and treating their language and culture at best with condescension, at worst with contempt. In 1855 the congregation in the large Anglican church at Amlwch, in Môn, consisted it was said of two or three publicans, a few paupers, a stray sailor or two from the port and the pupils of the church school, 'lost in the high pews and dreary galleries'.

In the external vestry door of the church of Llandetty on the banks of the Usk in Powys, there is a hole popularly supposed to have been caused by a gun-shot. If so, it is an early and dramatic memento of dissent against the Established Church in Wales. At the time of Cromwell's Commonwealth the church was taken over by the furiously Puritanical squire of the neighbourhood, Colonel Jenkin Jones, who used it as a barn. One day as he was supervising the milking of his ewes there news arrived of the return to England of Charles II, and the restoration of the Anglican Establishment. Instead of a lifetime of plain prayer and self-mortification, Colonel Jones must face the return of the Church in all its opulence. He lost his head. Mounting his horse, the story says, he cried 'Ah, thou old whore of Babylon, thou'lt have it all thy own way now!', and firing his pistol furiously in the direction of the vestry door, galloped away down the Brecon road, never to be seen in Llandetty again.

Hardly had the Puritan sects begun their work in England than they began to preach the word in Wales. Hardly was Catholicism outlawed than Nonconformity crept in! By 1593 John Penry of Cefn Brith, in Powys, who called the Anglican bishops 'soul murderers', was being hanged for treason, leaving behind his four daughters Deliverance, Comfort, Safety and Sure Hope—'a poor young man', as he described himself, 'born and bred in the mountains of Wales'. By 1639 the first Nonconformist chapel was established, on the New England pattern at Llanvaches in Gwent, by 1649 the first Baptist chapel, and by 1653 the most radical dissenters of all, the Quakers, had established themselves in the back-country ('very rude and wild and airy', George Fox thought them).

High on a hillside near Newtown, in Powys, stands one of their early meeting-houses, built in 1713 as remotely as possible, out of sight from highways and villages, for privacy's sake. The Pales is a plain thatched building, with a scrubbed and tidy schoolroom attached, a cottage adjacent with many cats, and a field next door with a horse in it. To this tranquil sanctuary a handful of Quakers still come for prayer meetings, or for funerals in the little graveyard, and after the meeting on Christmas Day tea is served, with mince pies. Elsewhere across Wales, too, there are reminders of the early Friends—a meeting-house here and there, but more often an old burial ground, miles from anywhere or hidden away now among factories and new housing, where you can just make out the names of the old greathearts lying there, staunch to the end in their unconsecrated ground.

But it was the rise of Methodism, in the eighteenth century, that was to transform the nature of Wales. The growth of Nonconformism then, its tentative and daring beginnings, its phenomenal spread, its tremendous eruption of faith, hope and sacrifice, left an effect upon the country like the passing of a hurricane. The Christian faith took centuries to root itself in Wales; Catholicism spread slowly, out of the Celtic Church; Anglicanism was imposed by writ of law; but the Methodist Revival, Y Diwygiad, hurled everything topsy-turvy, demolishing the social structure, transforming the culture, shifting the self-image and the reputation of the people, and eventually giving rise to a great convulsion of power that was truly a revolution.

The instinct of that hot-tempered colonel, aiming his pistol at Llandetty church, lay deep-rooted in the Welsh temperament: not perhaps in a severe or self-denying kind, for the Welsh loved their pleasures, but as an intuitive yearning for something more elemental than the lofty proceedings of Anglicanism. When John Wesley's ideas arrived in Wales in the mid eighteenth century (shortly to be followed by John Wesley himself, who came forty-six times in all, and thought the Welsh 'as pagan as Red Indians'), they spread like a bush-fire, releasing many a stifled emotion in the people, and spawning out of the Established Church sect after reformist sect, whose fiery Exhorters were soon snatching congregations in their hundreds from the appalled parish clergy, and whose numberless chapels grew bigger and grander and richer and more dominant as the generations passed.

The pace of it! An inspired and inflammatory company of preachers achieved it all within a century, and Wales reverberates to this very day, at least in chapel circles, to their terrific personalities—some great national figures in their time, like actors or politicians now, some celebrities of a more local fame, silver-tongued Ellis Gwynne of the Station Road chapel, or hypnotic Mr Thomas, Zion Baptist. Their rhetoric was often majestic, their techniques were theatrical. Christmas Evans, the one-eyed Baptist virtuoso of Llandysul in Dyfed, was said to make his congregation tremble just by his Cyclopian glare. John Elias of Môn held his listeners in so powerful a trance that he could manipulate their very senses: 'God's avenging bow is bent!' he cried on one famous occasion, bending his arm to an imaginary weapon, 'Look, the arrow of the Lord will strike the sinful!'—and instantly the congregation opened before him, to let the missile pass. Daniel Rowlands used to appear suddenly before his congregation at Llangeitho, in Dyfed, as though out of heaven itself, through a door at the back of his pulpit. In Gwent the Independent minister Edmund Jones, 'the Prophet of the Tranch', preached 511 sermons in 1773 alone (besides evangelizing a wide countryside from the saddle of his donkey, writing a famous book about ghosts, and decreeing that he should be buried in a separate grave from his dear wife, as he 'didn't want there to be any difficulty on the day of resurrection . . .').

People travelled immense distances to hear the great revivalists. Hundreds came by sea from North Wales to Rowlands's meetings at Llangeitho, landing at one or other of the little havens of the west coast and walking the rest of the way, and one of Wales's favourite stories tells of the 16-year-old Mary Jones, who walked fifty miles barefoot over the hill-tracks from her home in the Gwynedd mountains to get a copy of the Bible from the celebrated Thomas Charles of Bala. The people wept to the tears of the evangelists, they laughed to their laughs, they shared their joys, they believed their every warning. 'Go on, go on', congregations frequently cried, when preachers showed signs of concluding their addresses.

Sensual and even sexual instincts were quite frankly aroused by these charismatic performers—as William Williams the hymn-writer wrote of the movement, 'the flesh also insisted on having its share, and all the passions of nature aroused by grace were rioting tumultuously'. Bewildered Anglicans reported scenes of hysterical fervour, as the people succumbed to the effects of *hwyl*—which means 'mood' or 'spirit', but in a technical sense among the evangelists described a particular form of delivery, high-pitched, intense and sing-song, which seems to have had an intoxicating effect upon its hearers. Celebratory jumping for hours at a time, in heavy clogs, was a phenomenon unique to Welsh revivalism, and English tourists used to come across the border especially to watch it: jumpers claimed that they were only following biblical precedent—David danced before the Ark, the baby leapt in the womb of Elizabeth, and the man cured of lameness leaped and praised God.

It was a national ecstasy. We hear of people at the prayer meetings of revivalist Wales collapsing in tears of rapture or remorse, tearing their hair, fainting, wildly shouting *Gogoniant!* 'Glory!', singing and praying and clapping their hands for hours after the sermon had ended and the preacher gone home. As they left the chapel themselves, parting at the gate, they would point to the sky above, to remind each other that one day they would meet up there, never to be separated again.

To Authority, temporal and spiritual alike, these manifestations were subversive. They denied the glory of the Crown as God's surrogate in Wales, and they denied the status of the Anglican gentry as the ordained rulers of the land. In some ways they were like a return to the faith of the Independence: a sort of confession was a feature of Methodism, its hymns were often folk-tunes spiritualized, and the stylized rhetoric of the preachers was not unlike the chanting of the old priests.

Dissenters of all kinds were mocked, slandered and not infrequently imprisoned—the Quakers, the most dissenting of all, were so cruelly persecuted in Wales that in the end, though often rich and influential citizens, they nearly all emigrated to the United States. But this only made martyrs of them all, and there grew around the great names of the movement traditions as vivid as those of the Celtic saints. Up and down Wales their shrines remain places of pious pilgrimage. Daniel Rowlands stands in lugubrious effigy on the site of his chapel at Llangeitho, whose village square, once thronged on Sunday evenings with the thousands of his visiting congregations, now lies silent in the dusk, dominated by an ancient yew within a whitewashed wall like the plaza of some more southern sanctuary. A memorial marks the site of the first Welsh Baptist chapel, a little ruin reached only by footpath up a wooded valley near Ilston in Gŵyr—GORAU GOF, COF CREFYDD, it says, The Best Memory, the Memory of Faith, and a plaque nearby tells us that, such are the ironies of Welsh history, it was unveiled in 1928 by the Right Honourable David Lloyd George, lately Prime Minister of Great Britain, on land presented by Admiral A. W. Heneage-Vivian, Royal Navy. Many a pilgrim visits the village of Llanfihangel-y-Pennant, near the head of the Dysynni valley in Gwynedd, from where Mary Jones set off on her famous journey over the mountains in search of Truth. It was evidently always a holy place—the church has a circular churchyard—and is celebrated in Welsh history, too, for just down the road are the remains of Castell-y-Bere, one of the principal strongholds of Llywelyn Fawr. But its fame now is the fame of Mary Jones, and there is a memorial in the middle of the hamlet to recall her story, and bring a tear to the eyes of those who have grown up with its telling, Sunday school to chapel sermon to television half-hour.

Often the early Nonconformists, hounded by squires, clergy or outraged citizens, had to meet in private houses, and here and there in Wales chapel meetings are still held in farms. Every Sunday such an assembly is held in a ground-floor room of Devanna, a grand old house in Powys whose name, a corruption of Tŷ Faenor, Manor House, proves it to have been a grange of the Cistercians at Abaty Cwm Hir. It is a gauntly splendid building, all crooked wood and deep-set windows, with an elaborate oak staircase up the middle of it, doors as thick and heavy as fortress gates, and at the top of the house an attic marvellously full of jumbled bric-à-brac, saddlery, trinket-boxes, dusty photographs and unexplained iron things. Below the house an orchard runs away towards the river valley, and all is green and misty.

In 1818 the Griffiths family, ardent Methodists, moved into Devanna, and there being no chapel anywhere near, meetings were held in their downstairs parlour. They are still there today, and the meetings are still held in the same room. The minister comes from Knighton, Trefyclawdd, fifteen miles away, and the congregation consists almost entirely of Griffithses, all related to each other. The room must be very familiar to them. The three or four pews they move into the floor are the same pews they were propped upon in their infancies; the same pictures of Methodist divines look down gravely from the walls; the same harmonium plays the same hymns; Mr Griffiths's shotguns still hang incongruously on the beams above, and after service, as always, pots of good strong tea, with bread and butter, appear manna-like upon the big table in the middle of the room.

The effects of this religious convulsion are still with us, though gradually the power of the chapels wanes, and the hold of the deacons over public morality weakens into parody. To outsiders it was always rather absurd, matter for satirical contempt or music-hall mockery, and to many Welshmen, down to our own times, it has seemed repulsively pietist and kill-joy.

To many more Welsh people, though, Nonconformist Christianity became in the course of the Victorian century the very rock and meaning of existence, first of course as immortal souls and human beings, but secondly, hardly less strongly, as Cymry. In their eyes chapel morality was Welsh morality, self-restrained, teetotal, and the leadership of the chapels was the new Welsh aristocracy—how grand to see the minister of the great Tabernacle Chapel at Treforys, Morriston in Glamorgan, bearing himself as the equal of the industrial magnates of the town, and driving to Sunday meetings in his carriage wearing a silk hat and a frock coat! Even those Welshmen who flouted the conventions of the chapel, drank merrily in the pubs and brazenly fornicated, recognized its authority if only by defying it, and to many others the Welsh way of life was definitively embodied in the chapel way: even in 1982, when almost all Wales voted to allow the opening of pubs on Sundays, after half a century of Sabbath prohibition, sombre voices were raised, on television as in pulpit, to denounce the event as the Beginning of the End.

In some ways the Nonconformist ethos, as it became solidified in Victorian times, was alien to old Welsh instincts. Its Calvinist self-denial was at odds with the natural hedonism of a spirited and humorous people, and it did much to stifle popular music and dance in Wales. It was more effective than either the Catholic or the Anglican churches in suppressing the national penchant for the occult—just as after the Reformation Catholic priests were seen as the repositories of the old folk-wisdom, so later Anglican clerics assumed the improbable roles of exorcizers and magicians. In general, though, the movement really did express Welsh intuitions better than its predecessors, and perhaps more nearly fitted the national need than any form of religion since the age of the Celtic missionaries.

For one thing it was, despite a monolithic appearance to outsiders, furiously varied within. The theological differences between its various sects, Calvinist Methodist, Wesleyan Methodist, Baptist, Independent, might seem insignificant to churchmen or pagans, but were intensely important to their own congregations. In some parts of Wales men even cut their hair to sectarian modes, and districts of Dyfed which succumbed to the free-thinking Unitarian persuasion were known to Welsh chapel folk as Smotyn Du, the Black Spot. This fierce variety accounts for the vast number of chapels which arose in Wales. By the start of the twentieth century hardly a village was without its couple of chapels at least, Zion Baptist versus Bethesda Methodist, Calvinist Methodist sometimes cheek by jowl, in tiny hamlets, with a zealously competitive Independent. This suited the separatist ways of the Welsh, their preference for tight and local loyalties.

Then again, the democratic nature of the chapels was proper to the place. These were churches of the people. There were no Oxford-accented divines to preside over their sessions and Sunday schools, no hoity-toity squires to make those deacons feel inferior or self-conscious, no rectors' daughters plummily to discipline the choir. Social climbers and calculating tradesmen might prefer to worship with the gentry at the church, but the vast majority of the Welsh people preferred the populism of the chapels, where the ministers were men of the farms, shops and factories like themselves, and there were no gradations of birth, only of wealth or piety.

The life and politics of the chapel came to dominate innumerable Welsh lives, rather as bingo, sport or video were to obsess them later. The sonorous names of the chapels, often chosen very unexpectedly from the roster of the Holy Book, were like the names of football teams: Pisgah, Berea, Salem, Beulah, Libanus, Cephas, Ebenezer—names so overwhelming that often whole towns and villages were to be called after them. The Welsh came to know the Bible, it is said, better than any other people in Europe, and in mines, in quarries, on farms, on ships and even in taverns intense theological discussions were all the rage. Young men were proud to be called to the *sêt fawr*, the 'big pew' of the deacons, families were honoured to entertain visiting preachers to Sunday dinner.

The Sabbath was excruciatingly observed. Farmers would put off the ploughing of a furrow, even the milking of a cow. Drovers on the road, taking their herds of cattle to England, kicked their heels from

Saturday night until Monday morning. At sea the captains of Welsh ships not only conducted divine service morning and afternoon, but imposed on their crews an air of contemplative sobriety throughout the day, whatever the circumstances, however far from Salem or Ebenezer their little vessels rode the waves. At Llanuwchllyn, Gwynedd, in the 1820s, people would not even wind a clock on Sunday; in our own time the painter Nicholas Evans of Aberdare, Aberdâr in Glamorgan, would never paint a picture on the Sabbath, until he came to see it in later years as an act of worship in itself. Many people in Wales still regard Sunday newspapers as slightly sacrilegious, if only subconsciously, and when in the 1980s one was published in Welsh, for the first time ever, it did not last long.

The power of the chapels, for good or ill, became enormous. The Staff Rule Book of the Taff Vale Railway Company, 1856, declared: 'It is urgently requested every person . . . on Sundays and Holy Days, when he is not required on duty, that he will attend a place of worship; as it will be the means of promotion when vacancies occur.' In the coal-pit of Mynydd Newydd in Glamorgan, from 1871 to 1932, when the mine was closed, miners met at 6 a.m. every Monday for a service in the whitewashed underground chapel they had cut out of the solid coal in the Six Foot Seam, 774 feet deep. At Nant-y-Moel in Glamorgan the chapel-dominated Town Band would accept no players, even tuba-players, who drank: they were obliged to join a rival ensemble, known defiantly as the Beer and Bacco Band.

In the early years of Nonconformism Methodist societies were supposed to be, like Communist cells, mercilessly self-critical—there were interrogators to discover members' weaknesses, stewards to keep a register of attendances, and congregations were expected to share all their temptations and mystic experiences, as in the confrontation therapy of the 1980s. The pressure remained unrelenting even into the twentieth century. In 1900 one chapel in the Gwynedd quarry town of Bethesda (where there were at least half a dozen) organized a prayer meeting on Mondays, a procedural meeting on Tuesdays, five study classes and a literary society discussion on Wednesdays, four study classes on Thursdays, the Band of Hope on Fridays, and on Sundays a prayer meeting for the young, a morning sermon, Sunday school for all in the afternoon, a singing meeting at five o'clock and an evening sermon to bring the week to an end.

*

It could be stifling in its narrowness and intensity. As in all despotisms, busybodies thrived and hypocrisy was rampant; artistically and intellectually the nineteenth century, the great century of the chapels, was probably the dullest in Welsh history—even its theology was deadened by the force of chapel conviction. On the other hand the Welsh language was given new self-confidence. There were many English-speaking chapels, and you can still find chapels, side by side, conducting their Sunday meetings in different languages, but the Nonconformist movement in its prime was essentially a movement of the Cymry Cymraeg—comprising in those days perhaps three-quarters of the population. The revelatory preachers, the ecstatic hymn-writers, spoke and sang in Welsh. The tide of evangelical matter that swept the country, in magazines and memoirs, in books of devotion or philosophy, may mostly have been poor stuff, but at least gave the language new authority in the eyes of the people (besides leaving in its ebbing an inexhaustible deposit of improving matter throughout the second-hand bookshops of Wales). Around the chapels thrived a resurgent local culture of eisteddfod and literary meeting, even in the remotest country districts, which lingers still today, and has done much to bring the old language through doldrum and dangerous times.

Above all the chapels gave back to the Welsh, whatever their denomination, a sense of pride and enthusiasm. For all their sanctimonies, they demanded high standards of behaviour, and Welsh chapel people were scrupulously honest and temperate: the quarrymen of Gwynedd, said a local paper proudly in 1874, did not delight in cock-fighting, dog-fighting, pugilism, kicking, biting or other such brutal pleasures, but they went in their thousands to concerts and literary discussions. Strait-laced and disapproving though the Calvinist morality might seem, it was often translated into demonstrations of lively exuberance, and in later years the *Cymanfa Pregethu*, the outdoor preaching session, became almost as much a holiday as a spiritual occasion.

Thousands of people often assembled on a hillside, or beside a lake, for these marathon festivals, and we see them in old photographs, with their wagons and carts grouped around them, looking rather like emigrants on a western trail. Hour after hour the meeting would proceed, successions of preachers standing on makeshift platforms, shouting hoarsely against the wind as often as not, or bright-eyed and bareheaded in the rain. The vast crowd listened intently, weighing every word, pressing in ever more closely; and when all was over the meeting would end with some vast, grand and melancholy hymn, its theme rolling all around the empty countryside, echoing through the mountains, its last refrain repeated again and again, ever more emotionally, by the weeping, laughing, Hallelujahing and richly singing multitude.

All this time the Church of England, as in law established, clung to its embattled positions in Wales. We will visit now one of its more obscure strongholds, the church of Llanfrothen in Gwynedd. It is of no great architectural interest, is dedicated to one of the least recognizable of all the Celtic saints, the otherwise unknown St Brothen, and is to be reached only by way of a muddy winding lane, unfrequented between bigger roads. In the story of Welsh religion, though, it has twice played brief and curious roles of allegory.

In 1888 the vicar of Llanfrothen, the Revd Richard Jones, declined to allow within its consecrated graveyard the burial by Nonconformist rites of a local quarryman, Robert Roberts, whose daughter already lay there, but who was a prominent Methodist. Nonconformists had a legal right to burial according to their own rites in parish churchyards, but Mr Jones, a frenetic Anglican, maintained that the terms under which this particular plot of ground had been willed to the Church excluded it from the law. The vicar's attitude understandably angered people in Llanfrothen. Few of them were Anglicans, but most of them cherished the sanctity of a graveyard which had been theirs several centuries before the Church of England had been invented. The vicar was adamant however, and locked the churchyard gate against the quarryman's family. They in return, after taking legal advice, recruited a Methodist minister, borrowed a bier, broke open the gate with a crowbar, and buried the deceased within the churchyard in the next grave to his daughter's.

Wales has never quite forgotten this paltry squabble. The solicitor consulted by the family was Dafydd Lloyd George of Porthmadog down the road, then aged 25, and it was the Llanfrothen Church Case that first made his name. The case went to court, and was then appealed, and for months arguments raged about the facts of trespass, the nature of bequest, and the effect of the Church Burial Act, 1881, upon a conveyance of 1864. To Lloyd George however, as to the Welsh people at large, the issues were much greater than the legal niceties. When the Robertses finally won their case, and the old quarryman was left in peace in his grave beside his daughter, the victory was seen as a symbolic step towards the final liberation of the Welsh people from an alien Church imposed upon them three centuries before.

For by then the gulf between Church and common people was so deep that the official nature of Anglicanism was a farce. Among Welsh people who worshipped God at all, eight out of ten worshipped in Nonconformist chapels. The established Church in Wales had grown more English than ever, more blatantly allied to the landed classes, and much more out of touch with the needs of the people, who called it *yr hen fradwres*, 'the old traitress'—the Revd George Howell, who was buried at Llangattock, Powys, in 1884, was described on his gravestone first as Domestic Chaplain to the Duke of Beaufort, a great local landowner, and only secondly as rector of the parish. The payment of tithes for the benefit of this minority cult made the status of the Church as much a political as a spiritual grievance, and was grist to the mill of radicals like Lloyd George (who is alleged indeed by some mischievous critics to have spirited up the whole Llanfrothen affair himself). For generations Nonconformists had been agitating for the disestablishment of the Welsh Church, the ending of its official status in Wales: within the Church, too, many reformists argued for the foundation of an independent Welsh archdiocese.

The Llanfrothen decision changed nothing legally, but it seemed to give official recognition to a great wave of popular feeling. Not only were there riots in several places against the payment of tithes, but in 1904, as if to give the whole protest the divine support, there suddenly swept across Wales one last astonishing Nonconformist revival, gripping almost every neighbourhood in a visionary fervour of rededication, and compelling thousands more into the fold of the chapels. All the old excitement flared again! It began in south-west Wales, spread to the coal valleys of the south, and soon had every back-district aflame with salvationism. The country was transfixed. The winter carnival in the Pavilion at Caernarfon was cancelled for lack of merry-makers. Pit ponies stopped working because miners had given up swearing. In two years convictions for drunkenness in Wales were halved, and the mental hospital at Denbigh, in Clwyd, reported in 1905 that a quarter of new admissions were 'religious cases'. 'There came a sound', reported a worshipper at Bethesda in Gwynedd, 'like a sound from heaven, and it fell as a heavy shower upon the congregation . . . falling on everybody in the place until the place was boiling. Some weeping, some groaning, others shouting "Amen! O diolch! Bendigedig! Dyma ef wedi dod!"'—'Amen! O Thanks! Blessed! He has come!'

In all more than 100,000 conversions were claimed. The stately bishops, the Kilvertian curates, the studious vicars of the Church could hardly rival this measure of revelation, and in its wake, after years of discussion and negotiation, the Established Church of England quietly withdrew from Wales. The Welsh Church Bill Act was twice rejected by the Lords (whose hands were, said Lloyd George, recalling that many of them had been made rich by the dissolution of the monasteries, 'dripping with the fat of sacrilege'). In 1921 however it was at last decreed that the Welsh Anglican Church would henceforth be known as The Church in Wales, with an Archbishop to be elected from among the Welsh bishops. In a way it was a concession to reason: in another way it was a vindication of ancient instincts. The people's manner of worship had won, and the rites of the conquerors were cut down to size.

The Robertses still lie in Llanfrothen churchyard, round the back, and their grave is visited by television crews from time to time, for the making of historical documentaries, and by all biographers of Lloyd George. And in 1979 the church performed its second allegorical function. The death had occurred of the village landowner, the merry and patrician architect Sir Clough Williams-Ellis, who was much the best-known personality of the neighbourhood, but who had always cheerfully proclaimed himself an agnostic. An elaborate memorial was prepared for him, for erection in the church at which his ancestors had worshipped; but the parishioners, remembering his impious views, refused to accept it. So even the devoted flock of the Parson rejected, in the end, the most brilliant of Squires.

And presently, in a kind of exhausted repletion, the godly passion of Wales left the scene, as though its job were done. As the great beat of its wings died away among the mountains, something seemed to leave the soul of the country—or if not the soul, at least the sensibility. The gifts still lie on Rhulen font; the painted clock still stands awfully at five to twelve, as it always has, upon the chapel at Whitchurch, Eglwys Wen, in Dyfed; that blue-grey smoky haze still drifts through the cathedral of

Dewi Sant: but gradually, in the course of the twentieth century, this profoundly religious country has abandoned its religion.

It has long been strewn, of course, with the hulks of discredited convictions. For centuries the monasteries have been roofless and picturesque—Tintern in Gwent is one of the great tourist sights of Britain, Abaty Cwm Hir, where Llywelyn's body lies, is beset with conifers, in the old abbot's house at Llanthony, where Dewi had his hermitage, there has been for many years a flourishing hotel and restaurant (speciality *bara lafwr*, fried seaweed with bacon on top). The holy wells, all too often, stand scummy and rubbish-strewn, or are reduced to squelchy dingles. The wind blows through the last crumbled walls of the sea-shore chapels.

Here and there are reminders of yet more transient dedications. Up in the north-west, on the grand sea-coast of Ardudwy in Gwynedd, lies the once-celebrated prophetess Mari Evan, who in the late eighteenth century proclaimed herself the Betrothed of Christ, and went through a form of engagement ceremony in Ffestiniog church, wearing a red cloak and attended by many disciples. She was a lurid figure, given to preaching wild sermons on lonely sand-dunes, her white-robed disciples massed about her, and she claimed she would never die, but would await her lover until his second coming. When in 1789, aged 54 she *did* die, her followers would not believe it, but preserved her corpse until the parish constable decreed that it must be buried for hygienic reasons. She lies now in the churchyard of Llanfihangel-y-traethau, St Michael of the Sands, which stands at the end of a long lane on a hillock above the saltings. Her tombstone is a squat slate slab, crudely lettered, and it is sunk there almost surreptitiously, closely hemmed in by the stately stones and florid epitaphs of more conventional parishioners. Long ago some devotee scratched on the back her vatic pseudonym *Mari y Fantell Wen*, 'Mari Whitemantle': but the *Dictionary of Welsh Biography* identifies her simply as 'Evans, Mary, an impostor'.

Then in a gulley of the Black Mountains, higher up the Honddu valley from Llanthony, stand the remains of the monastery founded in 1869 by Joseph Leycester Lyne, a rebellious Anglican deacon ordained as Father Ignatius of Jesus by a Syrian Archbishop of debatable credentials. A Calvary marks the spot where, four times in 1880, the Holy Virgin appeared in a dazzle of light, and near by stand the gaunt white monastic buildings, long since secularized, and the roofless ruins of the chapel in which the founder, whose bardic name was Dewi

Honddu, surrounded by his sandalled homespun monks and nuns, prostrated himself before the All-Holy in the gorgeous ritual of his brief-lived Order, to clouds of incense, and a myriad flickering candles, and the thunder of an organ through the silent mountains. (He is buried there, under a big cross of stones spread-eagled beneath the open sky, and every year a pilgrimage to the site honours his flamboyant memory.)

And there are always others, to find in Wales some special inducement to transcendental experience. There are cultists of Alternative Societies, and devotees of the Magic Mushroom, and the disconcerting idiosyncratics who call themselves Mutants, and who were so feared and disliked in the 1980s that when they left their camping site in Dyfed huge boulders were placed all over it to prevent their return, like megaliths keeping evil spirits out. The Jehovah's Witnesses have done well in Wales; now and then Pentecostal preachers seem to spark some latent memory of Christmas Evans or John Elias; there are two Mormon 'stakes' or dioceses in the country, and their members like to recall that many Welshmen went with Brigham Young to Salt Lake City, to remind you that the techniques of the great Tabernacle Choir were based upon Welsh examples, and to suggest that if you are ever in those parts you might care to take State Highway 28 south from Provo and visit the old colony of Latter Day Saints called Wales, Utah.

But the vast energy of organized religion, which so galvanized and transformed Wales in its day, no longer sets the pace, decrees the tone, or even keeps the pubs closed on Sundays. Church and chapel alike have lost their hold, and the people have turned to other consolations. Are they the worse for it, or the less godly? Perhaps they are only returning to older intuitions still, which taught their remotest forebears that the divine was to be found in the stones, the springs and the trees. As Dafydd ap Gwilym sang:

> *Lle digrif y bûm heddiw*
> *Dan fentyll y gwyrddgyll gwiw . . .*
> *Ac eos gain fain fangaw*
> *O gwr y llwyn gar ei llaw,*
> *Clerwraig nant, i gant a gân*
> *Cloch aberth, clau ei chwiban,*
> *A dyrchafel yr aberth*
> *Hyd y nen . . .*

Holy Country

A happy place I was in today,
Under cloaks of lovely green hazels ...
And the eloquent slim nightingale,
From the corner of the grove near by,
Wandering poetess of the valley, rang to the multitude
The Sanctus bell, clear to its trill,
And raised the Host
As far as the sky ...

Now as then, perhaps it is in the place itself, ingrained in its soils and
floating in its atmospheres, that the true Welsh holiness resides.

4. In the Mind

'Those musicians that shall play for you', Shakespeare's Owain Glyndŵr promises his sceptical Hotspur, 'hang in the air a thousand leagues from hence, and straight they shall be here . . .' The culture of Wales was ancient even in Owain's time, the language had long evolved into maturity, and the particular shape and mood of the Welsh imagination was already formed. If we listen now, from our seats near the foot of Sycharth hall, to the conversation of the uchelwyr *at the top, or the words of Iolo Goch the praise-poet to his music, we are likely to find not just the notes and phrases familiar enough, but even the style of mind. The same chords, the same rhythms, the same laughter, the same chill down the spine when an adjective is just right, an idea especially apt, or a joke bitterly to the point, reach to us still from the hearths of Owain and his kind, and form the toughest of all the strands which link their Wales with ours.*

A THIN Welsh girl, with an elfin face, sits at a harp in a long green dress. She sits in a curiously posed way, face theatrically eager, rather as dimpled Chinese children prepare for xylophone performances. Then with a slight toss of her head, as if in ritual, she throws herself into a curious plaintive duet with herself. While her harp twangs to one melody, a few beats later her voice soars off to quite another, and so the two seem to struggle in rather metallic conflict, twisting about one another, clashing sometimes, at odds with each other's beat, until quite suddenly all is resolved, rhythm and harmony is unexpectedly restored, and the performance ends abruptly with a last apparently uncompleted chord, the girl bowing gravely over her instrument.

This is *cerdd dant*, 'art of string', or *canu penillion*, 'singing of verses', and we have been watching it on Welsh-language television, where it plays a popular part in musical entertainments of all kinds, interspersed with rock, male voice choirs and reggae. But we could have been watching something like it, live, at any time during the last thousand years: for not only has the plucked instrument always been the Welsh musical preference, but that particular taste of art, the bitter-sweet of it, the slyness, the queerness tamed by convention and brought to a not-quite-absolute concord—all this is characteristic of Welsh creativity. This is not a culture of sagas, symphonies, epochal discoveries, philosophical theories, but rather of allusive lyricism, quick humour, devices of piquant interest, passionate mysticism, romantic melancholy and meticulous surprise.

It is a populist culture. Whether it has expressed itself in Welsh or in English, in Wales the practice of art has been a public pastime. The Elizabethan poet Michael Drayton said the Welsh as a whole were addicted from birth to the art of poesy: on Sundays and holidays, another seventeenth-century observer reported, 'the multitude of all sorts . . . meet in sundry places whether on some hill or on the side of some mountain where their harpers and fiddlers sing them songs . . .'. Two hundred years later Wirt Sykes, United States Consul in Cardiff, wrote: 'To hear a poor and grimy Welshman, who looks as though he might not have a thought above bread and beer, talk about the poets and poetry of his native land, ancient and modern, is an experience which . . . gives a stranger quite a shock.' It startles strangers still, and not only in the Welsh-speaking heartlands of Wales, where poets of all sorts are conventionally expected to abound. Max Boyce, a comedian much beloved in the clubs of the English-speaking and industrialized south, appeared at a Royal Command variety performance in London in 1981, and when he ended his bubbling hilarious act with a song of compassionate lyricism about the sadness of the mining valleys, the audience seemed to respond with baffled, if not affronted, dismay.

Mysticism always gripped the Welsh creative imagination, as we can see from the few Celtic artefacts still extant in the country. There is nothing straightforward to the manner of these objects, nothing right-angled or self-explanatory. They are neither realist in style nor entirely abstractionist—pictures which have evolved into patterns, triangles blurred into rhomboids, ritual combinations of curls and circles which may have some magic meaning, but have been stylized into an art form. When living creatures appear, they are caricature humans, schematic animals, and time and again there emerges the strange triskele, the wavy pattern of connected spirals which seems to have had some arcane fascination for the Celtic mind.

Part conundrum part hyperbole, this was art for mystery's sake, and it was to persist. Nothing could be stranger than some of the mutations and transpositions of the ancient Welsh stories, which seem at first to be perfectly meaningless, but which so often have symbolic point. Take again the tale of Brân the Blessed. Mortally wounded in Ireland, Brân himself orders his companions to cut his head off and take it home with them. They obey him, and the story tells of their journeyings with the still-articulate relic, hearing strange and terrible news along the way, serenaded by magic bards, feasted at a feast that lasts seven years, lodged in a castle whose third door they must not open. Always the head stays with them, and they are called the Assembly of the Wondrous Head, and they are happy: but when they open the forbidden door they are suddenly conscious of every loss they ever suffered, every kinsman they ever missed, every ill that has befallen them. So they take the king's head to London, and they bury it beside the Thames, and there it remains, and that is one of the Three Happy

Concealments, for so long as it is hidden there no plague will come across the sea.

The Three Happy Concealments! Here are a few more such haunting categories of the Triads: Three People Who Broke Their Hearts from Bewilderment, Three Perpetual Harmonies of the Island of Britain, Three Men of the Island of Britain who were Most Courteous to Guests, Three Golden Shoemakers of the Island of Britain, Three Bull-Spectres of the Island of Britain, Three Prominent Cows, Three Slaughter-Blocks, Three Golden Corpses.

And these are the Three Elders of the World: the Owl of Cwm Cowlyd, the Eagle of Gwern Abwy, the Blackbird of Celli Gadarn.

No wonder there runs through all the literature of Wales, whether in Welsh or in English, a powerfully recondite strain, infusing even the least likely forms. The great wisdom of Dewi Sant, so his biographer Rhigyfarch tells us, was his ability to perceive 'the spiritual meaning within a literal statement', and the great strength of Welsh literature, which has been active without a break since the sixth century, is a similar fusion of the physical and the unearthly.

The *cynfeirdd* or First Poets, misty figures of antiquity like Taliesin or Aneurin, tremendously originated this tradition. Theirs is the oldest recorded poetry in any living Western language, the first to appear out of the confusion of the Dark Ages, and though they were official poets of a kind, concerned with bolstering the glories of princes, or telling heroic stories, their work was shot through with images of Fate and speculations about the meaning of things. In the ninth-century saga of Llywarch Hen, a tragic tale of war and bloodshed, the king mourns the deaths of all his twenty-four sons, and rages at his own old age, with this famous stanza:

> *Y ddeilen hon, neus cynired gwynt,*
> *Gwae hi o'i thynged!*
> *Hi hen; eleni ganed.*

> This leaf is chased by the wind,
> Alas for its fate!
> It's old; it was born this year . . .

Four centuries later an anonymous poet considers the ambiguities of springtime:

Ban ganont gogau ar flaen gwŷdd gwiw,
  Handid mwy fy llawfrydedd,
Tost mwg, amlwg anhunedd,
Can ethynt fy ngheraint yn adwedd.

When cuckoos call from the tops of fine trees,
  Greater is my sorrow,
Pain of smoke, sleeplessness evident,
For my kinsmen have gone to their death.

Ym myrn, yn nhyno, yn ynysedd môr,
  Ymhob ffordd ydd eler
Rhag Crist gwyn nid oes ynialedd.

On hill, in valley, in islands of the sea,
  Every way one goes,
From Holy Christ there is no escape.

And here, in the fateful year 1282, Gruffudd ab yr Ynad Coch climaxes his elegy for Llywelyn Olaf with a mighty appeal to the evidence of Nature itself:

Poni welwch-chwi hynt y gwynt a'r glaw?
Poni welwch-chwi'r deri'n ymdaraw?
Poni welwch-chwi'r môr yn merwinaw—'r tir?
Poni welwch-chwi'r gwir yn ymgweiriaw?
Poni welwch-chwi'r haul yn hwylaw—'r awyr?
Poni welwch-chwi'r sŷr wedi r'syrthiaw?
Poni chredwch-chwi i Dduw, ddyniadon ynfyd?
Poni welwch-chwi'r byd wedi r'bydiaw? . . .

Do you not see the path of the wind and the rain?
Do you not see the oaks beating together?
Do you not see the sea scouring the land?
Do you not see the truth preparing itself?
Do you not see the sun sailing the heavens?
Do you not see the stars fallen?
Do you not believe in God, simple men?
Do you not see that the world has ended? . . .

Five centuries on again, and half the Metaphysical poets, who specialized in 'spiritual meanings within literal statements', were Welsh by origin, if not by residence—John Donne, the two Herberts, Thomas Traherne and many more—and though they generally wrote in English they expressed just the same luminous association of things seen and unseen. Among them the closest to his roots was Henry Vaughan, 'The Silurian', whose whole life was spent in the ancient tribal territories of the Silures, along the lovely Usk in Powys. There he was born, there he ministered as a country doctor, and there he died, to be buried in the churchyard of Llansantffraid within sight of the river. The church was monstrously rebuilt by the Victorians, and a busy main road now separates it from the Usk, but still it is a magical sensation to stand there beside the Silurian's grave in the pale washed air of mid-Wales, looking across to the grand heights of Brycheiniog and remembering his poem about the afterworld:

> They are all gone into the world of light!
> And I alone sit ling'ring here;
> Their very memory is fair and bright,
> And my sad thoughts doth clear . . .

Two supreme Welsh poets of the eighteenth century expressed the visionary instinct in the idioms of the Methodist Revival. William Williams, an Anglican curate, of the farm Pantycelyn near Llanymddyfri in Dyfed, was one of the original geniuses of *Y Diwygiad*. In the flame of his conviction he wrote, besides immense works of inspirational prose, more than 900 hymns—'singing the Welsh towards God', they said of him—and some of these are not only recognized now as being among the greatest works of Welsh literature, but thanks to chapel congregations across the world, in their English versions at least are perhaps the best-known of all Welsh verses. Even more voluptuously mystical, though, was Pantycelyn's contemporary hymnist Anne Griffiths, a true ecstatic in the manner of St Teresa of Avila. It was on the farm called Dolwar Fach, near Llanfyllin in Powys, that this unlikely genius was called to her fulfilment. The property remains much as it was then, an isolated but comfortable smallholding of the lowlands, very simple still, with pigs and geese and innumerable dogs, and a few relics of the hymn-writer still in the front parlour, where pilgrims come from all over the world to sign their names reverently in the visitors' book. Until her marriage to a neighbouring farmer Anne Griffiths ran this place herself, helped only by an illiterate companion, Ruth Evans, and her poems came to her as she worked in the fields—when the inspiration came she would throw herself to the ground with cries of wonder. She never committed the words to paper, and they were preserved, we are assured, only by the memory of Ruth Evans, who dictated them after the poet's death (in childbirth, aged 29, in 1805). They are hymns of an almost erotic abandonment, in which all Anne Griffiths's emotions are sublimated in her passionate yearning for Christ, and she welcomes the Godhead, like poor Mari Evan the prophetess of Ardudwy, all but physically as her lover—*Oh! to linger all my life-time in his love!*

O ble deuai, cried in a famous line the poet Waldo Williams, who died in 1971, *yr un a fu erioed?*—'From where did he come, the one who was always?' For potently into our own century, too, the mysticism of Welsh thought has survived. Most of the best poets of the twentieth century have been essentially religious men, whether they have been priests like R. S. Thomas or Euros Bowen, academics like Roland Mathias or Bobi Jones, bank clerks like Vernon Watkins or apparently worldly reprobates like Dylan Thomas. And truest of all to the tradition, perhaps, has been Saunders Lewis, the author of plays, books of literary criticism, novels and poems, one of the few twentieth-century writers in Welsh with a European reputation, but for many Welshmen chiefly the keeper of the national conscience.

This strange man, a Liverpool-born convert to Catholicism, is thought by some to be the greatest Welshman of our time, and by others to be a seditious mischief-maker. His appearance is distraught —fierce burning eyes beneath a high, high brow, face intense with anguish or lyricism—and his attitudes have often been despairing too, as though he is fighting some fateful rearguard action against enemies most of us cannot see. His vision is catholic in every sense, searching for wider unities and more universal traditions, but the instrument of his passions has been Wales. If he has gloried in Wales as part of Europe, he has suffered for Wales as part of mankind, and in his successive battles for Welsh nationality, Welsh language, Welsh pride, which have made him many enemies, and bound to him many disciples, he has always seemed to be fighting for them as surrogates for still greater causes. He stands alone among his peers, the most metaphysical of patriots, and you can interpret his life and work in so many different ways that he is almost like an invented person, or at least the first dim delineation of a myth. Here is a poem, *Y Pîn*, 'The Pine', by this haunting genius, who retired to the respectable seaside resort of Penarth in Glamorgan, almost as far as you can get in Wales from the silent lakes of the night:

In the Mind

Llonydd yw llyn y nos yn y cwm,
Yn ei gafn di-wynt;
Cwsg Orion a'r Ddraig ar ei wyneb plwm,
Araf y cyfyd y lloer a nofio'n gyntunus i'w hynt.

Still is the lake of the night in the valley,
In its windless trough;
Orion and the Dragon sleep on its leaden face,
Slowly rises the moon and swims sleepily on her way.

Wele'n awr awr ei dyrchafael.
Chwipyn pelydri dithau o'i blaen a phicell dy lam
O fôn i frig dan ei thrafael
Yn ymsaethu i galon y gwyll fel Cannwyll y Pasg dan ei fflam:
Ust, saif y nos o'th gylch yn y gangell glaear
Ac afrlladen nef yn croesi â'i bendith y ddaear.

See now the hour of her exaltation.
At once you gleam before her with the spear of your leap
From root to top beneath her journey
Shooting to the heart of darkness like the Easter Candle beneath its
    flame:
Hush, stands the night around you in the shining chancel
And the bread of heaven crosses the earth with its blessing.

For all its dreams and visions, nevertheless, the Welsh imagination is
generally *precise*. Those enigmatic Celtic patterns were never enigmatic
in a fuzzy way: on the contrary, they were taut, calculated, balanced,
and the interweaving lines of their patterns could have been achieved
only by an uncompromising accuracy. The folk stories of Wales are
exceedingly detailed, even at their most fanciful. Welsh folk-dances,
before the chapels killed them, were unusually exact of step—in 1798 a
visitor found them so complicated that 'they would render an appren-
ticeship in them necessary to an Englishman'.

It is an imagination etched rather than sweeping. Internationally
celebrated painters have been few (Augustus John, his sister Gwen
John, Frank Brangwyn, Richard Wilson). Sculptors in the grand
manner have been fewer still (hardly a public statue in Wales seems *not*
to be the work of Goscombe John, RA, 1860–1952). The Welsh vision
often appears to be monochrome, and when Welsh artists have
experimented with colour they have sometimes seemed overwhelmed

by it. It was the Welshman Owen Jones who devised the gaudy colour scheme of the Great Exhibition at the Crystal Palace in London in 1851; the immense British Empire murals painted for the House of Lords by Frank Brangwyn in the 1920s were so violent in their greens and blues that their Lordships could not face them, and they hang today around the walls of the concert hall designed especially for them in Swansea Guildhall.

It is in definition that Welsh visual art has best succeeded. The stone walls of Wales are like wonderfully controlled abstractions, their unmortared stones fitted together with such infinite care and judgement, to be completed, as in filigree, by the mosses and ivies of time. The old custom of carving love-spoons, pairs of wooden spoons conjoined to represent true love, has often inspired a truly Celtic complexity of invention—mazy reliefs or incisions, spheres entrapped in cylinders, chain-like appendages of whittled wood. Wrought iron, too, with its capacity for twist and flourish, has suited the Welsh genius: the eighteenth-century Davies brothers of Clwyd were among the most accomplished ironworkers in Europe, and their masterpiece was the pair of gates which still stands at Chirk Castle in Clwyd—the Baroque Celticized in a pagan riot of iron flowers, birds, dogs, and foliage, and a great golden sun-face that might have been contributed by the Druids of Môn themselves.

The chief outlet for popular visual art in Wales has always been the tombstone. Today it is generally a horrible object, of speckled marble or crudely gilded slate. A century or more ago, in the days when popular religion, popular art and popular emotion were all one and the same thing, it was often very fine. Sometimes it had an original lyric elegantly chiselled on it, and sometimes it possessed a moving if simple symbolism. A grand example is the tomb of Anne Griffiths, a child who died in 1853, in the graveyard at Menai Bridge, Môn, which is surmounted by four unevenly truncated slate pillars, their shadows falling at different lengths upon the slab of the grave itself, and upon the letters of its disturbing epitaph: SHADOW OF DEATH WITHOUT ANY ORDER. Or there is a nineteenth-century monument beside the river Grwyne Fawr in the churchyard of Llangenni, Powys, which is a kind of revelatory totem: a grey obelisk, it is engraved all over with phrases and symbols, an all-seeing eye, I SAW HEAVEN OPEN, and the word Love multifariously engraved, Love in long swirly flourishes, Love in severe italic script, Love within concentric circles, the whole strange tall object standing there beside the river, at the foot of the churchyard, rather as though it has been tattooed.

The most famous Welsh lapidarists were the Brute dynasty, whose work you may find in many churches and graveyards of Gwent and Powys. For 200 years, almost into our own times, this family worked out of the village of Llanbedr in Powys, their heyday being the early nineteenth century. They were not very sophisticated craftsmen, and were prone to afterthoughts and spelling errors, but they liked to colour their memorial stones with an ochre dye of their own creation, its composition now long forgotten, which gives the slabs a naïve grandeur, and makes them feel much older than they are: while conversely the occasional insertion of a forgotten E, or the slip of a chisel on a slightly off-centre ornament, somehow suggest that Mr Bute and his assistant have just that minute left the church for dinner.

And out of the same tenebrous heritage, one supposes, came a uniquely beguiling visual folk-craft, the slate carving of Dyffryn Ogwen in Gwynedd. For some twenty years in the first half of the nineteenth century quarrymen in those parts practised at the end of their working day a curious art of their own, the etching of elaborate designs and pictures upon slate fireplaces. The work was neglected for years, almost forgotten, and it is only since the 1970s that its charm and fascination have been recognized. By now several hundred examples have been discovered, some still in houses, some used as paving-stones or thrown away as rubbish, and they show a festivity of imagination wonderful to find in those bleak and demanding uplands. Some designs are purely abstract, whirls, concentric circles, diamonds. Others represent ships, or flowers, or birds, or staves of music, or buildings, or the elaborated names of proud householders.

Up a steep little track off a country road near the village of Tregarth the pilgrim may discover the most remarkable example of this craft. A smallholder's house, a *tyddyn*, stands at the top there. Part of it is comfortably Victorian, but part of it is very old, and one enters it through a low door at the back, and through a stone-flagged dairy into the kitchen: and there around the stove stands a real prodigy of a fireplace. It is covered all over, every inch of it almost, with meticulously etched astronomical emblems and instructions—the signs of the zodiac, explanations of eclipses and the passage of comets, diagrams of the planets in their orbits. For many years this fireplace has been black-leaded, and now it gleams superbly there, and glints with the pale mountain sunshine through the window, like a black totem of omniscience made manifest in the farmhouse kitchen.

When it comes to romanticism in the Welsh intent, we can best turn to music, where the more tremulous side of the national imagination has most obviously, critics might say most blatantly, expressed itself.

Of course not all Welsh music has been rich and plummy. In a few Welsh country churches, at Christmas time, they still perform *plygain* carols—dawn carols, originally sung before the day broke on Christmas morning. These ancient hymns have been handed down orally, but several have been recorded, and so we can hear the voices of the *plygain* singers for ever in our own homes. They sound like voices out of the beams, or the rafters; dry, flaky old voices, carefully accentuating the rhythms, singing in unaccompanied quartet their innocent Christmas messages:

> *E bery cariad Iesu cu*
> *Fyth i'w ryfeddu'n faith;*
> *Datganu ei fawl, ryglyddawl glod,*
> *Sydd ormod, gormod gwaith;*
> *Hyn oll yn awr a allwn ni,*
> *Sef llawen godi llef . . .*

> The love of dear Jesus
> Will always be a wonderment;
> Sounding its praise, praising it worthily,
> Is too much, too much of a job;
> This is all that we can do now,
> Namely raising our voice merrily.

Then the harp, which can be slushy enough Heaven knows, but can also be distant and austere, is pre-eminently the instrument of the Welsh—more than that, a very part of the Welsh condition, the one possession which, in the medieval Welsh laws, could not be seized for debt. 'A pure Welsh harper,' wrote the eminent practitioner John Roberts in 1889, 'one who has love for his country, ought to be well averst with the history of his country—to be acquainted with the mountains, valleys, Rocks, Rivers, Dingles and Dales—so as to be able to give a true sound to his national music.' Among young Welsh patriots the harp is still popular. In the 1980s a busker regularly sang

Welsh lyrics to the harp among the ruins of Aberystwyth Castle in Dyfed, and as he sat there over his instrument in a long frayed overcoat, steel spectacles glinting above somewhat wispy moustaches, perfectly fulfilled old John Roberts's last precept for a true Welsh harper: 'He ought to have a Smile on his Face, or a Tear in his Eye . . .'.

The Welsh are fond of all corporate music-making: brass bands, jazz bands, rock groups, mouth-organ ensembles—at Nant-y-moel in the 1920s a harmonica band of sixty instruments used to provide incidental music for the silent movies at the Picture Palace. It is as choral singers, though, that they have always been chiefly known to the world. 'In their musical concerts', wrote Giraldus in the twelfth century, 'they do not sing in unison like the inhabitants of other countries, but in many different parts: so that in a company of singers, which one frequently meets with in Wales, you will hear as many different parts and voices as there are performers.' One still meets companies of singers frequently enough, and they will still sing in different parts. Whether it is a party of Welsh housewives on an excursion with their local branch of *Merched y Wawr*, Daughters of the Dawn, or a party of students on a cheap trip to London, or a coach-load of Rugby supporters going home well fuelled, sooner or later a voice will strike up a song, as the bus rattles and lurches through the night, and presently all of them, in the back seats, in the front, the shy young student teacher huddled in her scarf, dear old Mrs Evans taken along for the ride, the driver himself in his darkened isolation up front—presently they are singing not in unison like the inhabitants of other countries, but in a heartfelt harmony; and when they reach the last note of the song, ten to one the very last voice to be heard, outlasting all others by a determined quarter-beat, will be the richly vibratory soprano of hard-of-hearing Mrs E.

We cannot pretend that the Welsh are always good singers. They often sing badly out of tune, their emotional approach to the art driving them *en masse* sharper and sharper off key. On the other hand they do produce a remarkable number of excellent performers, from internationally famous opera singers or rock stars to a multitude of ballad tenors and delicate exponents of *canu penillion*, while the Welsh National Opera in Cardiff, which was founded as an amateur chorus by a dedicated businessman in 1946, has become one of the most generally admired companies in Europe. Welsh singers take their music very seriously, and are often resentful of the popular image of Welsh music, all throb and melody, when as they point out avant-garde

Welsh composers are producing music every bit as tuneless and arhythmic as their contemporaries anywhere else. Besides, did not Mick Jagger himself once call the Welsh 'real rockers'?

Sometimes a modern Welsh classical composer, William Mathias, Alan Hoddinott or Grace Williams, has given us Welsh music expressed in an international idiom: conversely singers like the remarkable poet Geraint Jarman have so brilliantly conjoined rock music with the Welsh language that some pundits have seen them as the chief cultural pioneers of the day. Like it or not, though, the most immediately recognizable Welsh music remains the sort of music, often maudlin, often jejune, but often moving too, which is summed up by the drear tourist slogan 'Wales, the Land of Song', and which reaches an apotheosis when on St David's Day each year several thousand Welsh exiles assemble at the Albert Hall in London to sing their hearts out with the all-too-familiar melodies.

The famous choirs of the South Wales valleys, the epitome of that image, used to be as much social as artistic phenomena—vehicles of mass feeling, or religious certainty, or universal taste. The statue that dominates the town square of Aberdare in Glamorgan (by Goscombe John, of course) represents no conquering general, statesman or even capitalist, but a genuinely native hero, Caradog the conductor, Griffith Rhys Jones, who twice took *Y Côr Mawr*, the Great Choir of the South Wales Choral Union, to victory in the Crystal Palace Choral Competitions of the 1870s. When the Victorian miners' leader William Abraham found himself faced with an unruly crowd, he had only to raise his hands and strike up a hymn, 'and hardly had he reached the second line', a wondering Scottish observer recorded, 'than he had the vast audience dropping into their respective parts, and accompanying him like a great trained choir'. Thousands of Welshmen still carry the given names, Haydn or Handel, first adopted by their grandparents in those open-throated years of long ago!

So there is only one way to end a passage about music in Wales: with a glimpse of that variously venerated and abhorred institution, the male voice choir. Mention Wales anywhere on earth, and if they have heard of the country at all, people will mention its male voice choirs. They are not so common as they used to be, but they thrive in all parts of the country, sometimes nowadays experimenting with atonal cantatas or dissonantic serenades, but more often still singing just as they always did, in the fervent Welsh way, to the old Welsh melodies.

The best time to catch a choir is at practice, when it has not been stiffened up with clean shirts and clasped hands for the concert. This is easy enough to arrange. In the country you may come across a chapel all ablaze with light on a weekday evening, and stopping to investigate, find its very structure shaking with the blast of baritones from within. And in the southern valleys, where the most worldly of the choirs are to be found, the ones that make European tours or visit Australian *eisteddfodau*, you can telephone in advance, and discover when the Treorchy or the Dowlais will be rehearsing this week, in their dowdy grey memorial hall or red-brick workmen's institute, down there among the terraces.

Wherever it is, whatever the standard of performance, the effect will be the same: a truly electric effect of irrepressible zeal. Nobody ever tried harder, than a Welsh amateur choir intent on getting an interpretation absolutely right. Just once more, cries the conductor —*unwaith eto, bois*—and the lady accompanist stiffens herself again at the piano, the stocky tenors, the well-paunched basses adjust their spectacles, smooth out the creases in their music-sheets and wait in tense taut postures, like tennis players awaiting a service, for the drop of the baton. The few people in the dim-lit body of the hall sit on the edges of their chairs. The rustlings and the coughings stop. Silence falls. The maestro crouches there before his men half-doubled on the dais, a demoniac figure, black of hair, swarthy of face, eyes gleaming. He may not be Caradog of Y Côr Mawr, but he is irresistible tonight. He raises his baton. The choir takes a breath. The pianist lifts her fingers. Crash, the place reverberates, the whole town surely, perhaps the whole of Wales, with the passion of the opening chord.

This is an old story concerning the magical place of music, and especially harp music, in the life of Wales: a man who had befriended fairies was asked what he would most like in the world. A harp, he said, which would play of its own accord—and hardly had the *Tylwyth Teg* left his house than a harp appeared beside the fireplace. He had only to touch its strings for it to burst into exuberant music.

Many people came to hear the marvellous instrument, and they found that so long as it was playing, they could not stop dancing—wild, mad dancing, whirling, prancing, leaving them when the music stopped laughing till they cried, and happily exhausted.

One day the man, in a fit of spite, would not stop the music, but kept the harp crazily playing, the people uncontrollably dancing, hour after hour into the night, until they were begging him to stop. He took no notice, but maliciously plucked away at the strings until at last, long after midnight he fell asleep over his instrument, and his guests collapsed half-dead on the floor.

Next morning the harp had vanished, and he never saw it again: nor did the *Tylwyth Teg* offer him another chance to do them favours.

Like everything else in Wales, art tends to be close-focused. An elegiac poet may summon all the effects of the empyrean into his metaphors, but he is mourning only the death of a local prince, a neighbour or the head of a family. Even the saga-like novels of modern Anglo-Welsh writers, Richard Llewellyn or Alexander Cordell, confine themselves geographically, more often than not, to particular valleys. Welsh artists have generally celebrated their own *bro*, their own chieftain, and in particular their own intimate experience of nature—nature in the detail, nature particular.

Hardly a beast, bird or fish has escaped immortalization—Dafydd ap Gwilym alone mentions some twenty species of bird—and they have generally been depicted or addressed familiarly, as equals, to be apostrophized man to man, or poet to owl, say (for the owl, as it happens, figures largely, and by no means always meritoriously). Often the creatures are enlisted as couriers, to deliver billets-doux or reproaches in a poetic device called *y llatai*, the love-messenger —Thomas Prys, in the sixteenth century, sent messages at one time or another by a porpoise, a mouse and a flea. Sometimes they are confidants, offered confessions or asked for advice—were not the Three Elders an Owl, an Eagle and a Blackbird? A few brief characterizations, then, from the grand menagerie of Welsh poetry:

Dafydd ap Gwilym, *c.*1320–*c.*1380, on the Owl:

> *Benfras, anghyweithas waedd;*
> *Lydandal, griawal groth,*
> *Lygodwraig hen lygadroth . . .*

> Large-headed, hateful of cry;
> Wide-browed, berry-bellied
> Hag-eyed old mouse-catcher . . .

❧ R. S. Thomas, b. 1913, on the Blackbird:

> A slow singer, but loading each phrase
> With history's overtones, love, joy,
> And grief learned by his dark tribe
> In other orchards . . .

❧ Llywelyn Goch ap Meurig Hen, *fl.* 1360–90, on the Coal-tit:

> *Gwyn a du yn gweini dail.*
> *Cyfaill dynionau ieuainc,*
> *Cyny bych mawr, cerddawr cainc . . .*

> White and black attending to leaves.
> A friend of young people,
> Though very small, a crafter of song . . .

❧ Christopher Smart, 1722–71, on the Cat:

> For he is the quickest to his mark of any creature.
> For he is tenacious of his point.
> For he is a mixture of gravity and waggery.
> For he knows that God is his Saviour . . .

❧ Huw Llwyd, *c.*1568–*c.*1630, on the Fox:

> *Dy ddannedd, rhyfedd yw'r rhain,*
> *Gefel chwith â gafael chwyrn*
> *Draw a wasgai drwy esgyrn.*
> *A'th lygad mor seliad sur,*
> *Hwn a droit fel hen draetur.*

> Your teeth, wonderful they are,
> Strange tongs with a quick grip
> That can crunch through bones.
> And your eye so sour of look
> You turn like an old traitor . . .

❧ Dylan Thomas, 1914–53, on the Heron:

> . . . the elegiac fisherbird stabs and paddles
> In the pebbly dab-filled
> Shallow and sedge . . .

And W. H. Davies, 1871–1940, on (for no creature has been neglected) the Rat:

> Shall I be mean, when all this light is mine?
> Is anything unworthy of its place?
> Call for the rat, and let him share my joy,
> And sit beside me here to wash his face.

The early Welsh poets were mostly professional poets of elegy or praise, dedicated to the glorification of their princely patrons. The rich amateur Dafydd ap Gwilym, in the fourteenth century, brought a merry new independence to the craft, and since his time elements of the comic and the iconoclastic have generally flourished in Welsh literature. The popular medieval story-tellers were full of fun, too, and some of their nonsensical fizz went into the folk stories still popular in the nineteenth century, like these from Llŷn:

Some yokels from Aberdaron, sold a cabbage at Pwllheli fair, are told it is a mare's egg. They have to cross a river on the way home, so lest they drop the egg during the passage they throw it into a gorse bush on the other side. This startles a hare, who leaps out of a bush: the yokels think the mare's egg must have hatched, and that a foal is running away.

A farm labourer, applying for a job, is asked why he left the previous one. It was the food, he says. When an old sow died they had nothing but bacon. When an old cow died they ate beef for months. When the farmer's mother-in-law died the labourer decided to find another job.

A similar tom-fool aptitude informs the national penchant for nick-names, of which these are a few from all ages, and all parts: Tom Twice (Thomas Thomas); Jones One Eye (who lived at no. 1 High Street); Dai Ding the bus conductor; Mrs Williams Move About; Twm Tobacco; Emlyn Kremlin the well-known Communist; Exactly Jones ('exactly, exactly', he was fond of murmuring); Dai Alphabet, who was much decorated in the Great War; Bob Ideal Milk, who talked rather grandly; Barry Central Eating (apocryphal one fears, but said to have been a man with only one tooth in the middle of his mouth).

But the mordant Welsh eye, if it can be funny, can be bitter in its vision too. Humour is often black, and mingled with despair. Thomas Edwards, 'Twm o'r Nant', most celebrated of eighteenth-century Welsh dramatists, made scathing fun of Squires Self-Esteem,

Vampire-Lawyers, Miser-Bailiffs and Reverends-in-Pigs'-Collars. Daniel Owen, chief of nineteenth-century Welsh novelists, introduced his readers on the very first page of perhaps his best-known novel, *Enoc Huws*, to a chapel elder of such nauseating humbug that he refused to speak to his only daughter as she lay dying on the bed of illegitimate childbirth—bold stuff, in the days of the Nonconformist hegemony. As for Caradoc Evans, the most brilliant short story writer of the next generations, he is remembered with contumely by some Welshmen to this very day, so savage was his assault upon the morality of rural Nonconformism, summed up in most people's minds by the macabre conclusion of his story *Be This Her Memorial*, which has the heroine, shamefully neglected for her sins by the sanctimonious chapel folk, finally eaten alive by rats in her lonely cottage.

One contemporary novelist of the Cymry Cymraeg, though, and that the most powerful of them, is universally recognized as telling the truth even in her blackest strictures. Kate Roberts, the chronicler of the North Wales quarry country, is often called the Welsh Chekhov. Certainly she peoples her narrow grey stage, in the quarry villages and smallholdings above the sea, with a Russian intensity. Her stories deal almost entirely with poor people leading harsh lives of struggle, lit sometimes by flashes of success, when scholarships are won, or beautiful babies are born. If her men are often weak and unreliable, and her minor female characters flighty, her central heroines are indefatigable, bearing upon their shoulders the whole burden of family responsibility or moral purpose, and even it sometimes seems of national identity—for in the best of her writing not just the world of the slate quarries, but the wider world of rural Wales itself is encapsulated.

In her old age Kate Roberts lived in Denbigh, and there a regular stream of pilgrims went to visit her in her comfortable but oddly incongruous 1930ish house, with its genteel lawns and mullioned windows. She was very frail by then, and lay often upon her bed almost unable to move: but so perversely wiry did she look down there, so hard and grey, with her sharp quick eyes looking out of her pain, and her hand resolutely on her walking-stick to heave herself into a position of welcome—so taut and gritty was her presence that it was rather like visiting one of her own stories, seeing the sentences hewing themselves out before you, and the hard attainment of adverbs.

*

For all its opaque and bemusing climate, better for impressions than for facts, Wales has been fertile enough in ideas. Perhaps solutions form themselves, or innovations fall, out of the morning mist! Here now are some notions that were conceived, some things that were invented, some men of perception who were born, some events that were first generated in this nook of a country.

*c.*380 Pelagius first preached his heresy, they say, from the tumulus still standing in the churchyard of Castell Cerinion in Powys: it declared man to be independent of God's will, spread through much of Europe until its extinction in the following century, and is now back in fashion.

1888 T. E. Lawrence, 'Lawrence of Arabia', was born at Tremadog, Gwynedd, the illegitimate son of an Irish baronet and his family governess: a plaque marks the house, and though Lawrence lived in it for less than a year, the chance of his birth there was to qualify him for his scholarship at Jesus College, the Welsh college at Oxford.

1982 Wales was declared the first nuclear-free country in Europe, all its county councils having agreed never to allow nuclear weapons on their soil (but the Royal Ordnance Factory at Llanishen, Cardiff, continued to make casings for nuclear bombs anyway).

1873 Lawn tennis was first played by Major Walter Wingfield at Nantclwyd Hall, Llanelidan in Clwyd: the historic court has not been preserved, and what might be one of the world's great sporting shrines does not encourage visitors.

*c.*1550 The mathematical sign for equality, =, was invented by Robert Recorde of Tenby, Dinbych-y-pysgod in Dyfed: he died bankrupt in a debtors' gaol, but never mind, a memorial in Tenby Parish Church commemorates him.

1841 Sir Henry Morton Stanley, MP, Knight Grand Cross of the Order of the Bath, was born at Denbigh, Dinbych in Clwyd, the illegitimate son of John Rowlands and Elizabeth Parry: he was brought up in the workhouse at St Asaph, Llanelwy, went to sea, was befriended by Henry Morton Stanley of New Orleans, and became the most formidable of all African explorers.

1568 Brass was first made by alloying copper with zinc, at Tintern, Gwent: or so it says on a plaque on a wall outside the Abbey.

1663   The first practical steam engine was built by Edward Somerset, second Marquis of Worcester, in Raglan Castle, Gwent: or so it says on a plaque in Raglan Church.

1771   Robert Owen was born at Newtown, Trenewydd, Powys, the son of an ironmonger: socialist, Utopian, 'founder of the cooperative movement', he returned to die there in 1858, and his florid tomb, embellished by admirers long after his death (he despised all forms of organized religion), is in the yard of the ruined medieval church.

1890   The Sealyham terrier was first bred, by John Owen Edwards, at Sealyham Hall in Dyfed: it was a mixture of the Corgi and miscellaneously apposite mongrels, was intended for otter-hunting, and was selectively evolved by pitting it against captive polecats.

1861   The first mail-order business was started by Sir Pryce Pryce-Jones of Newtown: among his customers was Queen Victoria, and his big red-brick emporium, which is still active, is called the Royal Welsh Warehouse.

1804   The first steam railway engine, invented by the Cornishman Richard Trevithick, made its first journey from Merthyr Tydfil to Quaker's Yard in Glamorgan, pulling ten tons of iron and seventy passengers at five miles an hour, and stopping several times for the removal of inconvenient trees.

1878   The Bessemer process of steel-making was perfected by Sidney Gilchrist Thomas and his cousin Percy Carlyle Gilchrist at Blaenavon in Gwent: their discoveries transformed the steel industry, and led directly to the industrial expansion of the Ruhr in Germany, and thus to the First World War.

*c.*1750   Copper sheathing for ships was first thought of, in Môn: it was noticed that the hulls of ships using the copper-polluted port of Amlwch never seemed to be fouled.

1872   Bertrand Arthur William Russell, philosopher, was born at Trelleck in Gwent: in 1955 he went to live at Plas Penrhyn, on a ridge above the sea at Penrhyndeudraeth in Gwynedd, and there he died in 1970, the world for all its horrors, he wrote, having left him unshaken.

1924   The first of all radio plays was written by Richard Hughes the novelist, and broadcast by the British Broadcasting Company Ltd.: it was called *Danger*.

1807   The first public passenger train, pulled by horses, ran along the coast road from Swansea to Oystermouth, Ystumllwynarth in Glamorgan: it continued to run, hauled later by steam engines, later still by electricity, and finally metamorphosed into double-decker trams, until the service was ended to scenes of public mourning in 1960.

1897   The first radio message transmitted across water was sent by Guglielmo Marconi from the island of Flat Holm to Lavernock Point, Trwyn Larnog, in Glamorgan: a commemorative stone is one of the few un-crumbled structures on the island, a plaque in a wall marks the place of reception, and in the National Museum at Cardiff is preserved the historic message itself—'Are You Ready?'

There have been a thousand other Welsh innovations of course, from the breeding of new grasses at Aberystwyth to the making of ice in Benares, first achieved in the eighteenth century by John Lloyd Williams from Dyfed. It is a varied roster, but we will narrow the focus now, and consider one field of mental enterprise in which Welshmen have traditionally specialized: medicine. Wales has always swarmed with doctors, qualified and unqualified, quacks and great specialists, back-country bone-setters and distillers of magic ointments to eminent brain surgeons and infallible psychiatrists.

The father of them all was perhaps Melus the Physician, son of Martinus, who is remembered in a fifth- or perhaps sixth-century Latin inscription on a churchyard pillar at Llangian, tucked away in a cranny of Llŷn. The tradition is more famously embodied, though, in the Doctors of Myddfai, *Meddygon Myddfai*, the supposed descendants of that Lady of Llyn y Fan Fach whose unsuccessful marriage we have already explored. She bequeathed to her mortal family, when she returned to the lake, a matchless body of medical lore, and her descendants made such good use of it that their curative skills became famous all over Wales, and *Meddygon Myddfai* became almost a generic name for Welsh physicians.

For centuries Myddfai, which is nothing more than an obscure hamlet, really was a centre of medical practice and research—the great

Lord Rhys of Dinefwr, one of the most powerful of the Welsh princes, was the protector, patron and no doubt grateful patient of its doctors. All around the district there are still place-names of medical connotation—Llwyn Ifan Feddyg, for instance, the Grove of Ifan the Doctor, or Llidiart-y-Meddygon, Gate of the Doctors—and the family that claimed to have started the tradition, back in the days of fairy-tale, actually did produce working doctors and vets until late in the nineteenth century: their last representative is said to have been Sir John Williams, physician and accoucheur to Queen Victoria of England.

The Myddfai School of medicine was inevitably confused with folk-wisdom and magic, as we can see from some of its recommendations, codified in the Middle Ages. For the extraction of a tooth, for example, the physician was advised to apply to the tooth a powdered calcination of newts: the tooth would presently fall out painlessly of its own accord. For the soothing or encouragement of the brain, the following were recommended methods: smelling musk, drinking wine moderately, keeping the head warm, washing the hands frequently, listening to music, smelling roses and washing the eyebrows with rose-water. As to that perennial concern of the medical profession, stress or depression, it could easily be cured by the adding of saffron to meat or drink—'but beware of eating over-much, lest you should die of excessive joy'.

Alternative medicine of one kind and another has always found receptive patients in Wales, and the lore of the country is full of such esoteric remedies, some of them still sworn by. There were the multitudinous panaceas of the holy wells, of course, but there were also cures specific to certain herbs or meats, or known only by particular families of curers—several families offered hereditary remedies for malignant ulcers, and others knew how to deal with snake-bites. Until the second half of the nineteenth century, at least, people believed that the grass in the churchyard of St Edern's in Dyfed, now an abandoned ruin, was a specific against rabies, and people bitten by mad dogs would travel from all over Wales to eat it in bread and butter sandwiches. Barmouth, Abermo in Gwynedd, produced a seaweed that was excellent for kidney diseases; oil made from Môn sheep's fat was indispensable to rheumatics; within living memory Welsh people were treating whooping cough with the juice of sugared slugs, earache with drops of human urine and incontinence by mixing roast mouse with bread and milk. Whooping cough could also be cured by the action of the sea

—stand at the water's edge and the ebb tide would remove the germ: in 1916 a mother took her sick child back and forth on the Severn ferry near Chepstow until the cough was gone.

Quacks flourished, and often succeeded by the force of suggestive power. Into our own times the patients of a medical conjuror living near Llangurig willingly submitted to various rituals of lesser mumbo-jumbo, like standing within chalked circles or listening to incomprehensible formulae, and thousands are said to have been cured of multifarious diseases by the Great Welsh Remedy which Gwilym Evans of Caergybi, Môn, touted in the nineteenth century—a medicine, he grandly claimed, of 'inherent and peculiar powers'.

But many able men, too, practised unconventional medicine. The combination of health salts devised by Evan Jones, a nineteenth-century healer of Whitland, became the basis of Ffynnon Salts, one of the most trusted of British branded health products. The Thomas dynasty of bone-setters in Môn produced the great orthopaedic surgeon Sir Robert Jones (1857–1933), and until the 1950s inhabitants of Llŷn trusted implicitly in the cancer-curing formula of Owen Griffiths of Llangwnnadl (they used to call a cancer *dafad wyllt*, 'wild sheep'). Another admired practitioner, Hugh Lloyd of Powys, is commemorated by an epitaph in the church of Michaelchurch-on-Arrow, just over the border in Herefordshire:

> A talent rare by him possessed
> T'adjust the bones of the distressed;
> When ever called he ne'er refused
> But cheerfully his talent used.
> But now he lies beneath this tomb,
> Till Jesus comes to adjust his own.

Many Welsh physicians are thus fondly recalled. The folk-memory is full of doctor-figures, quaint, lovable or sometimes insufferable —doctors who went off to sea each year, as ships' surgeons for their annual holidays—doctors with magnificent libraries, or wonderful ancient cars—traitor doctors, who diagnosed as the iron-masters instructed them, worker-doctors who would always give you a certificate of ill health if you had a ticket for the Rugby international—doctors immensely grand, like Fergus Armstrong of Tonpentre in Glamorgan, who habitually wore a sable fur coat from St Petersburg, and was known as 'The Baron', and doctors fabulously celebrated, like J. P. R. Williams, the star of Welsh Rugby stars in the 1970s. Sometimes Welsh families spawned generation after generation of physicians: the descendants of the Revd Henry Davies of the Rhondda, who died in 1766, have so far included fourteen doctors and another half-dozen, so to speak, doctors-in-law.

Here is a portrait, *con amore*, of a Welsh family doctor, of a kind only now being made extinct by social change and medical advance. Robert Rees Prytherch was born in Môn in 1908 of a ship-owning family, took a medical degree at Cambridge, and was for many years a general practitioner in the Gwynedd seaside town of Cricieth, dying there in 1976. An internationally famous fly-fisherman, a lifeboat volunteer in his youth, he was perhaps the best-known citizen of the little town: everybody knew him, and by the time of his death nearly everyone's father had known him too. He was, in his maturity, a slightly stooping man with hooded thoughtful eyes; his eyebrows were habitually raised as if in faint surprise, and his surgery, in his big Victorian house above the sea, was a brown jumble of this and that, books and bags and boxes, piles of medical journals, boots in a corner, pictures of ships, or local landscapes, or fishing rivers on the walls. His pace was slowish and measured, and entailed a good deal of conversation, and kept a queue of patients waiting faithfully in the gloom of the waiting-room outside.

But it was when Dr Prytherch went on his rounds that he came into his own. He was a tireless visitor, and knew the inside of everyone's home from Chwilog to Pentrefelin. Here he would come now in his estate car up the lane, wearing an angler's hat, and behind his seat would be his big black Labrador, and there would be a bag of rods propped against the back of his seat, and a twelve-bore, and a landing-net jammed in somehow, and a box of flies beside his doctor's bag. Out there on the farms in his muddy boots he was everyone's idea of a country doctor, welcomed like an old friend—'Ah, come in now, come in doctor, we've got the tea just on the boil, *yn arbennig ichi*, special for you mind!'—gossiped about like a neighbour—'I'm not saying a word against Robert Prytherch now, I'm only saying that he never *did* understand poor Elen . . .'—and frequently to be seen, at the end of the day, expertly casting his fly on his beat on the Glaslyn river (where he had a telephone for emergencies fixed to a tree) or labouring up the lane to his fishing cottage, in long thick oilskins almost down to his feet, clasping by its tail a glistening salmon.

When he died, people said *dewch*, there would never be another like him, one of the old sort he was, and half Gwynedd breathed an affectionate *requiescat* over his memory.

Midwives too were people of consequence. Meg, a midwife of Llangwrog, in Gwynedd, was approached by a tall handsome stranger at Caernarfon market one day and asked to come at once, his wife being in labour. Away they sped on his magnificent black stallion, fast as the wind, and through a wood, and over a ridge, and there stood the most marvellous of castles glittering below, and in it the loveliest of women in labour, and presently the most beautiful of boy babies was born in the splendour of her chamber. 'Rub this ointment on the child's eyes', said the man, 'but whatever you do, get none of it on your own.' Meg did as she was told, but accidentally allowed a speck of the stuff into her right eye, and instantly all was changed—the castle was a hovel, the magnificent four-poster bed was a pile of rushes, and the beautiful young mother was none other than Myfanwy, a poor young woman of Llangwrog.

With a scream poor Meg ran from the place, over the ridge, through the wood, never stopping until she was safe at home. Some months later she saw the man at the market again. 'How is Myfanwy?' she boldly said. 'Very well', said the man, 'but tell me, which eye do you see me with?' 'The right eye', said Meg. The man raised his stick without a word, and poked the eye out.

Medicine apart, and despite the prevalence of archaic Welsh names in the geological vocabulary (the Cambrian System, the Silurian System, the Ordovician), science in Wales has generally been confused in the public mind with wizardry of one sort or another—the only Absolute Truth is the Truth of God, and searching for alternatives must be devil's work. The great Elizabethan polymath John Dee, astronomer, geographer, political economist, mathematician, was best known in his native Powys as a necromancer, an alchemist and an exponent of the Black Arts, and many a country scholar had only to stay up late over his Virgil to be suspected of malicious sorcery. Such old prejudices still cloud the memory of the most celebrated modern scientific investigator in Wales, the late and mysterious Grindell Matthews of Craigcefnparc.

Craigcefnparc is a small village in the foothills north of Swansea, where the industrial coastland meets the raw high country of the interior. Here in 1934 Matthews, a much-publicized private scientist, allegedly got down to work to perfect a Death Ray that would make all other weapons obsolete. In the course of a long inventing career he had already pioneered developments in radio telephony (he produced the Aerophone in 1910), in light-controlled boats (his experimental *Dawn* had been demonstrated to the Admiralty) and in talking films. Now, it was said, he foresaw the coming of the Second World War, and was going to devote himself to weaponry. He set up his laboratory in a black and white bungalow which he built on the high moorland above the village, and there he lived for several years as a recluse with his housekeeper and his Persian cats, seldom appearing in public, and visited only, if we are to trust the folk-memory, by strangers in big black cars or aviators landing their monoplanes on his private landing-strip. Wild rumours surrounded his activities, sightseers crept warily about his property, and the London Press seized avidly upon the Death Ray Man and his Laboratory in the Mist. He was in short the very exemplar of the Welsh sorcerer, tinkering with the unknown up there, alone with his cats and his calculations.

His one biographer, E. H. G. Barwell, tells us that Matthews was thinking too about rocket power, aerial minefields, submarine detection and interplanetary travel, but to the local people he was always and only the Death Ray Man. He vanished from the moors soon after the start of the war. Barwell says he died in his bungalow, but the rumorists thought otherwise. Some said he had gone to develop his ray in a Government establishment somewhere, while others maintained that he had really been a German all the time, and had either been spirited away to Berlin, or shot in the Tower of London. As wizards do, he disappeared.

His laboratory is now used as a riding stables, but still looks lonely and suggestive up there on the mountain. Some local people swear that he actually perfected his ultimate weapon (though Barwell claims only that it could kill a rat at 60 yards): and there are farmers still around to tell you of the weird things that used to happen to the engines of their cars, when they crossed the invisible tracks of Grindell Matthews' projections.

Despite occasional appearances, and general reputation, Welsh creativity is unusually disciplined, for since the earliest times the Welsh artistic tradition has been governed by codes and conventions—perhaps since the Druids, relying as they did entirely upon their memories, drew up rules of composition to make it easier for themselves.

In the Wales of the Independence the bards and harpers were institutionalized, with their own allotted places in society, their established functions to perform. They regarded poetry and music as professions, for the practice of which one must qualify, like a lawyer or a doctor. There were agreed measurements of value for a work of art, and the subjects of poetry were formalized, consisting at least until the fourteenth century mainly of eulogies and elegies. More importantly still, the forms of art were governed. Musicians were restricted by intricate rules of composition. Poets were governed by the Twenty-Four Strict Metres of the classical Welsh tradition.

Among the Cymry Cymraeg the Metres still prevail. When Welsh poets speak of Free Verse, they mean forms like the sonnet or the ode, which obey the same easy rules as English poesy. Strict Metre verse still honours the immensely complex rules laid down for correct poetic composition 600 years ago. To foreign sensibilities they often seem crippling, and there have certainly been poetic talents stifled or misdirected by the authority of the Strict Metres: but they have also been the whetstone upon which the Welsh poetic genius has been sharpened—or the scaffold, perhaps, against which its energies have been strung and tautened, like the struts upon which the Catherine wheel spins around its nail, spitting sparks into the night.

Writers in English have often tried to adapt the sounds and rhythms of Welsh poesy to their own language, but it never quite works, for the rules of the system and the sounds of the Welsh tongue are made specifically for each other. The system is actually called *cynghanedd*, harmony—and was defined by Gerard Manley Hopkins, who tried to use it in his own English verse, as 'consonantal chime'. It is divided into three main types, depending partly on rhyme, partly on alliteration. Cross harmony demands internal alliteration, three-part harmony demands alliteration and internal rhyming, bridge harmony requires a kind of delayed alliteration. But within these kinds there are other conventions of more demanding complexity: for example the seven-syllabled metre called the *cywydd* also requires that an accented word should always rhyme with an unaccented word, while a still more complicated form, *croes cadwyngyrch*, insists upon complete alliteration of consonants within a line, together with consonantal harmony of initial letters of all the lines in the poem, and consonantal alliteration of the last words of one line with the first word of the next!

These laws of the Twenty-Four Metres make for an impression of complicated sound, interwoven with meaning, given fizz by intellectual challenge, and resolving itself, like *penillion* once again, into an unexpectedly harmonious whole. They mean that classical Welsh poetry is still essentially an aural pleasure, and they demand of its practitioners not only artistic gifts, but great semantic or even acrostic agility, rather as though every single line were to contain a compulsory anagram. There has probably never been a verse system more difficult, or more subtle.

In the hands of its masters *cynghanedd* has been carried to marvellous heights of virtuosity, binding the whole literary tradition together and giving to this little country the curious possession of a literature of lofty standard that cannot be properly understood, even in the most subtle and sympathetic translation, except by a minority of its own people. It is part of the secret otherness of the nation, very old, very hard to grasp, but still exerting so strong an appeal that every year scores of competitors submit to the judges of the National Eisteddfod epic poems of 500 lines, every single line observing the strict rules of *cynghanedd*.

But the rules are honoured by more ordinary craftsmen too, and particularly in the epigrammatic form of Welsh verse called the *englyn*, which is perhaps the most truly Welsh art form of all. Four lines long, with alliterations throughout, a curious sort of jerk or stammer to the scansion of the opening line, and a closing couplet in which a stressed syllable must rhyme with unstressed syllable, the *englyn* is sharp and to the point—there is something almost Japanese to its intricate small clarity, so abrupt, often so wry.

To illustrate the form, here is an *englyn*, on the will-o'-the-wisp, written in English by Robert Graves:

> See a gleam in the gloaming—out yonder
> It wand'reth bright flaming;
> Its force, that is a fierce thing!
> It draweth men to drowning.

And here is the real thing, in the hands of a contemporary master of the form, Alan Llwyd, writing about Cymru itself:

Fy ing enfawr, fy ngwynfyd,—fy mhryder,
Fy mhradwys hyfryd;
Ei charu'r wyf yn chwerw hefyd,
A'i chasau'n serchus o hyd.

My great agony, my bliss—my anxiety,
My lovely paradise;
I love her bitterly too,
And hate her affectionately always.

Among the Cymry Cymraeg the *englyn* remains a true folk-form. It appears on innumerable tombstones, it is thrown off extempore by poets in competitions, and it is composed still by thousands of domestic practitioners, who contribute it in columns to local Welsh-language magazines. What a quick, quaint, elegant device, to represent the sensibility of a people!

Once a year the Welshest part of the Welsh culture assembles its energies, so to speak, in an effervescent affirmation of its survival. The National Eisteddfod, held in the first week of August alternately in North Wales and in South, is one of the greatest folk festivals of Europe. Hundreds of *eisteddfodau* are held in Wales every year, from minute local celebrations like that in the Gwynedd hamlet of Garndolbenmaen, where the prizes offered in 1983 included £1 for the best *englyn* on the subject of Water, to the well-known International Eisteddfod at Llangollen in Clwyd, during whose week of activity in July songs in unknown tongues resound all along the Dee, and folksy aprons of many colours, hats of curious silhouette, are to be seen at the queues for fish and chips. Much the greatest of them, though, is the Eisteddfod Genedlaethol, the National Eisteddfod of Wales.

When the idea of such a national festival was mooted in the early nineteenth century, it was imagined as a direct descendant to bardic assemblies of ancient times, or even to rituals of the Druids. Its instigator was the immensely gifted but perhaps half-crazed littérateur Iolo Morgannwg, whom we shall meet again, and this is how he decreed that an Eisteddfod should be proclaimed, a year and a day before its opening each year, by a herald of the Gorsedd, the semi-fictional body of bards which he himself had resurrected:

When the year of our Lord is ——, and the period of the Gorsedd of the

Bards of the Isle of Britain within the summer solstice, after summons and invitation to all Wales through the Gorsedd Trumpet, under warning of a year and a day, in sight and hearing of lords and commons and in the face of the sun, the eye of light, be it known that a Gorsedd and Eisteddfod will be held at the town of ——, where protection will be afforded to all who seek privilege, dignity and licence in Poetry and Minstrelsy ... And thither shall come the Archdruid and Officers of the Gorsedd and others, Bards and Licentiates of the Privilege and Robe of the Bards of the Isle of Britain, there to hold judgement of Chair and Gorsedd on Music and Poetry concerning the muse, conduct and learning of all who may come to seek the dignity of National Eisteddfod honours, according to the privilege and customs of the Gorsedd of the Bards of the Isle of Britain.

VOICE AGAINST RESOUNDING VOICE

TRUTH AGAINST THE WORLD

GOD AND ALL GOODNESS

This pleasing gobbledegook was characteristic of Iolo's conception. He invented a bardic symbol for his Gorsedd, and explained it thus: 'And God vocalizing his name said /|\, and with the Word all the world sprang into being, singing in ecstasy of joy /|\ and repeating the name of the Deity.' So with the very voice of God the great annual jamboree was launched. After a fitful start in Iolo's day it began its modern career in 1858, and by the end of the century Herbert Herkomer, one of the most fashionable painters of the day, had created for its functionaries gloriously neo-Druidical robes and insignia of gold, velvet and ermine (the Archdruid's breastplate was designed to choke him, Herkomer said, if he gave a false judgement). The English found it all ludicrous: the *Daily Telegraph*, reporting the 1858 assembly, which *was* rather preposterous actually, called it 'a national debauch of sentimentality', *The Times* said it was 'simply foolish interference with the natural progress of civilization and prosperity—it is a monstrous folly to encourage the Welsh in a loving fondness for their old language'.

But that fondness was to prove irresistible, and the Eisteddfod Genedlaethol flourishes as never before, having matured from cranky antiquarianism through rigid chapel respectability to a fairly pragmatic tolerance of public views and social styles. Though its competitions are confined strictly to the Welsh language, and though even many Welsh-speaking writers and musicians prefer to have nothing to do with it, still it remains the chief public expression of the Welsh culture's continuing existence, the one occasion when a stranger can realize that the language is still creative, the traditions are not lost, and the loyalty of the Welsh people to their origins is by no means dissipated. Honorary membership of the Gorsedd is still the only honour the Welsh nation can bestow upon its sons and daughters, and in a kind of back-handed symbolism the British Government's Secretary of State for Wales is generally invited to open the festival's proceedings (generally having to learn a few words of Welsh in order to do so . . .).

The Eisteddfod in full fig is rather like a military encampment. All its tents and pavilions are erected around a big central space, the *Maes* or Field, which is usually scuffed and slippery with mud by the end of the week, Welsh Augusts being what they are, and throughout the festival hundreds of people are perpetually wandering around this arena, some perfectly aimlessly, licking ice-creams, some hoping to meet friends, or to run into some of the Welsh celebrities who are always obligingly to hand. Most institutions of modern Wales are represented on the *Maes*, Gas Board to University of Wales Press, the genteel Society for the Protection of Rural Wales to the fiery Cymdeithas yr Iaith Cymraeg, the Welsh Language Society. There are shops selling harps, and comic stickers, and *Lol* the lewd and racy student magazine, and pottery, and evangelical tracts, and lots and lots of books. There are advertisements for Welsh travel agencies, Welsh computer firms, video-cassettes of Welsh television programmes or the Roma House Hotel in London ('proprietor Talfryn Phillips, Tenor'). There is a tent especially for learners of the Welsh language, flooded in instructional materials, there is an exhibition of arts, crafts and architecture, there are pavilions where one may watch the television coverage of BBC Cymru, Teledu Harlech, or Sianel Pedwar Cymru, and there are restaurant-tents with long trestle tables and steaming tea-urns (but no alcohol—you must go down to the town for that, as all the young bloods will certainly be going tonight).

Satirical reviews are put on by students, and a bustling booming marquee is devoted to Welsh rock music, but the Eisteddfod is essentially competitive: there are competitions for *penillion*, and *englynion*, and male voice choirs, and poems in strict metre, and poems in free metre, and essays, and translations, and plays, and short stories. All over the field, warbling voices and twanging harps are relayed somewhat anaemically over loudspeakers: outside the *Pabell Lên*, the

Literary Tent, poets mutter couplets to themselves, or exchange bitter
bardic complaints. And twice during the week, for the Crowning of the
bard who writes the best poem on a set theme in free metre, for the
Chairing of the bard who writes the best poem in strict metre, the
whole assembly seems to turn towards the Grand Pavilion, claimed to
be the largest movable structure in the world. Multitudes jam its doors
then, television cameras swing about its gantries, and the worthies of
the Gorsedd of the Isle of Britain, robed in green, white and blue, are
unloaded from buses at its entrance.

Tara, tara, blare the trumpets on the stage, east, west, north and
south. *Oes heddwch?* demands the Archdruid of the great
gathering—'Is there peace?' *Heddwch!* responds the crowd, and the
Great Sword of the Gorsedd is sheathed for another year. How Iolo
must enjoy it! There on the stage all the members of his Gorsedd are
now assembled, some bespectacled, some with trousers showing
beneath their robes, but all looking properly learned or poetical, with
the Archdruid at their head in Herkomer's golden breastplate, and all
his acolytes, Herald and Recorder and Swordbearer, grouped pictorially about. Green-clad elves come dancing in, escorting a matron
with a horn of plenty. Harps play. Children sing. The tension mounts,
for nobody in that immense audience yet knows who is to be the
recipient of all this honour. The winning poet is somewhere among
them, but first he must be found.

A searchlight plays now along the rows of seats. There is silence, but
for the rustle and stir as four thousand people twist in their chairs to
follow its progress. Slowly it moves across the hall, tantalizingly
wavering now and then, jerking on, slowing down, while the cameras
follow from their high gantries, until at last it falls upon a particular
figure, dazzling him with its glare. The poet has really known for some
time that he is the winner, but he pretends a proper astonishment
anyway, and is raised faintly resisting to his feet, and out to the aisle,
and away up to the platform escorted by druids. The organ blazes a
grand march, the gathering rises to its feet, the cameras whirr, and the
bard is throned upon his bardic throne, attended by elves and
trumpeters and druids, in a haze of medallions, oaken wands, gleaming
accoutrements and banners talismanically inscribed.

Gently he is settled upon the Chair which is itself his prize, and he is
proclaimed a champion: not because he has won a war or a football
game, or even an election, but because he is judged by wise men of his

nation to have composed a worthy *cywydd* concerning the nature of clouds.

Behind it all, behind the noble literature, behind the quiddities of Welsh thought and invention, behind those guileless carvings of the fireplaces or the innocent progress of Dr Prytherch among his patients, behind the humour, behind the mystery, behind the spirit of the Welsh laws and the style of the great Eisteddfod—behind it all stands one supreme heritage of the Welsh mind: Cymraeg, which is spoken only by a fifth of the population, half a million in all, but which remains as vivid and as fertile as ever.

It is the oldest living literary language in Europe, and its historic epigraphs are among the chief treasures of Wales: the stone in the church at Tywyn, on the Gwynedd coast (flowers and Sunday School paintings propped against it) which is inscribed with the oldest of all Welsh inscriptions, or the cramped little memorial to the scholar Adam of Usk, in Usk church, which is the oldest Welsh text on brass. The very survival of the language is an astonishment. Once related languages were heard over much of Europe, in the days when the Celts were powerful from the Black Sea to the Atlantic, but today they are spoken only in Ireland, in western parts of Scotland, vestigially in Cornwall, in Brittany and in Wales (a proclamation is read in Manx at the opening of the Isle of Man Parliament each year, but probably not a soul there, except the Herald himself, can understand a word of it).

Of these survivors only Welsh can presently claim to be a completely contemporary tongue, spoken by hundreds of thousands of people as their ordinary vernacular, but expressing itself also in the full range of literature, journalism, radio and television programmes, rock lyrics, official documents, drama and satirical revue. The language is the truest badge of Welsh identity—*Yr Hen Iaith*, the Old Language of the country, as against *Yr Iaith Fain*, the Thin Language of the English. The literary tradition embodied in it is the grandest constant of Wales, and even in its most vestigial forms, in names on signposts, in bilingual warnings about the disposal of rubbish, it gives notice to all comers that Wales is still a separate place.

It is, as everyone agrees, a poetic language—even those who do not understand a word of it often marvel at its strength and resonance. Its characteristic sounds are part guttural, part slithery, like the consonantal *ll* which foreigners are so often reluctant to tackle; its flow is eased by the practice of mutating initial letters of words to relate to the word before, a practice called in Welsh *treiglo*, 'wandering', which prevents abrupt changes of timbre, and to the foreign ear makes everything slur into everything else. The pronunciation of Welsh is logical and straightforward—much easier than English, for instance. Its grammar is complex, and only in the 1920s was its orthography finally settled. Its nuances are subtle: the word *gŵydd* or *gwŷdd*, for instance, can mean according to context and accent a loom, a goose, a plough, a weaver, trees, wild or presence. There are strong differences of dialect in various parts of Wales, but standard written Welsh is the same everywhere, and in fact has changed in essence so little down the centuries that an educated Welshman can still read, without too much difficulty, the Welsh of the Middle Ages. It is a language wonderfully rich in idiom, and with an almost Arabic profligacy of proverbs—*Rhyw i hwch ei rhoch*, 'grunting is natural to a sow', or *Waethwaeth fel mab gafr*, 'worse and worse like the son of a goat'.

Welsh has taken some batterings in its time, is on the defensive always, and has been in numerical decline since 1911, when it reached an apogee of almost a million speakers. Cassandras constantly pronounce its doom. But it is sustained by a multitude of lovers and enthusiasts, and still stands at the very heart of Welshness. Without it, it can be said, there would be no Wales by now, only another province of England, speaking a dialect little more distinctive than Yorkshire or Devonian. The Welsh manner of thought, the Welsh style of things, even perhaps the Welsh face, all have been moulded by Cymraeg. It is a life-giving language. In those parts of Wales where it has died, leaving only fugitive verbs and spectral adjectives to give an enigmatic beauty to the names of places, something is missing, something saddened—*gaeaf cenedl*, the poet Waldo Williams called it in the 1950s, 'the winter of a nation', its cold heart *heb wybod colli ei . . . llawenydd*, unconscious of losing its delight.

But in parts where it is still vigorously alive, in Walia Pura, where it is still as Williams put it *goleuni blas*, 'the light of taste', its presence is a solace and a stimulation, sealing friendships, maintaining loyalties, and making everything seem more virile and vivacious. Often diffident and defensive when they are speaking English, Welsh people are superbly confident when they break into Welsh, releasing all the wit and speed of response that has always been noticed in them—the 'sharp and acute intellect' that Giraldus Cambrensis reported in the twelfth century, which made them 'more quick and cunning than other inhabitants of a western clime'.

The language also gives the Cymro Cymraeg, the Welsh-speaking Welshman, membership of a freemasonry. He has friends wherever Welsh is spoken—and more than friends, comrades, who will not easily let him down. His is like a secret inner world, within the half-private world that is Wales as a whole. Even Welshmen, if they speak no Welsh, know little of this underground, with its own pop heroes, television personalities, comedians and best-sellers (that is, novels selling 5,000 copies or more). A stranger without Welsh could live next door to a man for years, without realizing he was a celebrity in the culture of the Cymry Cymraeg: to the traveller who knows the language, another country altogether opens up before him as he wanders through Wales, like the country of the *Tylwyth Teg* themselves, rich in a pride and energy denied to mortal eyes.

All small countries, of course, have their own pantheons of gods and heroes, peculiar to themselves. Not many, though, possess a culture couched in a language almost unknown to anyone else. The great men of the Cymry Cymraeg are ciphers to the world at large—even those who are household names at home, like William Williams Pantycelyn, say, who is as familiar to Welsh people as Charles Dickens to the English, or Mark Twain to the Americans. In the 1970s the former county of Meirionydd, Merioneth, now part of Gwynedd, produced an atlas which enumerated all the famous men and women of the district. It makes inspiring reading for Welsh-speakers, but is likely to bemuse all others, even local residents. 'Cadfan' the notable littérateur? Ywain Meirion the distinguished ballad-writer? 'Betsi Cadwaladr' the celebrated nurse? Bob Owen the historian? John Davies the great bibliographer? What kind of celebrities are these? asks the sceptical outsider: but celebrities they are, stars, leaders, heroines, within their own ancient and still lively civilization.

Even more tellingly, after its sections on Water Supplies, Small Industries, Local Government since 1888 and Wool Factories in the nineteenth century, the Atlas of Meirionydd had a Folk-Gazetteer, from which you may discover where in the county the best-known giants lived, where children have most often been kidnapped by the *Tylwyth Teg*, or the best-authenticated habitats of wizards. The possession of the language gives Welsh-speakers possession of the landscape too, and of all that it recalls, allowing them a sense of unbroken continuity from the earliest years of the race-memory. Few peoples can claim such immediacy with their remotest origins: it makes most other national identities seem dim and parvenu, and most other patriotisms coarse.

We began this chapter with a girl at her harp: we will end it with the shade of a poet, for it is the image of the poet, above all others, that properly embodies the creativity of Wales. Literature is the first Welsh glory, poetry is its apotheosis, and the company of poets is the nobility of this nation.

Ellis Evans, whose bardic name was Hedd Wyn, was a farmer-poet of Trawsfynydd in Gwynedd, where a statue of him stands in the village street. His *awdl* in the Strict Metres on *Yr Arwr*, 'The Hero', won the Chair at the National Eisteddfod of 1917, held for once outside Wales, at Birkenhead in Lancashire, but he was not there to be honoured, for six weeks before he had been killed in action in France. His Chair, draped in black, stood empty upon the stage, and Hedd Wyn became a legend, a symbol and an inspiration to other poets. The Black Chair of Birkenhead was taken sadly home to Gwynedd, to be placed with the other trophies of Hedd Wyn's short life in the family farm above the Bala road, and there we may visit it still.

It has never been forgotten. A constant stream of visitors, patriots, poets, groups of schoolchildren, winds its way up the long farm drive, in the lee of the hills, to the old house among its clumped trees. It stands there all alone looking out magnificently over bare hills to the ramparts of Eryri in the distance—the very epitome of a Welsh view, all grandeur tinged with melancholy. The Black Chair is kept in a sort of shrine-room, dim-lit and cluttered. Around it three or four other *eisteddfod* chairs stand in attendance, like sacred stools in an Ashanti temple, and there are pictures of great occasions on the walls, and bound volumes of poems, or judgements, or testimonials lying on tables. The rooms is very quiet: and those tall shapes there, those heavy books, those inscribed texts looking down from the walls, make it feel like a reliquary of all that is oldest, and most secret, and most ineradicable in the mind of Wales.

5. Towards a National Character

Dimly we can see, or think we can see, what Owain Glyndŵr looked like. On his Great Seal he is shown sitting on a throne in the classic posture of a prince, sceptre in hand, dogs at his feet, staring directly at us hawk-eyed from beneath his canopy. He is fork-bearded and gaunt, he has a wart (we happen to know) under his left eye, and he looks, strangely enough, even in the plenitude of his brief power, more doomed than haughty. It is tempting to think of him as representative of a national personality, a summation of the Welsh temperament; but no, beside him we see grouped in his service an extraordinary company of individuals just as authentically Welsh, warriors, priests, monks, bards, lawyers, any one of whom might be called, in one sense or another, typical of his countrymen. Welshness is a matter of varied extremes, and in their personae as in all else the people of Wales are hard to categorize: if we climb up the dais now into Owain's presence, leaning our elbows perhaps, if we dare chance our luck, upon the arm of his gilded throne, we may see how far an inspection of personal manners and public traits will take us towards a national character.

'THERE are no better men than the best of the Welsh', wrote Giraldus in the twelfth century, 'and no worse men than the worst.' By and large this daring generalization may stand today. The ethnic composition of the Welsh nation has greatly changed since Giraldus's time (when there were probably less than 100,000 Welsh people anyway) and except of the Welshiest Welsh minority we can hardly talk of racial characteristics nowadays. Hundreds of thousands of English people have come to live in Wales down the centuries, some becoming entirely Welsh themselves, some remaining as English as ever, and there are minorities of Flemish stock, too, and Irish, and Italian, and black people in the southern seaports, and Polish refugees, and German former prisoners of war, and a sprinkling of Arabs, Indians, Pakistanis and Chinese restaurateurs. By now there can be few Welsh families, except in the remotest rural areas, who have not at some time or another bred outside the Celtic strain.

Yet climate, landscape, religion, have kept the Welsh recognizably Welsh; and more still, history, and the immense staying power of the Welsh culture, which inescapably influences the character of the people. One of the Welshest towns in Wales is Caernarfon, built as an utterly English fortress town; among the best-loved of modern Welsh singers are two at least who are black; the people of the south-eastern coal valleys, though half their forebears came from Birmingham, Bristol or London, speak almost to a man a dialect recognizably derived from *yr hen iaith*, and often supposed by foreigners, indeed, to be the Welsh language itself.

Superficially the Welsh have always been disparate. Until the modern roads and railways came most communities were terribly isolated, and developed strong characteristics of their own. Among those who spoke Welsh there were colourful variations of dialect, syntax and vocabulary. Among those who spoke English, diverse accents prevailed—the people of south Pembrokeshire spoke a sort of blurred Devonian, the people of the north-east preferred a pungent variety of Scouse. Then the people of Dolgellau were notoriously unwelcoming to strangers, the people of Y Bala were celebratedly pious, the people of Llŷn were poets one and all, and the entire county of Cardigan was supposed to be inhabited by tight-fisted opportunists.

If we were to emulate Giraldus now we might say that physically two principal types of Welshmen have emerged from this complexity, popularly maintained to be derived from separate branches of Celticness, but doubtless really the product of much more involved genetics. One is relatively tall, big-boned, rather patrician of bearing, quiet and thoughtful of response: the other is short, volatile, vivacious, all too quick to answer. The one sometimes seems, with his long thin face and his grey-blue eyes, like a visitor from the past: the other, with his flood of words, his penchant for the comic, the flash and quick chance, is sometimes almost excessively modern. But they have more in common than meets the eye. Both have an element of the sly to their nature, both are easily stirred to emotion, and both are essentially evasive—not necessarily in any malicious sense, not always to gain advantage, but as a matter of profoundest inherited instinct. 'Your Frenchman's truth', an American once said, 'is like a straight line, but your Welshman's truth is more in the nature of a curve.' So it is, for it is only by weaving and winding, by a gift for bemusement and a mastery of romanticization, the the Welsh have managed to stay Welsh at all.

Here are some more of Giraldus's sweeping propositions, which would probably be unpopular among sociologists today, but ring bells of recognition all the same:

- The Welsh of all classes have 'a boldness and confidence in speaking and answering, even in the presence of their princes and chieftains', which is denied to the English.

- They are a people 'quick in action, but more stubborn in a bad than in a good cause, and constant only in acts of inconstancy'.

- They are devoted to the defence of their country and their own liberty: 'for these they fight, for these they undergo hardships, and for these they willingly sacrifice their lives'.

- They are 'immoderate in their love of intoxicating drink', being parsimonious in bad times, but extravagant in times of plenty.

- They are very facetious in conversation. They exceed any other nation in attention to their teeth. They 'consider liberality and hospitality among the first virtues'.

- They are much given to incest. In war they are 'bold in the first onset, but cannot bear a repulse'.

- 'Because of the pride and obstinacy of their disposition they will not, like other nations, subject themselves to the domination of one lord and king.'

All honest Welsh people can see at least a few of these traits in themselves, and some of blinding self-perception may admit to them all. Most of them anyway are only the historical symptoms of a small people dominated by a mightier Power, struggling to maintain its identity sometimes by force, sometimes by guile. Many Welshmen have sought to escape from these inherited conditions, but they seldom entirely succeed: scratch the most urbanely Anglicized of London Welshmen, or the most exquisitely cosmopolitan of academics, and not far beneath the skin you will find Giraldus's Cymro. And his first and grandest maxim remains unarguable: the best of the Welsh are unbeatable, the worst are ghastly still.

If there is such a thing as a Welsh national character, it is certainly not self-evident. Welsh people are seldom simple, and tend often towards the actorial and the posed, masking their true personalities in layers of defiance, self-defence or affectation. From the limitless ranks of this kind, let us introduce ourselves to a couple of virtuosi, supreme exponents of camouflage or side-step in the art of Welsh living.

First, David Lloyd George, Dafydd to his compatriots, Prime Minister of Great Britain between 1916 and 1922, and for a few years one of the most powerful men on earth. He was born as it happened in Manchester, but he was brought up by his uncle Richard Lloyd, chapel elder and village cobbler of Llanystumdwy in Gwynedd. From that distant hamlet beside the river Dwyfor he went on to political achievements, personal failures, scandals, successes and innovations that were all monumental—as John Grigg his biographer has said, no Prime Minister has so changed the face of Britain: yet even at the height of his power, when he disposed the fleets and armies of the greatest of all the Empires, when he sat with his peers Wilson and Clemenceau in the Hall of Mirrors at Versailles, or decreed the fateful partition of Ireland, still he thought of himself as a Welshman first, surrounding himself with Welsh aides and advisers, and often conducting business at 10 Downing Street in the Welsh language.

The first thing people commented on, when they met this singular statesman, was his flamboyance. He was a marvellous exhibitionist, and bore himself always for maximum effect. With his bard-like flowing hair, his swirling cape, his flowing moustache like a Celtic warrior's, he was his own walking advertisement: everybody knew that figure, even those who had never set eyes on it, and every cartoonist, every music-hall comedian, fed satisfactorily upon the image, and propagated it more widely still—in 1934 the cartoonist Strube, in the *Daily Express*, pictured fifteen assorted character costumes worn by the old politician during his career, including those of Welsh Bard, Jester, Prime Minister, Wizard and Man Who Won The War. It was by no means an image always admired, but it was, like all the best advertising fancies, subliminally irresistible.

Next, everybody felt Lloyd George's charm. Even his enemies admitted it. Truly like one of the enchanters of the old Welsh tales, Lloyd George could alter people's responses, influence their behaviour, by the deliberate exertion of his own personality. His voice was a little shrill, but curiously beguiling. His command of the graceful compliment, or the shared confidence, was wonderfully effective. His eyes could twinkle so, his face could be so merry, that children always loved him, while there was a sensual insinuation to his presence, a whisper of virility only just under control, that women adored. Everybody agreed, even those who loathed him, that he could be terrific company, and he could move with an unaltered air of sincerity from country gossip with an Eifionydd farmer to diplomatic discussions with a visiting President.

He wore, or seemed to wear, his emotions on his sleeve. On great issues of State he appeared to speak with absolute heartfelt passion—on the Boer War for instance, when he braved physical violence and political ignominy to express his opposition. In personal matters he seemed always on the edge of his feelings, tears welling into his eyes, laughter bubbling up, anger striking. He looked all passionate spontaneity. When he visited French troops in the trenches during the First World War, he made some of them weep just by the fervour of his *Vive la France!*

And yet, and yet, except among his own particular people, nobody quite trusted him. His truth was curved—he took, says the historian

Kenneth O. Morgan, a 'romantic' attitude to facts and figures. It was not merely the scandal that from time to time surrounded him, the dubious acquisition of shares, the blatant selling of political honours for party funds—not even the famous affair with his English secretary and the notorious mistreatment of his Welsh wife. It was a flaw less specific, that made people feel he was seldom altogether straight with them. Was that flamboyance studied after all? Was that famous charm just play-acting? How truly from the heart did those quick emotions spring? There was something hard to pin down in his character, something shifting and almost mocking, which disturbed people often, and made them feel they had been hoodwinked.

Not so often Welshmen, though. Although many Welsh people excoriate the name of Lloyd George today, believing him to have deserted his own country for worldlier glories in the end—*Duw*, he even became an *earl!*—still only they, perhaps, really understood him. To foreigners he was always to remain an uncomfortable if dazzling sort of enigma—'a goat-footed bard', as John Maynard Keynes rather too imaginatively put it, 'a half-human visitor to our age from the hag-ridden magic and enchanted woods of Celtic antiquity'. To his compatriots his temperament was less exotic. Whatever they thought about Lloyd George's policies and private behaviour, they did not mind the theatrical complexity of Lloyd George's character. They were used to it.

Besides, in general Welsh people admire the bold gesture, and relish all kinds of picaresque effrontery. Our second virtuoso suited the taste exactly, for he was a genius of fine bravado, but of inexhaustible moral and intellectual complexity. On a wall inside the church of Flemingston in Glamorgan a stone in Welsh and English, somewhat shaky now, records the burial near by of a local stonemason, Edward Williams, who was born in 1747 and died in 1826. Few tourists go to see it, visitors seldom pay much attention, and nobody knows exactly where the actual grave lies: yet this is the burial-place of the poet, hymnist, antiquarian, scholar and forger who called himself Iolo Morgannwg, Iolo of Glamorgan, and whose passionate commitment to Welshness powerfully revivified the culture, and has confused Welsh scholarship from that day to this.

Iolo, as he is known among Welsh people still, was as clever a man as ever lived, and wonderfully gifted, but he was also perhaps a little touched, if only by the laudanum he took all his life to counteract his arthritis. He was touchy, hypochondriac and conceited, but he made friends and enemies with equal facility and satisfaction. A fiery radical in the age of revolution, he despised the existing order of things, and moved from trade to trade, place to place, with an ostentatious disregard of all precedents or convention. He was a pacifist, a passionate opponent of slavery, a Welsh nationalist and one of the founders of the Unitarian faith in Wales. In a London bookshop once Iolo encountered Dr Johnson, and plucked up courage to ask which of several books on display it would be best for him to buy. The insufferable sage so snubbed him that in a characteristic gesture of infuriated *hwyl* Iolo bought the lot.

Iolo earned his living variously, and precariously, as mason, as farmer, as journalist, as a businessmen of sorts: he owned a grocery store for a time, a lending library, even a trading schooner in the Bristol Channel, and he spent a useful year in the debtors' gaol at Cardiff, reading, copying manuscripts and playing the flute. He became however the most learned Welsh scholar of his time, devoting himself to the glorification of the Welsh culture in general, and in particular the culture of his own beloved Morgannwg, Glamorgan, to which he attributed all possible splendour and achievement. Wandering around the countryside on long journeys of discovery, visiting libraries, calling on scholars, he transcribed and annotated a vast body of the old Welsh poetry, half of it then forgotten. He was one of the great personalities of eighteenth-century Wales: a peaked and shabby little man, in a tall black hat, slung about with canvas bags of books and writing materials, spectacles on the end of his nose, refusing to ride or travel by coach out of respect, he said, for his fellow-creature the horse.

Iolo recognized, long before most of his countrymen, that the continuity of Wales lay above all in its literary traditions. But over the years this wonderfully percipient man, himself as talented a poet as he was imaginative a scholar, began to confuse fact with reality, even in himself. For one thing he convinced himself, in that age of fanciful antiquarianism, that the ancient order of the Druids had miraculously survived through all the centuries in his particular corner of Glamorgan, and that he was its last surviving master. He accordingly set out to re-establish it all over Wales, founding his peripatetic Gorsedd, awarding bardic degrees and freely inventing rituals. He did not work in any spirit of pastiche: he truly believed that the message of

God's utterance had been mystically passed down to him from the oak-crowned priests of Ynys Môn.

This cracked vision of the Welsh heritage he translated into literary terms too, and he began to augment the body of Welsh literature with fictions of his own. Since he knew more about Welsh classical literature than any man alive, he could do this with impunity, and over the years he invented so many medieval poems that the chief task of Welsh literary scholarship in the twentieth century has been the disentanglement of Iolo's forgeries from the real thing. Some of his poems are of an exquisite beauty anyway: others are such brilliant copies of a style that they really do seem to show some mystical immersion of one personality in another—literary shape-changing. The motto Iolo chose for his bardic order was *Y Gwir yn erbyn y byd*, 'The Truth against the world', and in his queer drugged way no doubt he was honouring truths of his own conception.

For a time, when these misdemeanours were discovered, the name of Iolo Morgannwg was not popular. He had become a cultural hero of Wales—in the 1880s there was even a tramp steamer named for him—and the truth about his forgeries and inventions seemed a public betrayal. Opinions presently changed though, the nation was mollified, his Gorsedd remains today the presiding body of the Eisteddfod Genedlaethol and his hymns are sung in chapels all over Wales. Even the scholars have been reluctantly reconciled. His chief unmasker G. J. Williams, who spent a lifetime exposing Iolo's forgeries, came in the end to admire him: and when in 1962 Dr Thomas Parry, the greatest living authority on the poems of Dafydd ap Gwilym, edited *The Oxford Book of Welsh Verse*, he included one exquisite piece attributed for years to that master, but now published under the name of his true creator, Edward Williams of Flemingston.

For many years the lifeboat at Tyddewi, St David's, was kept in the town square above the cathedral, to be pulled down to the sea by horses when the need arose. The practice was stopped, though, in 1888, by order of the Very Reverend the Dean: not because it was inconvenient for the lifeboatmen, or clumsy in an emergency, but because the townspeople got up to such shameless things beneath the tarpaulins.

This is a famously lusty people—it used to be said that Welsh sexuality was inflamed by the prevalence of mists!—and the annals are full of prodigiously virile exploits. Abroad Ieuan Wyn, a fourteenth-century soldier of fortune at the court of France, was so irrepressible a gallant that the French called him *le Poursuivant d'Amour*, the Love Herald. At home Thomas Parr of Middleton in Powys, a sixteenth-century celebrity known as 'the old, old, very old man', was over 100 when he had to do penance in church for getting a woman with child, and 120 when he married for the second time (and 152, it is wildly claimed, when he died from over-eating at a banquet in his own honour). As for his contemporary William ap Hywel ap Iorwerth, who lived near Llangefni in Môn, he fathered forty-three children by his five wives, and his eldest son was over 80 when his youngest son was born.

Welsh folk practices were popularly supposed by Englishmen to be disgracefully prurient, especially the old custom of courting in bed —'bundling', the English called it, semi-institutionalized pre-marital sex, noted by Giraldus as common in his day and never abandoned even in the heyday of the chapels. More often than not a healthy freedom had certainly governed the sexual attitudes of the Welsh. Dafydd ap Gwilym spoke for young Welshmen down the ages when he reported in verse his unsuccessful flirtations during sermons in Llanbadarn church, his plans for seducing an abbess, and his discomfiture when, surprised by a jealous husband, he was obliged to hide in a goose-shed (not to mention other exploits and predicaments, it is popularly rumoured, still suppressed under lock and key at the National Library in Aberystwyth).

Three hundred years after his time English visitors were astonished to find Welsh girls of all ages bathing happily in the nude along the sands of Dyfed, or pouring naked on to the beach, 'rabble from the hills', beneath the decorous villas of Penarth in Glamorgan. 'The lower classes here, as in many other parts of Wales', said an English guidebook to Aberystwyth in 1821, 'indiscriminately dress and undress on the sands, and pay very little distinction to their sex.' Thomas Lloyd of Coedmore, a nineteenth-century Lord Lieutenant of Cardiganshire, horrified an English judge, as they drove together to the Assizes, by telling him that both the coachman who was driving and the footman up behind were his own illegitimate children—there were several others, he added, working at this and that in his employ.

Victorian reformers were horrified by these tendencies, and put them all down to the base Welshness of the Welsh. In 1847 a Royal

Commission of Enquiry into the state of Welsh education attributed most of the evils of North Wales to promiscuity. Up there illegitimacy, which was far above the national average, was not regarded as anything shameful, and the sexual vigour of the people was more or less unbridled. The Vicar of Nefyn, in Llŷn, said he had been obliged to put bars across his chamber-maid's windows, to keep the young men out. The Bishop of Bangor reported that local farmers, when they hired servants, agreed upon convenient bundling hours, and went on to assert 'with confidence, as an undeniable fact, that fornication is not regarded as a vice, scarcely as a frailty, by the common people of Wales'.

All this in 1847, at the height of the Methodist Revival, when deacons stalked the land denouncing sinners, when unmarried mothers were pilloried before the chapel elders, and pulpits thundered with the lessons of Sodom and Gomorrah! Disapproving though they might be in public of sexual immorality, in private Welsh people were likely to be tolerant and understanding, turning a blind eye, whatever the bishops, the ministers or the Educational Commissioners said, to the young people in the hayloft or under the lifeboat tarpaulins.

Lusty the Welsh remain, and often frank enough in their sexuality, the young men and women of the southern valleys, in particular, often positively bursting with it, as they strut the raddled streets of their dejected towns, or race their gaudily painted old cars, full of sexy symbolism, with cassettes blaring through the night! And there are still many in Wales who talk about these matters, as the Bishop of Bangor reported severely to those Commissioners, 'without the slightest reluctance or modesty, and with a levity and confidence of manner which proves the parties to be quite lost to all sense of shame'.

Let us now consider Howel Harris of Trefeca, born in 1714, whose religious institution near Talgarth in Powys was a power-house of the Methodist Revival. Here's a tangle of another kind. Mystical but practical, simple but showy, devout yet irreconcilable, Harris illustrates the extra dimensions that so often enmesh the Welsh character when it is caught up in the fascination of religion.

Though he was to become one of the most famous of the revivalists, 'the Luther of Wales', Harris caught the ecstasy in the Anglican parish church at Talgarth. There, during Holy Communion on Whit Sunday,

1735, he was inspired to his mission. He came from an apparently unvisionary background. His father was a joiner; one of his brothers was a distinguished astronomer, another so prospered as a tailor that he became a considerable landowner and High Sheriff of Breconshire; Howel himself began life as a country schoolmaster. Yet within a few years of that Whit Sunday revelation, still in his twenties, he had established throughout South Wales his own system of reformed religion—a system of cells, meeting regularly for devotions and mutual confessions, which gave birth to the idea of the *seiat*, the Meeting, and was later to stand at the very heart of Welsh Methodism. Harris remained a member of the Church of England, and was indeed three times refused ordination by the Bishops: later in life he boldly went preaching in the churchyard at Talgarth himself (and converted to his idea of Christianity, on the very spot where he had been originally inspired himself, William Williams Pantycelyn).

But by then Harris was a kind of bishop himself. For seventeen years he conducted a furious campaign of evangelism, riding on horseback all over the country, preaching twice a day or more, holding meetings sometimes at midnight, sometimes at dawn to avoid molesting crowds (who often stoned evangelical preachers), busybody officials (who sometimes tried to press them into the navy) or interfering squires (who sometimes sent men with drums and trumpets to drown their exhortatory voices). Nothing daunted him for long. 'A breach made in Satan's Kingdom!' he would record in his diary at the end of the day. 'Love came down!'

He was an extremist among extremists. He threw himself into this mission, as into everything else, with an irresistible avidity—he was, wrote a contemporary, 'naturally of an open choleric disposition, undisguised in his words and actions, impetuous in his proceedings, would flatter no man ... nor give up a particle of what he was persuaded to be the truth to please his dearest and nearest friend.' In fact he frequently antagonized his nearest and dearest, and split the Welsh Methodist movement asunder, by his personal arrogance, and later by his declared belief that God himself, not simply the human Jesus, had died upon the cross.

Others he alienated by his curious relationship with one of his own disciples, the wife of a drunken Llŷn squire who called herself 'Madam' Sidney Griffith. Madam Griffith had the power of second sight, she said, and she took to accompanying Harris on his journeys as a mobile oracle, foreseeing circumstances favourable or unfavourable to his mission, sensing atmospheres and assessing graces. Harris became obsessed with her, and though the relationship was probably all spiritual, or perhaps occult, nevertheless the squire of Cefnamlwch publicly disowned his wife, and the affair became a public scandal.

The reformer was undeterred. Quarrelling with more and more of his comrades, he decided to establish a religious community of his own, and with the help of £900 contributed by Madam Griffith (who then died) in 1752 he set up the settlement at his old home of Trefeca. He himself designed the buildings, around the core of the family cottage, and some of them still stand: early examples of the Gothic Picturesque, with handsome Venetian windows, corner turrets and a tower in the middle, the whole surmounted by a golden angel weathervane, holding a trumpet and calling the dead to judgement.

Here Harris flourished anew, as sage, seer and progressive agriculturist. More than a hundred people joined his community, sacrificing all their possessions, but sharing all the profits of its 765 well-farmed acres. They kept pigs, cattle and sheep, they did carpentry and building work, they wove sheets out of their own flax, blankets from their own wool, they ran a printing press, and Harris led them like an unusually modernist squire, adopting all the latest techniques and inspiring the foundation of the Brecknock Society 'for the encouragement of Agriculture and Manufactures', the first such body in Britain.

It was a far cry from those clandestine sermons and midnight meetings, or even the blinding light of Talgarth: Williams Pantycelyn called the members of the Trefeca flock 'cold, barren, dry sheep'. Now Harris became a respected member of county society, in the very place of his birth—taxed with the grandness of his buildings, he wrote: ''Tis not too good for the Lord and for the Countess of Huntingdon's use.' In 1759, war having broken out between England and France, he and twenty-four of his disciples joined the Breconshire Militia, and when they were posted to garrison duty in England he marched off with them in full panoply of serge and brass as one of His Majesty's captains. He was a great monarchy man: we are told that when he failed to quiet an unruly congregation with the words 'In the Name of the King of Heaven', he cried 'In the Name of King George' instead, and got immediate attention.

For Howel Harris did nothing by half measures, and almost nothing ordinary. 'There is no jesting with God', he liked to say. He died in

1773, still officially outside the Methodist movement but reconciled with most of its leaders, and was buried in Talgarth church, where his long mission began, while 20,000 people jammed the village streets outside. His portraits show him, beneath his wig, fierce of eye and distinctly stern of mouth, and it was the absoluteness of him, that flaming choleric temper, that willingness to shock his own best friends, that made him such a power. Religion often takes Welshmen that way. Among all the famous Christians of this country, from St David himself with his unyielding asceticism to the relentless fundamentalists of our own day, few have been meek or mild: they have generally been intense, unaccommodating, always ready for a quarrel in their cause. They have not been saintly in the soothing kind. Their calls to salvation are generally apocalyptic of style, and their convictions are black, white and often maddening.

Heavens, the thunderous roar, part shouting, part cheering, part laughter, part a mighty blurred rendition of *Cwm Rhondda*, the noblest of Welsh hymn-tunes, which sweeps through the streets of Cardiff like the din of a revolution! A potent element in the Welsh character is a taste for sport, and nothing illustrates it better than the condition of Cardiff, the national capital, on the afternoon of an international Rugby match, when the whole life of the city seems geared to the great occasion, when almost the whole population seems to have squeezed itself within the high stadium walls of Cardiff Arms Park, when the streets around are deserted but for a few roisterers too poor, too late, or just too drunk to get tickets, and that immense noise from inside is like the concerted opinion of the nation.

The Welsh have always been a sporting people—too sporting, their supervisors have often thought. In 1573 the Lord President of the Council of the Marches, the English administration of Wales, complained that the people disgracefully neglected their archery in favour of Tables, Dice, Cards, Bowls and Quoits, while in 1799 a clergyman of Môn observed that the common people delighted in nothing except 'empty sport and carnal pleasures, playing with dice and cards, dancing and singing with the harp, playing football, tennis, mock-trials, and hostages, and many other sinful sports too numerous to mention'. (The dancing especially must have disturbed him, for Caergybi, Holyhead in Môn, was famous for its annual non-stop dancing competition, in

which scores of girls jigged to the fiddle hour after hour until they all
subsided in hilarious exhaustion.)

Often the church itself was the people's sporting centre, its walls
providing a court for games of fives, its churchyard excellent for
football. The great porch of Aberedw in Powys, which was used for
parish meetings on some days, was used on others for games of dice,
cards and ball. At Llanfair Discoed in Gwent a notice still in the porch
darkly warns the parishioners against Sabbath games within the holy
precincts:

> Who Ever hear on Sunday
> Will Practis Playing at Ball
> it May Be be Fore Monday
> The Devil Will have you All.

Though the Methodist revolution put paid to many of these cheerful
practices, the Welsh have remained adept at the robuster kinds of
sport. They hunt a lot, and shoot, and fish. The hunters are mostly
farmers, often hunting on foot in the mountains with mixed packs of
hounds and terriers, but they also include the equestrian colliers of the
Miners' Hunt, in the Amman Valley of Glamorgan. The anglers range
from punctilious fly fishermen working enormously expensive salmon
reaches of the Wye, to a multitude of village enthusiasts rushing out to
catch sea-trout with worms on summer evening floods, not to mention
poachers in every degree of skulduggery, endearing rod-and-line ras-
cals to poison-and-gunpowder thugs.

Boxing has always been a Welsh pastime, especially in the coal
valleys, where in the old days men would work off their differences by
bloody bare-fisted contests high on the bare moorlands, and where the
young bloods of today are just as ready for a pub fight or a street-corner
brawl. Huge crowds gathered to watch the bare-fisted champions of
the nineteenth century—'it lasted for about forty minutes', recalled an
eyewitness of one contest, 'non-stop mind, no rounds, but lam one
another till they collapse'. More recently a succession of internationally
famous boxers has fought its way out of the valleys—'Peerless' Jim
Driscoll, featherweight champion of the world, whose funeral in 1924
was watched by 100,000 Welshmen, Thomas Thomas, British middle-
weight champion in 1909, who habitually fought with a bull to save the
expense of sparring partners, F. H. Thomas ('Freddie Welsh'), world
lightweight champion, who in 1907 knocked out a lightweight, a

welterweight and a heavyweight all in a single day, Jimmy Wilde, world flyweight champion in 1916, who lost only four fights in 864, the former fairground heavyweight Tommy Farr, who almost beat Joe Louis in 1938, the beloved featherweight Johnny Owen, who died after a world championship fight in America in 1980, and is commemorated by the Matchstick Man pub on the hills behind Swansea.

Running used to be a Welsh speciality, too. In the early days of the iron-fields foot-races were held all over the southern valleys, sometimes along the tramways, and one of the folk-heroes of the age, still vividly remembered today, was Guto Morgan, known after his family farm as Guto Nyth Brân, Guto Crow's Nest. Even now many people like to visit the grave of this stalwart, which lies in the tumbled churchyard opposite the pub in the hamlet of Llanwynno, where in the opening chapter of this book we saw a young Welsh horseman riding from out the tavern yard. All sorts of legends have accrued about his life, and are still current—how he paced himself against hares, how his mother put the kettle on, and Guto ran the five miles to Pontypridd to buy tea, and was back again before the water boiled—and most often told of all, how in 1737 he collapsed and died of a burst heart on the spot, after running the twelve miles from Newport to Bedwas in 53 minutes. A broken heart is engraved on his tombstone, by the church door, and sometimes you hear children, wandering over the road while their parents sit at their beer outside the inn, exclaiming to each other, as of an old friend, 'There's Guto! That's Guto Nyth Brân!'

They play quoits in some parts of rural Wales, very solemnly in meadows on Saturdays, and a Welsh form of baseball in Cardiff and Newport. They play cricket, and not only in the more obviously Anglicized parts of the country: in the 1920s the Tywyn cricket team, in Gwynedd, was entirely Welsh-speaking, and today one of the most piquant sights in Wales is that of a game of cricket being played on some ridge above a coal-grimed valley of Glamorgan—the drizzle gently falling, as likely as not, the mist on the hills above, the long lines of grey houses deep in the vale below, and those impeccably white-clad figures poised so elegantly around the wicket on the levelled plateau of the pitch.

At half a dozen country race-courses, still, trotting ponies hurtle around the circuit with their sulkies; and just as a century ago Welshmen would make for the bare and lonely mountains to pit their fighting cocks against each other, out of sight of constables or censorious elders, so today on a Sunday afternoon many a high Welsh moor reverberates to the whine, roar and kick-change of the motor-bike bravoes, hurtling their machines through rock and bog, all scarlet helmets, mud and goggles, down to the motor-campers where their girl friends, in high cowboy boots and anoraks with team stickers, have already brewed up the tea.

But the sport of Welsh sports, and a powerful contributor to the contemporary Welsh character, is Rugby football, Union Rules. In its present form this is a purely English game: Welsh traditionalists like to think, though, that it is a relatively tame successor to the ancient Welsh sport of *cnapan*, which was played all over this country at least until the seventeenth century. This was really more a battle than a game, and it was played stark naked. In open country without goals or limits, anything up to 1,500 men fought to get the *cnapan*, a slippery bowl of heavy wood, into the territory of one village or the other. The play swung back and forth, over hedge, ditch and meadow, all those hundreds of nude figures racing across the churned-up fields, hurling the *cnapan* here and there, kicking, hitting and wrestling one another, sometimes urged along by horsemen, and forcibly bringing into the action anyone who happened to be near. At least according to one seventeenth-century observer, the game was played in good humour, and the players went home after the match, bleeding and bruised, 'laughing and merrily jesting at their harmes, telling their adversaries how he brake his head, to another that he strocke him on the face, and how he repayed the same to him again, and all this is in good myrth, without grudge or hatred . . .'.

Cnapan of a kind survived in Wales until 1922. At Llandysul in Dyfed a mass football game was annually played, with goal-posts eight miles apart, but by then the affair had become so disorderly, and the rules of the game, if there ever were any, had been so generally forgotten, that a Sunday school festival was substituted for the event. The good myrth however has been inherited by the Welsh Rugby players of today—who, though they become great national and even international celebrities, are amateurs at least in theory still, and distinctly retain some of the *cnapan* spirit. Rugby is in particular the game of South Wales, and the style of Welsh playing is very akin to the style of the valley people themselves. Stocky of build and fiery of temperament, Welshmen of the south are perfectly fitted to the quick changes of mood, the uninhibited rough-and-tumble of Rugby, and as a matter of principle Welshmen acknowledge no superiors in the game (except perhaps the New Zealanders, who nearly always beat them).

The popular reputation of Welsh Rugby is rather coarse, comedians and fiction writers having conspired to surround its images with a haze of bawdy, booze and maudlin sentiment—what a northerner, Lloyd George, once described as 'morbid footballism'. If you follow the hymns and the hullabaloo, though, to Cardiff Arms Park and that international match, you will find it not much like that. A few harmless hooligans may invade the pitch waving Welsh flags, a streaker may mildly amuse the crowd by weaving a naked escape, in truest *cnapan* form, through the clumsy black lines of helmeted policemen. On the whole however such an important game is rather a serious occasion, to be watched with the proper attention, to be judged as dispassionately as is human, and to be notched up carefully upon the register of life's experiences, rather as Spanish *aficionados* remember for ever the memory of a great bullfight.

Long before the game the crowd seethes on stand and terrace, waving red dragons everywhere, and when the band strikes up on the green, its dapper band-master tense with zeal, then the vast swell of voices that we heard from outside rises from the stadium like a flight of very heavy birds to swell across the city. From side to side of the arena the conductor marches his musicians, facing each quarter in turn, like a bishop and his acolytes waving incense from aisle to aisle of a congregation, or the trumpeters at the National Eisteddfod, and one by one the grand old favourites resound: famous melancholy hymns, jolly songs like *Sospan Fach*, 'Little Saucepan', and just before the kick-off, the tremendous national anthem itself, *Mae'r Hen Wlad Fy Nhadau*, 'Land of my Fathers', whose words only a quarter of that crowd, perhaps, could actually interpret, but which are sung with unanimous fervour anyway.

But the game's the thing. A polite round of applause greets the visiting players, in their white, blue or green jerseys, as they emerge at a fast and nervous trot from their tunnel beneath the grandstand; a colossal communal shout greets the Welsh, in their dragon-red; the crowd settles down to watch the play with a concentrated and critical attention. Every error is greeted with sigh or groan, boisterous shouts of reproach fly across the pitch, and when some splendid winger weaves his way terrier-like through the opposing pack, ball clutched like a treasure before him—around the hulking enemy backs—far, far up towards the distant touch-line—suddenly a thrilling expectancy seizes Cardiff Arms Park, the whole assembly turns as one man with that darting player, an eager buzz stirs through all the stands, and rises in crescendo, and hovers, for a second or two, almost breathless—until, as the player is thwarted at last, or alternatively throws himself in triumph over the line, it subsides as abruptly as it arose, or explodes into cheers, laughter, clapping, commiserations or congratulations.

Generally that lack of grudge prevails. The players, who have very likely engaged in apparently irreconcilable fisticuffs in the course of the match, leave the field all sentimental *bonhomie*. The crowd, as it jostles its way through the turnstiles after the game, continues its discussions without acrimony. 'Fair play man, *chwarae teg*, that Dubois runs like a bloody cat.' 'What about Evans, then? They ought to put the bugger out to grass. What a bloody shambles!' Or: 'They've never been the same since J.P.R. went, never the same at all . . .' And so they go their separate ways, tackles and hymn-tunes still in their heads.

The best-known of all Welsh soldiers is Shakespeare's Fluellen. He is not however really characteristic of the Welsh military men who have stormed in one cause or another almost without a break through history. He is a pedantic, studious soldier, a soldier by the book: more often the Welsh military genius has been of a fluid kind, better suited to guerrilla skirmish than protracted siege, adept at ambush, feint, luring enemies into bogs and the better part of valour.

It is only natural that soldiering should have bitten deep into the character of the Welsh. For nearly a thousand years the Welsh were engaged in almost incessant conflict, if not against foreign invaders, then against each other: Henry II of England described them as a people so implacable that 'though the beasts of the field over the whole face of the island become gentle, these desperate men could not be tamed'. And when the wars of the Welsh Independence were over, and the princedoms were at peace at last, Welsh captains did not hesitate to fight in other causes instead, with English armies against other foreigners, with other foreigners against the English. War was in their blood, and they were much in demand.

At the battle of Poitiers in 1356, for example, Welsh commanders were prominent on both sides. With the Black Prince of England fought Hywel ap Gruffydd from Gwynedd—Hywel y Fwyall, Hywel the Axe, so murderous a man with his battle-axe that for years after his death a feast was annually served before it, to be given to the poor afterwards in honour of his valour. With the King of France was a more famous Welshman still, Owain Lawgoch, Red Hand, the very epitome of European chivalry, who was a great-nephew of Llywelyn Olaf, and called himself the rightful Prince of Wales. This glamorous figure, the Bonny Prince Charlie of Wales, once actually captured Guernsey as a step towards the throne of his own princedom, but was condemned to live all his life as a mercenary in exile, and is commemorated in legend and folk-song in many parts of Europe—'Duke Yvain de Galles', as a Swiss song puts it, 'with his hat made of gold'. In the end the English had him murdered, an assassin creeping up on him, we are told, during the siege of Montagne-sur-Mer in 1378, and stabbing him in the back, poor vain Welsh champion, while he combed his hair.

Welsh officers were everywhere during the incessant wars of the sixteenth and seventeenth century, fighting indiscriminately for many masters. In the east Henry Lloyd of Gwynedd fought in turn for the Austrians, the Prussians and finally the Russians, in whose service he became a general, commanded armies in wars against the Swedes and the Turks, and wrote a famous textbook used in nearly every European military academy. In the west swaggered Henry Morgan of Gwent, whose capture of Panama in 1671, after a forced march across the fetid and fever-ridden isthmus, was one of the most audacious coups of military history: he went to the Caribbean as an indentured servant —'Henry Morgan of Abergavenny, labourer, bound to Timothy Townsend of Bristoll, cutler, for 3 years to serve in Barbados'—he died there deputy-governor of Jamaica and one of the great bravoes of universal legend. Coming as they did from circumstances so little-known, from a society so unlike others, with a history and culture so individual, for all their prowess such men were often considered, like Fluellen himself, figures of fun. Here is a description by the seven-teenth-century diarist John Aubrey of a visit by Cardinal Mazarin and Marshal Turenne to the camp at Dunkirk of the belligerent Thomas Morgan of Gwent, among the most successful of contemporary commanders:

Whereas they thought to have found an Achillean or gigantique person, they saw a little man, not many degrees above a dwarfe, sitting in a hutt of Turves, with his fellow soldiers, smoking a Pipe about 3 inches (or neer so) long, and did cry-out to the Soldiers, when angry with them, Sirrah, I'll cleave your skull! as if the words have been prolated by an Eunuch.

During the First World War Lloyd George wanted to create a Welsh Army of volunteers—'if we can only get the right type of young man to join we will have one of the most magnificent little armies ever turned out of this country!' Lord Kitchener the War Minister did not at all like the idea—he distrusted Welshmen *en masse* almost as deeply as he distrusted Irishmen—and the military authorities were also dismayed by the notion of a separate national army within the forces of the United Kingdom. Thousands of Welshmen were already in uniform anyway, but a Welsh Division was formed nevertheless, commanded by a Philipps of Picton Castle (its minimum height requirement, so many of the taller Cymry having gone before, being especially reduced to 5' 3"). It went to France at the end of 1915, 16,000 Welshmen together, and fought its great battle at Mametz Wood in July 1916, one of the most terrible of all the battles of the Somme, suffering 4,000 casualties in five days—'Mametz Wood', wrote Robert Graves, Royal Welch Fusiliers, 'A certain cure for lust of blood'. 'Why do they always sing those mournful hymns?' asked an English brigadier, as one of the Welsh companies waiting to go into the trenches broke into song. 'Most depressing—bad for morale. Why can't they sing something cheerful, like other battalions?' The writer Wyn Griffith happened to be there, and he gave the answer: 'They are being themselves, not men in uniform. They are back at home, with their families, in their villages . . .'

The Welsh soldier is still with us. He was ubiquitous in the Second World War, and it was a soldier of Llŷn stock, Colonel H. Jones —'Colonel H' to all his men—who posthumously won the only Victoria Cross of the Falklands campaign in 1982, having sacrificially led his soldiers to the capture of an Argentinian machine-gun post. For all the pacifist tradition of Welsh Nonconformity, which runs deep in this society, pride in soldiering remains part of the Welsh character. There are three Welsh regiments in the British Army, and many of their old comrades would be content with the epitaph by which Walter Jones, a seventeenth-century soldier of Gwent, is remembered on the walls of Usk Church:

> Walter Jones I doe him prayse
> A valiant soldiour in his days

Unto the wars would he goe
To fight against his forraine foe
To advaunce a pike before his queen
The which Elizabeth have seene
His sword and speare he did advaunce
And then he took his way to France
And landed on the Isle of Rhee
Where his desire was to be
And to the Lord he gave prayse
That he came home to end his days.

At the heart of a chapter about the Welsh character must stand a passage about Welsh women. Foreigners experiencing the conventional sights and sounds of a visit to Wales, watching a Rugby match, listening to male voice choirs, accepting cups of cottage tea, often assume this to be an incorrigibly male-dominated society, but it has never been so. Even the laws of Hywel Dda were feminist for their day—the legal worth they set upon a woman was six times higher than in contemporary England—and when in 1865 Welsh settlers established a colony in southern Argentina specifically to live by the Welshest of all Welsh convictions, theirs was the first society anywhere in the world to give women the vote.

Welsh women, as a whole, are Welshier than Welsh men, perhaps because of their often strikingly indigenous appearance. There are two particular types of Welsh female face, and they are equally distinctive. On the one hand there is a curiously *spiky* kind of face, high-boned, thin-cheeked, long and narrow: a slightly witch-like face perhaps, with very bright humorous eyes, and a pointed nose, which seems to speak of the immense antiquity of this people, and is easily to be imagined beneath the high-crowned black hat of the old Welsh peasant dress. On the other hand there is the kind of face conventionally attached to the idea of Welsh beauty, a face much rounder and gentler, with soft blue eyes set very widely in the head, with a small nose, and plump cheeks, and a general air of calm kindness, the generic face to be seen in eager ladies' choirs at *eisteddfodau*, and summoned up by the yearnings of Welsh parlour ballads.

Women have seldom been put on pedestals in Wales, in the manner of the Victorian English, or the Americans of the southern States—even the Virgin Mary was not particularly venerated in Wales until the arrival of the Normans. On the other hand they have seldom been ineffective, and as innumerable novels and memoirs demonstrate, have more often than not been the mainstay of family life, on the farm as in the pit or quarry village. Wales gave to the world, via Arthurian legend, the medieval idea of chivalry, with its idealization of women fragile in wimples on castle balconies, but it was never to find much confirmation in its own country, where women have always been, by and large, very well able to look after themselves. Even as late as the seventeenth century, Welsh women scorned to take their husbands' names: in parts of Dyfed, it is said, their husbands took theirs.

Welsh history is peppered with distinctly un-wimpled ladies. We read of the majestic Gwenllian, mother of the Lord Rhys, that in 1136 she led her own army against the Normans at Kidwelly, Cydweli in Dyfed, seeing one of her sons killed, seeing another taken prisoner, before going down fighting herself, to be remembered still by the name of the battle-ground, Maes Gwenllian, Gwenllian's Field. Heroic in a different kind was the stunningly beautiful Nest, the Helen of Wales, founder of more dynasties than it is polite to mention. Daughter to the last king of independent Deheubarth, she was mistress to Henry I of England, wife to Gerald de Windsor, Constable of Pembroke, was romantically abducted by Owain ap Cadwgan, son of the Prince of Powys, and is generally supposed to have had any number of other romantic liaisons—it is chiefly in Nest's honour, flexible though that was, that thousands of Welsh children are still called Nest today.

Or there was Catrin o Ferain, a sixteenth-century chatelaine of Clwyd—Katheryn of Berain, who shared with the island of Môn the sobriquet *Mam Cymru*, 'Mother of Wales', because of her innumerable descendants. Granddaughter to an illegitimate son of Henry VII, she married a succession of influential Welsh gentlemen. At the funeral of the first, two men proposed to her before she left the churchyard; she married one immediately, and upon his death moved on to the other, finally marrying for the fourth time, in 1583, the father of her daughter's husband. In myth she is more profligate still: she is supposed to have had six husbands in all, and to have killed five of them by pouring molten lead in their ears, until the last incumbent, foreseeing the worst, locked her up in her own house and starved her to death.

Another tough lady was Margaret ferch Evans of Penllyn, at the northern end of Llyn Padarn in the mountains of Eryri. For a great part of the eighteenth century she was well known as a boat-woman on the lake, but she was far more than a mere ferry-person. Not only did she build and repair her own boats, but she was a formidable huntress and fisherwoman, an excellent shot, a powerful wrestler until the age of 70, an accomplished harp-maker and a proficient fiddler. She made her own boots, she shod her own horses and she ran a pub at Nantlle. Margaret had innumerable suitors, but she treated most of them with contempt: when T. Assheton Smith, the millionaire owner of the local slate quarries, once pretended to make advances to her on her boat, she threw him into the lake, and when at last she gave her hand, so the antiquarian Thomas Pennant tells us, it was 'to the most effeminate of her admirers'.

For passionate commitment to Wales nobody could beat Lady Llanover, née Augusta Waddington (whose husband Benjamin, as Commissioner for Works in London, gave his name to Big Ben). Though she lived in a heavily Anglicized part of Wales, near Abergavenny, Y Fenni in Gwent, Lady Llanover turned her mansion and estate into a very hotbed of Welshness. She imported Welsh-speaking servants from the north, dressing them in neo-traditional costumes of her own design, and turned the estate village into an idealized Welsh hamlet, with a Temperance Hotel where the old Duke Inn used to be, and a Methodist chapel whose services were all in Welsh and whose minister was obliged to be bearded. Though her own command of the Welsh language was far from complete she adopted the bardic name Gwenynen Gwent, the Bee of Gwent, and around her person there occurred a truly remarkable renaissance of Welshness in those parts, so that for a few years Abergavenny really was one of the cultural centres of the whole Cymry Cymraeg. 'Big Ben' died thirty years before his remarkable wife, but they lie side by side in a magnificent melancholy mausoleum in Llanover churchyard, covered all over with Cymric texts and symbols, and surmounted by the arms the couple had devised for themselves upon Benjamin's elevation to the peerage, supported by a dragon and a horned goat. Here and there around them lie harpists and domestics, epitaphed all in Welsh.

It was a woman, Sarah Jane Rees of Llangrannog in Dyfed, who was the best-known navigational instructor of nineteenth-century Wales. Many schoolmistresses taught the subject, in the coastal villages of the west, but Sarah Rees was unique in that she had herself gone to sea, as a deck-hand on her father's ships, and had qualified as a Master

Mariner. Under her bardic name of Cranogwen, and as a lifelong spinster, she also won the Crown at the National Eisteddfod of 1865 with a poem on the set subject of 'The Wedding Ring'. She was a famous temperance worker, she edited a women's magazine, she was a dedicated exponent of the tonic sol-fa system of musical notation, and she looks out from her portrait in old age with an irresistible gleam of mingled sweetness, cleverness and sardonic amusement, wearing a lace jabot and gold-rimmed spectacles, and appearing perfectly ready, even then, to navigate a schooner round the Horn.

Even in the wings, Welsh women have often stolen the limelight. The battle of Pilleth, where Owain Glyndŵr defeated the English in 1402, is best remembered not for the victory itself, but for the fury of the Welsh women who are alleged to have swarmed on to the battlefield with knives to mutilate the corpses of the enemy. When the future Henry VII marched through Wales on his way to capture the English throne in 1485, he consulted a well-known Dyfed soothsayer, Dafydd Llwyd, as to his chances of success: it is Mrs Llwyd who is remembered now, for wisely persuading her husband to prognosticate certain victory, on the grounds that if it proved true the new king would load him with honours, but if it proved false he would be past caring. The last invasion of the British mainland, the French landing at Fishguard in 1797, is chiefly immortalized by the legend of the Welsh women, in their black hats and red flannel skirts, masquerading as redcoats on the clifftops, and by the feats of the formidable Jemima Nicholas, a cobbler, who is said to have taken several Frenchmen prisoner at the end of her pitchfork. Out of the long grey memories of the slate-quarries spring all-too-human figures of house-proud wives, with their passion for dainty ornament and their sacrosanct front rooms; out of the tumult and hardship of the coal valleys swarm armies of militant women, cheering on their men at pithead demonstrations, stridently resisting arrest, throwing stones at policemen or screaming abuse at colliery managers.

There is almost nothing Welsh women have not done. They have gone to foreign wars: Elizabeth Davies of Bala was one of the best-loved nurses of the Crimean War (though not by Florence Nightingale, whom she detested in return). They have gone to sea on fishing-boats and ferries: when, at the end of the eighteenth century, Grace Perry's boat was swept away from the Menai Strait and turned up at Liverpool, she walked the 60 miles to get it, and with the help of a hired hand rowed it all the way home. They have been famous in sport: Emmeline Lewis-Lloyd of Llwyn Madog, in Powys, once spent an entire night playing a great salmon in the Elan river, sustained by relays of people bringing her refreshments. They have worked in pits and foundries, dragging fearfully heavy coal-wagons, or tipping huge cauldrons of molten iron. And for hundreds of years they have gone out with their ponies and carts over the wide flat sands of the Loughor estuary, in Glamorgan, to gather their licensed quota of cockles—lonely little figures that the tourists love to see, far out there in the puddled wastes when the tide is low.

In our own times women have been pre-eminent in Welsh public affairs, too, as politicians, as writers, as actresses, as composers: they have even broken through the barriers of the Rugby football fraternity, and are to be seen skilfully scrutinizing scrum-half tactics or damning the ineptitude of referees. But they still contribute more traditionally, too, to the character of Wales. In 1981 the postmistress of Llangeitho in Dyfed, whose duties included witnessing documents, sending prescriptions by bus to the chemist in town and helping Welsh-language learners with their mutations, described her main task as 'keeping one little star burning to light up the darkness in the world today'.

Fizz is a Welsh characteristic. The Rugby men fizz with a vengeance. The young miners fizz, as they swagger into their pubs with their mugs clanking at their belts. Welsh comic writers tend to be heavily aerated, and Anglicized Welshmen of the southern intelligentsia all too often bubble with a relentless effervescence. Sometimes it is just a symptom of high spirits, often it betrays inner uncertainty: for the one reason or the other, and occasionally for a combination of the two, it has engendered down the years a long and well-loved line of Welsh eccentrics, some of whom have entered the Welsh pantheon, and become household names.

Richard Robert Jones, 'Dic Aberdaron' from Llŷn, was in all material respects a complete failure. He is famous not so much for what he did, as for what he might have done, not for his triumphs over adversities, like most national heroes, but for his patrician refusal to adjust to them. He was born in 1780 the son of a fisherman, and for a time took to the sea too, but he early discovered in himself a precocious gift for languages, and this was the end of him. He gave up gainful employment for the rest of his life, and instead took to wandering around the country learning new languages, translating foreign books and working upon ephemeral literary projects.

He was the very image of a tramp. Thickly-bearded, floppy-hatted, often wearing a brilliantly bright blue Dragoon's jacket with silver epaulettes, generally bare-footed, nearly always filthy, accompanied more than likely by an adopted stray cat, with a harp and a horn slung over his back and every pocket of his raggety coat bulging with books—accoutred thus, he was a familiar figure in the lanes of North Wales, at the houses of country gentlemen or parsons where he stopped for sustenance and intellectual encouragement, on the water-front at Liverpool, where he liked to practise his languages on foreign sailors, in the drawing-rooms of London Welshmen and even in Dover, where he enjoyed expressing horrifyingly subversive views to the soldiers of the garrison.

Dic was described by a contemporary as 'innocent as a child, but cunning as a serpent'. He is said to have mastered fourteen languages, and to have had a smattering of many more, and he was greatly respected in his own lifetime for his prodigious self-taught intellect. But he was also a sponger, a squabbler, and a distinctly unreliable protégé. Time and again he was befriended by men of substance, who often put him up for a time, lent him books or money, or commissioned translations from one language or another. He let most of them down, in one way or another, and was engaged almost all his life in quarrels and recriminations.

It is often impossible, even now, to disentangle his truth from his fiction. Could he really speak all those languages? If he knew their words, did he always understand their meanings? Possibly not, but now as then people prefer to give him the benefit of most doubts, so that to this day Welsh schoolchildren are taught to view him with respectful regard. Dic's only lasting creation was a mammoth Welsh–Greek–Hebrew Lexicon, never alas to be published, but there are young Welshmen still who see his way of life as admirable—a life full of aspiration and private satisfaction, but utterly outside the usual canons of success. Dic owned nothing at all but his books, his harps and his horn, and he lost most of them at one time or another. He died in 1843, and despite his atheist beliefs was buried in the churchyard of St Mary's Church at Llanelwy, St Asaph in Clwyd, where admirers who go to shed a gentle tear, and wish Dic's vagrant spirit well, will find this *englyn*, by Ellis Owen, carved upon his tombstone:

> *Ieithydd uwch ieithegwyr wythwaith—gwir ydoedd*
> *Geiriadur pob talaith.*
> *Aeth angau â'i bymthengiaith.*
> *Obry'n awr mae heb 'r un iaith.*

> A linguist eight times above other linguists—truly he was
> A dictionary of every province.
> Death took away his fifteen languages.
> Below he is now without a language at all.

Dic achieved nothing much in life: at the other end of Wales another idiosyncratic original, Dr William Price of Llantrisant in Glamorgan, achieved so much that he has permanently affected the laws and customs not only of Wales but of the English-speaking world. Born in 1800, the son of an indolent Anglican clergyman, he was a practising physician among the colliers and hill farmers of half-industrialized Glamorgan, but it seems to have been a precept of his life to be as totally dissimilar as possible to anyone else who ever lived. He was a violent radical in almost everything. A vegetarian, an animist and a revolutionary republican, when he was 81 he took to living brazenly with a common-law wife (he disapproved of marriage—it 'reduced the fair sex to a condition of slavery'), and named their two children Iesu Crist and Iarlles Morgannwg, the Countess of Glamorgan. His appearance was striking: a tall strong man with a hooked nose, glaring eyes, long hair and a long beard too, he normally dressed all in green, white and scarlet, and wore on his head a fox-skin with its front paws on his forehead and its tail hanging down his back.

As a doctor he concentrated on causes, not symptoms, charging his patients only when he failed to cure them, but declining to treat them at all if they smoked. He was a skilful surgeon—he once grafted a bit of bone from a calf's leg on to a miner's crushed ankle—and was so fanatical about hygiene that he never wore socks and washed every coin that passed through his hands. As a politician he was fiery but ineffective: he called the mine-owners of South Wales 'blood-sucking Pharaohs of Wales', but after the failure of the Chartist riots in 1839 ran away to France, where he spent seven years. He was engaged in constant law-suits, in all of which he insisted on pleading his own case, wearing around his shoulders a plaid shawl, and in at least one of which he was supported, as assistant counsel, by his infant daughter the Countess. Charged with perjury once, he ended his defence with these baffling but tremendous words:

Cannot her Majesty, as the mighty huntress, in her day, before the Lord, go out like the Sun to find beasts of prey enough for her bloodhounds without hunting them to sacrifice the liberty and life of an innocent man upon her criminal altars with the bloody hands of her priesthood? What! Does the equivalent Queen of Great Britain, the mistress of the civilized world, in her day, fear the light of the Sun, living in a drop of dew, and identified in the name of William Price? . . . Not guilty! Remember that my fate is sealed by the word of your mouth! Your will be done on earth as it is in heaven!

He was acquitted.

Dr Price was an addict of the Druidical mysteries. He haunted the great Rocking Stone, *Y Maen Chwyf*, which still stands on the hillside above Pontypridd in Glamorgan, often addressing meetings from its slightly tremulous surface, and nearby are the two great drum towers, now used as houses, which he built as the entrance to a proposed Druidical temple. Its centre-piece was to be a tower eight storeys high, with a camera obscura on top, and he himself of course was to be its resident Archdruid: but it came to nothing after all, for though he made so bold a start upon the project, almost nobody would subscribe to the cost.

In 1884 Dr Price's baby son Iesu, aged five months, died. The doctor was heart-broken—he had believed the child destined to restore to the earth 'the lost secrets of the Druids'—and taking the little body to Caerleon Field, above Llantrisant, he cremated it there with arcane lamentations. This was too much even for his tolerant and generally fond neighbours, who thought he had burnt the child alive; angry crowds besieged his house, and had to be driven off by the formidable physician, a pistol in each hand, and his mistress holding a shotgun.

Dr Price was arrested, and charged in Cardiff with the illegal disposal of a body. He defended himself implacably, wearing beneath his tartan a white linen smock with scalloped cuffs, and at Glamorgan Assizes in February 1884 he won a historic decision. The burning of little Iesu was declared lawful, and thereafter cremation was to become legal throughout the British possessions, all over the world. Today, in the village square at Llantrisant, there stands a splendidly gaunt and eerily robed figure of the doctor, by the sculptor Peter Nicholas, which was erected in gratitude more than a century later by the Cremation Society.

After his great victory Dr Price thrived. He got damages from the police for false imprisonment, he struck a commemorative medal of which he sold 3,000 examples, and six years later, aged 90, he sired another son, also called Iesu Crist. His enemies were mostly reconciled, his patients continued to swear by him, and when he himself was cremated in Caerleon Field in 1893 huge crowds of mourners, each bearing a ticket printed 'Cremation of Dr Price, Admit Bearer', watched his iron coffin grow incandescent in the byre. His last act on this earth—or as he put it 'in my present tenement . . . called William Price'—was to drink a glass of champagne.

Fizz! But we will leave the Welsh eccentrics with an original of a gentler kind. In the early years of this century the people of Porthmadog, in Gwynedd, were very attached to an odd-ball of their own, Wil Ellis, a vagrant who lived by running errands here and there, or holding horses' heads, and who was chiefly famous for his habit of instantly falling asleep, and loudly snoring, wherever he happened to settle—in chapels, in shops, in pubs, or even in the open street. When he died elegies were written for him by many local poets, and on his gravestone were written the words *Cysga Wil, a phaid â chwyrnu!* —'Sleep, Wil, and no snoring!'

Hospitality was always a boast of the Welsh. The archetype of all Welsh hosts, Ifor ap Llywelyn of Gwent, Ifor Hael or Ifor the Generous, was immortalized for his open-handedness by Dafydd ap Gwilym, and has been honoured ever since: he gave his name to an eighteenth-century benevolent society, *Yr Iforiaid*, the Ivorites, and up and down Wales you may still find houses named in emulation Llys Ifor, Ifor's Court, or pubs proud to call themselves, even if they have forgotten why, the Ifor Arms. His spirit survives, too. Knock on the farmhouse door, wherever you smell the wood-smoke from the chimney, and a cup of tea is almost certainly yours. Ask your way in Pontypool, and you may be chatting there for half an hour. *Dewch i mewn*, 'Come in', is a true Welsh catchphrase, and one of the prime ambitions of any self-respecting housewife is to offer her guests better cake, or more varied canapés, or most importantly of all more immediate tea, than anyone else. The philosopher Ludwig Wittgenstein liked to tell of staying in the house of a Welsh preacher with a somewhat diffidently hospitable wife. 'Would you like a cup of tea, now? Would you like bread? Would you care for a nice piece of cake?' From the room next door boomed the rich voice of the minister: 'Don't *ask* the gentleman! *Give!*'

Here is the Victorian poet Gerard Manley Hopkins on a memory of Welsh hospitality:

> I remember a house where all were good
>> To me, God knows, deserving no such thing:
>> Comforting smell breathed at very entering,
> Fetched fresh, as I suppose, off some sweet wood.
> That cordial air made those kind people a hood
>> All over, as of a bevy of eggs the mothering wing
>> Will, or mild nights the new morsels of Spring . . .

And here are the lines, allegedly translated from the old Welsh, which were inscribed by Lady Llanover over the great gateway of her house in Gwent (inhabited in the 1980s, by the way, by an exceedingly welcoming three-legged cat):

> Who are thou, visitor?
> If friend, welcome of the heart to thee:
> If stranger, hospitality shall meet thee:
> If enemy, courtesy shall imprison thee.

As it happens the hospitality of Llanover was muted, by the standards of Ifor Hael anyway, because its chatelaine so sternly disapproved of alcohol. Chapel people do not like to admit it, but the convivial side of the Welsh character has often been encouraged by a taste for strong drink. The Celts were notoriously fond of it, the Welsh princes of medieval times not only had their own breweries, but also imported wines from France, and the magnates and squires of later years drank terrifically. It was said by his neighbours that Sir Watkins Williams-Wynne died in 1789 because he drank too little—he seldom finished the pint of claret which was the normal dinner ration then. A century later, H. M. Vaughan the chronicler of the Welsh squires tells us, at one country house in Dyfed three bottles of wine were laid as a matter of course for each diner.

The ordinary people, too, seem in many periods of their history to have been besotted by drink. Every village had its well-known drunkard, even during the hegemony of the chapels, and on market days in the eighteenth century the country lanes of west Wales were infested with reeling drunks, crazily driven gigs and horses lost by their inebriated owners. Mead, made of barley and honey, was the poor Welshman's drink in earlier times: so strong was it that the Church tried to wean people away to beer by starting its own ale-houses—often still to be seen, named *Tai-yn-y-Llan*, Church Houses so to speak, converted into dainty cottages at the bottom of churchyards. Later ale itself became the popular addiction. In 1573 the Council of Wales and the Marches complained about the excessive number of country ale-houses, often 'in desert and secret places, or woods, commons, waste grounds and mountains'. As for the towns, in the eighteenth century there were several hundred ale-houses for the 5,000 people of Amlwch in Môn, eighty-two inns for the country town of Caerfyrddin, and it was in the pubs of South Wales that the whole cultural life of the people was concentrated, with tavern *eisteddfodau*, saloon-bar political clubs, literary discussions in the tap-room and conspiratorial conclaves in the landlord's private quarters.

For a time the ale-houses of Wales were inhibited by the teetotalism of the chapel movement, and among topers the Welsh acquired a forbiddingly disapproving reputation. In 1881 an Act of Parliament, the first ever to legislate specifically for Wales, forbade the opening of Welsh pubs on Sunday; presently though this was replaced by a referendum every seven years, entitling each district to vote for or against Sabbath opening, and gradually the dry areas were squeezed into fewer and fewer enclaves of the west and north, until by 1982 only two small districts in the whole of Wales honoured the Sunday prohibition. Today the pubs, mostly presided over by English land-lords, once again provide the chief social assemblies of the people. The wheel has come full circle. The grim Welsh Sunday retreats into anecdote, and when one of the big brewers wants to publicize a new ale on television, as often as not they are jolly Welshmen who are to be seen appreciatively quaffing it, wiping their mouths in an experienced way and saying droll Welshmen's things.

Tea, nevertheless, remains the chief vehicle of Welsh hospitality—tea and inquisitive conversation. Food figures less, if only because the Welsh have seldom been greatly interested in it, even when they could afford to be. Their habitual diet today consists of chips, potato crisps and miscellaneous convenience foods (which is perhaps why they have the highest rate of stomach cancer in the British Isles), and in the past it was even worse. The quarrymen of North Wales in the nineteenth century lived largely on bread and butter; in west Wales people lived almost entirely on potatoes, even making potato flour; and in Gwynedd a staple of the rural diet was a dish called *Sgotyn*—'break a slice of bread into a bowl, pour boiling water over it, add salt and pepper to taste and serve at once'.

Beside the road in the village of Llandinam, Powys, there stands one of the best statues in Wales, by the nineteenth-century sculptor Alfred Gilbert—a hefty bronze figure of a man, holding a document in his hand. Knowing through what godly country we are passing, in the heart of evangelical Wales, we might suppose him to be some eminent Bible scholar or missionary, holding the Book of Ezekiel. In fact he is David Davies, a multimillionaire, holding the plans of a profitable engineering project.

The Welsh are not generally thought of as capitalists, and most of the country's great businessmen and industrialists have come from elsewhere. They are, though, extremely canny with money, and there have been many exceptions to the rule—so many in the days of industrial boom, and so frequently honoured for their acumen, that Cardiff between the world wars was nicknamed The City of Dreadful Knights. There was the brilliant Thomas Williams of Môn, the copper king of the eighteenth century, known to his workers as Twm Chwarae Teg, Tom Fair Play, but to his rivals as one of the most ruthless and innovative tycoons of his day. There was Pryce-Jones of Newtown, the mail-order pioneer, whose marvellous headquarters still dominate the town, embellished with stained glass windows, royal crests and plaques recording triumphs at international exhibitions. And there was David Davies, Llandinam, the unmistakably Welsh founder and proprietor of the Ocean Coal Company.

Llandinam is a very small village in a part of mid-Wales where even now nothing much seems likely to happen from one decade to the next, and the world at large is excluded by the low rim of the hills around. Here David Davies was born, the eldest of nine children, in 1818. His father was a tenant farmer and ran a small sawmill, and the son became a farmer and sawyer too, his first nickname, Dai Top-Sawyer, sticking to him all through life: but he broke into that world beyond the hills by grabbing a share in the Railway Revolution. First as contractor, then as financier he had a hand in building at least seven Welsh railway lines, some of them farcical failures but some of them great successes, and so not only made himself rich, but acquired a second sobriquet, Davies the Railway.

Then, eyeing the vaster fortunes being made in the coalfields of the south, in 1865 he bought a mineral lease near the head of the Rhondda valleys, a still sylvan and secluded corner of Glamorgan. Down there he was an intruder. An uneducated, down-to-earth man of the people, Welsh-speaking and extremely religious, he offered a pungent contrast to the suave urban capitalists, mostly English and Scottish, who set the tone of industrial development in South Wales. He had no huge resources to back him, as they generally had. The City of London had hardly heard of him, and he was seen by the territorial magnates of Gwent and Glamorgan as a vulgar and probably misguided speculator.

Misguided, because although the upper Rhondda was known to contain coal, the seam lay at an almost unreachable depth. Davies was obliged to sink the two deepest coal shafts ever made, and for months the issue hung in the balance. So crippling was the expenditure that at one moment Davies decided to give up, and assembled his workmen to tell them so. All he had left, he wryly told them, was the half-crown in his pocket. 'Well, we'll have that too, then', one of the men shouted. Davies tossed it to him at once; the men volunteered to work a week longer without wages; on 9 March 1866 the coal seam was reached at 660 feet, and proved one of the richest on earth.

A Liberal all his life, Davies never did join the tight circle of South Wales industrialists. 'Where, I say', he cried at another meeting of his workers, 'where can you find better specimens of capital and labour than are here today? Here are myself and my partners—working men every one of us!' He much resented the pretensions of the Marquis of Bute, Scottish-born lord of Cardiff, who controlled both the railways from the coal valleys to the sea, and the docks at their terminals, charging exorbitant dues throughout. The railways were terribly congested, the docks were clogged with shipping, and in 1882 Davies, aged 65, decided to bypass the system altogether, and build his own railway from the Rhondda to the Bristol Channel, with his own port at the end of it.

An Act of Parliament was necessary, and this was frustrated for years by the House of Lords, ever loyal to its kind. By 1889 nevertheless railway and dock were completed, and in no time Davies's new port of

Barry, Barri in the Welsh, was one of the greatest coal-ports in the world, with a brand-new town exploding around it like a Klondyke camp. Davies became a supreme magnate of his age, retiring in the richness of years to the mansion he built for himself within sight of his family's old homestead at Llandinam, buying the local squire's house for his son, and when Mr Gilbert came to make that statue, it was a plan of Barry Docks that he put in the great man's hand.

Davies is remembered partly of course as the most successful of all indigenous money-makers, but partly because he remained always so robustly a chapel Welshman. Though he became an MP as well as a millionaire, to the end of his life he refused even to open letters on the Sabbath, or to allow alcohol in his house, while it was said of his ever-devoted wife that she knew the whole of the New Testament by heart, together with all the Psalms and the book of Isaiah. Though he once went to Russia as the guest of Alexander II, to advise him on railway development, he was often to be seen out on the job with his men, wearing top hat and frock coat on the construction site, and he never tired of telling audiences how absolutely self-made he was—when he did it once too often in the House of Commons Disraeli said how uplifting it was to hear the Honourable Member praising his creator.

David Davies was the image of the local man made good, patronizing but still endearing, insufferably pleased with himself but benevolent at heart. He loved to make a genial splash. He built town halls, hospitals, chapels and assembly rooms all over mid-Wales, he was the biggest single contributor to the funds of the University College of Wales, and he paid for the rebuilding of Owain Glyndŵr's supposed Parliament House at Machynlleth on the coast of Powys (where his own face has been given to an image of Owain in a mural). Within three generations Lord Davies of Llandinam was to be educated at Eton and King's College, Cambridge, and to have an heir called the Hon. Jonathan, but David Davies himself remained plain Mr Davies till the end of his days.

In old photographs of the South Wales coalfields long, long lines of coal wagons are to be seen travelling down the valley railways to the sea. They are painted with the lofty titles of their various companies—Marine and Naval, Navigation, Victoria Coal—but none are painted so bigly or boldly as the wagons of David Davies's company: OCEAN COAL COMPANY, they say, a name which was to be carried from those railway tracks all around the world, wherever ships were coaled or locomotives fuelled, and which was to give its creator the third and most sonorous of his nicknames, Davies the Ocean.

The Wales of the chapels, the Wales which is only now receding into history, was generally very well behaved. It was *gwlad y menyg gwynion*, 'the land of the white gloves'. The crime rate was very low, honesty was the rule in public matters, if not always in private, respect for public order was inherent: schoolboys on their way to school would tip their caps to the local policemen—'Morning Mr Jenkins', 'Good morning, boys . . .'

By 1924, though, we read about schoolboys in Ebbw Vale, Glynebwy, Gwent, behaving very differently: parading the streets foul-mouthed on the Sabbath, leap-frogging over tombstones, singing ribald ditties, stealing jam tarts, dribbling salmon-tins along the pavements and generally adopting, said the local paper severely, 'a devil-may-care attitude'. This was another return to form, for the Welsh character contains a strong streak of anarchic flair. Respect for the law is not as deep as it may have appeared to Constable Jenkins, and Authority, if it is less breezily flouted than it is in Ireland, certainly commands far less deference than it does in England. 'The tongue of man', observed a report to the English Parliament in 1283, 'can scarcely recount the vanity of tricks and plots by which the Welsh, in the manner of wolves, have afflicted us and our predecessors from time out of memory.'

Sometimes this piratical streak shows itself in cheerful roguery, sometimes in endemic venality, and there are obvious historical reasons for it—it is the inherited reaction of a people whose mores have been under attack for centuries, and who long ago identified authority as alien and hostile. Besides, the virtues instilled in the English by the public schools and ancient universities never were particularly admired by the Welsh: the stiff upper lip, the absolute respect for truth, deference to the social hierarchy—none of all that meant much to Welshmen, and even among the most godly and law-abiding citizens, different moral codes prevailed.

The criminal has often been the hero, in Welsh memory. Perhaps the long guerrilla wars against the Normans and the English saw to that—thousands of Owain Glyndŵr's soldiers, when the cause was lost at last, became outlaws and bandits for the rest of their lives, but were still known affectionately to the people as *Plant Owain*, and generally succoured. Squatters who defied tyrannical landlords, poachers who gaffed squires' fish or snared parsons' rabbits, rioters who broke down toll gates, smugglers who fought their endless battles with revenue men around the coasts of Wales, miners and quarrymen who struck for fairer shares in the wealth of the country—all these have been popular figures among the Welsh.

A taste for violence has often surfaced, too. Two of the most furious of buccaneers were Welshmen—Henry Morgan of Gwent, Bartholomew Roberts of Dyfed, 'the worshipful Mr Roberts', who always included musicians in his crew, who struck a true Welsh chord with his dictum 'better a pirate and a commander be, than a common man', and who, when the Royal Navy killed him at last in 1722, was thrown overboard at his own request in full piratical gear. Bandits of the most ruthless kind have often plagued Wales: the most famous of them, the red-haired bandit clan of Dinas Mawddwy in Powys, having had eighty of their number sentenced to death by Judge Lewis Owen in 1555, lost no time in murdering the judge in return. Wreckers were active into modern times: when in 1908 the Austrian steamer *Szent István* went ashore on the Dyfed coast, the looters were said by the local paper to include not only publicans and hooligans but 'deacons and respectable tradesmen' as well. And no explorer was ever more ruthless of method than Henry Stanley, né Rowlands, who once killed five Africans with four shots of his elephant rifle, 'loaded with explosive balls', he said, 'for this occasion'.

Several favourite Welsh legends tell the tales of malefactors, and are generally sympathetic to them. At Montgomery a well-worn track across the churchyard leads to the grave of Robert Newton, hanged in 1821 for alleged sheep-stealing. Newton swore his innocence to the last, and prophesied that grass would not grow upon his grave until his memory was cleared: and though in fact the spot is barely recognizable now for the foliage growing all over it, still the guidebooks fondly prepare their readers for a bare patch there, and hundreds of tourists every year go to look for it. Then in the churchyard at Presteigne is buried Mary Morgan, who was hanged in 1805, aged 17, for the murder of her illegitimate child: she was made pregnant either by a fellow-servant in the great house where she worked, or more probably by the young squire, neither of whom would accept responsibility, and having delivered the child all alone in her bedroom, immediately killed it with a pen-knife. The townspeople were horrified at her execution, and erected upon her grave a monument with the text 'He that is without sin amongst you, let him first cast a stone at her'. Flowers are still laid upon it on the anniversary of her death.

A slanting rock near Cilycwm, in the upper Tywi valley in Dyfed, is known as Twm Siôn Cati's Cave after a well-beloved rogue of the seventeenth century. A squire's son and an educated man, Twm Siôn took a sabbatical from the gentry life and turned highwayman for a few years, robbing only the rich of course, and establishing himself if only in hindsight as a champion of the common people. Whether or not he really lived in the cave up there, whether half his rollicking adventures really happened at all, he established himself so firmly in the public affection that in the 1970s they made a television series about him, and visitors are still shown the house to which in his maturity, as Thomas Jones, poet, antiquarian and Justice of the Peace, he retired to live respectably ever after.

Young Welshmen are still cheerfully ready to cock a snook at the police, but this independent attitude to the law has its seamier side too. The lesser fiddle, the illegal perk, have joined the folk-tradition now, part of the never-ending battle between Us and Them, Labour and Management, which sprang out of Tenant and Landlord long ago, and before that out of Welsh and English. Men who would not dream of cheating their pub-keeper or the corner shop freely cheat the factory canteen, and nobody in Wales in his right senses would hesitate to deceive the social security people. Hardly a soul cared when, in 1982, the supposedly amateur heroes of the national Rugby XV were proved to have accepted payments from a firm of boot manufacturers: for one thing the amateur rule seemed made only to be infringed, and for another almost everybody did it, and anyway nobody suffered, and the boys deserved a bit—Christ Almighty, look what the soccer stars get!

Corruption breeds corruption, and often enough this comradely mayhem infects the character of Wales in less generous ways. Corrupt councillors, corrupt officials, corrupt contractors cheat often enough for the narrowest of all comradeships, themselves. 'The Taffia', the allegedly self-perpetuating oligarchy of South Wales industrialists, officials, financiers, broadcasters and academics, has an unsavoury reputation, and some Welsh people oppose the idea of self-government on the grounds that an autonomous Wales would be irredeemably tainted by its own tricks and wolfish plots.

*

Being a poet is a characteristic Welsh condition. The percentage of practising poets among the Cymry Cymraeg is probably higher than anywhere else in the Western world, and to foreigners and indigenes alike a touch of the poetics is inescapable in any assessment of the Welsh character. From the long-haired romantic Dafydd ap Gwilym to the young practitioners of today, tousled and pugnacious at *eisteddfodau*, or lonely in milk bars working out their metres, there have been Welshmen in all generations perfectly fitting the world's idea of what a poet should be.

Most people might think Dylan Marlais Thomas the supreme example, and in some ways he was. In looks he was just right. He was rather fleshy of appearance, obviously liable to fatten with age, and extremely sensual of style. His mouth was a little loose, and a little mischievous: his eyes were beautiful, very deep and thoughtful, and with a trace of sadness to them, as though they offered a window into profundities. He looked the Welsh artist *in genere*. All his physical characteristics, the humour of the mouth, the lyricism of the eyes, the suggestion of bawdy, the hints of self-indulgence around the belly, the touch of the sly, the ever-lurking sense of melancholy—all these are characteristics of the breed.

But he was an example of a disturbing kind. In background Dylan (who pronounced his name, in English orthography, 'Dullan') was as Welsh as could be. Both his parents spoke Welsh, and they lived in the still very Welsh seaport of Swansea. Inexplicably however the boy was not brought up to speak the language, and all his work was to be in English. Here were the elements of a tragedy. All Dylan's incessant poses, his degradations in London and New York, his slow decline into alcoholism, his rudeness, his brutal ingratitudes, his ever sourer resentment of university audiences and trendy critics, speak cruelly of a spirit deracinated or dispossessed, cut off from the sources of its personality and its art—groping for the affinities of the Welsh tradition, even using, in a pathetic yearning for its own poetic origins, English approximations of the classical Welsh forms (and yes, instead of being read only by a small minority of a peripheral nation, becoming familiar, admired and spasmodically fashionable wherever the English language is understood . . .).

In all this Dylan was certainly an archetype. In his life and in his art, he represented the quandaries of Anglo-Welshism, a traumatic split of the emotions which can leave a sensitive man divided not only in his loyalties, but in his personality. The figure of Dylan Thomas, the world's idea of the Welshman, growing more volubly Welsh with every whisky, wandering the West End bars or the cocktail parties of Manhattan, is a figure to tug the Welsh heart, so poignantly does it suggest old betrayals and injustices. And what is one to think of his work, its parody-Welsh, its caricature Welshmen, but its genius notwithstanding, which distributed to a wider audience than ever before some of the authentic spirit and flavour of Welsh art? No wonder Dylan raises mixed emotions in the hearts of his countrymen. It is a comfort to think that perhaps he found a Welsh serenity in the end, when they lowered him into his grave in the rocky soil of Laugharne, on the Dyfed coast, beneath his English epitaph.

At another poetic extreme, no less disconcerting to other Welsh sensibilities, stands a figure whose every word, every action, is secured in the oldest succession of the Welsh. Dafydd Iwan is an authentic contemporary bard, combining in his career the bard's historical functions of entertainment and political purpose, and able like his ancient predecessors to stir the people into passionate emotion. *I'r Gad, I'r Gad!* runs one of his most grimly exuberant songs—'To Battle, To Battle!'; and tremendously sound the voices of his audiences, atavistic despite themselves, when they join in its dark chorus!

Dafydd Iwan is sure of a footnote in Welsh history because as Chairman of Cymdeithas yr Iaith Cymraeg in the 1960s he led a successful campaign for the official use of the Welsh language—a reversal of Government attitudes that had prevailed since the Act of Union in 1536. He and his comrades achieved this partly by propaganda and agitation, but partly by non-violent illegalities, and he spent some time in jail. If this made him something of a bogey-man to Authority and to many Anglicized Welsh people, it made him a champion of champions to young patriots, and a household name among all the Cymry Cymraeg. His power was that, like the prophetic and insurrectionary bards before him, his appeal was instant, infectious and essentially popular. He was not only a poet by vocation (and an architect, as it happens, by training), but also a gifted composer and folk-singer—'a bit of a troubadour', is how he described himself. He used all the techniques of contemporary popular music to distribute his message, and he became inescapable on Welsh television and radio, besides travelling the countryside incessantly, playing in halls, huts and recreation centres wherever Welsh was spoken.

Dafydd Iwan is a politician, a leading member of Plaid Cymru, the Welsh nationalist party. More than that, though, he is a poetic agitator. Much of the excitement of his performance is the *frisson* of inherited defiance, expressing in catchy tunes and fiery words, in a mixture of satire, pride and affection, aspirations that many Welsh people only half-recognize in themselves—in Prague or Kiev he would never be tolerated, and the old British Empire would not have liked him much, either. In his person, too, he is a symptom of historical continuity, for he is the son of an Independent minister: if he is a throw-back to the bards in some respects, in others he recaptures the *hwyl* of the great revivalists. To see him on stage really is like experiencing many ages of Welshness all in one evening. The platform is bare but for a few chairs and the tangled wires of microphones and amplifiers. The audience, Welsh-speaking to a child in arms, is muffled in coats, scarves and woolly hats. The supporting musicians are dressed in extreme casualness, jeans, jerseys, open shirts. And Dafydd himself, stocky and square of build, dark, with wide-apart eyes and an expression tinged, for all his buoyancy, with a certain gravity, looks for all the world like a wandering poet from the Age of Princes. Replace his guitar with pipe or harp, replace his check shirt with cloak or tunic, and he might have wandered in that evening on his way from one great house to another, or *en route* perhaps to Ystrad Fflur, to sing his message to us wondering peasants:

> . . . *mi ddawnsiaf ddawns y Gymru Rydd*
> *Mi ganaf gân y Gymru Rydd*
> *Ac rwy'n yfed i doriad yr hyfryd ddydd*
> *Y dydd y bydd pob Cymro'n rhydd!*

> . . . I'll dance the dance of Wales Free
> I'll sing the song of Wales Free
> And I drink to the dawn of the lovely day
> The day when every Welshman will be free!

There is a chapter of examples, then, to refute or confirm the ancient generalizations. Does there emerge from them a recognizable national character? Not on the face of things. Not in looks, or style, or even morals, not in degree or ambition or depth of feeling. A David Davies seems to have little in common with a Dic Aberdaron, and some of those fighting soldiers would certainly have looked askance at Iolo or the irrepressibly dissident Dr Price.

Yet set almost any two of them side by side, whatever their views, whatever their calling, from North or South, speaking Welsh or English, and they would feel a pull of kinship. Far more than most people, certainly far more then their English neighbours, the Welsh are subject to their heritage, a compatibility of Welshness impervious to politics or social nuance. Perhaps this *is* the national character: it hardly amounts to nationality, it does not always even aspire to patriotism, it seems beyond institutionalizing, it often does not show, but it is always there—an ancient stamp or shadow of comradeship, marking the Welshman as a member more than a subject, a colleague rather than a follower or a master.

It is this quality which successive patriotic champions have tried, with such transient success, to bring to national fulfilment—a tantalizing community of instinct or temperament, fragile and evasive, which slips away into nothingness when a leader tries to grasp it, or an author wants to put it in a book.

Interlude

By the summer of 1404 Owain Glyndŵr had achieved the fulfilment of Wales, and was recognized by most Welsh people as their only prince. It was a moment roughly half-way through the recorded history of the nation—six centuries since the making of Offa's Dyke, six centuries before our own time—and Owain had turned Wales into a State, presenting itself as of equal status among the Powers of western Europe. Though its population was small even by the standards of the time—perhaps 150,000 souls—still it bore itself with some grandeur, and its style was glittering. It was like a fictional kingdom of romance, out there on the fringe of Europe, sustaining itself by force of arms, dependent upon ancient myth, upon vatic declamations and suggestions of geomancy, to give it pride and confidence. Like some barefoot magnifico out of the western mountains, Owain Glyndŵr's princedom of Wales thrust itself into the company of the nations.

At its head, indisputably, stood the hero. His image seems to have been consciously arcane. If he had started life as a cultured country gentleman of distinguished stock, he had become in his middle years one of those self-recognized men of destiny who appear now and then in the histories of all nations. Descended on his father's side from princes of Powys in the north, on his mother's from kings of Deheubarth in the south, he was nevertheless a leader different in kind from the independent rulers of the old Wales. He had no indigenous rivals, for one thing. The Llywelyns had become rulers of all Wales by a process of long calculation and conflict, but Owain's princedom was, so to speak, his own invention: the old princely claims to sovereignty had long since lapsed, and Owain was less a dynastic revivalist than a political revolutionary. He claimed a throne that had never really existed, the throne of a Welsh State.

It was a visionary concept, and he achieved it by visionary means. Mystics and poets declared his divine calling. The whole teeming repertoire of Welsh fancy and folklore was summoned into the service of his cause. Prophecies of liberation were refurbished, newly interpreted or very possibly invented. Taliesin, the Old Man of Pencader, the birds of Llyn Safaddan, Owain Lawgoch, were conscripted as witnesses of providence. A web of fate was woven around the person of the prince, so that he acquired, among his subjects as among his enemies, a supernatural reputation: comets blazed at his birth, spirits obeyed him, the very elements were at his command.

He lived, in 1404, in the symbolic magnificence such a hero-figure needs. In the spring his soldiers had captured from the English the castle of Harlech, the most thrilling of all the fortresses Edward I had built to suppress the Welsh resistance. It stood in those days (for the geography has altered since) in a posture of supreme boldness on a high bluff immediately above the sea, and its four round towers could be seen in terrific silhouette from far along the Ardudwy coast, or stark against the mountainside across the water from Llŷn. To find Glyndŵr's ensign flying from the battlements of this prodigy must have been an inspiration in itself, but the meaning of his presence there was deeper still: for long before the English came to Wales at all, Harlech had been the seat of power of an earlier Welsh hero, Brân the Blessed himself.

Here then in the early years of the fifteenth century lived the Prince of Wales, with his wife Margaret, his six sons and three daughters, with his Chancellor and his chaplain, his military commanders and his constitutional advisers. It is hard to imagine a more high-flown court, so rich in allusions old and new, only a small Welsh village huddled around its fortress walls, before it the Celtic Sea, behind it nothing but the wild Welsh mountains. From Harlech Owain's emissaries went out to his commanders in the field, to his agents elsewhere in Wales, to his English confederates, to the Pope in Avignon, to the Kings of France, Spain and Scotland, to the chieftains of Ireland. Within the castle walls Owain received the envoys of his allies, accepted the submissions of his defeated enemies, and confined his principal captives and hostages. Sometimes a French warship, from the patrolling squadrons of Jean d'Espagne, lay at anchor beneath the bluff; often troops of horsemen could be seen travelling along the rough coast road that led, over mountain passes out of sight, to the scattered battle-fronts in the east.

For this was a State perpetually at war. Though Glyndŵr had driven the English from almost the whole of Welsh Wales, they had certainly not come to terms with him, and English columns incessantly probed and skirmished. Owain ruled his kingdom, nevertheless, as though it would last for ever. Twice he convened national parliaments, once at Harlech, once at Machynlleth, to which delegates from all the Welsh regions were summoned, and around him he assembled a formidable cabinet. His chief adviser, his Bismarck, was the brilliant Gruffydd Young, archdeacon of Meirionydd and doctor of canon law. His intelligence chief is likely to have been Edmund Mortimer, one of the greatest of the English Marcher lords, who had been captured in battle in 1402, had switched allegiance, and was married to Owain's daughter Catherine. He had the services of several eminent churchmen, many lawyers and innumerable propagandists. His Great Seal was of an imperial authority. His flag was the Red Dragon.

The princedom was unified, but in the Celtic way. There was no capital, Harlech being only the seat of Owain's own power, and Tyddewi the ecclesiastical centre. There was no permanent site for the national parliament. There was no army really, only a conglomerate of guerrillas under commanders who came and went. Owain planned to establish a Welsh university, but it would have been divided into two parts, one in the north, one in the south. The real unity of his princedom was in the idea of it—the notion of a Wales living in a Welsh way, under a Welsh Prince, governed by Welsh values in the Welsh language. This was all the prophets had promised the people: and for better or for worse, in 1405 Owain Glyndŵr had given it to them. His was a princedom as much in the mind as on the map.

And in the mind, it lives vividly to this day. That bony figure of the Welsh throne is commanding in the imagination even now. We can still see Gruffydd Young and John Hanmer, plenipotentiaries from Harlech, presenting their credentials to the chivalry of France, reminding the Frenchmen perhaps of the feats of Owain Red Hand and the Poursuivant d'Amour, and handing over that formal declaration of alliance, stamped with the seal of 'the mighty and magnificent Owen, Prince of Wales', which is still preserved in the French national archives. We see the French commanders disembarking at the Harlech sea-gate from their flagged pinnaces, or smartening up their bedraggled battalions, wet and hungry from the mountains, before marching into the castle forecourt. We see Owain's delegates cloistered in secret session at Bangor with the envoys of his English fellow-conspirators, Mortimer and the Earl of Northumberland, to divide the whole of the English realm between them—Northumberland to get the north of

England, Mortimer to get the south, and Glyndŵr's Wales to include a large slab of territory on the eastern side of Offa's Dyke.

We see the grandees and their trains of armed men making their way through the mountains, from Dyfed and Ceredigion, Clwyd and Eifionydd, to the Welsh assemblies. We see the traitor Hywel Sele, about to draw his bow on Owain, quivering with the arrows of the princely bodyguard, and dumped in that hollow tree to rot away for ever. We see one-eyed Dafydd Gam of Aberhonddu, plotting the death of the prince in the English cause, thrown ignominious in a dungeon. We hear the harps and bards of Harlech, the heady praise poems in the great hall, we see Owain over his wine at the high table, locked perhaps in conversation with Mortimer and Gruffydd, or laughing with Margaret and Iolo Goch. We see the little nation, in short, living epically, on the knife-edge of history.

It was only a dream perhaps—poverty stalked the land really, the Black Death ravaged it, all the waste and sadness of war blighted the brief glory: but in the Welsh consciousness, one dream fosters another.

Six more centuries pass, and we imagine now, without benefit of bards, Wales fulfilled once more, sometime in the twenty-first century perhaps. Let us see how the country might look in the eye of another generation of visionaries, cherishing still as Owain did the idea of a Wales controlling its own destinies, to its own tastes. We will fly into Wales this time, up the estuary of the Dyfi, the Dovey, half-way along the western coast, and there, clustered among green water-meadows below the mountains, stands the national capital of Machynlleth. It is not a very big capital—the smallest in Europe, in fact, except possibly Reykjavik—and it looks, as it always did, like a small market town: but the Red Dragon flies everywhere above its rooftops, a cosmopolitan crowd swarms among its pubs and cafés, and sometimes a big black car with Corps Diplomatique plates weaves a cautious way through the market stalls of Stryd Marchnad. Here are assembled the central institutions of Welsh sovereignty. Parliament meets on the very site where Owain's delegates assembled six and a half centuries before. The Prime Minister's office occupies the fine old building which has long been called the Royal House, and in which, it has always been said, Glyndŵr kept some of his prisoners. The President of the

Republic lives in the eighteenth-century mansion, Plas Machynlleth, which the Marquis of Londonderry gave to the municipality a century ago, and which has fine staterooms for the entertainment of eminent visitors, and a balcony with flagpoles from which the President waves to the assembled populace on St David's Day (now combined with Independence Day), and each year declares by satellite the opening of the National Eisteddfod, wherever it may be.

Offices of State are scattered piecemeal through the town—the Chancellery next door to the Wynnstay Arms, for instance, the Banc Cenedlaethol Cymru, the central bank of the Republic, occupying the somewhat enlarged premises of the old National Westminster, the Foreign Office in a long low building by the river (fishing strictly reserved, though, for members of the Dyfi Angling Society). Most of the accredited ambassadors of foreign Powers are based in London, but those who find it politic to have a legation in Wales occupy houses in the country round about—the English have lately bought Nanteos, for instance, the Americans have built a complex of air-conditioned bungalows on the seafront at Borth, and the Irish have been fortunate enough to acquire the former Brigands Inn at Mallwyd, which they have left fastidiously unaltered.

Though Machynlleth fulfils the normal functions of a capital, Wales is still not a centralist State. Most power is in the hands of the six regional councils. Most of the national bureacracy is still in the former capital of Cardiff, much of the private sector business community too, while the National Library is at Aberystwyth still, the National University is divided into five campuses across the country, the National Museum has branches everywhere and the headquarters of the Defence Force is at Aberhonddu, Brecon. A new motorway (*Sarn Elen Newydd*) brings almost all these institutions within two hours of each other, and is being paid for by tolls (60 *ceiniog* a passage).

Wales is a bilingual State, with priority being given to Welsh wherever possible, and only elderly citizens are now unable to speak Cymraeg. All civil servants, Members of Parliament and academics must be fluent in Welsh and English, and foreign students at the university are required to take courses in Welsh. Government business is conducted in both languages, and Members of Parliament may speak in either (though only a few veteran *Toriaid* now choose to use English).

The single-chamber Parliament is elected by proportional representation. This has meant that the numerical preponderance of the south has never been great enough for an overall majority, and Wales is habitually governed by coalitions. Deliberations are entirely informal, the only concession to English parliamentary practice being the fact that division bells ring in the Wynnstay Arms, the Red Lion and (it is said) in the front parlour of the Irish Embassy. When the President opens the legislative session each year he is robed as an Archdruid, and attended by that matron with the horn of plenty.

Wales became a republic after a hotly disputed referendum, rigged some say by patriotic extremists. It is a member of the European Community, and a founder-member too of the Neutral League—in many parts of the world Wales is represented by the League's joint diplomatic corps. The emphasis of Welsh foreign policy is on the European relationship, and the highest ambition of many of the cleverest young Welsh people is to represent their country in Brussels or Strasbourg. Relations with England are cordial: the border is open to travellers without passport, but there are strict regulations about the buying of property in Wales by foreigners, and this has vastly reduced the number of English residents. It is true that conservative English opinion still tends to look upon an independent Wales as a traitorous aberration, but the interests of the two nations seldom actually clash, and when the King of England recently paid a State visit to Machynlleth, except for a few catcalls he was kindly received, and at the Presidential banquet that evening made some amusing jokes about his boyhood impressions of Caernarfon Castle.

Economically Wales has thrived since the break from England. Freed from the restraints of British policies (and politics), the co-operatively owned steel-mills of the south, among the most productive in Europe, have dictated their own prices and found their own markets. The dozen or so surviving coal-mines devote their entire output to the coal-fuelled power stations that have replaced nuclear generators. Water and power are sold to England at a price agreed by independent arbitrators, oil coming by sea to the great refineries of the south and south-western coasts is subject to a special tax. Small industries have flourished as workers' co-operatives, with technical help from the Basques and the Jugoslavs, and even the least progressive of resort shopkeepers are obliged to admit that the independence of Wales, if it has somewhat inhibited mass tourism from England, has greatly increased the flow of more profitable categories from Europe and America: there are far fewer caravan sites, far more hotels of international standard—and the industry has been greatly helped, of course, by the recent inexplicable improvement in the Welsh climate.

The laws of Wales, hammered out by constitutionalists in the years after independence, are an amalgam of English Common Law and the Laws of Hywel Dda, embodied in an altogether new Code, *Cyfraith y Rhyddhad*, the Law of the Release. They are based upon the idea of contract, in both civil and criminal cases: keeping the peace and the faith is considered a universal contract between citizens, and its breach must be paid for, by cash payment, by service to the community, and only in extreme and obdurate cases by the punishment of the Republic. Judges are arbiters between claimants, and the principle of revenge, as against compensation or reconciliation, is abhorred. As for the national health services, under jurisdiction known as *Newid y Galon*, the Change of Heart, they are financed by that proportion of the national income reckoned to have been spent, under British administration, on the Crown, nuclear weapons, air defence and military intelligence, and are considered the most advanced in the Western world, inducing most of the best Welsh doctors, surgeons and nurses to remain in Wales, and offering completely free treatment and medicine of all kinds.

Wales being a neutral State, like Ireland, Sweden or Switzerland, it was only after long heart-searching that the founders of the Republic decided to have armed forces at all. The Defence Force that was finally decided upon, *Plant Owain*, is hardly an army really, but more a force of organized irregulars, wearing no uniform but camouflage fatigues, and trained solely for the guerrilla harassment of an occupying army: as such, it has been copied by small countries all over the world, and Welsh military instructors are much in demand abroad. Even so, it is embodied in the Welsh constitution that the republic should aspire towards a condition of absolute non-violence, and every seven years a public referendum decides whether the force shall be maintained at all (its members being guaranteed full pay for life if the people decide on abolition). There are no public military parades of any kind in Wales, and no pretensions to pomp, and the President and Prime Minister are guarded only by policemen in their denim dungarees. There are no official secrets whatsoever.

The strength of Wales has proved to be its smallness. A threat to nobody, a society of remarkable inner stability and contentment, its place among the nations is curious but admired. Welsh intermediaries are often invited to rule on international disputes, the Welsh voice in the United Nations, presented by a series of delegates of great intellectual force and wit, carries far more weight than might be expected. The bilingual newspaper *Cymru*, which brought back to Wales many of the best Welsh journalists of Fleet Street, is quoted all over the world as a mouthpiece of enlightened opinion—the *Manchester Guardian* of its time, it has been called. As the very model of a non-nuclear, neutral, un-militarist ecological State, Wales is a lode-star for young idealists all over the world. And the psychological serenity of the Welsh people, freed at last from the old anxieties about identity and national purpose, is the envy of far richer Powers, and the despair of hostile ideologues.

It is only a fantasy, like Glyndŵr's perhaps: but which is the more improbable, the one that came true in 1404, or the one that is still just a fiction for the interlude?

6. The Order of Things

Owain Glyndŵr's independent Wales was a social and historical experiment. Divided always by their centrifugal tendencies, split apart again by alien impositions, the Welsh were not obviously the stuff of statehood. Their cohesion, such as it was, lay so to speak in their lack of it—in the passionate precision of their loyalties, their rootedness in their own especial corner of the country. All this Owain tried to harness into rational organization, with the appurtenances of nationality. He was trying to give order to an innately disordered people: or rather, he was trying to make a contemporary kind of order out of a system of life that was based upon other values, other aspirations. He failed, and looking out with us over the same prospects today, while we find ourselves in a condition of déjà vu, *he must survey the state of Wales with mixed feelings of comfort and despair, marvelling that while so much changes, so much remains the same.*

THERE is no pretending that the Welsh are a well-regulated people, at least in public. The interiors of Welsh farmhouses are often exquisitely tidy, but outside they are generally an easy-going muddle of dilapidated outbuildings, abandoned implements and bits of disused fencing, the whole spattered or blown through by the discarded blue bags of artificial fertilizers. Nobody would claim for these people great powers of organization or discipline, either, and their moments of co-operation all too easily break down in angry dispute, whether they concern the governance of a country or the running of a snooker championship. 'There is no madness like contention', Non the mother of Dewi Sant is supposed to have said, but the Welsh have taken no notice. Contention is endemic among them, often enjoyably so, the quick riposte is more admired than the compromise, and they are almost never unanimous about anything. There is no easily definable hierarchy, no universal kind of patriotism. North Walians think, speak and look differently from southerners, worlds of style and experience divide the anthracite miner's family of Ammanford, the wine-bar *flâneurs* of the Cardiff suburbs and the severe Calvinist agriculturists of Y Bala or Tregaron. To observers from more logically arranged countries Wales seems to lack all qualifications or even instincts for cohesion.

Yet there is a Welsh order of things, of an abstract and private kind, which embraces most Welsh people, not least those of alien origins. It is an amalgam of character, temperament, climate and history, and its primary symptom is a certain tingle to the air of the place, which may be welcoming, or may be suspicious, but is nearly always apparent when visitors are around—a heightening of attitudes, an extra-smiling smile, an intensity of attention, a suggestion of collusion somewhere, that tends to put strangers warily on their guard.

The Welsh have survived as a nation chiefly by cunning and reserve. If they are more anxious than most to please, if their hospitality is deservedly proverbial, still in dealing with outsiders of any kind they are seldom uninhibited. They play for time, they fence, they scout out the situation, they do not commit themselves. Those sweet smiles are truly sweet, but they are well under control. It is a performance that greets you, polished and long practised, played on a deceptively cosy stage set with brass pokers by the fire.

It is the outward sign of a social order that is essentially communal. *Bradwr*, traitor, is one of the most expressive words in the Welsh language, far more bitter than its equivalent in English, and it can work on many levels. In successively smaller and tighter formations the Welsh are ranked, ready for all comers, from powerful combinations of political or economic advantage to the furious resentful pride of the Evans family, 24 Bryn Terrace, perpetually up in arms against the Social Security.

For first comes the family, *y teulu*—like the Jewish family, very firm, very demanding still. Sociologists tell us that even the car and the television have not much weakened the closeness of the average Evanses, who still tend to live as near to one another as possible, sharing their pleasures in prosperous times, closing ranks in times of trouble. The symbolism of family always was strong in this country. The princes called their bodyguards their *teulu*, Howel Harris called his community of disciples the Family of Trefeca, and the Welsh word for nation itself, *cenedl*, means no more than 'generation'.

The old Welsh laws recognized family obligations to the ninth degree of relationship, and Welsh blood-bonds are still ramified, subtle, and potentially dangerous. Mr Emrys Jones, treading a tricky anthropological path through the family connections of Tregaron in the 1960s, thought it was like walking in the nearby bog of Cors Goch—'if you depress the bogland with your foot it sags only a little, but fully 20 yards away tall grasses will sway gently in response . . .'. Nine degrees may be beyond the range of most Welsh people now, but they are still strong enough on third cousins, great-aunts by marriage and unsuspected connections in Ystradgynlais.

All this makes genealogy more important to them than to most people—the token of Welsh continuity was the *aelwyd*, the family hearth, whose fire was never allowed to go out. The Welsh interest in pedigrees has always been something of a joke to foreigners. Thomas Fuller, the seventeenth-century English antiquarian, suggested that any Welsh gentleman (if, as he wryly interjected, that was not a tautology) could find himself princely origins. Certainly many did. In Elizabethan times a popular way of spending a Welsh holiday was to assemble on a hillside somewhere and recite pedigrees, and they nearly all reached back to the ancient monarchies of the nation. Some went further still: several Welsh families claimed Trojan origins, one or two traced Knights of the Round Table upon their family trees, some proclaimed themselves descended from Noah and one or two from the Holy Family. Especially in the more rural parts of Wales this ancient preoccupation is far from dead. Welsh farmers are still liable to produce immense genealogical folios from beneath the dresser, to demonstrate to you their unchallengeable connection with Cunedda, Eliseg or the Royal Tribes, and Clough Williams-Ellis, when he built his pleasure-village of Portmeirion on the north-west coast, affixed to its campanile a plaque recording his direct descent from the princes of Gwynedd.

Actually, since there are only about two and three-quarter million Welshmen even today, any Welshman of reasonably settled pedigree is related to any other: and because there are so few family names in Wales every Welshman is able to recognize himself, however deceptively, in the annals of his country. It was only in the seventeenth century that the old patronymics and descriptive names were slurred into surnames—ap Rhys, 'son of Rhys', into Price; ap Evans into Bevan; Goch, 'The Red', into Gough; Fechan, 'The Small', which was the equivalent of Junior in American social parlance, into Vaughan. Several given names were turned into surnames simply by adding a possessive 's'—Robert into Roberts, William into Williams: it was paradoxically an English Christian name, John, which was to be majestically mutated into the name of all Welsh names, Jones.

All these remain overwhelmingly the family names of Wales, and appear over and over again in every record of Welsh affairs: 'a patronymical Bedlam', is how an English judge described the place, after a court hearing in Gwynedd in 1894 in which virtually all the participants seemed to be homonymous. Let us consider one of the middlingly common names, Morris. It is variously spelt, from the Latin Mauricius to the pure Welsh Morys, and is said to mean Moorish, referring to the saturnine looks of earlier Morrises, or perhaps to their supposedly African origins. Some 1,200 Morrises are to be found today in the Cardiff telephone book alone, and they have always been ubiquitous in the affairs of Wales. In our own time one has become Secretary of State for Wales, one has become Archbishop of Wales, and several have done the next best thing and played Rugby for their country: in the eighteenth century the Morris brothers of Ynys Môn, patriots, poets and men of letters, were so well known that they were simply called *Y Morisiaid*, The Morrises.

But they have come in all kinds. Valentine Morris was one of the most spectacular of eighteenth-century squires, who made his seat at Chepstow a showplace of the Picturesque; the Revd Ebenezer Morris was one of the most ferocious of nineteenth-century parsons, who fell upon dissidents with an iron hand, and was more than once indicted for assault; Mary Morris of Berriew, Aberriw in Powys, was one of the two wives whose corpses the eighteenth-century squire Sir John Pryce of Newtown kept embalmed, one on each side of his bed. An unidentified thirteenth-century sandstone head in the National Museum of Wales bears around its crown the inscription + MORUS (and looks rather negroid).

John ap Robert ap Morys of Gwydir, Gwynedd, was described in 1618 as 'a poore man, he liveth himsellf as a hired servant, his weif and three children allowed to begge in the parish'. On the other hand Robert Morrice was Bailiff of Monmouth in 1492, and Mrs Mona Morris was the first female mayor of Aberystwyth in 1978. It was 'a man named Morris' who, in the nineteenth century, found the crown of Rhys ap Tudur in a rock-cleft of the Rhondda, and kept it for himself. George Byng Morris owned the horse-drawn Mumbles railway. Morriston, Treforys outside Swansea, is named for Sir John Morris, a more than usually enlightened eighteenth-century industrialist. There is a lake in Gwynedd called Llyn Morys, after a man who drowned in it, and a standing stone in Gwent called Bedd Morus, Morus's Grave, but the hamlet of Morris Mawr, Great Morris, is buried beneath the steelworks of Port Talbot in Glamorgan.

Carey Morris was an eminent twentieth-century artist of Llandeilo, David Morris was a successful eighteenth-century banker of Caerfyrddin, Sir Cedric Morris was a celebrated artistic guru of the 1940s, John Morris was first lieutenant to Henry Morgan during his assault on Panama. Sir John Morris-Jones, died 1929, was the greatest of all Welsh grammarians, but Hugh Morris of Llanengan, Gwynedd, in 1797, lived in 'a small hutt', his son David having gone away to America and left him penniless. Tom Morris was private harper at the mansion of Eglwysfair, Dyfed, in the 1890s. The Porthmadog schooner *Miss Morris* was sunk by a German submarine in the Mediterranean in 1917. Lewis Morris, of Gwent stock, lived at Morrisania in New York

and signed the Declaration of Independence. 'By Christ', exclaimed
James I of England, looking more closely at the honorand after dubbing
William Morice of Gwynedd, 'I fear I have knighted an old woman.'

Morus Dwyfach was acclaimed the best poet in Wales at the
Caerwys Eisteddfod of 1568, Dafydd Morus was both a cattle-drover
and a famous hymn-writer, Huw Morus was one of the great lyric poets
of the seventeenth century, it was to Sir Lewis Morris, who complained
that the critics were silent about his poetry, that Oscar Wilde gave the
advice 'Join them, Lewis, join them'. And Edward Morris, a seventeenth-century drover-poet from the melancholy northern uplands
called Mynyddoedd Hiraethog wrote of his own house, Hafod Lom:

> *Mi af oddi yma i'r Hafod Lom,*
> *Er bod hi'n drom o siwrne,*
> *Mi gaf yno ganu cainc*
> *Ac eistedd ar fainc y simdde,*
> *Ac ond odid dyna'r fan*
> *Y byddaf tan y bore.*

> I'll go from here to Hafod Lom,
> Although it's a long journey.
> There I shall get to singing a song
> Sitting in the chimney-seat,
> And probably that's the place
> I shall be until morning.

There is no Morris clan, though, in Wales, no Chief of the Morrises,
no gathering at Castell Morys on St David's Day. Welsh affinities are
more exact than that, and when Morrises meet by chance on a bus, they
may ask each other if they happen to have any cousins Ystradgynlais
way, but show no further interest.

Above the family, other kinds of kinship. The tribes and princedoms of
ancient Wales were based upon complicated notions of inter-
dependence: the prince or chieftain at the top, the *uchelwyr* or great
men around him, the privileged bards, the freemen—all united, in
theory anyway, by descent from misty common ancestors of tradition.
This made for stout comradeships, but narrowed horizons too. Wider
visions were obscured by the sharp little perceptions of the day, and
civilization seemed to revolve about each petty court or castle. There is

a place near Mold, Yr Wyddgrug in Clwyd, where this ancient compression of emotion is expressed with just the right mixture of romance and provincialism, and tells us in an allegorical way why the Welsh social system has always been at once so intense, so confining and so paradoxically grand.

It is the ruined castle of Ewloe, which was built by the Welsh probably in the thirteenth century, when the English were pressing into Wales all along this frontier. It seems a remarkably unassertive fortress at first. Though it stands only a quarter of a mile from the busy road between Mold and Denbigh, and is actually overlooked by a modern housing estate, you cannot see it until you are almost within its gates. It is sunk in a thickly wooded dell, with a ravine full of undergrowth dropping away behind it. You would never know it was there, were it not for the Ancient Monument sign beside the passing road: and even that somebody with a paintpot, pursuing perhaps an immemorial instinct of concealment, has lately done his best to obliterate.

The castle stands there in a more or less perpetual half-light, dappled by the trees: a neat and elegant little stronghold, all alone, deep in its secret hollow. In the days when battles raged to and fro across this countryside, when ruthless English generals came storming this way and that across the Marches, it must have seemed a very bunker of Welshness in that wood. How tight a comradeship sustained the prince and his soldiers down there! How magically exclusive harp and Welsh voice sounded, muffled through those oaks!

When the tribe or the princedom was gone, subsumed in entities too remote for such camaraderie, there remained the neighbourhood, the *bro*, and the Welsh became no less fervently attached to a particular country community. People became identified, as they still are, by the names of their homes—Owen Parry Trefan, say, or Betty Jones Pentwyn. A new sort of tribalism arose, and the Welsh devoted their loyalties to Eifionydd, or Penllyn, or to many another small corner of Wales whose existence was generally unknown to all the others. A kind of social Balkanism splintered the country, divided as it was by hard terrain and miserable communications, and its effects remain with us today, in an inability to combine on public issues, but a staunch fellowship in private. 'The work people are very kind to each other', said an observer of the southern coal valleys in the 1830s, 'and will help each other in time of distress to an extent that would scarcely be believed'; and so, to an extent still unimagined by most strangers, the Welshier Welsh remain today.

Your country Welshman is seldom alone. In life he is sustained by a web of neighbours and relations, ready to help with the shearing, sit with the sick, give a second opinion on a used car, combine for an hour's gossip at the Red Lion or a package tour to Alicante: and when he dies, ah, even in these ungodly times what a sad strength of fellowship his departure illustrates, the kind attentions of neighbours, the silent tearful visits to the coffin in the front room, the long lines of cars crawling along the winding lanes to the chapel cemetery, the almost ritual display of public sorrow, the not too surreptitious examination of the cards on floral tributes, the sly-solemn reminiscences, the plate for charitable contributions and the strong sweet tea in the curtained parlour afterwards!

In the industrial areas the brotherhood is more often of terrace, or calling, or Rugby team, or pit. At Old Cwmbran in Gwent there is a small square of houses built for the local mining community—ten or twelve houses around a green, with a chapel in one corner, the Squirrel Inn at another, and a little shop in the middle. People still alive remember when the whole of this little community, if not actually related, operated like a family unit.

When there was a childbirth, you never had to run for a nurse . . . There was always someone there to see to it, you know, you were never left on your own . . . We would be in and out of each other's houses, well, not every day, but if you ever wanted anything . . . Nobody ever shut their doors . . .

Even today, when people of the southern valleys take the car to the hypermarket to do their shopping, and run down to Cardiff now and again for a show or a restaurant meal, pride of place and community often manages to survive the challenges of economic depression, as it resists the corruptions of prosperity. There is no club like the club of a South Wales coal-pit, for however tough things are up above, however uncertain the future seems, an almost theatrical brilliance of comradeship shines below. Everyone knows everyone else down there, and the long tramp to the coal-face, through the awful clattering din of the conveyor belts, the whoosh of the ventilation, the banging of tools and machinery, is an exhilarating succession of greetings and *badinage*. Near the coal-face, where the men are crouched in their alcoves with picks and drills, the blackness is broken only by wavering helmet-lights, but when a beam falls upon some coal-grimed face, instantly, even in that grim place, it lights up with a welcome. A consciousness of shared trust, danger and fun compensates for the miseries of the mine, and few young colliers readily leave the calling, for all its hardships, just as they seldom willingly move from the terraces on the valley floors to the semi-detached and centrally heated gentility of the city suburbs—'not such a bad place', they bravely say, stepping from the cage at the end of the shift, and surveying the long lines of houses snaking away among the abandoned pits and half-derelict factories —'not what it used to be mind you, but it could be worse . . .'.

In 1981 the people of the former quarry village of Porth-gain, on the Dyfed coast, scraped up the money between them to buy the whole village from the English colliery firm which owned it, and make themselves its freeholders. It cost them £55,000, and the deed of sale still hangs in the tap-room of the Sloop Inn, above the harbour.

'Love one another' is a favourite Welsh sermon text, and the Welsh memory is rich in illustrations of it. The artist Elis Gwyn Jones, in an essay about the personality of Eifionydd, his native *bro* in Gwynedd, tells a quaint and touching story about two poets of the place, Eben Fardd (né Ebeneser Thomas) of Clynnog and the invalid Siôn Wyn of Chwilog. In 1838 Eben walked over to Chwilog to take a present of five shillings to his colleague, but pretended he was bringing it on behalf of somebody else, who wished to remain anonymous—'here's a letter to explain'.

'Well', said Siôn, reading the letter, 'people *are* kind. But who is it, Eben?'
'I've been warned to keep it a secret.'
Siôn Wyn looked closely at the writing. 'You know what, I'll swear a woman wrote this.'
'Really?' Eben saw his plan to hide his kindness working better than he expected.
'Yes, only a woman could write so nicely.'
And after his benefactor had said goodbye, the bed-ridden poet slipped the envelope under his pillow, smiling to himself: 'Woman indeed! I'd know Eben's writing anywhere.'

*

These instincts of community were recognized in the ancient legal system of Wales, presided over by the symbolic figure of a king, Hywel Dda, Hywel the Good of Deheubarth, who in the tenth century extended his rule over most of the country. By then a rich and varied body of law, more customary than formal, already governed the various Welsh societies, differently applied in different parts, and open to disparate interpretations. According to tradition Hywel convened an assembly of the wisest men of all Wales at his palace of Tŷ Gwyn ar Daf, the White House on the river Taf—modern Whitland, where the event is commemorated by a garden and a plaque: and placing them in the charge of Blegywryd ap Einon of Gwent, 'a man of singular learning', he ordered them to pull this raggety legislation together, and codify the laws of Wales.

So say the chroniclers (though actually Blegywryd, it is now thought, was the happy invention of Iolo Morgannwg). The old Welsh laws have ever since been called *Cyfreithiau Hywel*, anyway, and prized by Welsh patriots as a great monument of the Welsh order. More than thirty medieval manuscripts survive to record the system for us, in Welsh as well as in Latin, and they really do show it to have been among the most advanced and equable of its time, regulating all aspects of life with an almost Islamic thoroughness, but with a secular dispassion.

Some of its rules seem eminently commonsensical. If something is to be divided between two people, for instance, one is to do the dividing, the other the choosing. Marriage is to be regarded as an agreement, not a sacrament, to be ended by common consent. A doctor is liable for the death of a patient unless he has taken an assurance from the patient's family beforehand. Bastards have the same rights as legitimate children. In civil matters contract is stronger than legislation. In criminal matters the laws aim at recompense and reconciliation rather than revenge: the intention was to re-establish social harmony, and the more terrible penalties of English law, the torturings, the gibbetings, the disembowelments, were unknown in independent Wales—even public whippings entered the country only with the Tudors.

Here are some assorted decrees of civil law traditionally ascribed to Hywel Dda and the wise men of Tŷ Gwyn ar Daf:

If a woman, wanting to leave her husband, claims that he is impotent, they must have intercourse on a clean sheet. If the man ejaculates upon the sheet, she must stay with him: if he cannot, she may leave him and take all her property with her. If a man abducts a virgin, and before they have intercourse she asks *Beth a rody y mi?*, 'What will you give me?' and he specifies how much he will pay her, and then denies it afterwards, then the girl's word is conclusive.

The Mediciner of a household must give free treatment to everyone in the house, except for a blow on the head to the brain, a blow on the body into the bowels, and the breaking of a limb: for any of these the Mediciner is to be paid 180 pence and his food, or one pound without food, and also his patient's bloody clothes.

The value of a kitten from the night it is born until the night it opens its eyes is one penny. After it starts to kill mice, its value is four pence, and so it remains. Anyone who sells a cat must guarantee that it does not caterwaul, that it does not eat its own kittens, that it has eyes, teeth and claws, and that it is a good mouser.

This was an order of fellowship: even in criminal cases it was not Crown or State versus the People, but People against other People, preferably coming to an agreement—*Volksrecht*, Dafydd Jenkins the legal historian tells us, as against *Kaiserrecht*. It was very different from the body of law built up by the English, based upon a strongly hierarchical system of society, upon discipline rather than settlement, order before justice. The Welsh laws were extinguished by the English, but only gradually. As late as 1536 Henry VIII's Act of Union could still deplore the fact that the Rights, Usages and Customs of Wales were 'far discrepant from the Laws and Customs of this Realm': and long after that again Welsh people often preferred to settle their differences and organize their arrangements by the old traditions—even in the 1800s, in some parts of Wales, the laws of Hywel Dda were still quoted as ultimate arbiters of civilized behaviour.

Actually the style of them has lately come back into fashion, as the States of the Western world desperately try to solve their problems of crime and social *malaise*: divorce by consent is now the general custom, and the idea of community service as a penalty for antisocial behaviour is truly in the Blegywryd spirit. The English knew, though, that nothing identifies a nation more exactly than its legislation. If Wales, like Scotland, had been allowed to retain its own body of law, every session of the justices would have advertised a national continuity extending back to the Golden Age of the Independence, before the conquerors came.

As it is, only the flavour or application of the law occasionally retains a Welsh dimension. When, in 1970, Dafydd Iwan was imprisoned in Cardiff for refusing to pay a fine incurred by his patriotic activities —disfiguring road signs, that is, which were not in the Welsh language—a group of twenty-one Welsh magistrates, obeying the emotion of comradeship rather than the reason of authority, clubbed together to pay his fine and arrange his release. Their overlord in London, the Lord Chancellor of England, was very shocked.

For the English imposed a different kind of order upon Wales, a vertical as against a horizontal order, and for centuries it was administered by a powerful and privileged caste, the landed gentry. This has almost vanished now, but here and there across the country one may still see the traces of its lost supremacy. It may be some great memorial chapel: the wonderful chapel of the Wynns of Gwydir, a prodigy of woodwork, alabaster, brasses and armorial bearings attached to Llanrwst church in Gwynedd, or the chapel of the Mansel family, at Margam in Glamorgan, whose great marble effigies are ranked tightly side by side, flat on their backs with their hands jutting in parallel prayer, in an unforgettable concentration of consequence. It may be a style of building, giving to some otherwise unexceptional hamlet the tinge of a squirely taste—Llanfachreth in Gwynedd, for example, whose goblinesque manner reflects the preferences of the Vaughans of Nannau, or Angle in Dyfed, whose oddly flat-topped houses and colonnaded Globe Inn reflect the participation of Colonel Richard Myerhouse in the South African Wars. Or it may be just a blush of feral shrubbery up a shaly mountainside, which shows where the gardeners of some long-vanished mansion once cultivated their rhododendrons.

It was a far cry from the social system envisaged by the learned Blegywryd to the system dominated by this powerfully Anglicized élite in the heyday of the English supremacy. By the eighteenth century the ownership of the land had settled into a purely English pattern, and there had come into being an all-powerful territorial hierarchy ranging from immensely rich magnates to a host of petty backwood squires. Between them they owned almost all the land of Wales. The ordinary people were absolutely in servitude to the landlords; in Gwynedd a smaller proportion of the people owned their own land than in any other part of the British kingdom.

Thirty or forty families were politically dominant, and many of these were the inheritors of Norman baronies, still holding the same lands, and still almost as powerful: of the twenty estates exceeding 20,000 acres in extent, three-quarters had been in existence at least since the fifteenth century. The Philippses of Picton in Dyfed, the Mostyns of Clwyd, the Morgans of Tredegar were all ancient and powerful houses, but the three greatest of them all were the Somersets of Raglan, Dukes of Beaufort, the Pembrokes of Glamorgan, and the Powyses of Powys Castle. These families lived in vice-regal state—the Beauforts possessed three castles, plus Tintern Abbey. Justices of the Peace were in effect their appointees; Members of Parliament were their creatures; clergymen were subject to their patronage; almost nothing could happen, in all the wide lands of Gwent, Powys and Morgannwg, without the sanction of Beaufort, Powys or Pembroke.

Other families of the oligarchy were more recent arrivals. The Bute dynasty of Cardiff, like many another immigrant clan, had come into its Welsh estates by appropriating a Welsh heiress. Scots by origin and by principal loyalty, in their nineteenth-century climax the Butes were among the richest people in the world. They lived in Cardiff Castle, when they were not on their Scottish island, their London home or their country houses in Ayrshire, Northumberland or Bedfordshire —'air the castle', the Marquis would wire his agent, when he proposed to visit his Cardiff property—and thanks to their ownership of the neighbouring hill country, became landlords of half the South Wales coalfield, besides being proprietors of its chief port, much of its railway network, its daily newspaper and 20,000 houses in Cardiff alone. The half-blind second Marquis of Bute, the most overwhelming of them, lived like a monarch in his castle: retired soldiers in the Bute livery manned his gates, women curtsied as he passed, an entire aisle of St John's Church was his private chapel, he was served by hereditary functionaries and his land agent was also Town Clerk of Cardiff. Later Marquises reacted differently to their wealth. The third, the original of Disraeli's Lothair, became a Catholic and an implacable opponent of blood sports, wrote a book about the ancient language of Tenerife, acquired an estate in Palestine and had Cardiff Castle done up in a fantastically Gothic merriment. The fourth spoke fluent Welsh and sold most of his Glamorgan estate. The fifth, in 1947, gave Cardiff Castle to the municipality and left Wales for good, to a ceremonial lowering of the Bute standard and a fly-past of aircraft.

Other grandee families again were native Welsh by origin, having acquired their estates by more ancient opportunism (by supporting Henry VII, by acquiring the lands of dispossessed monasteries, by acting as stewards to English lords or by opposing Owain Glyndŵr). Their epitome was the Williams-Wynne family of Wynnstay in Clwyd, whose estates were so wide, whose influence was so overwhelming, whose personalities were so large and whose pedigree was so long that for generations they were nicknamed 'The Princes' in Wales. By family tradition the eldest son was always named Watkin, and so through many decades one Sir Watkin Williams-Wynne after another dominated the annals of north-eastern Wales—even today, when the family estates are vastly reduced, perfect strangers may tell you, if you ask them whose land you are trespassing on, 'Why, Sir Watkin's, of course'.

In their prime they ruled an empire. Within their own estates there were resources of coal, lime, lead, tin, copper, corn and timber, and they were part-owners of the turnpike roads and railways that ran through their properties. They had a theatre at Wynnstay, a chapel too; when in 1770 the young heir of the day came of age, he and his 15,000 guests, including all the tenants, ate 30 bullocks, 50 pigs, 50 calves, 80 sheep, 660 fowl, 73 hundredweight of bread, 125 plum puddings, 60 barrels of pickled oysters and 18,000 eggs. By and large the Williams-Wynnes were considered benevolent overlords—in 1831 Sir Watkins, as Lord Lieutenant of Denbighshire, was summoned to London by the Prime Minister himself to explain his reprehensibly sympathetic attitude to miners on strike. They also remained distinctly Welsh, maintaining private harpers and habitually speaking Welsh as late as the 1860s: a nineteenth-century lithograph entitled simply 'Romantic Wales' showed at first sight the conventional assortment of mountains, bridges and waterfalls, but revolved sideways turned out to be Sir Watkin Williams-Wynne in profile.

Whole slabs of Wales were saturated by the presence of such families as these. The Windsor family, twelfth-century custodians of Windsor Castle, married into the family of the Earls of Pembroke, thereby acquiring lands in Glamorgan, and established their headquarters at the fortified mansion called St Fagan's Castle, outside Cardiff. In the nineteenth century part of their estate was developed as the new port and seaside resort of Penarth, and the street names chosen for it then, and still in use today, perfectly reflect their status.

Windsor, Plymouth and Mountjoy were all titles within their family tree. Pembroke, Bute, Archer, Bradford and Clinton were all titles they had married into. Herbert, Lewis, Clive, Bridgeman, Hickman, Albert and Paget were all families linked by marriage. Harriet, Victoria, Charlotte and Agnes were daughters and stepdaughters of the Earl of Windsor. Arcot, Plassey and Lucknow were victories won by Lord Clive, whose grandson a Windsor had married, while Ludlow Road was so named because a Windsor was Member of Parliament for North Shropshire. There were also thoroughfares named Baron Street, Earl Street and Countess Street, and streets magnanimously named for the Earl's estate agents, Messrs Maughan and Forest.

So the annals of an Anglo-Norman clan were ransacked to give cachet to a small Welsh town: and in the end the Windsor family, before fading from the Welsh scene, repaid their debt to the country in another kind, for in 1946 they gave St Fagan's Castle to be the nucleus of *Amgueddfa Gwerin Cymru*, the Folk Museum of Wales, where the skills and customs of the tenantry have outlived their splendours after all.

The English writer George Borrow, walking through Wales in 1854, wandered up an avenue leading to the house of John Johnes, Esq., near the village of Pumsaint in Dyfed. The country was fine, a beautiful stream ran beside the drive, noble oaks lined it, and the mansion when it came in sight was plain, gentlemanly and comfortable. 'With what satisfaction I could live in that house', said Borrow to himself, 'if backed by a couple of thousand a year!'

As it happened enviable Mr Johnes was presently to be murdered by his Irish butler in that very building, but in principle Borrow was right: given an adequate competence, nothing could be more pleasant than to live the life of one of the lesser Welsh landowners, in one of the more genial and productive parts of the country. Nearly everybody wanted to do it—as soon as a Welsh lawyer made enough money, or a Welsh nabob came home from the east, he acquired an estate and became a country gentleman. For every Somerset or Williams-Wynne there were a dozen John Johnes, and a hundred lesser squires again, lording it over estates of more manageable size, and living in manor houses that ranged in style and effect from elegant small palaces to mere farmhouses, distinguished from their tenant neighbours only by gable-ends or grander chimney-pots. This was the true Welsh squirearchy, descended generally from the native line, usually Anglicized according to the fashion, but often unmistakably Welsh of spirit or of tang, and often still close to the Welsh earth—when the young Pryse Pryse of Gogerddan in Dyfed went off to Eton in the 1840s he wore a suit of homespun made from the wool of his father's sheep, put together by the local tailor.

All through the pleasanter, easier lands of Wales, up sheltered valleys into the rolling hills where the sheep roamed, scores of squirely families lived in those days in mostly unostentatious comfort, one estate adjoining another. Anglican and Tory almost to a soul, and so in many ways cut off from their overwhelmingly Nonconformist and increasingly radical tenantry, they would have been most affronted nevertheless at the suggestion that they were any less Welsh than their underlings. Many spoke their own sort of Welsh—Squire's Welsh, the people used to call it; many bore old Welsh names; they prided themselves often on princely pedigrees, some of them doubtless trumped up by compliant genealogists long before, and they believed themselves to be the natural and necessary leaders of the people.

More often than not their lives revolved about the running of their estates, together with the local hunt, the shooting season, and in the particular case of the squires along the Teifi river in the west, the tennis club at Castell Emlyn Newydd, Newcastle Emlyn in Dyfed, which held its convivial meetings, appositely enough, on the lawns behind the Norman castle there. They were generally high-spirited people, sometimes excessively so, fond of the grand gesture and the sporting escapade. The Kemeys-Tyntes of Cefn Mabli in Gwent maintained a second mansion a few miles away across the Bristol Channel in Somerset, and lived for alternate periods and in equal grandeur in each. The Newboroughs of Ynys Môn built their own forts, and installed their own cannon, to guard the entrance to the Menai Strait during the Napoleonic Wars. When a railway was run into the Black Mountains of Gwent in the 1900s Mr Richard Baker-Gabb, the local landowner, built his own private waiting room (now neatly metamorphosed into Lavender Cottage) across the track from Llanfihangel station, while it was the proudest boast of Ferdinand Capel Hanbury Williams, squire of Pontypridd in Glamorgan, that in 1872 he killed three foxes, shot two brace of partridge and caught a salmon, all in one day, all on his own land.

But they included many people of more sensitive originality, too. The Wynnes of Peniarth in Dyfed, the Vaughans of Hengwrt in Gwynedd, built up priceless collections of Welsh manuscripts, later to form a nucleus of the Welsh National Library. Sackville Gwynne of Llanfair-ar-y-bryn in Dyfed was a great eighteenth-century patron of Welsh harp-playing, and a distinguished harpist himself. George Powell of Nanteos was a poet and an aesthete, friend of Swinburne and of Longfellow, translator of Icelandic legends and loather of blood sports. The Yorkes of Erddig in Clwyd made of their mansion a very temple of eccentric liberality, hung with commissioned portraits of the family servants, each with its tributary verse, while the Inglis-Joneses of Derry Ormond in Dyfed not only erected a family monument exactly like a factory chimney on the hill above their mansion, but so manipulated the flow of a passing stream that it provided power for the organ in the village church. Sir John Philipps of Picton was an eighteenth-century champion of schooling in the Welsh language; Sir George Cornewall Lewis of Harpton Court in Powys (Eton and Christ Church, Oxford) was described by Walter Bagehot, on his death in 1863, as perhaps the most completely educated man of his time.

And the caste's own social chronicler, H. M. Vaughan of Plas Llangoedmor in Dyfed, left us in his *South Wales Squires* (1926) some of the most engaging English prose ever written about the matter of the Welsh, whether he was discussing the appearance of a well-known sportswoman ('she bore some resemblance to a jolly dignitary of the Roman Catholic Church'), or reporting the habitual response of Colonel John 'Blundy' Howell of Glaspant to a successful joke—'Haw! Haw! Very superior!'

Meet a couple of squirely extremists.

First, R. J. Lloyd Price of Rhiwlas, Y Bala, the enterprising, versatile and eccentric scion of a family which had been enriched by its support of Henry VII. Price, who was born in 1843, was very Anglicized but extremely proud of his Welshness, and knowledgeable about Welsh literature and traditions. He gloried in the distinctly unreliable legend that the medieval chieftain Llywarch Hen, the subject of one of the oldest of all Welsh poems, had lived on Rhiwlas land, and he cherished a peculiar pebble which was said to foretell, by the widening of a crack in it, the imminent death of the head of the family. He rejoiced too in his full-blooded and sometimes equivocal ancestors: Cadwaladr Price, outlawed in 1598 for embezzling armour and illegally imprisoning people, or Richard Watkin Price, inventor of the sheep-dog trial, who pursued and caught the last two felons ever hanged for sheep-stealing.

R. J. Lloyd Price was a man of ebullient originality. At Frongoch, near Y Bala, he caused to be built a Home-Made House, still standing there, with a proud plaque claiming it to be constructed entirely of materials from the Rhiwlas estate. He patented a brand of Welsh whisky, made with Rhiwlas water, and also bottled the water of a local holy well. He was a prolific if variable author. He adored dogs—his books included *Dogs' Tails Wagged* and *Dogs Ancient and Modern*—and he once refused 500 guineas, a fortune then, for his cherished Belle, champion pointer bitch of the world. He loved horses too, not least betting on them: in 1899 he backed the winners of the classic double, the Oaks and the Cesarewitch, having been tipped their names by his deceased mother in a dream, and when he died in 1923 there was engraved upon his tomb at Llanfor the following grateful acknowledgement of another punting success:

> As to my latter end I go
> To win my Jubilee,
> I bless the good horse, Bendigo,
> Who built this tomb for me.

But like most of the squires, R. J. Lloyd Price was not averse to killing animals, either. On one July day in 1885 he and a party of friends, including a Wynne of the scholarly Peniarth Wynnes, two lords, an earl, a duke and a baronet, killed 5,106 rabbits and other animals—'as yet', he proudly reported, 'the largest known number of living creatures brought to bag between the hours of 10 and 5 of the clock upon a single day . . .'.

A different superlative of squiredom is remembered by an arch of roughly-hewn stone which spans the road from Pontarfynach to Cwmystwyth, in Dyfed. It stands in the middle of a conifer forest, miles it seems from anywhere, and while it ostensibly commemorates the accession to the English throne of King George II, it more famously marks the frontier of the estate of Mr Thomas Johnes; who having been born in England of old Dyfed stock, inherited in this harsh and astonishingly inaccessible place the mansion called Hafod Uchtryd ('Hafod' meaning simply 'summer dwelling', a memory of the days when the Welsh mountain pastoralists, like their colleagues in the Alps, moved from one house to another according to the season).

By the time Mr Johnes had done with it Hafod, as it became known, was one of the most spectacularly romantic houses in all Europe. This was the high point of the Picturesque, an enthusiasm with strong Welsh connections, and Johnes turned his home into one of its most celebrated examples. Over the bare mountains of his property he planted some four million trees, transforming the very nature of the countryside, and around the house he created a rustic paradise of grottoes, falling streams and hanging gardens, with a brand-new church on the hill above. As for the house itself, we can envisage it best through the painting that Turner did of it, during a visit in 1798: a shining, gleaming Welsh Xanadu, created partly by John Nash, with slender chimneys, tall ogee windows and an octagonal library of vaguely Chinese affinity.

Hafod was burnt down in 1807, but Johnes courageously built it all up again, and in this tremendous retreat the squire spent his years doting upon his only daughter Marianne, a beautiful cripple, translating old French chronicles, entertaining celebrities of every kind and attending to his private printing press; until like many a squire before him he sank into bankruptcy and despair, losing daughter, library, house, forest, mountains and all, and dying prosaically, in 1816, in Devonshire.

Long ago the squires lost their power over the people. Just as the Church of England was alienated from the mass of its Welsh parishioners, so in the course of time the landed gentry antagonized the mass of their tenantry. Occasionally sheer arrogance undid them —greedy enclosures of common land, cruel evictions on the Irish pattern, or even simple brutality of character: the terrible Herbert Lloyd of Peterwell in Dyfed was a kind of bogey-man to his people in the late eighteenth century, and is most vividly remembered even now by the famous story of his agent dropping a stolen sheep down a farmer's chimney, in order to incriminate and evict him. Sometimes their vulgar privilege was just too much to stomach: in the 1870s the 22-year-old George Assheton-Smith, whose English family had bought the slate-rich Vaynol estate in Gwynedd in the previous century, was a magistrate and a Deputy Lieutenant of the county, owned 33,000 acres with annual rentals of £42,000, and lived all alone with fourteen unmarried servants in his showy mansion beside the Menai Strait. Sometimes they had never really taken root: the Buckleys, who bought the manor of Dinas Mawddwy, Gwynedd, in 1856, just had time to build themselves an enormous house, have the Buckley Arms named for them, open a quarry and found the Buckley Otterhounds, when in 1876 Sir Edmund Buckley lost all his money, and they left the scene for ever.

Much more tellingly, though, it was their own fear of political reform and social revolution that disinherited the Welsh squires in the end. When ordinary people got the vote it badly scared them. They had thought themselves the unchallengeable Tory lords of the countryside: now, they found, their own tenants were all too liable to cast their votes for some damned Liberal. Disgraceful coercions were used to make the country people of Wales vote the way the squires preferred, and all of a sudden those genial families, so proud of their Welshness, were found to have a less benevolent side. Those endearing Prices of Rhiwlas, those ingenious Inglis-Joneses of Derry Ormond, those guardians of the Holy Grail at Nanteos—all threatened their tenants with instant eviction, if they dared to vote Liberal. As Lord Cawdor's Dyfed tenants were told by his agent in 1837, 'I shall depend upon you to plump for Colonel Trevor at the coming election, who is the only candidate supported by your noble landlord, and I have no doubt that you will do so.' Or as Mary Morrice told her people in Dyfed in 1860, 'my conscience forbids me to allow you to use the advantages which come to you as my tenants to support principles which are contrary to those of the lady who owns your land'. Thousands of people were overawed into compliance: hundreds were thrown out of their houses for daring to disobey.

More and more, too, the rival power of the chapels jarred upon the squires, and disturbed their equanimity. They mocked the Nonconformist ethos, and made fun of chapel worthies, but they were apprehensive too. When at Y Bala in 1838 the Price of the day flatly refused to serve on the local bench of magistrates because a Methodist grocer had been appointed to the bench, an official inquiry declared his attitude truly patriotic, 'the spirit of aristocracy in a country magistracy being the salt which alone preserves the whole mass from inevitable corruption'. So the *noblesse oblige* was lost, and the old relationships of the land went sour. 'The gentry', wrote Saunders Lewis, looking back at the scene from the 1920s, 'betrayed their birthright, behaved like rich bourgeois and denied . . . the civilization which they boasted they were cherishing.'

These attitudes rebounded. Already socially, linguistically, religiously and perhaps philosophically estranged from their landlords, in the late nineteenth century the Welsh people rejected them politically. In the General Election of 1868 twenty-one Liberals were elected to Parliament, as against twelve Conservatives; in 1885 only four Tories were returned in Wales, in 1892 only three. Radical Liberals were triumphant everywhere, and the order of the landlords was doomed. Some sold up their estates there and then, many more left after the First World War, and since then the revolution has been all but completed, and the Welsh gentry as a class is dead or gone.

A few of the landed families remain and flourish, of course. The Prices still live genially at Rhiwlas, the Philippses are still at Picton Castle, there are Mostyns about, and Williams-Wynnes. The Tractarian Raikes of Llangesty in Powys are still in their manor house beside the lake, and the family graves in the churchyard await new recruits to join the general, the admiral, the couple of colonels, the sergeant-pilot and the colonial medical officer, 'died of plague, Singapore 1929', already awaiting them there. The 7th Marquis of Anglesey sits in his study beside the Menai Strait writing the definitive history of the British cavalry. The Newboroughs still possess a private fort, offering joy-rides from the air-strip nearby and on ceremonial occasions even firing its cannon. Colonel Myerhouse's grandson still drives each day, from manor house to home farm, past the neo-Natalian estate houses of Angle.

But most of them have vanished. Some proud dynasties have, as the Irish say, returned to the bog, and become ordinary Welsh people like everyone else, but far more have left Wales for ever: even their last maidenly relatives, having lingered on in dower house or cottage, have retired to nursing homes far away, to be near their married nieces, or lie beneath English epitaphs in distant and more cosy churchyards. Erddig, having been presented to the National Trust by the last of the Yorkes, an actor, is one of Wales's most piquant tourist sights. Hafod Uchtryd was blown up as an unsafe ruin in 1958; its church had been burnt down in 1932, and almost all that is left of Johnes's lovely dream is a memorial to Marianne, by Francis Chantrey, which was rescued

from the fire and set up in the reconstructed church—a sadly calcin-
ated lump of marble, hardly recognizable as a memorial at all, which
stands eerily shrouded in an alcove of the nave. And all along the happy
valley of the Teifi, where the gentry once rode so blithely from hunt to
dinner-party, and the cries of 'Good shot!' or 'Jolly well played!' rang
with such *bonhomie* across the tennis-courts beside the castle, the
comfortable country houses have fallen into decay, forlornly
masquerade as hotels, or are restored with brown paint and plywood
partitions as schools and institutions.

Rural Wales has reverted to its own, and has become essentially a
country of smallholders. All over the country, with the decline of the
gentry, tenant farmers bought at last the land their families had often
farmed for centuries, crowds of neighbours cheering them on to
success at auction-rooms from Clwyd to Glamorgan. The process is
remembered in a generic way by a memorial in a field near Ambleston,
Treamlod in Dyfed, which represents in life-size marble detail two
such self-liberated tenants, John and Martha Llewellin. Staunch, stern
and buttoned they stand there, as though for chapel, and on their plinth
it says that by the blessing of God, and by their joint undertaking and
thrift, they bought their farm and handed it down without encum-
brance to their heirs. 'Endeavour to pull together as they did. Union is
Strength.'

It was also fulfilment, for this possession of the land seemed to many
Welsh people a kind of national redemption. The poet William
Roberts, writing at the end of the century, expressed the depth and
poignant satisfaction of it all:

> *Rhy ddrud, ddywedsoch, am bedwar cant*
> *Tyddyn fy ngeni a chartref fy mhlant.*
> *Nid prynu yr oeddwn 'r hen fur a'i do*
> *Na'r tipyn daear o'i amgylch o.*
> *Rhy ddrud, ddywedsoch, am bedwar cant*
> *Tyddyn fy ngeni a chartref fy mhlant.*

> Too dear, you said, at four hundred pounds,
> The farm of my birth and the home of my children.
> I wasn't buying the old wall and the roof,
> Nor the bit of land around it.
> Too dear, you said, at four hundred pounds,
> The farm of my birth and the home of my children!

*

The valley called Cwm Cywarch is hidden away in the Arennig mountains of Gwynedd. It is narrow and very secluded, twisting between high hills on its three-mile course to the wider valley of the Dyfi below, and at its head, where the Cywarch river springs from the mountain cirque, there lies a wide flat glacial bowl, rather like a yak-pasture in some greater range. Black cattle graze the meadows, twisted sessile oaks give intricacy to the scene, and in this quintessentially Welsh backwater you may sense the kind of order the nineteenth-century Welsh established for themselves, when they were free of landlordism. The farms of the valley are scattered, blobs of grey stone and jumbled outbuildings on both slopes, with steep tracks leading up to them from the road below, but their inhabitants formed a strong, well-organized little society of their own, self-contained within the womb-like shelter of the valley. They helped one another with sheep-shearing, walling and fencing, they met in each other's homes for the occasional *noson lawen*, the 'merry evening' of song and poetry which is perennially popular among the Welsh, they competed against each other in local *eisteddfodau*, they worshipped together in one or other of the two chapels, Tarsus (now full of hay) or Bethlehem (still active in the cause). The few score people of the *cwm* worked, played and worshipped communally, or rather *locally*: not always indeed in unity, because family antipathies sometimes split them, and the chapels were inevitably in contest, but to a universally accepted code of tastes and values. Everybody spoke the same language, literally and figuratively too.

In the Welshest of Welsh communities it is still so, the spectre of class hardly arising. The essence of traditional Welshness is the belief that social worth and cultural achievement need not be related to worldly success, and the Welsh words for upper, middle and lower class are all translations from the English. Social categories, though often tartly summoned, are lateral, not layered—*pobl y capel, pobl y dafarn, bois y pop*—chapel people, that is, pub people, or pop boys. Poets greatly honoured work as garage mechanics or small farmers: lawyer and plumber meet on equal terms, the one supplying his expertise to the other. Since the nineteenth century the leaders of this people have nearly all been of simple origin, and among the true glories of Wales are the modest houses from which the great men of the nation have sprung: the thatched cottage of Bishop Morgan, below the forests of Penmach-no—the remains of the lonely hut, in the Pumlimon foothills, in which

Sir John Rhys the great Celtic scholar was born—the little house next to the cobbler's shop, in a terrace at Llanystumdwy, Gwynedd, where Lloyd George began his climb to the political summit of the world.

This particular manifestation of the Welsh order reached its apogee at the end of the Victorian century, and at its root lay a passion for education. In the first years of that century Wales had virtually no schools to call its own—a few very English grammar schools, a few private academies for Nonconformists—and the one Welsh university college was Jesus College, Oxford, which was open only to members of the Anglican Church. In the previous century the Anglican clergyman Griffith Jones, of Llanddowror in Dyfed, had succeeded in bringing literacy to many thousands of Welsh people with his Locomotive Schools, travelling academies which taught religious subjects in the Welsh language. When the flush of his campaign died away, though, and the Locomotive Schools petered out through lack of funds, the Welsh were left once more with a miserable rag-bag of educational establishments, some started by religious bodies, some simple dame schools, some set up by retired or disabled seamen, dispossesed farmers or miscellaneous drop-outs. Standards were often terrible. According to a well-loved Swansea anecdote of the 1820s Mrs Silvanus Padley, committee member of a charity school there, was told by one of the teachers: 'I teaches them their needlework and spinning all right, Mrs P., but their three Rs, well, I simply grounds them in it.' 'I know you does, Mrs J.', sympathetically replied the philanthropist.

When the Welsh were literate, they were generally literate only in Welsh, and to many people this now seemed a contradiction in terms. It ignored the truths of history. It cut off the people from the world at large. It kept the Welsh incorrigibly and perhaps dangerously Welsh. The antiquary Thomas Stephens of Merthyr in Glamorgan, Welsh-speaking himself and one of the cleverest Welshmen of his day, believed that Welsh should be reserved for the chapels and for poetry, leaving practical affairs to be conducted in English. Why, cried a successfully Anglicized Welshman, William Williams, MP, if the Welsh had the same educational advantages as the Scots, who did all their schooling in English, 'they would, instead of appearing as a distinct people, in no respect differ from the English!' (Besides, as Williams ominously and revealingly added, 'a band of official schoolmasters is kept up at much less expense than a body of police or soldiery . . .'.)

In 1846, at William Williams's instigation, a Royal Commission was established to inquire into the facts. Its members were three very sharp young English barristers, all Anglicans, none of them Welsh-speaking, and their conclusions were predictable. After a close investigation of the state of Welsh education (and so, by implication, of Welsh society), they decided that its lamentable condition was due chiefly to the perverse addiction of the Welsh to their own language. Here are some extracts from their reports on individual schools:

Trelustan, Powys. 'Upon my asking for some account of the "disciples", mentioned in the lesson (Matt. xviii 1) a girl replied that they were "little children"; another said they were "the bloody Jews".'

Craig-y-Don, Llandegfan, Gwynedd. 'One of them said, that Eve was the mother of Jesus Christ.'

Trefriew, Gwynedd. 'Some of the first class said that Moses was the husband of the Virgin Mary.'

Jameston, Dyfed. 'Did not know who Jesus Christ was. Had never heard of Virgin Mary. Had never heard of Our Saviour's coming on earth. Master, a farm labourer, aged 72, stated: "It is something like remarkable that you reads and hears sermons, and don't recollect nothing that you sees and hears."'

Caernarfon, Gwynedd. 'It is remarkable that they could define all the islands in the Indian Archipelago . . . whereas the national scholars in the first class were unable to name the English counties.'

Kerry, Powys. 'Geography is professed, but only one out of the three best scholars was able to find England on the map.'

One guesses that the Commissioners and their agents were sometimes being teased, especially as they generally had to question the children through interpreters. They concluded nevertheless that the Welsh language not only kept the Welsh people in a state of intellectual backwardness, but worse still, encouraged them in the most depraved and promiscuous habits—bundling, fornication, and all manner of other sexual misdemeanour. It was not easy indeed, the Commissioners reported, to overestimate the evil effects of the Welsh language. 'It dissevers the people from intercourse which would greatly advance their civilization, and bars the access of improving knowledge in their minds.' As a proof of this, reported those three English gentlemen blandly, 'there is no Welsh literature worthy of the name'.

The report was received without much surprise in England, and the London Press had no doubt about its meaning. The Welsh, declared the *Morning Chronicle*, were fast settling down into the most savage barbarism. They had the habits of animals, said *The Examiner*. On the strength of the Commission's report the whole Welsh nation was branded in English minds as irredeemably backward and depraved, and its effects are not entirely expunged even today—when you hear a snide Welsh Joke in an English pub, or a sneer about Welsh windbaggery from a political commentator, you are probably hearing late cheap echoes of the Royal Commission on the State of Education in Wales, 1846.

As for the Establishment in London, it heeded the advice. 'It must always be the desire of a government to render its dominions, as far as possible, homogeneous', observed Matthew Arnold, Inspector of Schools, in 1852. 'Sooner or later the difference of language between Wales and England will probably be effaced ... an event which is socially and politically desirable.' 'The Welsh language', said *The Times* more succinctly in 1865, 'is the curse of Wales.' In 1880, when a State education system was established in Wales, the Welsh language was outlawed from its schools. In some class-rooms childred were fined $\frac{1}{2}d$. every time they talked Welsh, the proceeds to go to those who never did. In others a placard was hung around the neck of any child caught speaking the language, bearing the words 'Welsh Not': it was passed on from culprit to culprit, and the pupil wearing it at the end of the day was thrashed for his presumption.

The Welsh responded to the report very differently. Many indeed were convinced by it that the Welsh language really was the badge only of impotence and ignorance, and that Englishness was essential for success in nineteenth-century Britain: a host of Anglicized private schools sprang up, to which ambitious Welsh parents sent their children not only to perfect their English language, but also to master useful English skills, like water-colour painting, deportment, or what one Gwynedd prospectus called 'proper bearing towards servants'. But a more sophisticated minority, more sure of their own moral codes and intellectual vigour, were so maddened by the report that their reactions were to transform once again the order of things in Wales.

These infuriated patriots, who thought the report biased in its approach, unfair in its methods and insulting in its conclusions, called the whole affair *Brad y Llyfrau Gleision*, the Treachery of the Blue

Books, a name that has stuck. They pointed out that in a country overwhelmingly Nonconformist, three times as many Anglicans as chapel people had given evidence to the commission; and anyway, sending three English barristers to inspect the state of Welsh education was like inviting three Welshmen, without a word of English between them, to investigate the schools of Norfolk. The attack on Welsh culture was crass and ignorant. The attack on Welsh morals was an insult. From the *Llyfrau Gleision* a great swell of patriotism flowed, and in years to come Welshmen were proud to boast how often the Welsh Not had been hung around their necks—even more often, perhaps, in the memory than in the fact. 'Every day', gloriously reminisced the scholar O. M. Edwards half a century later, 'every day the Not . . . would find its way from every corner of the school to my neck. This is a comfort to me even today.'

Language (Welsh) and religion (chapel) were allied in this surge of righteous outrage, and in time it gave paradoxical birth, in the later decades of the nineteenth century, to a moment of triumphant national assertion—a public apotheosis, as it were, in its devotion to tongue and tradition, of the society that flourished with such private intensity in places like Cwm Cywarch. It was a cultural revolution! The country, still 80 per cent Welsh-speaking, was flooded with Welsh books. An endless sequence of tracts, memoirs, novels, collections of verse, essays, dictionaries and even travel books poured from the presses of Wales. There were dictionaries of Welsh biography, there were multi-volumed histories, there was a massive encyclopedia, *Y Gwyddoniadur Cymreig*, whose twelve volumes were so eagerly bought that they had to be reprinted almost at once. Scores of Welsh-language magazines appeared, and a ferment seized the people as they grasped at any kind of education—the miners' libraries of South Wales, by the end of the century, had 750,000 books on their shelves. At Sunday schools, at chapel meetings, at pit-head breaks, people earnestly discussed the newest economic theories, Darwinian evolution or *Y Pum Pwnc*, the Five Canonical Subjects of Calvinist doctrines. Earnestness indeed was the keynote of it all. 'I never had such a job keeping myself from laughing', a Gwynedd quarryman told Sir Ifor Williams, an eminent educationalist, after a lecture in which the sage was disappointed to find all his jokes falling flat.

*

Sir Ifor was an archetypal hero of this new order. Most of its heroes were men of learning. They blur in the memory now, if only because so many of them liked to be called by their initials, S.R., O.M., a practice which carried among the Welsh in those days impressive overtones of cultural distinction and academic authority. But anyway they were only the commanders of an army rich in strong and individual characters —as strong at least, and often just as original, as the Prices or Johneses of the previous dispensation. They were ubiquitous, north and south —Thomas Jones, writing about the mining town of Rhymni, Rhymney in Glamorgan, in the 1880s, recorded that in one small stretch of High Street there lived two poets, two clergymen, a cobbler who learnt a new chapter of the Bible every week and a whole family of musicians—but we will choose one late exemplar, Bob Owen of Croesor in Gwynedd, to show how liberating, how elevating, was this climax of the Welsh native order.

We will visit him first at his daily work, as a clerk in the office of the quarry company in his home village, high in the hills above Llanfrothen. He is, in late middle age, a small shy man with a high wrinkled brow, a white moustache and bushy eyebrows, respectably dressed as befits his calling in jacket, waistcoat and unassertive tie. He is very well known up there in Croesor. He was born just down the hill, in a little house called Weasel's Hole—they used to call him Bob Owen Twll Wenci—and he has worked for the company for thirty years. Also he is one of the prominent characters of the place: a tremendous talker, a merry practical joker, a chain-smoker of Woodbines, a chapel man of strong views, besides being a whizz at mental arithmetic, and so indispensable on pay days. Everyone knows Bob Owen. The quarry could hardly work without him.

When at the end of the day, though, Mr Owen returns to his square grey house in the hamlet below, where his wife has supper ready for him, his manner of life abruptly changes: for the moment he opens the front door he is hemmed in, towered over, squashed in, squeezed down by a multitude of books. He is said to have collected some 47,000 in his day, many of them valuable manuscripts and rare editions in Welsh and in English, and he never stopped buying them till the day he died.

Nor was he a mere collector. He was a scholar of infinite diligence, historian of the Welsh overseas, antiquarian, archaeologist, bibliographer, genealogist. He was friends with most of the great Welsh academics of the day, all the Sir Ifors, all the O.M.s, was consulted frequently by libraries and universities, lectured all over the place, broadcast often, and corresponded with researchers in many parts of the world. In his old age the University of Wales gave him an honorary degree, and he in return left his collections to various libraries of the University of Wales. He was a celebrity of his day. From Môn to Morgannwg people knew the name of Bob Owen Croesor.

He was unmistakably a child of the Welsh patriotic resurgence, with all its qualities and all its weaknesses too. He never gave up his job in the office, until the quarry closed in the 1930s, and remained always a man of the chapel, the evening institute and in later years the county council. He travelled around by bus, when he could not get a lift, and his closest friends were men like himself, self-educated and rooted in the *bro*. He was dazzled by education in its simplest kinds—the amassing of facts, the accumulation of books—and he was not without conceit, or free from hero-worship.

In a way he was the last champion of that Welsh renaissance, for he long outlived it, its triumphant liberalism and its unchallengeable Nonconformism. Before he died in 1962, to the consternation of some of his admirers he accepted from the hand of Queen Elizabeth, the Queen Mother of England, the insignia of a member of the Order of the British Empire. 'I think, Mr Owen,' said Her Majesty, 'you take an interest in history and literature.' The old quarryman, out of his natural element, was rendered incoherent at last. 'Yes, My Mother', replied Bob Owen Croesor.

The grandest effect of this flush of Welshness was the establishment, in 1872, of the first Welsh University College, the first national institution really, on the promenade at Aberystwyth. Much of the money for this came from the small contributions of at least 100,000 ordinary people, mostly Nonconformists—the chapels started a special festival, *Sul y Brifysgol*, University Sunday, whose collections all went to the fund. It was collected in shillings and sixpences, at prayer meetings, at miners' clubs, at local *eisteddfodau* all over the country; and supplemented by money from Welsh people abroad, and large gifts from one or two great Welsh industrialists, in the end it brought forth the College by the Sea.

Although in later years the University of Wales was to prove less than zealous in its devotion to the Welsh order of things, still to this day for many Welsh people the heart of the culture remains this original building on the sea-front. Its functions have mostly been usurped by more modern buildings now, but it is the symbolic core of Welsh academe. Built originally as a very grand hotel, its richly effusive Gothic, all multi-coloured spires and pinnacles, makes it seem an ironic monument indeed to a movement that depended so largely upon the sober ethos of chapel and self-improvement: but never mind, old Aberystwyth students have a special affection for it all the same, and whenever they walk along a seaside promenade, anywhere in the world, they still kick the railing at the end of the corniche, as they were accustomed to on their student walks from the College by the Sea, discussing the social implications of Unitarianism perhaps, or the poems of Goronwy Owen, through the winds off the wide Welsh bay.

Other institutions followed, in those great days of self-assertion—a National Museum, a National Library: but perhaps a truer memorial to the times is a more modest building altogether, the Memorial Institute at Glynceiriog in Clwyd. Glynceiriog had always been a nest of poets, and in 1910 it was decided to build a village hall and institute permanently to commemorate three of them—John Ceiriog Hughes, a nineteenth-century railwayman, Huw Morus, a seventeenth-century farmer's son, Robert Ellis, a nineteenth-century Baptist minister. The hall was to be a centre of cultural activity for the whole district, and it was built with proud care and craftsmanship.

It stands there still, and remains in an almost fossilized way a very repository of Welsh chapel and liberal values. It has a library for the reading of poetical works or evangelical tracts, and a room for the composition of lyrics or the glossing of genealogical documents, and it is full of literary and religious mementoes of the *bro*, and its walls are pierced by a series of fine stained glass windows honouring poets and holy people of Wales, hymnists, bards, translators of the Bible and well-known local worthies—the whole maintained with loving diligence, and smelling fragrantly of stained wood, and books, and floor polish, and some essence of confident piety no longer so readily available.

For in its turn the order of the schools, the chapels, the miners' libraries, Sir Ifor Williams, Bob Owen and the College by the Sea has long faded now. The Glynceiriog Institute is not so well frequented as it used to be, and you must look hard to find a Cwm Cywarch still living in the old way. By the 1930s Liberal idealism had been displaced by earthier Labour, only 30 per cent of the people spoke Welsh, evangelical Christianity was giving ground to secular materialism, the lust for education to the lust for entertainment—'cinema and billiards going strong', reported Thomas Jones of Rhymni in 1934, 'education going weak'. Half a century later the reaction had gone further still: by 1983 only 20 per cent of Welsh people spoke Welsh, the miners' libraries had been dispersed, and of the 38 Welsh MPs 14 were Tories, 8 of them educated at English public schools. That moment of public promise had passed, and the Welsh order of things was private and particular once more.

But then it has always been an inconstant order, evasive, coming and going. Sometimes when you look out of a Welsh window all seems lost—or if not lost at least permanently suspended in a hangdog limbo. The drizzle seems never likely to stop, the mountains look permanently concealed in mist, the sea is grey and queasy, the town damp and dingy—you can bet your life it's early closing day. The sheep in the field out there are huddled miserably against the wind. The river roars sullenly beyond the wood. Nothing, one feels, is ever going to change, or even perhaps to happen.

But then suddenly out of the west a fine bright breeze comes marching in, and everything is different. High, wide and blue stands the Welsh sky now, and the hills are sharp-edged against it, and the sheep nibble vigorously, and Mott the dog chases his tail from sheer high spirits, and a little blue train comes chugging down the line from Pwllheli, and prosperity seems to radiate from the windows of the Stryd Fawr shops. Is there anywhere on earth to beat Wales? you ask yourself then. Could anywhere be lovelier, fabled shore or wine-dark sea —could anywhere be more certain of success, than Wales on such a morning?

These are the poles of the Welsh condition, which swings perpetually from elation to despair. As the Spaniards move between *sol* and *sombre*, sun and shade, the Welsh fluctuate between *hwyl* and *hiraeth*, between crests of exuberance and troughs of desolation. It is these extremes of spirit, these emotional tugs and distractions, that foster the Welsh Way of Life, a kind of substitute for a social order. This is a popular conception among Welsh people themselves, who often like to talk of it, but generally raises a laugh among Englishmen, who believe the Welsh Way to be, by this time, virtually the same as their own. After all, they say, is not Wales an integral part of the United Kingdom of Great Britain and Northern Ireland, sharing not only its Government, but also its language, its economy, its public affairs and its soap-flake special offers?

They are wrong, though. Except in the most Anglicized urban enclaves, where one discovers, all too frequently, a tiresome pastiche of English manners and aspirations, in fundamentals everything is different in Wales even now. The history is different, the talk is different even in English, and so is the manner of life, which is more volatile, moody and intense—*hwyl* and *hiraeth* made human, so to speak. For all its faults it truly is a people's way, as truly egalitarian as you can find anywhere in the Western world, and now as in the days of Hywel Dda it is inspired by a powerful sense of personal worth. Just as most of the farmland of Wales is owned today by small farmers, so the vast majority of the industrial terrace houses are owned by the families who live in them, and very few Welshmen, even the most down-and-out, can easily be patronized—they are too touchy, or too proud, and often too humorous.

It is a kind way at heart, quick to sympathy for all its defensiveness —Wales is a good place to be, all in all, if you are destitute and despairing: and though the Welsh are apt to denigrate themselves, declaring themselves incapable of self-government, or too venal to be trusted, still most of them, whatever their political views, however shallow, profound or confused their sense of Welshness, are immensely proud of being Welsh. Those old loyalties, so local, so specialized, do extend in a more haphazard way into wider fellowships. Just as the Evanses stick together through thick and thin in their battles against Authority, or the supporters of Tonypridd Rugby club stand by their players through their most dismal ineptitudes of the scrum, so when they face the world at large Welshmen of all kinds stick together to support the Welsh Way.

Mind you, they often support it most fervently when they are far away from it—*Cymro gorau*, goes the saying, *Cymro o'r cartref,* 'the best Welshman's the one away from home'. When in the 1980s Max Boyce gave a concert in Sydney, New South Wales, he was disconcerted to discover that after his performance more than a thousand members of his audience showed no sign of leaving the hall. Instead they started singing Welsh songs themselves, moved by the message he had brought, and the fun he had transmitted, from the valleys so far away; and so they lingered there, singing and laughing and reunited in their deepest instincts, until the lights of the hall were dimmed at last, and they went out into the streets Australians once again.

7. Earning a Living

Seated upon his throne at Harlech, holding the sceptre of his sovereignty, Owain Glyndŵr contemplated a Wales that could be rich. Vast forests of timber covered its foothills then, oaks for the beams of houses and the keels of ships, beeches for the charcoal pits, yews for the weapons. The country teemed with game, the seas with fish, and up the sparkling rivers numberless salmon and sea-trout leapt to their mountain spawning-grounds. There was gold to be dug, lead, copper, coal and iron in profusion; huge herds of sheep grazed the sheep-walks of the monasteries, fat cattle were at pasture in the rich river lowlands. In the 8,000 square miles of Wales there was plenty for all. Yet in this as in so much else, when we survey the condition of Wales at the prince's elbow, we see only disappointment in the end. All those riches were never to be exploited for the good of Wales; the fat profits of the land have mostly gone elsewhere; and the Welsh people struggle still to earn an uncertain living from their all too often illusory Paradise.

YOU can see almost at a glance, from a map or a satellite picture, how the Welsh have generally earned their livings. Running down the spine of Wales are the brown splodges of mountain and moorland, interspersed with bog—the hard wet country of the shepherd and the forester. All around them, through the passes, up the valleys, along the coast, broadening now and then into green pastures, lie the lands of the dairymen, the potato growers, the arable farmers of Môn and Dyfed, which include some of the most fertile country in the British Isles. Little ports stand like specks around the coast, and finally in great black patches and streaks, in the far north-east, in the hilly south, you may see the deposits of heavy industry, the coal-mines and steelworks and smelters, together with the big cities and seaports that support them. The pattern has shifted over the centuries—those black patches would hardly have shown 200 years ago—but the fundamentals have remained the same, and the Welsh have always survived partly by grazing and tilling the land, and partly by carving it up or burrowing into it. The rubble-walled fields of Stone Age farmers still survive in places—wobbly squares and asymmetrical enclosures—and in the National Museum at Cardiff they preserve some of the axe-heads cut out from the quarries of Penmaenmawr in Gwynedd two or three thousand years ago. The Welshman's living has generally been elemental. He does not so much make things: he grows things, or gets them, or takes them somewhere, and sells them when he can.

In the eighteenth century an English Board of Agriculture official reported that the Welsh plough was 'perhaps the most awkward, unmeaning tool to be found in any civilized country'. Late in the nineteenth century Welsh farmers were still dragging hay about on ox-drawn sledges, and consulting conjurors when their beasts fell sick. By nature the Welsh have always been stockmen rather than ploughmen, and one gets the feeling sometimes that subsistence has always been prosperity enough for them, that they do not wish to develop nature, or change their techniques with the changing times, but are happy enough to ride the seasons as their fathers did, complying where necessary with the regulations of the Milk Marketing Board, inoculating where required, pasteurizing if they really must, but generally leaving things as much as possible as they always have been, including that drooping fence of old wire and baler string down by there at the bottom of the pitch.

This is misleading. Welsh farmers are more astute than they allow, and often richer than their husbandry suggests—or used to suggest, until a sudden re-fencing of half Wales with posts and webbed wire followed the announcement of a Government fencing subsidy. Look at the names of the great London department stores—Dickens and Jones, D. H. Evans, Peter Jones, John Lewis—and you will see how often canny Welsh dairy farmers, having made themselves rich selling Dyfed milk to Londoners, successfully broadened their investments.

The cattle-drovers of Wales, in fact, were the first Welsh entrepreneurs. For several centuries the livestock of this country travelled to the markets of England on its own feet, shod according to its kind—quarter-circle shoes for the hoofs of cattle, woollen socks with leather soles for pigs' trotters, pads of sand or crushed oyster-shells for the waddling webs of geese. The cattle mostly went to London, East Anglia, the east Midlands, or to Kent to be fattened up, the pigs often to Wiltshire to be turned into bacon and pork pies, and the great herds of creatures passing out of Wales, anything up to 400 head at a time, with their yapping Corgi dogs and the drovers wide-hatted on their ponies, were part of this country's everyday life. They were Wales's *llongau Sbaen*, said Archbishop John Williams in the seventeenth century, its ships of Spain, its treasure-fleets.

Drovers had to be officially licensed to pursue, as the sixteenth-century form had it, 'their mystery and sciens', and they often became important men in Wales, men of trust and standing, who acted as brokers and agents, carried confidential messages, and brought back from England all the latest intelligence, from news of foreign wars to samples of the latest dress fashions. They were entrusted with large sums of money, and sometimes with gold from the Welsh mines, for investment or the settling of accounts, and some of them went on to found the original Welsh banks: Banc yr Eidion Du, for instance, the Bank of the Black Bullock whose sign still swings outside the National Westminster Bank at Llanymddyfri, or Banc y Ddafad Ddu at Aberystwyth, the Black Sheep Bank, whose £2 note was engraved with two sheep, whose £1 note showed one, but whose ten shilling note portrayed only a little lamb.

Often the drovers were poets and scholars too: a famous phrase by Dafydd Jones, an eighteenth-century hymn-writer, likened the arrival of souls in heaven to the converging of his own cattle herds upon the Dyfed hamlet of Caeo. Some became country gentlemen, and built themselves grand houses in the English styles they had admired on their journeyings—the dormer windows and free-standing gatehouses you see in parts of Gwynedd are thought to have been copied from the Cotswolds. Others remained rough, ready and rowdy to the end, and were held up by disapproving parsons as models of how not to be.

All over Wales there are still Drovers' Inns and Black Ox pubs, and place names like Smithfield Lane, Little London or Maes-y-Gofaint, Blacksmiths' Field, which recall the old connection. *Hupla, Hupla!* the cry used to sound across the hills, as the herds made their slow way eastward, twenty miles a day if all was well, and when the mood of the morning is right it is as easy to think you hear it still, with the shuffling and lowing of the cattle, the clatter of the ponies, the barking of the dogs, the cackle of the weary geese along the upland tracks. The drovers avoided lowland roads, to save paying tolls, and in many places their routes are clearly recognizable. Here the uncommonly wide verges of a country road show where the herds used to loiter; there a turfy lane in the foothills, or a vivid patch of unexplained green on an otherwise brackeny hillside, remembers a drovers' resting-place; in the village of Cilycwm, in Dyfed, there survive the wide cobbled gutters, each side of the village street, at which the herds were watered as they passed. It is like a huge scattered scar across the land, the communal trail of a million living creatures, moving in migration west to east over the centuries: and when you see three lone Scots pines in the Welsh landscape, generally where the bare hill country reaches down to the cultivated valleys, there you are likely to find some old farm or tavern where the drovers used to spend their nights—blowing their horns to announce their coming, corralling their beasts in the Halfpenny Field behind, and settling down themselves to ale and roistering.

When they got to London, or Canterbury, or Calne, the drovers, having sold their beasts, often spent a week or two in England transacting private business of their own, or signing up new customers. Their dogs frequently went home ahead of them, and given affectionate slaps upon the rump, trotted back along the well-known route, befriended sometimes by colleagues on the way, clean across England into Wales, to the grey smoke-fragrant farmhouses of Ty Coch or Tan-y-Bryn in the mountains far away. The women then, hearing the scratching of paws upon the kitchen door, would know that their husbands were not far behind.

Your modern Welsh farmer frequently numbers drovers on his family tree, and has often inherited the drover's money-touch as well. Though he likes to speak of difficult times, and sticks to second-hand cars generally, he takes quick advantage of the small print in leaflets about Common Market benefits, and seems to have no trouble arranging overdrafts. Much the most efficient organization in Wales is the great mechanism by which all the millions of gallons of Welsh milk, from all the thousands of small Welsh dairy farms, are collected in tankers and sent away in bulk to their markets, as swiftly and expertly as the fish-men of Spain send their mullet and lobsters down the midnight highways to Madrid. In the days when milk was still moved about in churns the biggest churn-handling plant in Europe was at Whitland in Dyfed: now that it travels in refrigerated tanker-trucks, all over Wales in the early morning you will hear the hum of the electric coolers, keeping the milk fresh and sterile for collection.

And anyone deceived by the easy dishevelment of the Welsh smallholding would do well to visit the Royal Welsh Agricultural Show, which is held each year outside Builth Wells, in the geographical centre of Wales: for there, besides the parades of cattle and horses, the goat competitions, the rabbit classes, the speckled hens and the Singing Friar with his guitar, there are wonders of more contemporary sorts: six-wheel buggies for mountain farming, radio transmitters for vets or shepherds, amphibious pick-ups, and pamphlets about the very latest antidotes, Government-tested beyond the concept of the old conjurors, for foot-rot or sheep-fluke.

In some ways nevertheless the Welsh farmer remains profoundly traditionalist, and especially depends as he always did upon ancient local networks of co-operation. At harvest time, when people are rushing to get their hay in before the weather breaks, the young bloods of the agricultural community roar from farm to farm in their Ford Capris (black, very likely, with rally-type headlights), billowing plumes of dust behind them as they race down the lanes between the little oaks, and blaring snatches of rock music through their open windows. And at shearing time in summer on the mountain farms you may still occasionally see one of the great gatherings of sheep-farming families which have, for hundreds of years, assembled one day here, next day somewhere else, to clip the sheep's wool, and dye them with initials or a farm mark.

Nowadays the shearers themselves are sometimes peripatetic Australians or New Zealanders, travelling with their electric shears and generators around the hill farms through the season. In all other ways, though, the occasion is much as it always was, and offers haunting vignettes of the old Welsh Wales. Best not to go too close, but to stay at a distance with a pair of binoculars, and then the scene can seem an encapsulation of time itself—trapped in your lens, in the still of the mountain morning! The shearing-pens are usually on some flat ledge on the lower slopes of the hills, and long before you can see them you can hear the bleats of the sheep echoing in plaintive chorus over the ridge. Find a rock on a crest then, and settle down to watch.

Through the naked eye it might be a camp of gypsies there, or a prayer meeting of the old revivalists. But through your glasses one by one you can pick out the images of the occasion. Here the shearer is bent intensely at his work, zip, zip, turning the writhing animal on its back, zip again—fling it away, and off it bounds, wriggling and shivering, out of your focus into the pen. Shift your eye a little, and there are the farmers, cloth caps tipped to the backs of their heads, stumpy cigarettes perhaps in the corners of their mouths, laughing and talking and sometimes seeming to look you straight in the binocular, merry-eyed and stubble-chinned, as they mark each sheep with paint out of a bucket on long sticks. Along the ridge, past the big rock, you will find a composition of women, easily grouped within the circle of your vision: laughing, smiling, rosy faces, rolled-up sleeves, big pots of tea, or soup, or stew, on the ground before them, and children messing all around, lying flat on their backs with grass-stalks in their mouths, or reading comics on their bellies. And all around the flanks of them, as you turn your binoculars, the inescapable dogs are there, tongues lolling, eyes darting, crouched on their paws or slinking around like wolves.

It is like an altogether separate, private world up there. When you put your glasses away, and steal away over the ridge, the bleats of the animals linger on the air, and sometimes shrieks of laughter, with a rise or fall of Welsh cadences, follow you down the hill. Otherwise it might all have been some summer dream.

Click-clack-click-clack, down by the bridge at Llangollen, above the rushing of the weir and the rumble of the traffic you can hear the working of a loom—one of humanity's primary noises, with nothing metallic or electronic to it, only a shuttling and knocking of wood, and a whirring of wheels somewhere. It feels perfectly natural in the handsome little town, and goes well with the bustle of the old stone bridge, and the foam of the weir, and the smoky stoniness and busyness of everything.

Perhaps a dozen woollen mills are still clack-clacking in Wales today, but once the sound was ubiquitous, and in countless isolated mills of the river valleys, in a myriad upstairs workrooms of Newtown or Llanidloes, Welsh wool from Welsh sheep was being turned into Welsh textiles. They were not generally very high-class textiles, and they were nearly all marketed by English middle-men in Shrewsbury, but still the wool business was for several hundred years an organic adjunct to Welsh agriculture: in the little country town of Tregaron, in 1851, there were 176 hosiers, 63 tailors, 15 woollen manufacturers, 15 cloth dealers, 17 hatters, 36 seamstresses, 6 shawlmakers and 3 woollen mills, supporting a population of less than a thousand.

The very word flannel, it is said, comes from the Welsh *gwlanen*, and there used to be many people in the world who had heard of Wales only because of its wool. In Spain caballeros wore shirts of it. In the Caribbean slaves wore trousers of it. In India soldiers wore red coats of it. The woollen Monmouth Cap, Thomas Fuller tells us, was 'the most ancient, general, warm and profitable covering of men's heads in this island' and an edict of Elizabeth I of England (13th Eliz. c. 19) actually made its wear compulsory on Sabbaths and holy days, 'on pain of forfeiting ten groats'. Especially in the country around Y Bala, in Gwynedd, the knitting of woollen stockings was a universal occupation, among men as among women: people knitted all the time, indoors and out, while they walked, while they gossiped, to the accompaniment of harp, fiddle or poetry at the *noson lawen*, or at great alfresco knitting meetings in the sunshine. When squatters wanted to establish their right to land, in those parts, they sometimes staked out their plots with yarn and knitting needles.

Fishing was another branch of agriculture then. Every method of catching lake or river fish has been used somewhere or other in Wales, and nearly all are still used somewhere today. On the Teifi, Tywi and Taf, in west Wales, salmon fishermen still work from their leather coracles, using the same nets, talking the same jargon, as their medieval predecessors. On the Severn shore long rows of putcher-baskets are ranged diagonally into the mud, solitary fishermen wade through the shallows with huge lave nets, and the elver-traps at Chepstow usually catch about 60 tons of baby eels each spring (they are sold in the local shops in glutinous blocks, like nougat, but mostly go to Holland). At the Conwy estuary the Hughes, Jones, Roberts and Craven families are licensed to gather mussels, like their ancestors before them. On the Dee the Bithells are still catching salmon as they have since 1600. On the Taf, in Dyfed, the one single person authorized in Wales to get salmon with a wade net may sometimes be glimpsed up to his neck in the water with the pole of his primitive implement. Around the coasts at every river-mouth a few men have the hereditary right to fish with seine nets, and even the fish farms begun by the Cistercians (who sometimes used to put golden collars on their trout) have been revived as farms of rainbow trout, where heaving masses of fish, like water-vermin, thresh in their concrete tanks below the floodlights.

All these activities find their focus as always in the market towns of Wales, founded mostly by the Normans, which have maintained their characters and their purposes through every change of country life, ox-plough to artificial insemination. The service trades of agriculture were always concentrated in these towns, the saddlers, the joiners, the blacksmiths, the masons, the coopers, the nail-makers, the clog-men, the glaziers: they are mostly there still, plus the supermarkets, the TV rental shops, the garages, the dress shops, the travel agents for package tours to the Algarve and the Old Copper Kettle Tea Room for coffee and biscuits on market day.

A good specimen is Abergavenny, in Gwent, which stands between the industrial valleys of South Wales and the pastoral country of the interior. It is not a very beautiful town, though its setting among the hills is almost artificially picturesque, and on five days in the week is not very interesting, either. On Tuesdays and Fridays, however, it comes boisterously to life, as farmers from fifty miles around, shoppers from coal valley as from countryside, peripatetic salesmen from the English Midlands and livestock traders from half Wales stream into the place, jamming its car parks, filling its covered markets with stalls, and mustering in its every pen and paddock thousands of cattle, sheep, pigs and ponies. The streets are commanded then by stocky Gwent and Powys farmers, with cloth caps, knobbly sticks and big boots, and crowded with vivacious shabby shoppers from Ebbw Vale or Blaenafon, loaded with carrier bags, smoking cigarettes, and sometimes exchanging Rabelaisian quips across the stalls. Moos, grunts, neighs and barks sound from the livestock market, and a fine old smell of dung and animals mingles down there with the fish and chips.

Twelve pounds of gleaming Usk salmon lies in the window of Vin Sullivan's, the posh food store, along with laver bread from the coast, potatoes from Dyfed, Brazilian papaws and East African chillis; people peer over one another's shoulders at the property announcements in J. Straker Chadwick's—Magnificent Livestock Farm, 1,000 Yards Both Bank Fishing, Lovely Position But In Need of Improvement, Well-Restored Georgian Country House; Giant Prawns are selling well at the Great George (which shows George Bernard Shaw on one side of its inn sign, and George Washington on the other); the saddler's in Cross Street is busy with breezy women buying snaffles; farmers in pairs inspect the second-hand Volkswagens in the yard at Whittall Williams'. It is like a boom town, all astir, all talking, all cash.

But when the livestock sales are over, towards the middle of the afternoon, when Mrs Jones and Mrs Morris Fforest Coalpit have finished their weekly luncheon treat in the Country Kitchen dining-room of the Angel, when the Land-Rovers and horse-boxes have manœuvred themselves out of the car parks and the very last of the Pakistani salesmen are packing into their vans their unsold tea-sets, T-shirts and gadgets to prevent the milk boiling over, then a wistfulness descends upon the town, with the litter blowing through its streets and those market-day smells surviving, and all the life of Wales seems to have ebbed away again into the country all about.

In seaside towns and villages live the sea captains—or more often die, alas, for they are a passing breed. Solid respectable houses they have generally retired to, with sea-views if possible of course, dignified without being showy, with jugs and figurines on their window-sills, shells and Chinese fans and ivory elephants in glass-fronted cabinets, and paintings of sailing-ships just to be glimpsed through bay windows above living-room mantelpieces. You meet their owners sometimes on promenade benches, fine old gentlemen with trilby hats, carrying walking-sticks. You see their names on lifeboat committee lists, Captain Robert Evans, Glan-y-Môr, Captain Humphry R. Williams, Marine Parade. Sometimes they write their memoirs, locally printed and prominently displayed on newsagents' counters, and occasionally you see them interviewed on television, recalling their days at sea in apposite detail—'Oh yes, I remember we went to Sydney once, Tom Williams Amlwch was my first mate then, and his brother Bob was in the engine-room, he married my second cousin Dora you know, and it was *her* father I was telling you about before, commanded one of the old Bibby Line ships before the war . . .'

For Wales and the sea go together—the very word *hwyl* originally meant a ship's sail!—and the seaman's calling has always been a domestic affair in this country, like the farmer's, linking the genera-tions, the marriages and the neighbours too. In 1287 the worldly possessions of a man of Nefyn, Gwynedd, were recorded as being one cow and one fishing-net, and today many a builder or shopkeeper keeps his lobster-pots in Cardigan Bay, or chugs into the Bristol Channel in his shabby old fishing-boat when the day's work is done. In many families it used to be the accepted thing that younger sons went to sea, there being, on coastal smallholdings far from towns or railways, nothing much else they could do.

Luckily until the present century there were plenty of berths going. Fleets of smacks and schooners traded along the coast. Hundreds of bigger ships carried Welsh slate across the oceans, and brought back from foreign parts timber for Welsh pit-props, phosphates for Welsh smelters. There was a great fishing port at Milford, Milffwrd, in Dyfed. There were oyster-fleets of Mumbles and Môn. The coal ports of the south were home to thousands of colliers, and close at hand were the two great English seaports of the western seas, Liverpool and Bristol, whose ships almost always carried Welsh crewmen.

Ships were everywhere around the coasts of Wales. Every small seaside town had its own complement, often built in its own yards, and locally owned too: for instance the ketch *Mouse*, which brought wines to Aberteifi in the 1890s, was jointly owned by a wine-merchant of the town, a brickworks manager and a cabinet-maker. From Solva, no more than a hamlet on the coast of Dyfed, emigrant ships used to sail direct to New York. From Abermo, Barmouth in Gwynedd, Welsh wool was shipped direct to South America. From Porthgain in Dyfed, into the 1930s, a fleet of six diminutive steamships, warping their way cautiously out of the crooked little harbour, regularly carried roadstone to Dublin, Bristol and London. On almost every beach of Wales the smacks would ground themselves at one time or another, while the horse-drays toiled up the shingle with their cargoes of lime or gravel, the village women strolled down in twos and threes to buy their Bristol hardware, and the small boys rushed around making a nuisance of themselves at the ropes. Far up the Wye the town of Monmouth was a thriving river port; the long inlets of the Cleddau estuaries, in the west, were alive with grain ketches, anthracite barges and ferry-boats; and Nefyn, where the man with the cow and the net had lived, was said to be outclassed only by Appledore in Devon as the most absolutely maritime community in the British Isles.

Often a port was specific to an individual mine, or quarry, or coalfield, and had its own small transport system connecting it with the source of its cargoes: horse-drawn trollies or narrow-gauge railways, from the slate quarries to their private quays, or the Glamorganshire Canal which took the iron ore of Merthyr Tydfil (or Tudful) to the Bristol Channel, or later the mesh of railway lines connecting the coal-pits with their own ports. Often they produced particular kinds of ships, too. Porthmadog slate ships were known for their exceptional speed, the phosphate schooners of Swansea, built to sail around the Horn for copper nitrate, were particularly tough—the young Swansea masters that Joseph Conrad admired would sail, it was said, where nobody else would go. Swansea also produced a particular kind of pilot boat, two-masted and very graceful, while up the river Severn sailed the heavy trows that were built especially to ride out the great tides of the estuary, or defy its spectacular spring bore.

Welsh seamanship was hereditary, and often rule-of-thumb. The seamen of Caernarfon, it was said sneeringly in the 1860s, navigated only by 'a sort of knack'—they got to Hamburg or the French coast just by the help of 'certain clues'. But they really got there on the strength of their accumulated experience, which was immense, and wonderfully varied. Consider for example the maiden voyage of Captain D. J. Jenkins of Llangrannog, when he first went to sea in 1897 as deck boy and cook on the barque *Foxglove*, with a crew of six Welshmen under a

Welsh captain. First they went to Buenos Aires with a cargo of coal, then to Galveston in Texas, then around the Horn to get guano from Peru: to Liverpool next, and without disembarking around to Tyneside for more coal, to Buenos Aires again, to Valparaiso in ballast for a cargo of nitrate. On the way back to the Gulf of Mexico with it the *Foxglove* went aground in a storm at Tobago, sinking in two minutes, but young Jenkins, shipped home again to Wales, spent only a week there before finding another berth and setting off again for the River Plate.

A sort of knack! No wonder in the fullness of their seamanship Welsh seafarers were always in demand, and Welsh masters commanded every kind of ship, from Australian paddle-steamers to Atlantic liners, before coming home to those decorously house-planted, text-framed and binoculared villas above the seaside promenades.

The most exciting of all the small Welsh ports was Porthmadog in Gwynedd. It was founded in the early nineteenth century specifically to handle the slate of the Ffestiniog quarries in the mountains to the north, and was linked to them by a narrow gauge railway running over that embankment upon which we stood, admiring the most magnificent of all Welsh views, in the opening chapter of this book. The port was consequentially all of a kind, all functionalism. Its terraced rows of houses were neat, square-windowed and substantial, ship-shape houses in fact: villas for masters, owners, merchants and shipbuilders on the Garth above the sea, more modest homes in ordered ranks on the flat land below. A dredged channel gave entrance to the harbour out of Porthmadog Bay, and around it were grouped the yards, the chandlers' shops, the cranes and the loading quays. Even today, though they are only yachts, launches and an occasional fishing-boat in the harbour, the slate-roofed harbour-master's office is still in good condition, the mariners' inns are flourishing still (the Ship with a windjammer model above its porch, the Australia's sign showing Captain Cook and his *Endeavour*), and miscellaneously maritime concerns occupy the various shambled structures of the quays.

In its prime this little port was world-famous, for Porthmadog men not only sailed their ships to all the seven seas, but also built the lovely top-sailed schooners known as the Western Ocean Yachts, considered by specialists to have been among the finest of all small merchant sailing-ships, of which thirty-three were launched between 1891 and

1913. Porthmadog schooners, having taken their slate to America, Europe or Australia, picked up local cargoes for destinations anywhere, and so became as familiar in the ports of the Mediterranean or the west African coast as they were on the Elbe or in the Caribbean. A typical voyage might take a ship to Germany with Welsh slate, to Cadiz with German manufactured goods, to Newfoundland with Spanish salt, to Greece with Canadian salt cod, to London with Greek fruit and oil, and so home at last in ballast to Porthmadog. Sometimes a ship was away for a couple of years: at Gibraltar in June 1899 seventeen ships from this remote small port of the west all lay below the Rock at the same time.

We know from old pictures how dynamic Porthmadog looked then. Ships by the score crammed its quays in a dense mesh of masts and riggings, and out in the bay, waiting for the tide, scores more lay at anchor, or were roped up to the steam tug *Wave of Life* for the difficult tow over the harbour bar. The little trains huffed and chugged across the embankment, at the builders' yard another schooner was sure to be taking shape amidst its scaffolding, on the wharves the slate lay in gigantic heaps, shifted laboriously here and there by teams of horses. The whole life of the town was geared to the coming and going of the ships. Hardly a family did not have maritime connections, as sailors, as builders, as slate agents, as insurers, often as part owners, and pride in the ships was intense—what rejoicing when the *Blodwen*, 129 tons gross, beat all records by sailing from Newfoundland to Piraeus in twenty-two days flat! Porthmadog sailors loved to swagger the streets in the bright cravats and unfamiliar headgear they had picked up in Aruba or Casablanca, and when a new schooner was launched all work stopped, the school was given a holiday, and the whole town went down to the yards to applaud.

It was life lived intensely, just for a few years—the slate industry collapsed after the First World War. Some Porthmadog sailors came home moderately rich to retire to those comfortable sash-windowed houses on the hill, but many never came home at all: for of all the lovely Western Ocean Yachts, launched with such bravado from the yards of Mr David Jones or Mr David Williams, sent to sea with such pride behind the heaving paddles of the *Wave of Life*, cheered on their way by half the population from the point at Borth-y-Gest, from the beach at Cricieth, from headlands all down the coast of Llŷn—of all those thirty-three swift and beautiful vessels only five went to the breakers' yards in the end, and all the rest were lost at sea. The last of them all, the *Gestiana*, 124 tons gross, foundered on her maiden voyage, six miles east of Newfoundland, 4 October 1913. Her owners included a grocer, a dentist, three physicians, three solicitors, two quarry managers, a nurse, David Williams her builder and Lloyd George's wife. Her master was Captain Griffith Pritchard, Tremadog.

Very occasionally a ship still puts in to Porthmadog, escaping a gale in the Irish Sea, giving its crew shore leave from oil prospecting, or evading a Liverpool dock strike. The Irish packets sail from Abergwaun (Fishguard), Pembroke Dock and Caergybi, tankers disgorge their oil into a pipeline at Amlwch, a handful of trawlers work out of the west coast, now and then a coaster or a small tanker ties up at one of the infinitesimal harbours of the northern coast or Bristol Channel. More often, though, the little Welsh ports are either resurrected as yacht havens, or lie gradually rotting and silting down the years, jetties, docks, customs house all deserted, only a few ramshackle boats of part-time fishermen beached upon the mud.

All the remaining ocean ports are in the south, along the shores of the Bristol Channel, and its outlet to the Irish Sea and the Atlantic. Most of them were made great by the Industrial Revolution, when the products of the southern valleys, the iron ore, the steel, the unimaginable quantities of coal, were shipped through them to the world. In their day they were all immensely rich and busy, and though most of their traffic is lost now, and there are generally no more than three or four ships to be seen among their derricks, some grandeur of their black zenith still clings to their docks, impregnates their muddy waters, and gives them a nostalgic fascination. Monumental stand the port offices of these once mighty havens. Penarth's is like a country hotel (though actually a Social Security hostel) beside the forlorn remnant of its coal harbour, which once handled four million tons a year, and is now home only to a few yachts and a couple of fishing-boats. Barry's is soberly neo-classical among a wasteland of mostly empty docks and a vast marshalling yard filled with derelict rolling stock. Cardiff's stands bold as a castle, luxurious as a mansion, with the hills of Glamorgan visible behind it, and cranes and derricks all around—still polychromatic with stained glass windows, still fragrant with its old mahogony, still to be seen like a major-domo on its waterfront greeting its twenty or so ships a week as once it greeted the fleets of colliers hastening in their hundreds night and day towards its bunkers.

Farther east Newport, the first of the coal ports, now ships no coal at all, but thrives moderately as an importer of cars and general cargoes (and out to its offshore sandbanks men in engineless barges still allow themselves to be carried by the tide, to scoop up the coal-dust sedimented there and be borne by the waters home again). Farther west Swansea, which preceded the Industrial Revolution, has survived its waning too, and there are still tankers to be seen waiting for the tide in its bay, and ore carriers easing their way into the deep-water docks of the Port Talbot steelworks. But above all the big ships still come and go into the harbour of Milford Haven, Aberdaugleddyf, in the far south-west of Wales, which Nelson once described as the best harbour he ever saw, except only Trincomalee.

It is a long and complex inlet from the sea, guarded by rocky headlands, opening into a majestic fiord, and running away inland in myriad creeks, rivers and marshes. In the eighteenth century the British Admiralty built a dockyard at Pembroke on the southern side, and from the elegant yards that still stand rotting there, nicely interspersed with small mansions for admirals, several hundred warships were launched. In the nineteenth century Isambard Brunel the engineer built his South Wales Railway to the very shore of the haven, intending to run passenger services to New York with his mammoth steamship *Great Eastern* (he never did, but there is still a Great Eastern Terrace at Neyland on the northern side). Fifty years ago the haven was one of the great fishing centres of western Europe—in 1932 more than a hundred trawlers were based there. During the Second World War it was a chief assembly point for the Atlantic convoys, and through its headlands the freighters laboured by the thousand for the terrible crossing.

The little town of Milford itself, Milffwrd in Welsh, was planned from scratch as a new port under the patronage of Sir William Hamilton the local landowner, husband of Nelson's Emma: it is still trimly nautical of style, with three parallel terraces along the sea, and plenty of pubs along the waterfront, and all around the haven are old symptoms of maritime importance, like lighthouses, and coastguard stations, and mooring-buoys, and hulks abandoned on foreshores, and the skeletonic remains of ferry-boats.

Only in our day, though, has Milford Haven really fulfilled the potential that Sir William and Lord Nelson foresaw for it, and become a port of world importance, for in the 1960s the international petroleum industry fell upon this distant corner of the British Isles, and developed it as the chief point of entry for the oil of the Middle East. One by one, in the green countryside around the haven, there arose the gleaming stacks and convoluted mechanisms of the refineries, and the serried tanks of the storage depots, and the 700-foot chimney, highest in Europe, of an oil-fired power station; and far into the water there stretched the long, long jetties of the supertankers, the biggest ships on earth.

There you may see them lying now, immense and remote, huge, metallic, and apparently lifeless, hardly touching Wales at all, just mooring themselves at their silent piers, discharging their oil, and sailing away again through the headlands for the jetties of Arabia. In terms of tonnage handled this is the third or perhaps fourth busiest port in all Britain—4,500 cargo ships in and out each year, far more than all the other ports of Wales put together: but nowhere could be much more alien to the homely cluttered docksides of old Wales. The masters of the Western Ocean Yachts would scarcely recognize those behemoths as ships at all; the Victorian portmasters of Cardiff, peering through their ornamental windows, would be stunned by their clinical cleanliness, and the small boys of the haven villages, if they ran down to help with the ropes when one of these monstrous vessels sailed in, would get no further than the guard at the refinery gate.

Suddenly, on the wild mountain road between Llanidloes and Pontarfynach, everything is sterile. The grass is dead, the river below looks grey and sullen, mounds of broken stone cover the ground entirely, as though nothing soft or succulent has ever existed there. Shells of old buildings protrude, broken pipes and old rails lie about, but no life stirs. No sheep come near the place, and even the birds stay clear. It only lasts half a mile or so—just around the corner the greenness returns, the trees grow cheerful again, the little river sparkles: but it leaves a queer uncomfortable feeling in the mind, as though one has passed through an absolutely used-up patch of the earth's surface.

All over Wales you will find such places, scrawny places, little desolations, signs of the immemorial process by which mankind has extracted the wealth from the substance of this country, cleaned a corner out and moved on. On the Llanidloes road it was lead whose toxic substances killed everything in sight, blighted the hillside and polluted the river, and a long succession of lead-miners, between the Middle Ages and the 1940s, who earned their livings there. Elsewhere in Wales it was copper, or manganese, or tin, or iron, or gold, or coal: the industries of Wales have nearly all been brutally extractive. One by one they have burst into activity, made a few people rich, mostly foreigners, sustained a community perhaps for a generation or two, and then, having exhausted the matter beneath, declined into lifelessness: and so in every part of the country, like the scabs of old wounds, those countless workings remain today dead and abandoned, cherished only by industrial archaeologists, unless they are prettied up with information centres and numbered walks as attractions for the tourists.

Among the oldest and deadest of them all are the supposed remains of the Roman gold-mines at Pumsaint in Dyfed. These are said (by those who believe them to be gold-mines at all, for some archaeologists don't) to have been the second largest in the whole Empire, and technically the most advanced, being worked probably by slaves under military engineers. You would never guess it. They are queer little burrow-like mines, their entrances often grown over by the roots of trees like elves' holes, or badgers' setts: yet they were among the Roman Empire's chief sources of bullion, and half the Roman organization in Wales, its roads and garrisons, its towns and naval bases, was constructed around the presence of their treasure.

The relics of many another gold-mine litter the back-country of mid-Wales, like the huge abandoned engine-shed deep in the Gwynedd forest of Coed y Brenin, or the carefully padlocked level up the lane above Bontddu on the Mawddach estuary, half-hidden among the leafy glades. Gold mining is still fresh in the Welsh memory. People still alive can remember the miners tramping over the hills from the coast to work those Bontddu diggings, and it is less than a century since Dolgellau, at the heart of the workings, was a proper boom town, with speculators and prospectors cramming its pubs, with wagon-loads of equipment rolling through its streets, with thrilling whispers of new discoveries, offers of new shares, spilling through the market crowds and filling the columns of the local newspaper. Nor is the gold exhausted yet. Now and then the Bontddu level is reopened for a few years, as one speculator after another decides to have a go: and in sweetened parody of old tributes, when a prince or princess of England gets married, the wedding ring is habitually made of Welsh gold.

Welsh lead was also worked by the Romans, largely for the silver in it (at Llanymynech in Powys, they say, by slaves living for ever in underground man-made caverns). Later the Adventurers of Mines, a monopoly of the English Crown, invested in Welsh lead, later still multifarious private enterprise took over, and in the eighteenth and nineteenth centuries the lead-mines of mid-Wales were famous and highly profitable, their great water-wheels turning on the moorlands, their tunnels like warrens all over the place, their poisonous wastes polluting innumerable streams (the menagerie elephant who died at Tregaron in 1848, and is buried behind the Talbot Hotel, died of lead poisoning). Big communities grew up around some of the mines, and at Fan, near Llanidloes, you can still see the ghost of one in the gentle Powys foothills: chimneys, rows of houses half-ruined, the remains of a chapel or two; and a huge flat rubbly space, now partly filled with water, where once all the trollies and wagons of the mine bustled night and day, to a clashing of metal from its crushing plant, clouds of dust, the rush of water from water-channels high above, and the snorting of the trains running away to Llanidloes and England.

It was copper they extracted from Parys Mountain, on Ynys Môn. For half a century indeed copper *was* Parys, the richest source of it on earth, and in the heyday of the copper-bottomed ship vast fortunes were made from the mountain deposits—the British, French, Spanish and Dutch fleets were all sheathed with Welsh copper. A smallish un-thrilling hill near the island's northern coast, in the second half of the eighteenth century Parys Mountain was scooped and burrowed with mines and quarries until the whole of its middle fell in, leaving a huge horrible hole, filled over the years with water so vicious that a key dropped in it would be copperized in three seconds. The workings were a favourite subject for Picturesque painters, with their allegorical confrontation of Man and Nature—Nature so huge and awful, Man so puny but so daring, as he swung over the orifice on precarious gantries, or was lowered down the cliff face in buckets, or just dangled there at the end of a rope hacking away at the mountain mass.

In its time Parys was the greatest enterprise in Wales. The nearby village of Amlwch, hitherto no more than a fishing hamlet where English was never heard from one year to the next, was transformed into a tough and rumbustious industrial town, full of English immigrants. Parys had its own port blasted out of the sea-rocks, its own ships to carry the ores away, its own copper coinage with a druid's head upon it, and its acrid smelters poisoned all vegetation for miles around, even to the moss and lichen. Amlwch lived in a perpetual thick yellowish haze, and its curate was entitled to a special stipend for Smoke Trespass.

Today it is all gone, not a man works on the mountain, not a ship sails from the harbour, not a smelter seethes. The mountain, with a derelict windmill on its summit, still smells pungently, and looks like a huge long-disused rubbish dump, or perhaps the remains of some fearful explosion—covered all over with grey, red, brown, orange and yellow deposits, surrounded by an air of bitter exhaustion, and riddled everywhere, among its struggling heather, with perilous shafts and galleries.

There have been stone quarries in Wales since, well, since the Stone Age, and much of the countryside has been pitted at one time or another with quarry workings. Limestone, granite, sandstone, they have all been in demand in their day, but the essential Welsh stone is slate, and in the late nineteenth century the slate industry of North Wales was the quintessential Welsh industry. Its scale was tremendous, Welsh slate being shipped all over the world in huge fleets of sailing vessels, to roof the houses of the British Empire, America and the new industrial Europe. Its exploitation, mostly by alien or alienated landowners, was often ruthless. But the working society it brought into being was close-knit and exceedingly Welsh, and the very title of a quarryman (who was often a miner, actually) has a special meaning in Welsh life, lore and literature.

The hooter sounds at the end of the quarry shift; a pause; and then, clattering down the hill towards the hamlet far below, the quarrymen of Ffestiniog, or Bethesda, or Nantlle, come running—not lackadaisically, not casually, but at a deliberate steady dog-trot, all the way down the rough track home. They always ran home. It was a custom. They also habitually wore bowler hats at work, and met at dinner-time in discussion clubs called *cabanau*, cabins, and sometimes carved astronomical fireplaces, and very often doubled the industrial life with the agricultural, farming smallholdings on the side. They were chapel almost to a man, they were wide readers of literary and theological journals, and many of them were able poets.

Of all the Welsh industries this was the most cohesive, because its work-force was purely Welsh. Very few outsiders came to work the quarries, which were mostly in the remote north-west, and fewer still ever mastered the secrets of the craft. The language of the labour force was entirely Welsh, and its skills were jealously guarded—the infinitely delicate art of splitting slates, the subtle knack of judging, by the colour or the lie of the stone, just what kind and quality was there for the quarrying. 'I have read the best German, American and English authors on geology', said a writer in the *Mining Journal* in 1865, 'and I have not seen one single passage in any one of their works that can help, assist or enlighten a [Welsh] quarryman in any one of his operations.' The quarrymen agreed. *Rhaid cael Cymry i dorri'r garreg*, said one of their songs, *nid yw'r graig yn deall Saesneg*—'You must get Welshmen to cut the stone, the rock doesn't understand English . . .'.

Family traditions were strong among them—most quarrymen had fathers, brothers, sons or even grandfathers working with them—and the institution of the *caban* was family-like too, having been likened to an *eisteddfod*, a friendly society and a trade union all rolled into one. Its midday meetings were formally arranged, with an elected chairman, and the men all addressing each other as *Brawd*, 'Brother', but its activities were wonderfully varied. In the course of the year 1902 the *caban* at one Blaenau Ffestiniog quarry, for example, which met over jam-jars of tea by candle-light in a damp tunnel, organized a mental arithmetic contest, a singing contest, a discussion on the recent Education Act, a lecture on the subject 'How much greater is a Man than a Sheep', a spelling bee, a contest to create Welsh words, a discourse on Vanity, a debate on 'whether a wife is a choice or a necessity', a quiz on the Bible, a debate on whether ministers should be appointed for life, a contest to interpret a set poem and several competitions concerning the writing and memorizing of verse.

There is still some slate quarrying in Gwynedd, but the gargantuan activity of the industry in its prime is now no more than a memory, and the workings have become a sort of museum—the vast terraces and enormous pits, some of the biggest ever excavated, which distorted the skylines up there, created entirely new landscapes of grey slag, shifted the shapes of lakes and diverted river courses. In the mountain quarry town of Blaenau Ffestiniog, in particular, you can still sense with an astonishing vividness what life was like in the age of slate. Blaenau (which simply means 'tops of the valleys') has been almost perfectly preserved, and is now one of Europe's most fascinating sites of industrial archaeology. From its railway station the little steam train still puffs down its tracks to Porthmadog; above it still loom the slopes and plateaux of waste slate; all around the sombre mountains of Eryri stand in splendid cirque. The town itself is less like an industrial settlement than a conglomeration of so many country cottages, uprooted from the hills around and stuck together here into long lines of terraces—some a natural grey, slate-grey in fact, some brightly washed, and nearly all with a rural intimacy still. It is a tight, clamped town. The great grey chapels dominate it still, Bethesda and Bethania, Gwylfa and Tabernacl; a stony toughness informs the place; and from a distance, seen against that mighty background of the hills, below a leaden Welsh winter sky, with only sudden shafts of sunlight falling here and there through breaks in the cloud, Blaenau can look theatrically complete and powerful, as though an entirely separate society, fierce, odd and homogeneous, is still discussing the definition of Vanity behind its stout wooden doors down there.

All these were rural industries, crafts really, country callings. Before Wales could become a modern industrial nation, in the age of steam, foundations had to be laid. Until the eighteenth century there were hardly any roads in Wales—in Gwent, it was said, none at all, so that people had to move around in ditches, and the main street of Monmouth itself was described as 'a barbarous hollow way as deep as a horse's back'. We read of tracks so deep in mud that sixteen horses were needed to drag a single wagon, of sledges heaved miserably over snow-bound mountain passes, of long muddy strings of pack-ponies, huge logs across their backs, moving down the valleys to the coal-pits—like the pony-caravans of Colombia, a Spanish writer thought them in the 1820s. Then turnpikes began to appear, privately financed generally by local landowners, and a Government-backed highway was thrown across North Wales to connect with the Irish packets at Caergybi, and then the canals were dug, with their pretty paraphernalia of locks and keepers' houses, and finally the railways came, and slashed their way through all the hills and valleys of Wales, and changed everything for ever.

Wales was one of the first railway countries. The very first passenger train, drawn originally by horses, and on one unnervingly experimental occasion by sails, ran along the seafront at Swansea to a shattering din of iron wheels—'sufficient to make one reel from the car', reported a passenger in 1813, 'in a state of dizziness and confusion of the senses'. The very first steam train, built by the Cornishman Richard Trevithick, made its very first journey in 1804 down a tramline from Merthyr to Abercynon in Glamorgan, very slowly, and losing all the water from its boiler when a bolt broke. By 1816 troops were being brought into Wales by rail to deal with insurrectionary disturbances, and by 1860 you could leave Euston Station in London at 7.30 in the morning, and be at Caergybi, at the very north-west tip of Wales, just after two in the afternoon.

The railway mania which seized England in the middle of the Victorian century fell upon Wales no less crazily, and grandly named companies sprang into being in the remotest country districts. Half of them were pipe-dreams. The Wrexham, Mold and Connah's Quay railway never got to Mold, the Manchester and Milford never got either to Manchester or to Milford, the Lampeter, Aberayron and New Quay, whose seal depicted a powerful 4-4-0 tender engine, never owned an engine at all. The Newtown and Llanidloes, which did not reach Llanidloes, was so isolated from all other systems that its first engine had to be taken majestically to Newtown on a dray pulled by fourteen horses, with seven more pulling its tender behind.

Others were enterprises of wonderful style and success. Some of the greatest of contemporary viaducts, some of the deepest of cuttings, were made by the railway engineers in Wales. A mesh of tracks was built out of the coal and iron valleys to the sea. A line was thrown across the treacherous Cors Fochno, where the Great Toad lived, and another was laid to the summit of Yr Wyddfa, Snowdon (though its very first locomotive, built in Switzerland, came off the track on its opening service up the mountain in 1896, and from that day to this the Snowdon Mountain Railway has never had a Locomotive No. 1). Little trains ran to the smallest market towns of mid-Wales, big ones thundered, drawn by hefty Pacifics of the London and North Eastern Railway, or elegant brass-capped Castles of the Great Western, magnificently to meet the Irish packets at Abergwaun or Caergybi.

You could not escape the railways. At Raglan in Gwent, in 1863, Miss Anne Bosanquet, giving a new clock for the parish church tower, stipulated that it must not have a dial on the side facing the railway station, and so pandering to the nasty dirty things. On the other hand at the mansion of Pale, near Y Bala, a proudly sculpted locomotive and the motto *Ex Fumo dare Lucem* testified to the progressive achievements of its squire, the railway engineer Henry Robertson. One way or another, the coming of steam affected everyone: by the 1880s the occupations recorded in the baptismal register of the remote country parish of Eglwys Fair Glantaf, Dyfed, hitherto confined to labourers, saddlers, carters and the like, burgeoned every year with gangers, wheel-tappers, linesmen and locomotive engineers. Here is part of a poem by the late Mr William Jackson, engine-driver, about a journey on the little railway run by the Abertillery and District Water Board into the wild Black Mountains, where Richard de Clare was ambushed and Isio the martyr had his cell, soon after the First World War:

> Through the Cwm, where snakes abound
> And many foxes may be found.
> We roll along, the air is clear,
> The top of the bank does now appear.
>
> Past Llwyn Celyn, below the hill
> Where Bill can now relax his skill.
> Dai rubs the handbrake, all is well,
> The whistle is blown, clear as a bell.
>
> Bill shuts off steam, his work is done,
> A very good engine is this one;
> Then into the yard they come to rest,
> Just one more trip, they have done their best.

The train is still more familiar in Wales than in most places. Though most of those little country lines have long since gone, still there are trains at work, of one kind or another, throughout this country. The super-trains come from London to Cardiff in an hour and a half, the time to Caergybi is cut to $4\frac{1}{2}$ hours, in the coal valleys long lines of wagons are shunted desultory down their gloomy tracks. Trains still meander charmingly along the Heart of Wales line from Shrewsbury to Swansea—'Speed, Comfort, Efficiency, Safety', as it says on four pillars at Pen-y-Bont station near Llandrindod. Locomotives Nos. 2, 3, 4 and 5, all nearly ninety years old, still labour their way up Yr Wyddfa, and several little steam trains, lovingly restored, hiss, chuff and judder here and there through the green countryside, from the Welshpool and Llanfair Light Railway, which trundles along three perfectly flat miles of Powys meadowland, to the glorious little slate train which still climbs heroically off the embankment at Porthmadog, up daunting mountain gradients, through woodlands and groves of rhododendron, past lakes, over rushing streams, through a long tunnel in the slate, to its station at Blaenau Ffestiniog.

They suit the place. Those London expresses look fine, as they streak along the Bristol Channel shore, and Wales would not be Wales without the trains of the Cambrian Coast line, blue, cream and yellow pairs of diesel coaches, touchingly toy-like against the imposing mountain landscapes, which weave and wind a busy way over the estuaries and through the little seaside towns, tooting a horn now and then, waved at by holiday-makers from pebble beaches or caravan sites, and pulled up short only by the buffers at Pwllheli, far out in Llŷn, where all railways end.

So: the canals were dug, the tracks were laid, the roads were paved: the stage was set for the most fateful and ferocious of all man's successive assaults upon the matter of Wales, the attack upon the iron and coal deposits of the south which reached its climax in the first decades of the twentieth century. There are mines and heavy industries in the north-east too, but they have never caught the world's imagination as have the pits and mills of Gwent and Glamorgan, so rich in pathos and tragedy, so fecund of talent, celebrated by so many poets, novelists and playwrights. This was more than just an industrial revolution. It changed the face of an entire landscape—a thousand square miles, an eighth of Wales. It changed the lives of hundreds of thousands of people. It transformed South Wales socially, economically, morally. It made enormous fortunes, it caused appalling hardships, it brought to Wales multitudes of immigrants, and made it for a generation or two the America of Europe.

It was a harbinger of what was to happen in many other societies, East and West, from that day even into our own: for in half a century it turned a quiet pastoral country, heather moorland and sweet river valleys thick with trees, into a teeming, blackened, vastly profitable and socially iniquitous warren of townships, from Gwent in the east in a wide swathe all along the southern coast to Swansea and Ammanford in the west. Today when most people think of South Wales, even perhaps of Wales itself, they think specifically of this industrial belt, and in particular of the serrated mass of hills, cut by deep and narrow valleys, in whose rocks the early industrialists found first their iron, then their coal, and beside whose filthy rivers the celebrated workers' towns, Treorchy, and Tonypandy, Treforys and Merthyr Tydfil, Ystrad Mynach and Ebbw Vale, evolved in a mixture of hope and hardship their particular brand of Welshness.

In the 1840s, we are told, 'a Sabbath stillness' ruled the valley of the Rhondda Fawr, sixteen miles long and never more than a mile wide. 'The people of this solitudinous and happy valley are a pastoral race, almost entirely dependent on their flocks and herds for support.' Not for long: forty years later 115,000 people were living in Rhondda, and 40,000 miners worked its fifty coal-pits. The speed of growth was breakneck. Merthyr Tydfil had a population of 7,700 in 1801; by 1861 it was 70,000. At the start of the nineteenth century Cardiff, with 1,870 people, was the twenty-seventh town of Wales: by the end it was the biggest of all, with 164,000. The coal port of Barry, started from scratch in 1889, had a population of 27,000 within ten years. By the end of the nineteenth century migrants were arriving in the industrial valleys at a rate almost as high as the United States', and much the highest in Europe. By 1913 a quarter of a million men were working in the coal-mines alone.

The profits grew fantastically too. At Merthyr a lease worth £28 a year came up for renewal in 1847: it was raised on the spot to £30,000 a year, and the leaseholder accepted it eagerly. He knew his business. Vast quantities of iron, coal, steel, zinc, copper and nickel and tin plate were about to pour out of the mines, mills and smelters of South Wales, until in the whole world only the Ruhr and the United States matched the region for industrial power. A third of the entire world's coal exports emanated from those valleys. They called Llanelli 'Tinopolis', and Swansea had the largest nickel works on earth. Heating all over Europe, railways all over the world, steamships on every sea depended upon Welsh raw materials: by the end of the century 17,000 ponies worked in the pits, and the chief source of income of Ynys Dewi, Ramsey Island far away off the Dyfed coast, was the breeding of fat rabbits for the South Wales valleys.

For about a century the plunder boomed on, in an apparently irresistible cycle of extraction, production and profit, making many millionaires, and creating a new kind of Welsh society, vividly cosmopolitan in the eastern valleys, mutated rural Welsh in the west. South Wales became a prime boast of British power and expansion—did not the railways of Empire run upon Welsh tracks, was it not Welsh coal that those sweating stooping labourers, bent double beneath their sacks, loaded into the bunkers of the world's merchantmen from Halifax to Hong Kong?

At Tredegar in Gwent they preserve a characteristic memento of those heady times, surrounded by railings and overgrown bushes in the shabby municipal park. It is a solid fifteen-ton block of coal, cut by Mr John Jones (*Colinr Mawr*, 'Big Collier') especially for display at the 1851 Great Exhibition at the Crystal Palace, that exuberant advertisement of British pre-eminence. Beside it is the wooden trolley especially built for its transportation, and it sits in the shadows in a sanctimonious posture, like the fetish of some old religion whose gods were wealth and power, and whose hope of redemption was ever greater profit (though from time to time, it is alleged, people have clambered sacrilegiously over its railings to chip a bit off for the front-room fire).

Let us exert a literary prerogative, play about with time in the Welsh way, and travel from end to end of industrial South Wales through its various moments of climax, as its emphasis moved from iron and copper to coal and steel, as its fortunes shifted from ruthless optimism to resentful despair.

The place to start is undoubtedly Merthyr, the first of the iron towns, for in the early 1800s this was not only the biggest town in Wales, it was also the greatest industrial phenomenon of the world. People came from all over Europe to marvel at its incandescent enterprise, and artists by the dozen painted its marvels. There it stands now in one of their amazed delineations, sprawled below a bare moorland near the upper limits of the ore-field, and it seems to be in a condition of volcanic explosion. To the left of the picture, it is true, serenely stands Cyfarthfa Castle, the picturesquely castellated mansion recently built, in twelve months flat, for the almost unbelievably rich ironmaster Mr William Crawshay. Everywhere else, however, is a colossal detonation of smoke, steam and fire. Tall black chimneys, like hideously etiolated tree-trunks, forcibly eject their smoke into an almost solid mass across the top of the scene; the swarming figures of the ironworkers, labouring with shovels and sacks and trollies and steel chains, are silhouetted against the fires of the open furnaces. In the foreground are the long mean terraces of the workers, a chapel here and there, an inn or two, and in the very foreground crowd the shambled huts and shanties of 'China', the maze-like haunt of the whores and the robbers, festering there in the glare of the furnaces, but fortunately out of sight of Cyfarthfa.

For half a century indeed the Merthyr furnaces cast their glare all over the surrounding countryside, and could be seen shining with an eerie radiance from the pristine pastoral valley of the Usk on the other side of the hills. To some it was the radiance of success: the Merthyr works were prodigious enterprises, sending their chains, rails and girders all over the world, paying high wages by Welsh standards and making dynastic millionaires of their proprietors. To others it was the flame of torment: 'Ah me!' Thomas Carlyle wrote after a horrified visit, 'it is like a vision of hell, and will never leave me, that of these poor creatures toiling all in sweat and dirt, amid their furnaces, pits and rolling mills . . .' Merthyr was one of the catalysts of Welsh history. While the Crawshays of Cyfarthfa, the Guests of Dowlais, progressed from one million to the next, thousands of country folk flocked into the town in search of new lives, with children fresh from the farm working as puddlers in the mills, and women who had spent all their lives in windswept moorland cottages doing their best to keep those smoke-black tenements spick and span. At Merthyr a Welsh working class was coming into being, and the balance of Wales itself was being fatefully shifted.

Then away to the west stands Swansea, an old seaport by origin, but transformed in the early nineteenth century by the discovery of iron and coal in the valley of the Tawe, and the development of copperworks and tin-plate factories all along its banks. If Merthyr looked seismic in its heyday, Swansea in the 1860s, say, when its Metal Exchange was the copper centre of the whole world, seemed to have been visited by some horrific plague. Visitors approaching it by train from the east, seeing for the first time the green and sulphurous glow of its smelters, finding their carriages darkened by the black of its atmosphere, above all perhaps smelling its chemical fumes seeping and swirling all around, were sometimes terrified by the experience, so absolutely of another world did the place seem, and so poisoned by its own exhalations.

Hundreds of ships crowded the quays of Swansea, and the town itself, clustered below its hills beside the sea, was a rich, raffish and often violent confusion of nationalities: but it was the works on the river banks that everyone remembered, for they cast a shroud-like spell.

Everything was dead along that shore. All the grass was blistered off, all the water was fouled, not a tree lived, not a flower blossomed. A pall of vapour lay low over the valley: no birds flew through it, only the chimneys contributed their filth, and the flicker of the furnaces was reflected eerily in its clouds. J. M. Neale the ecclesiologist said he could imagine no scene on earth more nearly resembling hell: George Borrow, walking this way up the valley to Castell Nedd, Neath, thought it all a fit subject for Hieronymus Bosch.

To Cardiff now in the prime of its fortunes, perhaps in the early years of the twentieth century. Here the 4th Marquis of Bute presided over a sense of furious opportunism. Here the coal of the eastern valleys rolled down to the sea in endless lines of railway trains, night and day, clanking through the city streets to the magnificent Queen Alexandra Dock which the Marquis himself had lately brought into being. Cardiff, which had been a port of sorts since Roman times, was by now one of the world's busiest, with twenty-four consuls and fourteen vice-consuls maintaining offices in the town. It felt as though its pace would never flag.

There were few factories in Cardiff, and uptown, around the castle, its air was surprisingly clean and fresh. Down by the docks, though, all was grimed with coal-dust, and the streets rang always with the clatter of coal being tipped from wagons into the holds of ships. Down there was Tiger Bay, the district between the docks and the tidal flats known vividly as East Mud: one of the best-known and toughest of all the world's sailor-towns, with its teeming communities of blacks and Arabs, its prostitutes and its drug-pedlars, its gambling dens and Chinese doss-houses and multitudinous taverns. Hundreds of footloose seamen, Germans, Swedes, Russians, Norwegians, Danes, Finns, made Cardiff their home port; crimps with names like 'Jackstaff' Rafferty, 'Nigger' Toole or 'The Swede' haunted the pubs; hundreds of half-caste children roamed the streets; around their church of St Paul the Irish in their thousands honoured all their native enthusiasms of wake, jig and whiskey.

Behind the waterfront there was no escaping Cardiff's consequence. The streets of Butetown, the commercial quarter, were metropolitanly grand, the offices of shipping companies and coal factors were wonderfully dignified, flags flew from the offices of those consuls, a great Coal Exchange, rich in gilded panelling and commercial symbolism, presided over Mount Stewart Square: and stupendously above it all, from the fantastically decorated living-quarters of his castle at the top of the town, the Marquis looked over the rooftops of his indefatigable fief—to the sea one way, where the coal of Wales went streaming off to the markets of the world, to the hills the other, where in valleys hidden from his view the miners toiled to dig it out.

And into those valleys we now go ourselves, up the winding narrow road through Treorchy and Tonypandy, twenty miles up to the archetypal mining village of Maerdy, at the very top of the Rhondda Fach, the Little Rhondda—not in one of its periods of prosperity, which nobody remembers much, but in those of the Great Depression, in the 1930s, which were to stamp the images of these valleys for ever on the world's imagination. Maerdy stands at the very head of the Rhondda, where the road ends abruptly at the escarpment above: beyond the village street there is nothing but bare ribbed rock-face, like Iceland perhaps, or Afghanistan, with only a rough track running over the eastern hills to the next valley. The river there is like a little glacial stream, the grass is brownish and stubbly, and the sheep that graze it are dingy with coal-dust. It is a bleak and lonely place. It has a church, six chapels, six rows of terraced houses, a police station, a school, a post-office, two pubs, two banks, a handful of shops and a big Workmen's Institute (including a ladies' reading-room) to whose meetings members are called by a bellman ringing through the streets. But all is dominated by the four great pits, above and below the village, whose scaffolds with their spoked pit-wheels seem to stand there like living things. Everything in Maerdy, all its work, all its thought, is governed by those whirring wheels, and every building is subsidiary to them, from the manager's house, once the farmhouse of the upper valley, to the pubs and chapels down below.

Things are hard in Maerdy in the 1930s, in the depths of the depression. The main street badly needs some paint. The women standing at their doors in flowered aprons and slippers, babies wrapped in shawls, looked pinched and anxious. They call Maerdy 'Little Moscow, because of its militant trade unionism, and God knows it seems a proper place for revolution. The tuberculosis rate is terrible, diseases of lungs and eyes are rife, many a Maerdy miner suffers from permanent and unremitting back pains. Half the children go barefoot, nearly all are undernourished, and the infant mortality rate runs at about seventy deaths per thousand.

But wait! down the road from the pits above there comes marching in cheerful disunity the Maerdy Kazoo Band, on its way to the Saturday afternoon meeting in the square! And suddenly, for all its miseries, Maerdy comes alive. The women rush indoors for their coats, small boys come whistling and dancing down the steep wide streets. Mr Evans the grocer looks benignly out from his poster-plastered door (avoiding the eye of Mrs Thomas No. 9, who owes him £2. 10s. 2d.). Dr Morris, JP, pauses to watch for a moment on his way to visit old Tom Williams Edward Street, whose back, poor old chap, is long past treating anyway, and all around the bare bleak valley, as the band strikes up, melodies of rag-time and coon-show echo in merry anomaly, breaking the sad silence of the hills, and cheering up the residents of the communities further down the valley, Blaenllechau, Tylorstown, who can hear the Kazoo-horns faintly blaring.

And so finally, half a century later again, we find an allegorical conclusion to this tour. By now the great adventure is over, the storming and the shovelling is nearly done, the upheaval has quietened, the profits and the injustices alike have both been muted. Steel is still being made in South Wales, a handful of nationalized coal-mines are still working and a clutch of little private ones, but the dynamic force has gone. Let us end our journey, *circa* 1980, with a visit to Blaen-Cwm, one of the smallest of the Glamorgan mining villages, in a side-valley near Treherbert. They closed the pit there in 1966, filled in its shaft and capped it with concrete, and it stands there now as a lump in an empty green, like a tumulus, with only a couple of worn old tracks leading up to it. All its works, all its yards, all its railways and pit-head baths and cage-towers and rescue huts and power-houses and helmet-stores and canteens and managers' offices—all have gone. The village stands quietly below the empty site, and out of the wooded hills above a little river tumbles in a spendid waterfall. Sometimes you see people climbing up the hillside with carrier-bags, beyond the plugged pit, to collect loose lumps of coal from the mountainside.

Twenty miles over the hills from Blaen-Cwm, on 14 October 1913, an explosion occurred in the underground workings of the Lancaster Pit at Senghennydd. The pit-cage was blown clean out of its shaft into the air. Harry Wedlock, aged 14, who had begun work in the pit that morning, started to cry and asked one of the miners what was the matter. 'I told him it would be all right . . . I gave him some water and he got all right.' It was not all right, though. A great fire swept through the workings, 439 miners never came to the surface, and the whole community was felled by the disaster. At 40 Ilan Road Mrs Benjamin Priest lost her husband and both her sons, aged 16 and 14. At 68 Commercial Road the widowed Mrs Twining lost all her three sons, the youngest aged 14. Among the residents of Commercial Street, forty-five died, among those of High Street, thirty-five. More than sixty of the dead were less than 20 years old, and eight were only 14. It was Senghennydd, 1913, that first presented to the world the saddest image of Wales—the terrified women waiting with their children pale-faced at the pit-head, the ambulance men with their stretchers pushing a way through the crowd, the exhausted rescue men with their masks and lanterns, the Salvation Army women with their mugs of tea, and all around the village, on the slopes above the pit, the little knots of people waiting, murmuring to each other or quietly weeping.

They were images already familiar enough to the Welsh. The Senghennydd Explosion, as miners have called it ever since, was the worst mining disaster in British history, but it was only one of hundreds of tragedies that punctuated the industrialization of Wales. This was brutal business. Between 1837 and 1934 more then seventy disasters were recorded in Welsh mines, and in eleven of them more than a hundred miners were killed in a single day. And the saddest of them all, perhaps, was one of the latest, when on 21 October 1966, at Aberfan in the Rhondda, 116 children and twenty-six adults were killed by a landslide from the coal tip above the town. A generation was lost there and then, and scarcely a family in the whole community was without its sudden tragedy.

They buried all the bodies in one long row on a hill above the town. Behind the graves scrubby grassland rises towards the open mountain, with cattle grazing there: below them the town clusters hugger-mugger around the pit that has always been the reason for its existence, and was the cause of its catastrophe. It is an emblematic site, so utterly Welsh, so tightly contained within the valley wall, and emblematic too is the parade of gravestones. 'In memory of our darling little maid', the epitaphs say, or 'Richard Goldsworthy, Aged 10, Who Loved Light, Freedom and Animals', or

Earning a Living

The parting was so sudden,
One day we will know why,
But the saddest part of all,
We never said goodbye.

Down in the valley, at the spot where the tip came sliding so
dreadfully down the hill that day, Authority has made a small memorial
garden, with flower-beds in it, benches, and a little summer-house.
I'r Rhai a Garwn ac y Galarwn o'u colli, it says in Welsh, and in English
'To Those we Loved and Miss so Very Much'. It seems to mean
nothing to the people, though, and is blown about by litter, and
desecrated with graffiti.

Undeterred by mishap, striding lordly through their properties, risking
tremendous stakes, grabbing colossal fortunes, here we see the
industrialists of Wales, a small company of men whose energies, over
the generations, routed and scooped and blasted and gouged the
wealth out of the substance of this country, keeping much of it for
themselves. Some of them were Welshmen, especially the coalmasters,
many more were English or Scots immigrants, and though they
included many villains, their vision was often heroic. Half of them, in
the amplitude of their success, acquired comically anomalous titles,
and became the Lords Rhondda, Pontypridd, Swansea or Merthyr:
and in fact far more dramatically than any lost prince of the Welsh
tribes, or lord of the Norman Marches, they stamped their will upon
the nature of Wales, and decreed the way Welshmen should earn their
livings.

Some are remembered now chiefly by the monumental houses
which, when their fortunes were established, they lost no time in
building. Mr George Dawkins, for instance, having succeeded his
great-great-uncle Richard Pennant as owner of the Bethesda slate
quarry system in Gwynedd, assumed the name Pennant himself and
proceeded to build, with the help of William Hopper the architect, a
castle that any conqueror would have cherished—Penrhyn Castle, a
vastly towered pile beside the sea outside Bangor, with enormously
feudal halls and staircases, daunting portcullises and drawbridges, and
in its principal bedroom a gigantic four-poster made entirely of
Bethesda slate (especially for a visit by Queen Victoria).

Penrhyn Castle was frank in its allusions. It was pointedly Norman (though the Lancashire Pennants, as it happened, who had first been enriched by West Indian slaves and sugar, claimed Welsh descent). It was surrounded by a huge park, like a field of fire. It was next door to the private port, Port Penrhyn, through which the Bethesda slate was shipped. It faced southwards to the stern hills, their silhouettes flattened here and there by decades of quarrying, out of whose mass the Penrhyn fortune had been made. And just outside the park stood the parish church, as Norman priory might stand outside city wall, in which old Richard Pennant, the originator of all this grandeur, who died in England in 1808, was remembered in a recumbent effigy of white marble—with sustaining images of cherubs cutting stones, tending goats and holding sickles—with a quarryman, dressed in Roman style and holding a long staff, looking sadly down at the sarcophagus—and with a crowning motto, ironically honouring a clan of such well-attested rapacity, to the effect that 'he improved the condition of the peasantry, exciting them to habits of industry by employment'.

Others of the great magnates live on by reputation. In the valley of the Ebbw Fach in Gwent stand the sparse but ominous remains of the house the brothers Joseph and Crawshay Bailey built in the 1820s above their ironworks at Nant-y-Glo. The cottages of their labourers, some of the meanest in Gwent, stood on a lower level, and so as not to overlook their mansion, had windows only on the other side, facing the hill. The mansion itself has been demolished, but the remains of its park can still be discerned, anomalously consequential beyond a new housing estate, and more to the point, on the slope immediately behind stand two squat round towers, with a barrack-like block between them. These were the Baileys' personal fortifications, against the fury of their horribly ill-used workers: in the barracks they kept a detachment of armed men, and to one or other of the towers, which were armed with artillery, they proposed to escape if ever there was a revolution.

The Baileys were nephews to William Crawshay, whose house Cyfarthfa we have already glimpsed at Merthyr, and were only the most notorious of a legendary clan. Some of the early Crawshays and Baileys were in fact much less nasty than others, but the whole lot have gone into the demonology of South Wales. It is true that at Rugby club dinners, and at Labour Party shindigs too, they often sing a ditty which commemorates the family connection with the first of all steam trains:

Crawshay Bailey had an engine
She was puffin' and a-steamin',
And according to her power
She could do four miles an hour ...

But not all the verses, which are innumerable and sometimes impromptu, are complimentary to the clan, and the most popular conclusion to the song runs:

And when Crawshay Bailey died
How all the people cried!
And they raised two hundred pound
Just to put him underground.

Another Crawshay *bête noire*, Robert T. Crawshay, is buried in a cold grim churchyard at Faenor, Vaynor above Merthyr, looking over the deep ravine of the Taf Fechan river, and upon his grave is deposited a huge block of concrete, ten inches thick and weighing ten tons. Some say it is there to keep his ghost down, others to make sure that he misses the resurrection, and there are more serious suggestions that Crawshay himself ordered it as a protection against his wife's predilection for cremation. Certainly Robert T. Crawshay decreed the words which are, very properly in the general view, deeply incised upon it: 'God Forgive Me'.

Remorse did not however prevent others of the line turning themselves, over the generations, into high-class country landowners. Though the old county families long tended to shun them at garden parties, and neglected to send them invitations to weddings, gradually the Crawshays and the Baileys, solid Yorkshire by stock, moved out of the valleys they had so ravaged into more gentlemanly country to the north and west, the lovely Usk meadowlands, the genial Bro Morgannwg, Vale of Glamorgan. Soon they were behaving in very squirely ways, Mrs Crawshay of Dan-y-Parc taking tea in her pew during services at Llangattock, Mr Bailey of Glanusk setting up his mistresses, so gossip said, in his discreet pleasure-villa in the Black Mountains. Joe Bailey's grandson presently became the first Lord Glanusk, and around Crickhowell administered the only one of the really great estates of Wales which was not based upon hereditary possession of the land. Far behind them now were the pits and furnaces! Honourable Baileys became officers in the Brigade of Guards and the Royal Navy, and in the church at Llanilltyd Fawr there is a memorial to a twentieth-century Crawshay who so fulfilled the clan's baronial aspirations that he was christened De Barri Crawshay.

Other tycoons, less grasping or gargantuan of reputation, are all but forgotten now. Archibald Hood, coal owner of Llwyn-y-pia near Tonypandy, is remembered even by most local people only for the brightly coloured statue of him, in pale buff trousers and a grey coat, which stands outside the old Workmen's Institute there: he points his walking-stick benevolently towards his pit, across the road, and after the effigy was raised in 1906, 'by his workmen and friends as a token of regard', there was enough money left over to pay for a fountain in Tonypandy Square. And Thomas Hill and Thomas Hopkins, who founded the great Blaenafon ironworks in 1789, at the beginning of all this, are remembered simply by their technology: they themselves built St Peter's Church, Blaenafon, in which they both lie, and almost everything in it, pillars, font, window frames, tombs and all, is made of Blaenafon iron.

Today even the ferment of the southern valleys has died away: the wealth of Wales remains evasive, at least to its own people. The copper and the iron ore is all gone, the coal is ever more expensive to extract, the steel mills work at half capacity. Industrial Wales has never recovered from the depression of the 1930s, and from the extinction of the great British Empire which provided so many of its markets. The heady immigration of the nineteenth century was matched by a despairing exodus in the twentieth, when 400,000 people left the South Wales valleys for ever; the unemployment of the 1930s, said *The Times*, 'descended like the ashes of Vesuvius and overwhelmed whole towns', and some of them have never been the same since, never quite recovered their old squalid but defiant buoyancy, never teemed and sizzled in the old way. Often, with the closure of a pit or a mill, a community has lost its sense of purpose, even of reality, and no longer feels quite natural: it is like a man without a face, or a great city with its heart ripped out by bombs—its wholeness gone, and half its identity.

It is not for lack of trying. For half a century they have been trying to give new life to industrial Wales. After the Second World War they optimistically opened vast new steel mills, some of the biggest and most advanced in Europe, whose mighty forms still dominate the coastline

near Swansea and Newport: but they were out of their time, and no longer have world markets at their feet. Then they have repeatedly tried to start new kinds of industry, less thunderous, more amenable than the old. Bits of washing-machine are assembled, toothpaste is put in tubes, sweets are tinned, aircraft engines are mended, silicon chips are chipped. Japanese managers commute from their country bungalows on the Usk to the electronics factory at Bridgend. The British Royal Mint is at Llantrisant, in Glamorgan, and all British motoring documents are processed, sometimes as it seems through a Celtic mist, at Swansea.

They are only palliatives though, and they come and go. Hardly does a firm announce its opening in the Aberpandy Industrial Estate than one reads about its bankruptcy. Hardly is an export order proudly reported than another couple of hundred workers are laid off. The only consistent growth industry of modern Wales is tourism, and this casts a feebler kind of blight, meaner, more finicky, from one end of the country to the other.

The first tourists came to Wales in the eighteenth century, when the Romantic movement first convinced English people of taste that wastelands could be beautiful, and mountains sublime. We see them in old prints embarking upon Wye pleasure-boats, escorted on board by solicitous inn-keepers 'so that the ear is not pained with the coarseness of language too frequently heard from the navigators of public rivers'. We see them clambering up Cadair Idris with donkeys and Dolgellau guides, or setting up their easels to paint Caernarfon Castle in the setting sun, or even going to the races in the spa town of Llandrindod Wells.

The spas in fact were the first proper tourist resorts in Wales, and they began, we are assured, when in 1732 the learned vicar of Llanwrtyd in Powys, the historian Theophilus Evans, being almost worn out, as he said, by a 'radicated scurvy', was told of a neighbouring spring of curative powers. Its evil smell easily led him there, and as he sat beside it wondering what to do next, 'a frog popped out of the bottom, looked cheerfully, and, as it were, invited him to taste of the water'. Thus encouraged, he drank half a pint of it, and if not immediately cured of his radications, at least went away feeling fine. In no time at all Llanwrtyd had become Llanwrtyd Wells, and after it, wherever sulphurous or chalybeate springs were found, spas arose, and little resorts around them.

Llanwrtyd itself became the resort above all of the Welsh Nonconformist middle classes, who spent decorous holidays there taking the waters and walking the hills. Near by at Llangamarch Wells valetudinarians of more sporting turn could combine a course of the waters, in the pretty little bath-house on the bank of the Irfon River, with a fishing holiday at the adjacent Llangamarch Lake Hotel. In the far north Methodist ministers, in particular, frequented the spa at Trefriw in the Conwy valley of Gwynedd, first exploited by the Romans, whose 'airy but cosily furnished Spa House lounge', its brochure says, was 'the gathering-place of the pilgrims to this veritable Mecca of Health'.

But the most famous of them was Llandrindod Wells, in Powys, which for a few years in the nineteenth century became the most fashionable resort in Wales. If the Welsh Nonconformists went to Llanwrtyd, Anglicans and Englishmen preferred Llandrindod, where they were provided not only with Universally Approved Chalybeate Waters, but gaming-houses, assembly rooms, a boating lake, string orchestras at tea-time and a little race-course. Actually the first incarnation of the spa, in 1749, was rather *too* racy, and became a rendezvous, says Samuel Lewis's *Topography of Wales* (1833), 'chiefly of gamesters and libertines'. But in its Victorian prime, when the railway reached Llandrindod, and 80,000 visitors came to the little town in a single year, it was so absolutely respectable that the Pump Room Hotel had two tariffs, like the railway itself—one for First Class Guests, one for Second.

It remains a spa town *in excelsis* to this day. The boats still paddle about the lake, you can still take tea on the lawns of the Metropole Hotel, the Albert Hall still functions, the trains still run, in the hideously refurbished Grand Pavilion the Anglican Archbishops of Wales, attended by the ghosts of so many visiting parsons, are elected to office by their peers. And though Ye Wells Hotel in Rock Park is now a Further Education Centre, along the winding paths of the park, below the bowling-green among the trees, you may find the neat little pavilions of the pump house still warm with sulphurous vapours.

When the seaside became the thing, the English upper-middle classes hastened to Aberystwyth, the Brighton of Wales, where long rows of lodging-houses soon extended all along the front, or to the handsome resort of Llandudno in Gwynedd, built by the enterprising Mostyns as a speculative venture. Welsh communities hitherto utterly self-sufficient now became adopted by gentlemanly English families, who went year after year to Cricieth or to Tenby, to Aberdyfi in the west where they soon had a golf course going, to Rhosneigr on Ynys Môn where they built themselves ginger-bread holiday villas above the sea. For many a child of Kent or Warwickshire the grandest thrill of every summer holiday was their first sight, as the brake from the station rounded the sand-dunes, of faithful Mrs Williams from the village waving them a welcome with her duster from the verandah of Sŵn-y-Môr!

In late Victorian times the style of the industry changed, and mass tourism fell upon Wales. Some of the new visitors came by bike. The tea-gardens which still thrive at Llanferres in Clwyd, and which look like some pleasure-bower from the Indian hill country, were within convenient cycling distance of Liverpool in the days when every up-and-coming young gent joined a cycling club. 'Push your bike, sir?' was the only English phrase known by Jack Roberts, aged 10, when in the 1900s he used to hang around the bottom of Penrhyndeudraeth hill awaiting the bicycle tourists. Others came by boat, on paddle-steamer excursions from Bristol and Merseyside: one of the highlights of the Liverpool outings was the firing of a gun off Ynys Seiriol to send its hundreds of thousands of puffins squawking and flapping into the sky. But the great body of visitors came by train, and all around the coasts of Wales modest resorts sprang up to handle them, boarding-houses and private hotels proliferated, piers were hurriedly built, putting courses were laid out, scenic railways were commissioned, and from Chepstow to Caergybi the old salts of the waterfront baited their hooks for the family mackerel fishing.

Many of the Victorian holiday places have flourished to this day, but others, like so many of the railways that brought them into being, were never a success. All that is left of the chain of fashionable hotels planned by the entrepreneur Thomas Savin is the glorious old hulk of the College By The Sea, and in the Preseli hills of Dyfed you may find the poignant remains of a misguided mountain resort called Rosebush: this was planned in the 1870s by a nephew of Lord Macaulay the historian, who intended to bring tourists in by a railway which would take out stone from the nearby quarries, but it dismally failed, and all that is left of it is the ghost of an ornamental garden and the Rosebush

Inn, which is made all of corrugated iron, and looks less like a health resort for the English middle classes than a ghost town saloon in Nevada.

Today tourists mostly come by car, and in summer they are inescapable. Half a million a year crowd their way through Caernarfon Castle; like shift-workers they come and go, every weekend, from the holiday camps of Pwllheli and Barry Island; mile upon mile of coast is a wilderness of caravans. Along the northern shore, within easy reach of the Merseyside conurbation, Colwyn Bay, Bae Colwyn, Rhyl, Y Rhyl, and Prestatyn form one long jolly resort between the mountains and the sea, with all the statutory accessories of disco, ice-rink, hot-dog stand, indoor surfing centre and trailer camp suburb. The passes of Eryri, in the climbing season, are encrusted with tents and bivouacs; lolloping in their morose and apprehensive hundreds the pony-trekkers of the southern mountains are led up their rocky bridle-paths; armadas of bright yachts flicker across the bays and estuaries, or are marshalled through megaphones by umpires with Birmingham accents.

Here as everywhere, tourism is a corrosion, or a corruption. What farmer can resist the extra income of a caravan site on his stoniest and bumpiest meadow? Why bother to put up your signs in your own language, if all your customers are English? Tourism feeds upon parody, on self-mockery even: ludicrous stereotypes of this grand old country, women dressed up in tall hats and aprons for the selling of fudge, cheap and shoddy love-spoons wrapped in plastic, tea-cloths with ill-printed images of poets and heroes, to raise a cheap laugh in a Leatherhead kitchen. And as it enriches, so it sterilizes: there is nothing fertile to it.

It is an unworthy way to make a living, for such a people as the Welsh. In 1984, alas, no much grander new vocation offers itself for description, but at least we can end this chapter of functions with some snatches more organic: white superstructures of freighters, among the grey derricks and warehouses of Newport docks—distant lonely figures of shepherds and their dogs—a pit-wheel still revolving somewhere, or the drone of a tractor on a summer evening—the spectacular white spouts of the coolers at Port Talbot, and the red flare of furnaces staining the sea at night.

Or better still, we can stand on the flattened patch of shale and turf which has been made into a belvedere above the town of Treorchy. Below it the valleys extend at once wrecked and exalted by the onset, the apogee and the decline of heavy industry. Behind it the raw hills run away to the west, towards the green dairy valleys and the pasturelands. It is a landscape part gentle, part brutal. It suggests at once the nobility of the long Welsh labour, and the pathos of it—so much struggle, so much fire, and nobody much richer in the end. A text in Welsh has been placed there, from Psalm 104—'O Lord, how manifold are thy works! in wisdom hast thou made them all: the earth is full of thy riches . . .'.

At first sight the valley floors below you seem to be one inexorable mass of masonry, terrace after terrace, town after town, punctuated only by the gaunt forms of the chapels, the pit-scaffolds and the works. It is as though some huge black sediment has been laid all down the river banks, never to be expunged. A century ago, when these places were in their climax, it must have seemed that there was no holding back the triumphant course of industry over the Welsh hills. Look more closely at the prospect now, though, and you will find the tide already turned. A film of green is reappearing around the jammed townships below. Forests spring up where railway yards once sprawled, slag-heaps sprout with tender grass: gradually the balance is restored, and nature reasserts its primacy.

8. Building Wales

The Renaissance was entering its glory when Owain Glyndŵr came to power in Wales, and all over Europe wonderful buildings stood testimony to the age. The Doge's Palace rose pinkly over Venice, Toledo's steeple soared, Bruges Cloth Hall already had its belfry and they were about to start work on the chapel at King's College, Cambridge. Owain's Wales could boast of no such marvels, except for the colossal fortresses of its English occupiers. Its buildings were mostly small and often mean—even the vaunted halls of the uchelwyr *were hardly more than barns—and all its artistic imagination went into more ethereal forms, into poetry, and music, and disputation. It has always been so. The building styles of this country are either importations from outside, symptoms of alien power, influence and initiative, or else those of the simple vernacular, close to the earth. It is as though the Welsh, in their distrust of time and history, have declined to invest emotion in anything so fissile as walls, roofs and chimney-pots.*

T HERE is no such thing as a Welsh architecture, but the man who came nearest to achieving one built his buildings on the other side of the world. Frank Lloyd Wright was Welsh on his mother's side, and never forgot his links with the country, naming his home in Wisconsin Taliesin and adopting as his own motto, though he never knew its source, Iolo's *Y Gwir yn erbyn y Byd*—Truth Against the World. Lloyd Wright wrote of his Welsh grandfather, Richard Lloyd from Dyfed, that he was 'in league with the stones of the field', and he himself made buildings, even offices and institutional buildings, that were like artificially moulded outcrops of the earth itself: huge rocks formed the walls of living rooms, streams flowed through patios, great open fires burnt like fires in caves, and a Lloyd Wright house was often so sunken in its surroundings, so unobtrusively married to the rock and scrub around, that from the outside it scarcely looked like a human artefact.

He codified this practice in a famous principle. 'Never be *on* the hill', he said, 'but *of* the hill: make the hill better.' And this conciliatory power, the ability to unite a structure with its setting, and make it feel a part of nature, is the one distinctive hallmark of the building art in Wales. If you can judge a civilization by its buildings, then the civilization of Wales is *osmotic*.

The fundamental Welsh house-type, the *tŷ hir* or long-house, was nothing if not organic. Made always of the local stone, it was a single-storey building often on two levels, fitted laterally into the slope of a hill, with only a step and a corridor dividing the living quarters of the farmer and his family from the living quarters of their cows and horses. Life was not so very different on each side of the passage. Beasts and humans each had a single room, and if the cows were encouched in straw in byres, the people slept in straw mattresses in shuttered alcoves of their living-rooms. Warmth doubtless drifted from one to the other, from the byre the sweet natural warmth of the animals, from the parlour the smoky warmth of the open fire, with its wide stone chimney at the end of the little building. When the beasts came home from the field, when the humans came home from market, they entered by the same central door, like neighbours.

The long-house probably first came into being in the early Middle Ages, but all over Wales you may detect, rather than actually see it still. There may be a few conservative farmers who still keep their cattle across that passage; there are thousands more who have long since converted the byre into another sitting-room, or have built extra storeys above, or encapsulated the whole structure into something grander. Drive around the countryside, and by peering intently at the passing farms, disentangling in your mind their outbuildings and aggrandizements, often you may see still embedded in the heart of them the long-house of their origins. Step into any of a thousand houses, and by readjusting the topography of sitting-room and fully fitted kitchen, presently you will be able to smell the hay in the vanished stalls, and the milk in its churns along the dairy passage.

So long, so stony, the long-houses fitted easily into the contours of Wales. When farmers became more ambitious, and began to build themselves houses of more than one storey, they stuck to the style, and merely made them seem like taller, stouter outcrops. These are the dominant buildings of rural Wales today, plain functional buildings without ornament or fancy. Sometimes they are whitewashed, sometimes not; sometimes their stones are carefully dressed, sometimes they are left rough-hewn and rugged; some have sash windows, others still keep their tiny panelled glass; some are their original four-square selves, others have been successively enlarged and amended, with Georgian porches perhaps, with bay windows or carports roofed with plastic; they vary in detail from *bro* to *bro*—all sealed in, roof and all, with white cement, or hung all over with slates, in parts of Dyfed equipped with massive external chimneys, in other places brightly colour-washed, in pinks and reds and ochres. Yet they remain all of a kind, and even when they are cosmeticized with stucco and picture windows, their native strength redeems them.

Close to the earth too were the first churches of Celtic Christianity in Wales. The very first of all were doubtless no more than mud, thatch and wattle huts, but when they started building churches in stone they were long low buildings not at all unlike long-houses—into which indeed, far down into historical times, the faithful habitually took animals for divine service. The oldest ones still standing are the ruined chapels of the sea-shore saints, but there are many others which, though successively altered over the years as new styles and rituals gained ascendancy, are still recognizably structures of the Celtic Church. They are inclined to be stumpy, without aisles; without tower, only a bell-cote at the west end, and they are often surrounded by the stone circles of earlier convictions, and sometimes attended too, like a magician with his familiar, by an enigmatic standing stone.

There is one such building now, down there to the left beside the coast road from Aberdyfi to Tywyn. It is the church of Llangelynnin, and it stands on the very edge of the sea as if to welcome visiting holy men from their curraghs, with the steep escarpment of Ardudwy rising over the coast road behind. It is not a church of conventional beauty, indeed it hardly looks like a church at all. It has no tower, only a small belfry above its porch, its deep narrow windows contain only plain glass, and it seems to huddle there in the lee of its sloping churchyard, among the handful of grey stone houses that are its hamlet. In all essentials it is a Celtic sanctuary still, after a thousand years and two changes of ecclesiastical allegiance, fulfilling (every so often, anyway) its original functions. We approach it through a stone lych-gate, floored with very bulky pebbles, and so the stoniness of its style is established from the start: and when we pass through its stout protective porch, standing sideways to the sea, with a holy water stoup made of a big sea-pebble hollowed out by the tides, we find ourselves in a rough stone structure of absolute simplicity.

It is very bare. Nothing decorates its stone walls, not even whitewash, and there are only a couple of illegible memorials. The floor is stone-flagged, and a bit muddy, the font has a lid of rough wood, the seats are of crooked oak with names of old pew-holders painted on them —David Pughe, Bron-Llety-Evan, Gent., or the three Misses Edwards, Cefnfeusydd, Tyddyn Ithel and Pantgwyn. The altar is a plain stone table. The only suggestion of ritualism is the primitive wooden screen, a little lop-sided, which divides the chancel from the nave. The only overt symbolism is achieved by the old bier which hangs from the roof at the bottom of the church, and which, carried by a horse at each end, used to convey the coffins for their burial from the high mountain farms above. You can hear the sea through the open door, and smell cut grass on the air.

Where there was a Celtic *clas*, grander churches arose. As the years went by they were Normanized, given cruciform shapes and towers of consequence, but some of them are still lofty memorials to the days when the Welsh scholar-saints lived and worked there among their monkish pupils. One such is the church of Llanbadarn Fawr, outside Aberystwyth. This stands like a small cathedral on the edge of the foothills, looking down to the sea, and has been a holy place since the sixth century, when St Padarn founded his monastery there. It is a solemn building, very powerful, very spare. Outside it is plain, inside it is almost overwhelmingly austere, bare stone, bare floors, whitewash, tall, dark, cool, its ancient presence easily absorbing the florid memorials of eighteenth-century gentry plastered on its walls, and the impertinent restorations of the Victorians.

And easily accepting too, one likes to think, the irrepressible shade of Dafydd ap Gwilym, for it was under the auspices of this severe building, while the Sunday candles flickered, that he used to flirt with the girls of Llanbadarn long ago.

The Normans came, and the English after them, and for several hundred years there was nothing very Welsh to the holy buildings of Wales, but for a trefoil here and there, a totem-stone built into a porch, or the glory of a rood screen, carved by some anonymous local craftsman in a late flowering of Celtic decoration. Separating the chancel from the nave, the rood screen gave a dark intimacy to the rituals of the altar, like the iconostasis of Orthodox churches. Figures of the Rood, the Crucifixion, stood on top of it, blocking the whole chancel arch, and its own wooden arches were often so narrow, its ornamentations so thick and elaborate, that the shadowy altar beyond, the shifting figures of priest and acolytes, the smoky radiance of candles, must have been awe-inspiring indeed to the simple congregation in the nave.

Many Welsh churches still possess parts of their rood screens, though the figures on their lofts were, without exception, destroyed or removed by the iconoclasts of the Reformation. Some are superbly carved, with a heady richness of foliage, saintly figures, beasts, birds and sacred emblems, and these are often cherished by romantics as direct descendants of the earliest Celtic art forms. The screens that stand most truly in the line of Welsh Christian continuity, nevertheless, are the ones that do not flaunt the grandeur of the Godhead, but emphasize its ascetic mystery. Of these, perhaps the most moving of all is the oak screen at the church of St Ellyw at Llaneleu in Powys, a diminutive building in a high meadow, almost an alp, in the northern foothills of the Black Mountains. It is a simple thing, roughly hewn; the tympanum above, reaching to the roof, is painted red, and decorated with spattered white roses and a big white painted cross; the screen below is pierced peculiarly by five asymmetrically carved squint-holes. But it possesses a nobler symbolism than more famous and sophisticated examples, for it seems to stand there between the nave and the altar, a little tilted with age and perhaps with woodworm, not to keep secrets or amaze the superstitious, but simply in mystic demarcation —between the earth, stone and sweat at one end of the church, the fire and holy water at the other.

Up a farm road near Tremeirchion in Clwyd there stands a very strange structure indeed. It is evidently all that is left of a much larger building around an open court, and it is built of red brick on a palatial scale, and has classical pilasters attached to it, and is hugely embellished with the initials RC and the date 1567. It does not feel like Wales at all, but more like the yard of a Swedish castle, or something in Jutland. It was an early example of exoticism, not to say high jinks, in the houses of the Welsh gentry.

True, Sir Richard Clough's Plas Bach-y-Graig was an eccentric affair from the first. Clough himself was unusual enough—a draper's son from Denbigh who made an immense fortune in Antwerp, returned to Clwyd to be one of Katheryn of Berain's husbands, and died in his forty-first year—and his great house was much in his own style. It was the first Welsh house to be built of brick since Roman times, the bricklayers, it is said, being brought from Holland, and it was built to a spectacularly ostentatious design—an almost pyramidical house, its steeply sloping roof peppered with dormer windows, clumped with groups of amazingly tall chimneys, and crowned at the top with a cupola. It was a wonder of the age: fashionable visitors came to stare at it, local people thought it had been built by the Devil, but it was demolished by Gabriele Piozzi, husband of Dr Johnson's friend Mrs Thrale/Piozzi, who used its materials to build himself a more convenient mansion nearby. All that is left is the princely stable block, and the abiding legend of The Pyramid House.

Nobody actually copied Clough's audacious design—the nearest approximation was a smaller town house he built himself in Ruthin, eight miles away, which is now part of the Castle Hotel, and remains a lesser prodigy of tight-jammed dormers on a steep-pitched roof. All over Wales, though, the gentry, newly emancipated from their old ways by the accession of the Tudors, hastened to build themselves similarly fashionable seats, rather than simply improve their ancestral halls. Some were preposterously incongruous—huge Renaissance palaces, piles more suitable to Hertfordshire than to Ceredigion—but in the eighteenth century a number of Welsh gentlemen, led by Sir Uvedale Price of Aberystwyth, embraced the wildly influential cult of the Picturesque, and by applying it to the embellishment of country houses gave to the Welsh building art a glamorous new twist.

The cult advocated the worshipping, even the manipulation of Nature for Beauty's sake, 'picturesque' being nothing more nor less than something proper to be pictured: the river Wye, for instance, was thought to be exquisitely paintable, though William Gilpin the landscapist, who first publicized its beauties, thought that Tintern Abbey could do with a little more demolition to fit the precept absolutely. These notions very well suited the more imaginative of the Welsh squires, whose estates were a very epitome of the Picturesque anyway, and who eagerly adapted their property to the fashion. All over Wales sham castles went up, romantic battlements were added to sober old mansions, Gothic fancies and Sublime arbours made their appearances in hitherto workaday Welsh gardens. The twin glories of the movement were Thomas Johnes's Hafod Uchtryd, described by Borrow as 'a truly fairy place . . . beautiful but fantastic', and Valentine Morris's Piercefield outside Chepstow, which combined views of the Wye itself with wonderfully romantic plantations, glades, cliff paths, grottoes and woodland dells, open by the squire's command to all.

Many of the best-known architects of Welsh origin were to be exponents, in one way or another, of this attitude—not so much a style exactly, but a kind of architectural temperament, fizzy, graceful and hedonistic. John Nash, who was born at Haverfordwest, Hwlffordd in Dyfed, was a very prophet of the Picturesque, bringing the idea to its permanent culmination in the Prince Regent's pavilion at Brighton. And in our own time a late disciple of Sir Uvedale, and a late descendant as it happens of Sir Richard Clough, was Clough Williams-Ellis, who was to build the most entertaining and ambitious of contemporary follies in his seaside resort of Portmeirion, on the perfectly Picturesque coast of southern Gwynedd.

This was not, we are assured, designed just as a folly, but as a statement of aesthetic principle—the principle that profitable development need not clash with natural beauty. It became, though, a delightful expression of architectural *joie de vivre*. Part Italianate, part Welshy, mostly eclectic, it was a community of varied buildings grouped around an eighteenth-century mansion, the whole forming at once a hotel and a kind of pleasure-garden. Williams-Ellis's gift was for the vista rather than the building, the space rather than the bulk, and so his brightly coloured structures, with their whimsical rooflines, their balconies, their oddities of decoration, were like some floating fantasy above the sea. The sands of the Dwyryd estuary lay below Portmeirion, a promontory planted on a Himalayan scale with azaleas and rhododendrons protruded into the sea behind, and the whole thing was clustered with an airy flimsiness on its steep slope, as though one day it might slide all on top of itself into the water. Uvedale Price would have loved it, and Sir Richard Clough of Bach-y-Graig might have recognized something of himself in its exuberant excess: but after Williams-Ellis's death in 1978 some virtue left Portmeirion, if only temporarily, and when the American writer Paul Theroux went there in 1982 he thought it looked like a faded movie set.

Ah, but you do not think of festive mansions or *plaisirs*, when you think of Welsh buildings. You think more probably of chapels. Most of the churches of this country have been so altered by time and dogma that they are now hardly Welsh buildings at all, but nothing could be more absolutely Welsh than Ebenezer Methodist when the Sunday hymns are rattling its windows, Bethel Tabernacle in the mutter of its mourners, or Bethsheba deserted and alone among the oaks of Llŷn.

Actually the very first of the Welsh Nonconformist chapels were light of style and easy on the eye. There is a delectable example at Maes-yr-Onnen near Clyro in Powys, which has remained almost unaltered since it was built in 1696, and which still breathes a spirit of elated discovery. Simple without being in the least austere, it is happily cluttered with chairs, benches and lamp-brackets, is equipped with a piano and a harmonium too, has slate floors, a list of former ministers largely displayed upon its pulpit, and an electric fire with sham coals. It does not feel old at all—rather young and sprightly in fact, still shining with the excitement of its beginnings, when all was fresh and spanking among the Independents, and a morning prayer meeting was a joyous defiance.

Some of the remoter early chapels were even simpler. The first to be built in Llŷn, in 1769, was just a barn really. It is still there, up a muddy lane near the village of Nanhoron, and it is still floored with packed earth, and still lit by oil lamps for its rare meetings, and its only furnishings remain its original rough wooden pews, whitened now by ancient bird-droppings. And in the wild mountain country of the Welsh Desert, in northern Dyfed, stands the famous chapel of Soar-y-Mynydd, built in 1822, now accessible by motor road, but not long ago only to be reached by foot or pony-power—probably the remotest place of worship, the guidebooks say, in the entire British Isles. To this solitary whitewashed building, throughout the nineteenth century and longer, farmers and their families flocked each Sunday morning from the scattered sheep-farms of the mountains, on horses, in wagons and many walking. Attached to the chapel were lodgings for the preacher, together with stabling for his horse, and the congregation we are told was lively and devoted: all hundred seats of the chapel were generally full at Sunday services, everyone stayed on for Sunday school, and once a year there used to be a *cymanfa* in the field next door. They still have occasional services at Soar-y-Mynydd, but mostly the old place stands silent now among its little grove of beech trees, the river running gravelly below, the empty hills all around, and the couple of graves in its burial yard looking like the graves of lost travellers in an oasis.

The great age of the chapels was the Victorian age, when they sprang into being in their thousands up and down the length of Wales—at least 1,600 in the industrial south alone, forming one of the thickest concentrations of sacred edifices in the world. In these structures the Welsh achieved other variations of their vernacular. Experts assure us that the different sects built differently, but to the lay eye the chapels seem to present an organic homogeneity, based robustly upon a box with a pitched roof—stone sometimes, brick sometimes, sometimes hung with slate, or ornamented with classical pilasters, or eaved, but essentially tall, oblong, and steeply pitched. They announce themselves magnificently with their resounding biblical names, and they bear themselves magnificently too, for they deliberately set out to be boldly different from the buildings of the Anglican Church. From the outside they often look less like religious structures than municipal offices or assembly rooms, and they are sometimes built on so bulky a scale that they dominate their towns and villages as authoritatively as any city hall. Inside their design is deliberately plain, to act as foil to blazing sermons and the passionate singing of hymns, and they are like sober theatres, all their stalls facing the preacher's platform, or looking down to the anatomy demonstration.

Gothic was the stylistic rage of the day, but the Welsh Nonconformists thought it smacked too obviously of Anglicanism, so the chapels were more often neo-classical in their references (though one or two toyed with Romanesque, and one at least, Capel Heol y Crwys in Cardiff, bravely experimented with Art Nouveau). It was in their façades that the designers released their visions of splendour. They did not bother much about the back and sides: it was the front that counted, and there they let themselves go with mighty Corinthian columns, Doric balustrades, great triple windows and huge doors of polished mahogany. The flagship of all these sacred battleships was the Tabernacle at Morriston outside Swansea, known proudly if inappropriately as the Cathedral of Welsh Nonconformity. John Humphreys of Swansea designed this memorably hideous structure, and he was troubled by no inhibitions—its façade is hugely classical, but a tall Gothic spire rises unabashed above it. Even among its own flock, the Tabernacle has aroused mixed feelings. Spiritually it has been attacked as being altogether too self-important, architecturally it has been called an abortion, but it has been much loved and praised too, and it remains one of the emblematic buildings of Wales. In the 1870s, when it was new, it was like a mighty smack in the eye of the Anglicized Establishment; now, in its dingier old age, it is still famous among Welshmen the world over as the home of the Morriston Orpheus Choir, one of the most stirring of them all.

Grander even than the Tabernacle though, sounding their messages even louder than the Morriston Orpheus itself, the most assertive of all the buildings of Wales are organic in quite another way: the castles which, for all their splendour, are emblems only of wasted glory and despair. Humped on hillocks, flaunting themselves on cliffs, half-hidden in forest glades, towering over country towns, the castles of Wales are inescapable. There are said to be more than 600 of them—more to the square mile than anywhere else in Europe. They range from the simplest motte-and-bailey castles of the first Norman invaders, or fortified towers that look like strongholds from Oman or Afghanistan, to the fearful stone colossi of the Edwardian conquest, and they make this country a tragic but incomparable exhibition of the castellan craft. Some were built by Welshmen, some by Normans, some by Englishmen, and in their desuetude at least they vary in character as they vary in size, from the sweetly evocative to the still alarmingly overbearing, from the morose to the exuberant.

The most insensitive castle in Wales is the castle of Caernarfon, the prime symbol of English suzerainty, 'the most magnificent badge of our subjection', as Thomas Pennant called it in the eighteenth century, which Parliament ineffectively ordered demolished in 1688, but in which the English Princes of Wales are still invested with their grandeur in trumpery pomp and extravagance. On the other hand the most conciliatory castle is Harlech down the coast, which was built as an instrument of English oppression too, but which was Owain Glyndŵr's headquarters in its time, and which anyway stands so handsomely on its cliff above the sea, suggests such gay glitter of flags and pageantry, that the angriest Welsh separatist can hardly resist its charm.

The most astonishing Welsh castle is Caerphilly, all bashed about and leaning, which is surrounded by acres of artificial lake and occupies like an immense medieval incubus the whole centre of an otherwise ordinary industrial town. The cheerfulest castle is Kidwelly, which does not feel like a fortress at all, but stands beside the river Gwendraeth, opposite its sister priory, more like a huge and happy folly. The nastiest castle is certainly Pembroke, whose awful control tower, domed at the top like a gigantic helmet, is the stuff of nightmare. The most elegant castle is Biwmares in Môn, which is all curvilinear symmetry, and has a little toy harbour tucked neatly in its flank. The most romantic castle is Carreg Cennen, sprawled like a dream on a rock above the Tywi, with a secret cave inside it, and only the skies around.

The most brutal castle is Chepstow, like a huge fist of grey rock at the very gate of Wales. The friendliest castle is Cricieth, which is half Welsh and half English, and which stands on a sea promontory in the middle of the little resort as though it was put there for purely ornamental purposes. The poshest castle is Raglan, which is as much a sumptuous great house as a fortification, and the most secretive is Ewloe, hidden away there in its dell like a robbers' hideaway. The most forlorn is Dinas Brân, which was once a glittering centre of princely power, but which now stands like a set of rotten old teeth on top of a hill above Llangollen.

The jolliest castle is Oystermouth, Ystumllwynarth, which is all muddled up with the holiday shops and recreation grounds of Mumbles. The castle most conspicuous by its absence is Castell Dinas, which once magnificently commanded the strategic pass of the Rhiangoll near Talgarth, but is now an indistinct pile of rubble. The most Picturesque is Denbigh, which stands on a hill above its town in a lovely Tuscan pose. The most haunting is Dinefwr, stronghold of the great Lord Rhys, which stands all on its own, brambled and choked with scrub, high on a bluff near Llandeilo. The most nicely domesticated is Manorbier, which has a house inside its walls, and much the most comfortable is Powis, which began life as a Welsh fortress, but for 350 years has been a luxurious country residence.

The silliest castle is Gwrych in Clwyd, built in 1815, which has eighteen towers on its curtain wall, but is just a rich man's fancy. The most vulgar is Penrhyn, whose overwhelming mock-Norman grandeur came from the sweated labour of the quarrymen. The daintiest is Penhow in Gwent, a charming fortified villa with a church attached. The most exhilarating is Cardiff, whose Roman walls and Norman keep were brought to life in the nineteenth century by William Burges's stupendously decorated additions, and the most beguiling is its sibling along the road at Tongwynlais, where Burges turned the medieval remains of Castell Coch into the setting for a Rhenish fairy-tale. The most misleading castle in Wales is Morlais, above the Taf Fechan near Merthyr, which looks like nothing at all above ground, but secretes a marvellous crypt beneath. The most boring castle in Wales is undoubtedly Abergavenny.

The most exciting castle is the fiercely brooding Welsh stronghold at Dolwyddelan, in the mountain heartland of Eryri. The most suggestive is Castell y Bere, a fortress of the princes of Gwynedd in the valley of the Dysynni, between the rock of the cormorants and Mary Jones' village. The most pathetic is Newport, which is lapped by mud when the tide is low, and swamped by traffic always. The breeziest is Aberystwyth, which stands on a hump above the promenade, a carefree partner to the hardly less derelict pier around the corner. The most intriguing is Aberteifi, presently occupied by Miss Woods and her six cats.

And for any good Welshman the saddest of all the Welsh castles, and perhaps of all Welsh buildings too, is the hilltop fortress of Dolforwyn, overlooking the Severn valley in Powys, and only now being stripped of its turf to reveal its forgotten secrets: for this was the castle that Llewelyn Olaf founded in 1273, in defiance of the English, and which helped to bring upon Wales the full might of English fury—the last of the castles the Welsh princes of Wales ever built, upon the soil of their own country. A steep and squelchy track, more mud than grass, winds its way to this fateful bastion: and on the slope of the hill an ancient yew grows, old enough they say to remember when the prince was there.

Wales being a country rutted all over with chasms, valleys and declivities, washed by a thousand rivers, bridges have always played a more than utilitarian role in its affairs. *A fo ben, bid bont*, says an apophthegm inherited from the Mabinogion—'he who is chief, let him be a bridge'. The imagery of bridges was ancient, linking Life and Death, the Known and the Unknown. Their symbolism was potent —bridges marked frontiers in Wales, bridges linked traditions, or separated dialects, and it was on bridges that agreements were made. The bridge aesthetic, too, is as important to the Welsh scene as it is to the Spanish, and eighteenth- and nineteenth-century landscape painters found a bridge somewhere in the picture essential to their romantic conception of the country. 'I have always had a vision', wrote Kilvert in 1871, 'of coming to a Welsh town about sunset and seeing the children playing on the bridge . . .'

Scores of Welsh folk-tales concern themselves with the bridge, and this is the most famous of them. A woman stands beside the flooded ravine of the river Mynach, in Dyfed, wondering how to reach her cow which is stranded on the other bank. 'May I help you?' says a smooth soft voice behind her, and she turns to find a cowled monk standing there, rosary in hand. 'How can you help me?' says the woman. 'Can you get me over the river to that cow?' 'I certainly can', replies the monk, 'and I can easily span the chasm for you.' 'Well', says the old woman, 'that would be a kindness, but how am I to pay you?' 'Ah', the monk smiles quickly, 'simply let me have for myself the first living thing that crosses the bridge when I have built it.' *'Da iawn*, righ you are', says the woman.

But she was no fool, and she did not like the sound of all this. When in a remarkably short time the monk had finished the bridge, and called the woman from her cottage to get her cow, she brought with her a loaf of bread and her small black dog: and rolling the loaf across the bridge, she ensured that the dog, eagerly scampering after it, was the first living creature to cross the bridge. The monk swore a most unmonkly oath, and with a fizz and a strong smell of sulphur, disappeared. The old woman recovered her cow. The bridge is still to be seen crossing the dark gulley of the river. It probably was built by monkish hands, from the nearby monastery of Ystrad Fflur, and is known in Welsh as Pontarfynach, Bridge on the River Monk: but in English they call it Devil's Bridge.

It is supplemented now by two later bridges, one above the other, and the sight of the three of them there, the most ancient deep down and knobbly among the greenery of the ravine, the second gracefully eighteenth century, the third iron-railed by the Victorians for the tourists, is a particular delight to bridge-lovers. But there are examples no less alluring all over Wales, which must be one of the bridgiest countries on earth.

They come from all ages. At Ogmore Castle, Castell Ogwr in Glamorgan, the river Ewenni is crossed by the most primitive of all bridge forms, a causeway of stepping stones: and since the village of Ogmore lies on the other side of the river, as you precariously make the passage across their worn and toppled slabs you may sympathize with the soldiers of the Norman garrison, eight or nine centuries ago, returning to barracks after an evening with the natives. At Monmouth stands the splendidly fortified Monnow Bridge, like something from a Book of Hours, which the Normans built to guard the entrance to the town; at Llanrwst is Pont Mawr, the Great Bridge, reliably said to have been built by Inigo Jones, in the seventeenth century, and revolutionary for its day—so sensitively balanced, they say, that the whole thing shivers if you hit the centre of the parapet with your fist. And at Pontypridd in Glamorgan is the celebrated bridge thrown over the river Taf in 1756 by the Revd William Edwards, a Methodist minister proclaimed (in his epitaph) 'Builder to Both Worlds': in its day this was an engineering legend, the longest single-arch bridge in Europe, and old paintings of it, made in the days when the Rhondda valley was still sylvan countryside, show it almost surrealist against the green background of the hills, so daringly functional is its shape, yet so rainbow-like too. It made the minister-engineer famous, and after him his three sons, too, became bridge-builders, and have left their work all over South Wales—'that's an Edwards bridge', connoisseurs say, as others might identify a piece of china, or a claret worth remembering.

In South Wales several tremendous bridges of the railway age were world-famous in their time. The most spectacular of them was the viaduct which spanned both the Ebbw river and the Glamorgan Canal at Crumlin in Glamorgan—the 'train-in-the-air bridge'. It was built in the 1850s by a local contractor, T. W. Kennard, whose works stood in its shadow and whose family seat, Crumlin Hall, was on a nearby ridge, and for years it was a wonder of the valleys. An astonishingly delicate-looking structure of steel meshwork, 1,500 feet long and 208 feet above the valley floor, it was the third highest viaduct in the world, and the steam trains clanking across it, so high above the pit-village below, really did seem to be traversing the sky itself. Excursions were made especially to watch them, with picnics and parasols on the grimy flats below, and countless water-colours of the viaduct were painted, countless prints put on the market, until it was tragically demolished, as being too costly to maintain, in 1965.

Up in the north the English engineer Thomas Telford, building a highway to Caergybi for the Irish traffic, and a canal to Llangollen for the coal trade, built some of the grandest viaducts of the age—his glorious aqueduct at Pont-y-Cysyllt in Clwyd, which carries the Llangollen canal in an iron-bottomed trough 125 feet above the Dee valley, was described by Sir Walter Scott as the most impressive work of art he had ever seen—and when he came to bridge the Menai Strait to Môn, he did it with the very first of the great iron suspension bridges of the world. By a fortunate chance another engineer of genius, Robert Stephenson, was later commissioned to throw a railway line across the Strait, and he did it with an equally daring structure, the Britannia Tubular Bridge: and so to this day these two great things stand side by side, half a mile between them, offering bridge-lovers one of the supreme experiences of European travel.

Both bridges had to be built high, and archless, because the Admiralty insisted that big ships must be able to pass beneath them along the tricky shallows of the Strait, but the two solutions are majestically different. Telford's bridge was a graceful iron suspension bridge, the longest single span of its time, sustained at each end by four round-headed arches. Stephenson's was a four-span bridge of iron and brick, whose three Egyptian pylon-towers supported an immense rectangular iron tube, containing the double track of the railway line. One was elegant and airy, one all thrust and muscle, and though the tube has been removed now from the Britannia bridge, and an extra carriage-way has been added above, still both are in essence much as they were, and the holiday cars tumble across the one, the trains rumble over the other, just as the two masters would wish it. They provide a dual focus for a noble view—the calm water of the Strait stretching away to the open sea beyond, on the one side the green flatlands of Môn, on the other the mass of Eryri—and they powerfully affected people from the start. When the first chain of Telford's bridge was winched from one shore to the other, Mr Hugh Davies, stone-mason, Mr John Williams, carpenter, and Mr William Williams, labourer, were so excited that they immediately walked across the chain itself, nine inches wide, from one shore to the other.

All the same, the most memorable of all the bridges of Wales is one that Telford, Stephenson, Kennard and the Revd Mr Edwards might have found a little clumsy. The Usk, a serenely beautiful river, flows from the Mynydd Du, the Black Mountains of Dyfed, through marsh and hill-bog, across rocky shallows and deep green salmon pools, some fifty miles to the Bristol Channel at Newport, where it subsides bathetically into the sea in a last gurgle of mud-flats. It is crossed by all manner of bridges along its route, girder bridges of military urge, delicate suspension bridges for the convenience of anglers, tough railway bridges, two or three bridges by the inescapable Edwardses, an alcoved seventeenth-century bridge of marvellous quaintness at Llangynidr in Powys, an adorable canal aqueduct near Abergavenny, and a bridge at Crickhowell which has gone into the folklore, because it seems to have more arches on one side than on the other (though since the Bridge End Inn, the Six Bells, the Vine Tree and the Horse Shoe are all within staggering distance, the explanation may be less than mystical).

And at the very end, when the river flows through the murky dockland of Newport into the open Channel, there stands the Newport

Transporter Bridge. In 1902 the French engineer Ferdinand Arnodin was commissioned to bridge the river here to enable the road traffic of the then flourishing docks to pass from one quay to another. The problems were extreme. The tide there is one of the highest in the world, and big ships had to pass beneath the bridge. Arnodin however knew the answer, for he had bridged the harbour mouth at Marseilles a few years before. On each side of the river he built a tall trellis-work pylon, and from a lattice girder between the two he slung a movable platform, suspended by a cat's cradle of chains, and powered by an electric engine. The Newport Transporter Bridge was opened to astonished acclaim in 1906, and its platform has been plodding to and fro, between Brunel Street and Stephenson Street, back and forth across the brown waters of the river mouth from that day to this.

It is now one of the two last such bridges in the world, Arnodin's Marseilles masterpiece, the *pont transbordeur* beloved of Dufy, having been torn down. Crossing it is rather like experiencing a page of Jules Verne, or perhaps the Mabinogion. You drive your car on to its platform to be greeted by a functionary in a captain's cap, who presently disappears up a ladder into his cabin, a merry pavilion with a steeply pinnacled roof, painted blue with a bobble on top. A bell rings, the platform shudders a little, and off you glide silently high across the water. It is an eerie sensation. It is half like being in a ship, and half like being in the basket of a balloon: and since in fact not much traffic uses it nowadays, it possesses also a remote sensation of fantasy, as if you are all alone in the world with that faery captain in his gazebo, riding the wild Welsh winds above the wasteland of the docks.

Beneath the castles, over the bridges, towns arose. They did not exist in independent Wales, and town planning hardly suits the temperament of the Welsh, or the ravishing style of their landscapes. History, though, has paradoxically given this country several textbook examples of urbanism—anti-vernaculars, you might say.

To start with Edward I, in his measures to keep the Welsh in proper subjection, not only built his great castles all around the perimeter of Gwynedd, but established in their shelter several bastide towns, on the French pattern. He meant them to be proper colonies, largely self-sufficient communities of English settlers who would establish the presence of the Crown immutably among the unruly indigenes. They were planned along military lines, like the Roman camps before them, or the British cantonments which fulfilled a similar purpose in India later. The first of them was Flint, in Clwyd, whose grid system of streets, though split by a railway track, can still be traced among the supermarkets and car parks; the most important was Caernarfon, around the Eagle Tower and the King's Gate of its terrible fortress; but the most handsome was undoubtedly Conwy, and it remains one of the best examples of a walled town in Europe.

It was built at the spot where, in countless battles of the past, invading Norman and English armies had failed to force a crossing of the Conwy river. Never again! The new town was laid out in a commanding triangle between the river and the sea, surrounded by a high wall with twenty-seven turrets. The wall stands there still, complete in circuit if a bit knocked about in parapet, straight and flat at the water's edge, dipping and climbing along the high ground behind the town, where its sentries looked out to the threatening fastnesses of Eryri to the south. Within it the town survives much as it was, with its main roads driving north to south, east to west, between the four town gates, with its market square in the centre, its ancient inns, and looming above it all, at the eastern end beside the river, its powerful six-towered castle, controlling the waters and flatlands all around. Especially from a distance, Conwy still looks as tough a nut as ever: with the blue-grey mountains behind it, with the sea in front, a fierce little fortress-town cap-à-pie against its enemies.

Thirty miles away, several centuries later, there arose in Gwynedd a planned town of a very different nature. In the 1800s the English entrepreneur William Madocks, who was later to build the slate port of Porthmadog, conceived the idea of a new route from England across Wales to Ireland, avoiding the long haul over Ynys Môn to Caergybi, and instead embarking the traveller at the undeveloped haven of Porth Dinllaen, on the north coast of Llŷn. Resolutely acquiring land rights all over the place, he set to work to build a harbour there, traces of which remain, and some twenty miles to the east he established a kind of staging town, where travellers could stay on their way to and from the packets, and where an agreeably civilized community could be established upon a route that was sure to be frequented by all the best Anglo-Irish society.

He named it Tremadoc, at once after himself and the legendary Welsh explorer Prince Madog, and he designed it according to the latest tenets of the Picturesque. Its setting was naturally fine, at the foot of a line of craggy rocks, on the edge of the reclaimed estuary of the Glaslyn, and its buildings were made of rustically dressed stones, with wide eaves like Alpine houses. It was entirely symmetrical, a T-shaped village with a central square, and it was very complete: church, chapel, market hall-cum-theatre, hotel, two inns, wool factory, livery stable— all were neatly disposed, and on the edge of the town Madocks planted a fine nursery of trees, to ensure its perpetual Picturesqueness.

It is all there still, the church still a church on its artificial hump, the chapel a chapel, the market, after housing Breton onion-sellers for a time, now a crafts and souvenir shop. The factory is a laundry, the livery stable is a garage, the hotel is still the Madoc Arms and the two little inns still face one another across the square. The nursery has gone wild, and is now a properly Romantic wood, and only a modern housing estate and a few straggling bungalows tatter the effect of the plan. (But if aesthetically Tremadog, as it is now spelt, has been admired ever since—'one of the very last distant echoes of the Baroque movement', thought the French architectural historian P. Lavedan —functionally it was a total failure. The Porth Dinllaen route to Ireland never came about, not a single coach-load of Dublin swells came rattling into dinner at the Madoc Arms on their way to catch the morning boat, and the only reminders now of the village's bold ambitions are the names of the streets that lead in and out of it: to the east, London Street, to the west, Dublin Street.)

Another curious showpiece is the elegant little seaport of Aberaeron in Dyfed. A mere cluster of fishermen's cottages until the end of the eighteenth century, this place at the mouth of the Aeron river, half-way down the west coast, was seen by an astute local clergyman, the Revd Alban Thomas Jones Gwynne, as a new port of entry for the whole of mid-Wales. Fortunately he had come, by a sensible marriage, into the possession of a handsome estate, and thus was able to put his vision into practice. He dredged a harbour at the mouth of the river, and built a town to go with it, some say to plans by John Nash. It was centred upon an incongruously large plaza, named after its proprietor Alban Square, with terraced houses along the river-front between it and the sea. It was a high-flown kind of project, an attempt to bring the grandest ideas of contemporary planning to this remote tract of the Welsh coast, and Aberaeron remains an ordered delight of Georgian houses and grey stone harbour works, with an effect of space, ease and leisure very rare in Wales.

Mr Gwynne, though, like Mr Madocks, would be upset by the state of his creation now, for though Aberaeron flourished for a time, with the end of the coastal shipping trade it lost its occupation, and the town never was completed with all the arcades, monuments and gentlemanly merchant houses its pretensions required. Today the harbour is frequented only by yachtsmen, commerce is mostly for the tourists, and the plaza is not paved or gravelled, as its founder doubtless envisaged it, perhaps with an obelisk in the middle to commemorate him, with iron chains around it, and bronze pineapples at each corner—Alban Square is not the urbane centre of life and business that he meant it to be, but has long been roughly grassed, and is used sometimes as a cycle track, and sometimes for football.

Mr Gwynne chose the wrong industry. On the northern coast the immensely rich Mostyn family, one of the oldest and most resilient clans in North Wales, were more far-sighted when, eyeing the trend in holiday tastes in the 1840s, they realized that one patch of their enormous estate might make a profitable seaside resort. It was the neck of land that lay between the bays of Llandudno and Conwy, in northern Gwynedd, overlooked by the high and beautiful peninsula called the Great Orme. Fortunately the Hon. E. M. L. Mostyn was Member of Parliament for those parts, so he ushered through an Act for the Improvement of Llandudno, and thus brought into being the very crown and epitome, the very essence and apex, of the Victorian seaside resort. From the start it was fastidiously organized, the intention being, it was said, that 'the town . . . shall resemble, as far as is practicable, the "country"'. The existing fishing village was left strictly as it was, and in a wide crescent along Llandudno Bay, and in elegant grid behind it, an archetypal pleasure-town was evolved. By the end of the nineteenth century it was more or less complete, the Mostyns were richer than ever, and Llandudno had entered the English language, variously mispronounced, as a synonym of respectable holiday recreation.

For a time it was tremendously fashionable. The shops along Mostyn Street were smart and expensive—Wartski the jewellers had a branch in Bond Street, London, but their headquarters at No. 93. All the best performers played the Pier Pavilion, and Jules Rivière, the French conductor of its orchestra, used to beat time with a bejewelled ivory baton, sitting in a gilded armchair facing the audience, and wearing a huge spray of orchids in his velvet jacket. The grand hotels along the front were patronized, as their advertisements loved to say, by Titled Families: Napoleon III and Bismarck both came to Llandudno, and for five weeks in 1890 Queen Elizabeth of Rumania lived in the town, casting such a spell upon its burghers that three streets were named for her, and a new civic motto was adopted from her farewell message to the town—*Hardd Hafan Hedd*, 'Beautiful Haven of Peace'.

Socially Llandudno has lost some cachet since then, trains and better roads bringing, as the Queen of Rumania's wine merchants might say, customers of a different class. Physically it is much the same as ever. The hotels still swing in a fine wide sweep along the bay, the boarding-houses still extend in their hundreds in that careful grid, the Isle of Man steamer is waiting for us still at the pier. A quaint old electric railway takes us rather creakily towards the summit of Great Orme, where a café and a souvenir shop await us, and a helicopter stands by for joy-rides: along the wide sands below the donkeys continue to trot, the beach-balls bounce and the striped umbrellas cheerfully tilt. Nothing much changed, we laugh in relief, just like last year, for to many people Llandudno is like a family possession—a family toy, perhaps, of the old sort: in winter it is generally packed away, but in summer it is taken out of the cupboard, dusted down and painted up, and is seen to work just as well as ever, from one generation to another.

In the thirteenth century it was decided to start a town at New Radnor, in Powys, Old Radnor having lately been destroyed in a battle. The site seems made for more than just a town, but a great city: a wide shallow bowl in the hills where road and river meet—just the place one might think for a Welsh Florence, spires, domes and statues among the poplared gardens down there in the valley haze. The first structure that greets you, indeed, is a memorial of truly metropolitan scale, honouring the local Victorian celebrity Sir George Cornewall Lewis and built by John Gibbs, designer of the Shakespeare Memorial in Stratford-upon-Avon. It is, however, the only metropolitan kind of thing that ever happened to New Radnor, for so unsuccessful was the promotion of the city by its original developers that to this very day some of its lots have never been taken up, and the whole grand idea has shrunk into a silent hamlet. The railway never bothered to go to New Radnor, the highway bypasses it, High Street, Broad Street, Water Street, New Gate Lane and its other village lanes afford only an ectoplasmic kind of city centre, within a spectral city wall.

Wales is not city country. There are only two towns in the place that would be recognized as cities anywhere in the world, and they are both on the southern coast, with thirty miles between them, and about a quarter of the entire Welsh population living within their limits. They are inevitably rivals, but they are also in some ways antitheses: different in history, different in personality, and very different in looks.

Swansea is much the *nicer*. Everyone knows that. Swansea is fun. Kingsley Amis the English novelist, who spent some years teaching at University College, Swansea, called it in retrospect the happiest time of his life. Dylan Thomas called Swansea an ugly lovely city. Swansea is part Irish, which gives it an extra slightly raffish fizz, but it is also backed by the strongly Welsh anthracite valleys of west Glamorgan, which keep it very Welsh. To Swansea market, the liveliest in Wales, come the cockles of Penclawdd and the edible seaweed: the port of Swansea is busy still, and ever and again into the Swansea sky, long since cleansed of its noxious copper fumes, those huge plumes of white steam erupt magnificently from the coolers of the Port Talbot steel-works, just around the bay.

Most of downtown Swansea was destroyed by German bombing during the Second World War, and architecturally the town is scarcely monumental. Its vestigial castle is almost hidden by the curtain walling of a telephone exchange, its once-dominant Royal South Wales Institute stands forlorn among the ring roads, even the famous covered market is now housed in a shopping centre of modish banality. The one great public edifice is the City Hall, bravely built in the 1930s to provide work for the unemployed, but less moving than bathetic—exquisitely made, fitted out with loving craftsmanship, its Great Hall decorated with Frank Brangwyn's flaming murals, yet somehow as unexciting as a cake that has failed to rise.

But the whole of Swansea, as against the detail, is a delight. It is rich in pleasant Edwardian terraces, breezy modern housing estates crown its heights, and the whole town looks down upon one of the grandest of all possible urban views—the wide sandy expanse of Swansea Bay, there at the very foot of the city, with the rocky headland of the Mumbles bounding the view in one direction, and those mighty white geysers like a civic symbol over the foreshore in the other. Better than the Bay of Naples, the writer Walter Savage Landor once declared this prospect, and the real beauty of Swansea lies in the grand release of it: behind, the tight winding valleys of the coalfield, their villages cheek by jowl, and the hinterland of Wales so introspective, so tangled in doubt and hazed in folklore—in front, that fine fresh crescent of the bay, that shine of the sea, those ships passing and re-passing out of the Atlantic and all the chance of the wide horizons!

Cardiff, however, is the capital of Wales, and Cardiff is where the TV studios are, and Cardiff Arms Park, and the Welsh National Opera, and the *Western Mail*, and in Cardiff the chocolate-voiced all-but-English businessmen drive about in their Mercedes, or scoff at the Welsh language in lounge bars ('Though mind you, I'm as good a Welshman as any one of them . . .') while their wives practise their Knightsbridge idioms over calorie-light lunches with Perrier. Cardiff docks are quiet these days, and hardly a ton of coal passes down the railway tracks from one year to the next, but the city has bounced back from successive depressions, all the same, in a heady effervescence of opportunism, fuelled frequently with nepotism and publicity campaigns. Cardiff is Post-Industrial Wales, living by its wits and its service trades: and less than a dozen miles from the acheing sadnesses of the Rhondda, where a way of life, a language and a faith was still wasting away in redundancy and unemployment, in 1983 a third of this city voted Conservative.

Bright, brash, profitable, clever and cosmopolitan though it is, Cardiff is weak on *presence*. It tries to be a national capital, but it remains a witness to the political impotence of Wales, and to the innately centrifugal instincts of the Welsh. In the days when it was the Marquis of Bute's coal port it had a functional cohesion, suspended between the poles of docks and castle: now it lies there more indeterminately, weakened by parks and demolition areas, with no powerful focus or density of form. The castle is still there, of course, and with its great gates and towers, and its long surrounding walls strewn with sculptured lions, bears, monkeys and dragons, provides as splendid and unexpected a centre-piece as any city could want. But it is only a show-place now, not a power-house, just as the glorious old commercial centre of Butetown is half moribund, half self-consciously resuscitated, and is surrounded by a waste of apparently abandoned developments. Solid bourgeois shopping streets, where once the trams and hansoms lurched, have been prettily converted into pedestrian precincts with potted shrubs and tessellated pavements: Tiger Bay is all gone, all its squalors, sprees and dangers, and down at the docks, where the colliers filled their holds to that clang and clatter of the tippers, a Museum of Maritime Affairs has been opened in a gaily done-up warehouse.

Superimposed upon it all, too late perhaps for conviction, are the institutions of a capital. There is a national concert hall (built partly with funds from the European Community), there is a national stadium, and a school of music and drama; and at a confusing angle to the lie of the city, in the first half of this century there arose a monumental centre of officialdom—a long grass rectangle surrounded by buildings, the National Museum and the Welsh Office and the University and the City Hall and the County Offices and the Temple of Peace and Health—imposing portentous structures, ornate with texts and statuary in the Washington or Canberra mode, with a national war memorial in the middle and flags flying here and there. It is fine enough in its way, and impresses foreigners expecting only coal-grimed slums and dereliction: but it is hardly Cardiff really, and for that matter hardly Wales.

No, a more truly Welsh city than either Cardiff or Swansea, the only city indeed truly unique to this country, is one that is not a city at all by conventional standards: the spider-city that fills the valley bottoms of the Gwent and east Glamorgan coalfields. For all those townships of the pits do form an urban unity, Treorchy running into Treherbert, Abercynon looking round the corner, or over the mountain hump, to Porth or Pontypridd. If its plan is fortuitous, following the coal-seams of the valley bottoms, in some ways it is a model of urban enlightenment, for always close to hand, however dense the streets, the bare open mountains rise above, making the whole seamed massif half town, half country, half tight neighbourly terrace, half empty moor. Each township has its own shops, its own chapels and churches, its own cinemas and bingo halls and choirs and multitudinous pubs and Rugby teams and local prides: yet nobody would deny that to the coal valleys as a whole—The Valleys, as all Wales calls them—there is a corporate personality, a temperament and a style as strong as any of those of any of the world's more ancient and more recognizable cities.

But there are many ridges up on those mountains where, by the nature of the terrain, the valley floors are entirely out of sight, and it is as though Aberdare and Abertillery have never been built at all. Only the rolling empty moorland shows, heaving away to the summits of the distant Brecon Beacons: and then it seems that the urban idea is only an irrelevance anyway, in this country of stones, winds and high empty places.

But now, what generic building shall we choose at last, to stand example for the whole Welsh art of building? The farm, only the farm! We will pick just one, out of so many. It is not one of your pristine specimens, such as English searchers for second homes prefer. It is not the simplest kind, nor the grandest. It is just an honest Welsh working farmhouse, called Pentwyn or The Pant or any other of the dozen or so familiar Welsh farm names that occur all over this country. It stands sheltered in the lee of a hill, and it has a small scrubby garden in front of it, with a low stone wall and a central pathway to the front door. A windbreak of pines or beeches, perhaps, was planted long ago to the north, and there are rooks up there, while a somewhat scratchy-looking vegetable patch can be glimpsed around one corner, running away to the fields behind. It is not a very tidy place. Its outbuildings, barns and garages are cluttered any old how around a concreted yard, and there are disused bits of machinery here and there, and cars parked messily on the grass outside, and petrol cans, and plastic bags. From the open door of the cow-house, as likely as not, a bucket of brownish fluid comes swooshing into the yard as you watch, and on the flagged path beside the front door a child's bicycle is tilted on its side, together with an old biscuit tin and one small gum-boot. Radio music sounds somewhere. The inevitable couple of farm dogs eye you warily. Swoosh, comes another bucketful of watery dung.

But sturdily there stands the old, old farm. It has been there, very likely, for 500 years. They have added a kitchen behind, with a roof of corrugated zinc, and there is a television aerial fixed to the chimney, but it does not matter. The front door is still a fine old slab of dark oak, clamped together with supplementary strips; the walls, though there seem to be one or two cracks in them, are three feet of stone and rubble; and though the windows seem inexplicably to have been twisted a little in their sockets, giving the whole structure a faintly relapsed appearance, still it stands there indestructible. There are initials and a date above the door—IB, 1695—but they bear no relation to the age of the house, recording only the day when Iorwerth Bevan decided to improve it with his posh new porch (stone seats on either side, roof of

rough stone slabs). It has no age, really. It is all Welsh ages subsumed into one, and is as far as the Welsh have ever gone in expressing themselves in architecture. It is perhaps not art, not poetry in stone or music made solid, but it certainly obeys Frank Lloyd Wright's injunction, and genially improves the hill it sits beside.

9. Wales and the World

To Englishmen, in the fifteenth century as in the twentieth, Wales often seemed on the edge of the earth, far from the sources of power or inspiration, away on civilization's wet and windy bounds. To Owain Glyndŵr it seemed very different, for if the mountains secluded Wales from England, the long coastline was like an open door to the world at large. Wales stood at the heart of the Celtic communities, with Gaelic Scotland, Ireland, Brittany and Cornwall in a crescent all around it, and for centuries it had been in contact with the continent of Europe. It was natural for Owain to look to France for allies, and offer his nation's allegiance direct to the Papacy. Only the course of history, coupled with the accident of geography, made Wales seem provincial or dependent: seen in another projection, or from another perspective, it was not on the periphery at all, but plumb in the world's centre!

FROM the summit of Holy Mountain, near Caergybi in Môn, the whole world can be seen. The oceans lie in a gleaming arc around, and are speckled here and there with the distant humps of continents, rising majestically from the surface of the water, and sometimes tipped with snow. No matter that it is only the Irish Sea really, that those beckoning lands are only the mountains of Ireland, the English Lake District or the Isle of Man: on the right day it is the world and all its oceans, and its grand presence out there to the west, uncluttered, free, has summoned Welsh people always out of their narrow valleys and frustrations.

Into that prospect, we are told, in the year 1170 the Welsh Prince Madog ap Owain Gwynedd, son to the royal house of Gwynedd, sailed away and discovered America. Two places confidently claim to be the site of his departure. Near Porthmadog stands the rock called Ynys Madog, Madog's island, which is no longer an island really, but just a craggy eminence above a wood: from here the prince and his thirteen ships sailed off, they say, through the treacherous bar without benefit of the *Wave of Life*, down the coast of Llŷn, past Ynys Enlli to the open sea. Alternatively, built into the rock garden of a pleasant seaside house at Rhos, near Llandudno, behind the now heavily embanked seafront, is an old structure of flint and stone, sweetly flowered, said to have been the actual quay from which the adventurer sailed: and not merely said to have been, indeed, but adamantly declared, for affixed to it a plaque simply announces: 'Prince Madoc sailed from here to Mobile, Alabama.'

Madog did not return to Wales—he was, a Triad tells us, one of the Three Who Made A Total Disappearance From the Isle of Britain—and he was supposed to have settled with his Welsh crews somewhere in the New World. This obscure legend was to have fateful consequences. In the sixteenth century the English revived it as a claim to historic rights on the American continent: if Prince Madog had gone there from Britain so long ago, it was ingeniously asserted, the English Crown had a prior claim to sovereignty in the New World. In the eighteenth century it was used again during the Anglo-Spanish struggle for the control of the upper Missouri valley: if proof could be found of an ancient Welsh presence there, all the West might be British.

Fortunately several explorers claimed to have encountered, far in the interior, tribes of distinctly Welsh characteristics, and these were enthusiastically identified as the descendants of Madog's original companions. A flood of stories came out of the hinterland, of Indo-Cambrian traditions, of Indian chieftains with Welsh names and white men saved from certain death by the intervention of Welsh-speaking elders. In particular a tribe called the Mandans, who were rather light of skin, were said to be just like Welshmen. They fished from coracles, they buried their dead in Celtic mounds, they spoke a language that shared many words with Cymraeg: for example *cwm* in Welsh, a valley, was *koom* in Mandan, *prydferth*, 'beautiful' in Welsh, was *prydfa* in Mandan, while the words *hen* (old), *glas* (blue), *aber* (a river mouth), *mawr* (big) and many more were claimed to be identical in both languages.

British settlers on the American seaboard were thrilled by these suggestions, which became one of the great myths of the country, and Welsh origins became highly fashionable among the colonists. No less excited were Welsh patriots at home, who saw in the affair confirmation that they were one of the seminal nations of the earth. Iolo Morgannwg proposed the establishment of a Welsh colony in the Mandan *bro*, and for a while spent his nights in the open, toughening up for the enterprise: and in 1792 the Welsh literati of London really did finance a more suitable Welsh traveller, John Evans of Waunfawr in Gwynedd, to go out there and discover the truth, not so much for the aggrandizement of Great Britain as for the glory of Wales.

Indeed it was under Spanish auspices that Evans went into the American interior, thus becoming one of the very last and most improbable of all the conquistadors; but he failed to find the Lost Tribe, and like Madog himself never came home to Wales, dying in New Orleans in 1798. The Mandans themselves were eventually exterminated by smallpox and Sioux, and the quest for the Welsh Indians petered out. Their legend has never quite died, however, and though it has not lately been claimed, as it used to be, that Montezuma was a Welshman, from time to time researchers still discover apparent Welsh affinities among the North American tribes, be it a similarity of numerals among the Kutenai of British Columbia (identical with the Welsh except for suffixes), or remarkable resemblances between the castle of Dolwyddelan and pre-Columbian earthworks in Tennessee.

A tantalizing fable! In its half-legendary origins, in its subtle ramifications, in its derring-do and its absurdities, the story of Madog, the Mandans and John Evans Waunfawr is like a protracted allegory: and in a way it is, for one can read the tale of the lost prince and his followers as a figure of ancient Welsh impulses. Facing the open liberty of the sea from their always circumscribed homeland, the Welsh have habitually sailed away in search of foreign truths and advantages, and in return have absorbed over the generations countless strangers bearing examples from other shores.

A strange and magnificent stone stands inside the parish church of Llandudoch St Dogmael's, on the estuary of the Teifi river in Dyfed. Down one edge it has a strange series of slashes, like axe-cuts, some long, some short: on its face it bears the Latin words SAGRANI FILI CUNOTAMI. This is the Rosetta Stone of Wales. From its texts, we are told, in 1848 scholars first deciphered the meaning of the Ogham script, whose letters are those variegated slashes, and whose riddle was left behind on the shore by the first and most consistent of Wales's foreign visitors, the Irish.

It is only sixty miles across the Irish Sea at its narrowest point. In the earliest times, in the half-imaginary times recorded by the tales of the Mabinogion, Ireland was closer still; Brân was able to wade through the water to Dublin, and there was a constant coming and going of kings, giants and wizards. More than fifty stones in Wales bear Ogham messages, many an ancient circle is named still for the Irish, and the very word *Gwyddelig* came in later years to mean, in a misty kind of way, extremely old. Often and again, in lonelier and flatter and wetter parts of west Wales, some indefinable combination of atmosphere and allusion makes one feel that Irish spirits are about.

After the Roman withdrawal the Irish became the familiars of Wales, raiding the coastlands, settling here and there, even establishing transient kingdoms—Brycheiniog, Breconshire to the English, was named for its Irish founder, Brychan Brycheiniog, Llŷn bears the same name as Leinster. Welsh place-names ending in *-ach* are generally supposed to be mementoes of Irish governance long ago, and many Irish words have gone into the Welsh language: in some parts of

Dyfed, when they count the cows, they do so in an antique Irish numerology.

Then the Irish saints came, too, bringing with them their skills of Celtic decoration, and the students for the Welsh monastic centres, probably the first overseas students ever to come to Britain—St Patrick, who may have been a Welshman anyway, is said to have been educated at the monastery of Llanilltyd Fawr. A well-beaten path across the peninsula of Dewisland was followed by Irish missionaries on their way to Brittany and the evangelical fields of central Europe: Samson, for instance, who was born in Ireland, established several churches in Wales and ended up as St Samson of Dol, one of the best-loved of the Breton saints.

And besides these holy persons, thousands upon thousands of simpler immigrants came from Ireland into Wales. In the Middle Ages the clan of witches who overawed the people of Llanddona, Môn, and who were said to have arrived out of the sea in rudderless craft, were probably only poor Irish malefactors, pushed out to sea in an open boat as the Irish custom was. In the seventeenth century George Owen reported that whole parishes of Dyfed swarmed with Irish refugees from one trouble or another, who rode around the country on horseback selling poteen. The roads, railways, bridges, dams, canals and power stations of Wales have largely been built by Irish muscle, and in the years of the South Wales industrial boom the Irish formed teeming colonies of their own, working for the lowest wages of anyone, and expecting the least comforts—they were often brought to Wales as ballast in returning colliers. In the big southern towns Irish quarters came into being: Ethel Street in Canton, Cardiff, staunchly chapel on one side, was solid Irish Catholic on the other.

They are still around. There are still Irish people in Ethel Street, and the English spoken in Swansea still has a recognizable brogue to it. Just as Irish pedlars used to roam the Welsh countryside, so Irish tinkers in their shambled cars and caravans are familiar figures today on the roads that lead to the western ferry ports. Wherever the Irish have settled the Catholic Church has survived too, and sometimes it puts down new roots when fresh tides of Irishmen arrive to build, dig or demolish something. The Irish radio services are listened to everywhere, if only inadvertently by motorists twiddling their knobs at random, and on the north coast Irish television provides a couple of extra channels for Welsh viewers, with a Gaelic option now and then for eager pan-Celticists. Ironically in the footsteps of St Patrick came, fifteen centuries later, the Revd Ian Paisley, the most irreconcilable of Ulster Protestant militants, to learn his theology at the South Wales Baptist College, Barry.

Yet for all the ancient continuity of these links, for all those moments of sudden Irishness, for all the fact that the Welsh seals of the Dyfed coast frequently swim across to the rocks of Wexford—even so, the present links between the peoples are not intimate. Brân did not cross to Dublin in any spirit of fraternity—he went to revenge the wrongs suffered by his sister Branwen, who was made to work as a cook in her Irish husband's court, and had her ears cuffed daily by a butcher. If Celtic Christianity formed a bond between the two countries, the Celticity of language did not help for long, because by the Middle Ages the two branches had widely diverged, and today are almost foreign to each other. The Welsh have by no means always welcomed the Irish communities in their midst, either: in the industrial valleys they were often detested as under-cutters and strike-breakers, and suspected as bringers of disease, resulting in squalid ghettos of wild papist aliens within whose confines no self-respecting Welshwoman would care to be seen.

The temperaments of the two people are very different, for all their ethnic connections—the Irish so stormy, so obdurate, the Welsh so evasive, but generally so conciliatory—and in modern times it is really only the idea of nationalism that has given them much in common. The political passions of the Irish have often found their echoes and sympathies in Wales: as long ago as the 1840s, when the English were applying the harsh dogma of imperialist market forces to the ameliora-tion of Irish famine, it was noticed that officials with names like Griffiths, Evans or Thomas were distinctly more sympathetic to Irish feelings than the Bullingdons or the Harcourt-Smiths. Occasionally it is rumoured that there are connections between the most violent of Welsh nationalists and the Irish Republican Army, but generally the collusion is less precise: graffiti on Welsh walls support Irish hunger strikers or imprisoned activists, processions march sometimes, and on the day of the Prince of Wales's wedding, in 1981, several score young Welsh republicans took the boat to Dun Laoghaire and spent the day carousing merrily with sympathetic Irishmen in the pubs of Dublin.

*

Another old colony in Wales was the plantation of the Flemings. Unlike the Irish, they put down roots in particular parts of the country, and an ancient border still divides their chief settlement from Walia Pura, Wales of the Welsh.

It is called the Landsker, a Viking word it seems, and though it is unmarked, you know you are crossing it when you pass through the rocky gorge of Trefgarn, in southern Dyfed, which is fortified on either side by ancient earthworks in the woods. It was here that the Normans advancing from the southern coast were held by the Welsh, and there was established a no man's land running from coast to coast of the Dyfed peninsula, mostly low hills and marshland, with a line of strongholds to prevent its violation. Until the Second World War this cultural frontier was maintained: south of the line no Welsh was spoken, north of it little English, to the south were great estates, to the north it was smallholders' country. Even now most of southern Dyfed hardly regards itself as Welsh at all, and is innately suspicious of everything north of the Landsker.

Some time in the Middle Ages a colony of Flemings was established, under English patronage, along this line, their headquarters being an expanse of flatland, Y Rhos, which was protected by the various winding branches of the Cleddau rivers. They were, reported the *Bruty Tywysogyon* fastidiously, 'a certain folk of strange origin and customs', who drove out the local inhabitants and gradually extended their presence over a wide countryside around. Flemings also settled in the peninsula of Gŵyr, and other parts of Glamorgan, but this was their chief stronghold, and it became a powerful factor in Welsh affairs.

Nobody is quite sure why the Flemings came. Some say they asked for asylum when their own lands in the Low Countries, then ruled by the kings of England, were disastrously inundated; others believe they were forcibly transferred to Wales. However it happened, they proved invaluable allies of the English power. Dogged, efficient, excellent soldiers, as alien as they could be to the tumultuous and unpredictable Welsh, they adopted the English language and were so loyal to the Crown that English people even now like to call the southern part of Dyfed 'Little England beyond Wales', and often prefer to spend their Welsh holidays in its less foreign atmosphere. The Flemings never compromised with the Welsh, and fought them ferociously on behalf of the English. They provided some of the toughest opposition to Owain Glyndŵr, and never did accept his authority—150 years after the event a doctor of Flemish descent, Thomas Phaer of Cilgerran in Dyfed, wrote a soliloquy in thirty-four stanzas entitled 'Howe Owen Glendour seduced by false prophesies, tooke upon him to be prince of Wales, and was by Henry then prince thereof, chased to the mountaynes, were he miserably dyed for lacke of foode . . .'.

Over the years the Flemings became indistinguishable from English people, and to this day they hold themselves separate from the Welsh. In Gŵyr as in Dyfed a recognizable no man's land, of common and rough pasture, separates the old Flemish territory from the Welshry to the north, and 'up in the Welsh' say people disparagingly south of the Landsker, when they want to refer to the rest of Wales. It is not surprising that the most absolutely un-Welsh of all the towns of Wales is the old seaport of Tenby, which the Flemings made rich by their skill and industry. Though this was celebrated by Welsh poets long before the Flemings came, and is now also known on signposts once again as Dinbych-y-Pysgod, Little Fortress of the Fish, it is otherwise all but innocent of Welshness, and stands above its twin bays, on one of the grandest stretches of the South Wales coast, as though it has been deposited there *in toto* from somewhere altogether different.

As it happens it is the most amiable of all Welsh seaside resorts, too. Surrounded still, in its ancient centre, by a stout town wall, it is not in the least like a castle town. It is not aristocratic, but thoroughly mercantile, and feels full to this day of plump hard-working burgher-folk, complacent about their profits, proud of their aldermanic rights, aloof to all the doubts and anxieties, of language, of loyalty, of nationality, that plague people 'up in the Welsh'. Hugger-mugger run the streets of Tenby, this way and that inside the walls, and there are fine Georgian houses along the sea-cliffs, and a tall-steepled parish church, bang in the middle of town, which speaks spaciously of old wealth and satisfaction.

Today it is all tourism. The harbour built for the merchantmen and the fishing-fleet is given over to pleasure-craft, and most of those waterfront houses are hotels and boarding-houses. Still, the little town feels above all industrious and astute, as though its merchants are still hard at work at their lading tables, or awaiting a shipment from Flanders on the rising tide.

Weaving their circumspect way through this far corner of Europe we see the two great wandering peoples of the earth, the Jews and the Gypsies, achieving their Welsh incarnations.

The Jews came early, perhaps in Roman times, when they were dispersed among the nations after the fall of Jerusalem—Leland, writing in the sixteenth century, says that when the Welsh dug up Roman coins, they called it Jewish money. The oldest surviving sign of their presence in Wales, though, is a graffito scratched long ago by some intrepid heretic upon a wall of St Winifred's miracle-working well at Holywell—Hirsh Winshook Shacklickson, it allegedly says in the Hebrew script, and one wonders who would have been the more horrified to find it there, the Catholic guardians of the shrine or Mr Shacklickson's rabbi. By the early eighteenth century Jewish names were cropping up in the cosmopolitan community of Swansea, and soon Jewish settlers were appearing in small numbers all over Wales. One hears of a Jewish banker at Haverfordwest in the 1800s, and a Jewish Mayor of Swansea in the 1840s, and by 1909 the Wartskis had set up their celebrated jewellery shop in Llandudno, setting out direct from Mostyn Street to buy the gems of the Russian royal family and King Farouk of Egypt's Fabergé collection. In 1910 the great industrialist Alfred Mond became a Liberal MP for Swansea despite violently anti-Semitic opposition from the Tories—'Vales for the Velsh', their posters mockingly proclaimed. The reclusive painter Heinz Koppel, a German Jew who came to Wales during the Second World War and died there in 1980, revolutionized attitudes to art in Merthyr Tydfil, is represented at the Tate Gallery and is thought by some connoisseurs to have been a kind of genius. In Cardiff in our own time the Abse family have produced one of the most resilient of Welsh politicians, Leo Abse, and one of the most gifted of Anglo-Welsh poets, Dannie, while the Russian Jewish family of Pollecoff, far from all fellow-religionists at the extremity of Wales, gave the little Gwynedd town of Pwlhelli not only a mayor, but a member of the Gorsedd too. In 1982, for the first time in recorded history, a prayer was said in a synagogue in the Welsh language: Rabbi Kenneth Cohen had learnt how to say it from a Teach Yourself Welsh cassette.

This is how Israel Firman, a well-known herbalist and conjuror of Gelli-groes, Gwent, was described by a not very friendly newspaper reporter in 1839: 'attenuated and sapless frame, tall, gaunt, withered . . . a profusion of long, grissly hair flung back from his wrinkled and projecting forehead . . . sunken hollow cheeks, shelving eyebrows, piercing, jet-black eyes'. But in general the Jews have been easily absorbed into Welsh life, sometimes indeed giving up their faith and becoming ardent chapel-goers. In many ways the Welsh are very like Jews themselves, in looks as in temperament, in their love of words and music as in their clannishness. Jewish names are very common as Welsh surnames—Jacobs, Isaacs, Samuels, Moses—and in their chapel heyday the Welsh were conditioned to think of themselves as the Lost Tribe, living as they did in villages like Nasareth (Gwynedd) and Bethlehem (Dyfed), and knowing, thanks to Sunday school, the map of Palestine a great deal better than they did their own.

It was indeed George Adam Smith's historical atlas of the Holy Land that Lloyd George, as Prime Minister of Great Britain, sent to the British commander in the Middle East, General Sir Edmund Allenby, on the eve of his advance into Palestine in 1917—with its maps of Gilead and Hauran, its assessment of Palestine in the time of the Maccabees, it would be, he thought, 'a better guide to a military leader whose task was to reach Jerusalem than any survey to be found in the pigeon-holes of the War Office'. And perhaps it was partly Lloyd George's lifelong familiarity with the lands of the Bible that led him, that same year, to approve the Balfour Declaration promising a Jewish national home in Palestine—a Welsh Baptist from Llŷn opening the first fateful door towards the foundation of the State of Israel.

There have been Welsh gypsies for generations too, well known on the old circuit of itinerant pedlars and craftsmen, horse-dealers and fairground boxers: but just outside the porch of the little church at Llangelynnin in Gwynedd, which we visited in the last chapter, a stone in the ground commemorates the man generally accepted as the Father of Welsh gypsydom proper: Abram Wood, patriarch of *Y Teulu Wood*, a clan of true Romanies who settled in Wales at the beginning of the eighteenth century, and who called themselves simply and grandly The Welsh Gypsies.

Wood had come to Wales from Somerset in England, where he was known as a Gypsy King, and in 1799, at the end of a long life, died in a cowshed on the hill behind Llangelynnin. He was probably carried to his burial on the horse-bier we saw hanging in the church there, and was entered in the parish register as 'Abram Wood, a travelling gypsy'. Though he must have been an intermittent church-goer at best, they buried him in a place of honour, immediately outside the porch, and there on a slab of slate you may see his initials still.

His descendants presently forgot where he was buried, remembering it only as 'a lonesome quiet little place by the seaside'. They themselves prospered, and growing Welsher as the generations passed, became well known and well respected all over the country. For a century and a half, until the end of the nineteenth century, they lived the classic life of the gypsy tribe, moving from county to county in a great company of horses and donkeys and dogs, playing their violins and laughing as they went, with an old grandmother, we are told, habitually bringing up the rear on a white ass. They spoke Welsh as well as Romany, they knew every salmon pool and trout stream there was to be fished, they found seasonal work on farms or lived by horse-dealing, basket-making and fortune-telling. They were welcomed nearly everywhere, and 'in truth', as one of them wrote in retrospect, 'those days were good days, the old country was like heaven on earth then'.

Presently *Y Teulu Wood*, nevertheless, abandoned their migratory ways, married into Welsh families, and became known above all as musicians. Like gypsies everywhere they adopted the music of the country, and by the nineteenth century they were not only the prime fiddlers, but even more the prime harpers of Wales. Among Abram's own grandchildren, three became harpists and one a fiddler (two were fortune-tellers and only one, as the family records say, 'had the misfortune of being Transported'). Some took jobs as resident harpists in grand houses, others wandered the country playing their music anywhere it was wanted, in pubs, in farms, at weddings and dances. By the third generation John Roberts had become the most famous of Welsh harpers, and he raised an entire orchestra of musicians to support him. They travelled the country *en ensemble*, he and his wife and eleven of their children, riding a huge horse-drawn dray loaded with all their harps and violins. They were billed as The Famed Family of Welsh Harpists, or The Original Cambrian Minstrels, they were engaged to play for innumerable visiting swells, and their crowning glory came when they were all taken in a special train to Y Bala to entertain Queen Victoria of England at Pale Hall, the house with the sculpted railway engine on it, when the whole clan, in tails and boiled shirts, performed upon their gleaming triple-stringed harps in the great plushy drawing-room.

This was the climax of Welsh Romany, and the Robertses basked in its glory. Though Lloyd W. Roberts of Machynlleth still described himself as a Harpist, Fishing Attendant and Fly Dresser, J. L. Roberts of Llandrindod announced that he had played before Queen Victoria, King Edward VII, the Queen of Rumania and the Empress of Russia, while Albert Roberts of Newtown claimed to be Chief Harpist According to the Ancient Rights and Privileges of the British Bards. The patriarchal John Roberts died in 1894, honoured by then as The Oldest Living Welsh Harpist, and though there are descendants all over Wales still, the old tradition of *Y Teulu Wood*, The Welsh Gypsies, died in Newtown with him.

You will not often see a true Welsh gypsy now, the strain having long been dispersed and disseminated, and the old *joie de vivre* of the wandering Woods has been degraded into the harassed squalor of mumpers and drop-outs. The tradition seems mostly forgotten. 'We're not gypsies really', says an old lady resignedly in the gypsy camp at King's Moor outside Tenby, where generations of gypsies have stayed, where the young Augustus John used to go to paint the dark romantic faces, but which now looks, with its semi-permanent shacks and hangdog trailers, more like a South African location than a Romany encampment—'gypsies came from a foreign part', she says, 'Rumania or some place like that . . .'. Just occasionally, though, in the patrician stance of a scrap-iron merchant, or the speckled scarf of a dealer at the Llanybydder horse-fair, you may recognize a flash of the old heritage, to remind you of the days when the Welsh gypsies used to gather for their merry assemblies at Craig Aderyn, the rock of the cormorants, dancing and fiddling and harp-playing far into the night, telling tales of legendary forebears and eating feasts of stolen salmon beside the blazing fires.

The French have come! They came in the guise of Normans, they came as monks to the monasteries, they came as Gascon knights to quell the Welsh rebellions, they came with ships and men to help Owain Glyndŵr, and in February 1797 they came in two frigates, a corvette and a lugger, under the command of a 70-year-old Irish-American, to launch the last foreign invasion of mainland Britain.

A small slab above the sea, a few miles west of Abergwaun, marks the site of this desperate enterprise. The invasion force consisted in the main of a thousand untrained convicts especially released from gaol, and dressed in dyed uniforms captured from the British. Its commander, William Tate, had been ordered to destroy the ports of Bristol, Chester and Liverpool, to divert attention from a proposed French invasion of Ireland, but finding this task beyond his powers, he had decided to invade Wales instead, hoping that disaffected Welsh patriots would rise to his support. This was a mistake. The corps of criminals, once ashore, immediately set about looting, eating and getting drunk, never advancing more than a mile or two inland. The Welsh did *not* rise in sympathy. The ships hastily withdrew. Two Frenchmen were killed by a farmer and his son, another was run through with a pitchfork, and when the Militia and the Fencibles arrived in Abergwaun under the command of Lord Cawdor, after less than twenty-four hours General Tate sued for peace—as he convincingly explained it, 'the circumstances under which the body of the French troops under my command were landed at this place, renders it unnecessary to attempt any military operations, as they would tend only to bloodshed and pillage'. The surrender was negotiated in the Royal Oak inn at Abergwaun, where they still preserve the table on which it was signed, and all those scallywag commandos were imprisoned (though twenty-five of them, having chatted up some girls in Pembroke, enlisted their help in escaping, and in a stroke of brilliant impudence sailed away to France in Lord Cawdor's own yacht).

It was reasonable of the French, all the same, to suppose that the Welsh would rise in their support against the English monarchy, for the *cognoscenti* of the country were enthusiastically in favour of the French Revolution. Two Welsh thinkers in fact had played important roles in it. The radical ideas of Dr Richard Price of Bridgend, author of *The Nature of Civil Liberty*, were profoundly influential among the French Jacobins—when he died in 1791 the French Assembly went into mourning for him. And even more respected in Paris was another Welsh dissenting minister, David Williams of Eglwysilan in Glamorgan. In 1782 he had published his *Letter of Political Liberty*, a blueprint for revolutionary reform so explosive that when it was put into French its translator was promptly committed to the Bastille, and after the Revolution he was invited to Paris to help write a new constitution, and made an honorary citizen of the Republic.

The English, too, suspected the Welsh might collaborate with General Tate. In fact, far from inspiring any Welsh *sans-cullottes*, the landing at Abergwaun frightened many Welsh radicals into more conservative views, but there were dark accusations of collusion all the same, and nasty things were said about those girls at Pembroke and the fate of Cawdor's yacht. To the Welsh no less than the Scots, after all, France had always been the hope over the water: it was from France that Owain Lawgoch plotted his ascent to the throne of Wales, from France that Glyndŵr got his foreign fleets and armies, and from France that Henry Tudor had landed in Dyfed to seize the English crown.

The Welsh have always been closer to the French than the English have felt themselves to be. In later years the greatest of all foreign markets for South Wales coal was France—in the 1900s one French shipping line had a fleet of thirty ships carrying nothing else but steam coal from Port Talbot to Rouen, and hundreds of other ships took coal to Nantes and Bordeaux in return for French pit-props. Many French firms opened offices in South Wales, and French families became prominent in local affairs: one of the archetypal sounds of Penarth in the 1920s was the peculiar whoop of the steamer *St. Andresse*, owned by a well-known resident Frenchman, which used to come in on one tide for its cargo of coal for France, and leave on the very next. At the same time a generation of Welsh seamen learnt to know the harbours of northern France, and were familiar customers in their bars and cafés, just as today there are many Welsh truck-drivers who, in the course of their great journeys across the motorways of Europe, take the Red Dragon and the Welsh voice into vinous restaurants of Provence, and snug routiers' havens of High Savoy. The Welsh and the French generally get on well: they are temperamentally compatible, by and large, and no insuperable barrier of history divides them.

In 1812 another French prisoner of the Napoleonic wars, a Lieutenant Augeraud, found himself immured in one of the most isolated, not to say dead-and-alive, of all Welsh market towns, Llanfyllin in the heart of Powys. He was a fine fellow, 25 years old, brown eyes, five foot eleven, and he amused himself by painting a series of cheerful murals on the walls of his billet—still to be seen, endearing naïfs of waterfalls, sheep and rather Chinese-looking Alps, in a room above Jones the chemists—and by falling in love with the rector's daughter. The Revd William Williams, whose face Augeraud had repeatedly caricatured, it is said, during sermons in the parish church, was adamantly opposed to the romance, and arranged to have the lieutenant repatriated. He thrived, had the Legion of Honour pinned to his breast by Napoleon himself, and went on to enjoy a distinguished military career; but he did not forget Miss Williams, and when the wars were over he came back to Britain, married her, and took her home to France, where they lived happily ever after.

Long years afterwards, when Colonel and Madame Augeraud had died in the fullness of their years, and the whole romantic tale had gone into antiquarian lore and Welsh legend, their grandson returned to Llanfyllin, where it all began: and he is buried there now, in the churchyard of St Myllin, in the same tomb as his great-grandfather the irreconcilable rector.

A young man from Tregaron, or perhaps Llanystumdwy, plays a guitar in Rennes, the university town of Brittany, and sings in a resonant baritone an old Welsh lyric:

> *Rhodio yr oeddwn, a'm calon yn brudd,*
> *Ar ddydd Llun y bore, ar doriad y dydd;*
> *Mi glywn y gog lwydlas yn tiwnio mor fwyn*
> *Ar ochr bryn uchel, ar gangen o lwyn . . .*

> Strolling I was, my heart sad,
> On Monday morning at the break of day;
> I heard the grey cuckoo tuning so sweet
> On the side of a high hill, on a branch of a bush . . .

If the people hurrying by notice at all, they do not seem surprised by the performance. The young man does not look in the least foreign to them. The tune sounds vaguely familiar. The lyric seems to be in a blurred approximation of the Breton. For Wales and Brittany are linked by an unbreakable umbilical, the Celtic connection: not just the misty connection between Gauls and Ancient Britons, but more exactly the fact that Brittany was colonized in the fifth or sixth century by Celts from the British Isles—Great Britain was called 'Great' in the first place only to differentiate it from that smaller Britain over the Channel.

Though the languages of the two peoples have diverged since then, still this association has never been broken. In the Age of the Saints there was a traffic of wandering holy men between the countries, and when the Normans arrived in Wales they brought with them many Breton soldiers, if only one assumes to ease the language problem. The town of Monmouth, in particular, was a stronghold of Bretonism in Norman Wales: its garrison was always Breton, and Breton priests were also stationed there—among them, very likely, the town's most celebrated son, the historian Geoffrey of Monmouth who first propagated the Arthurian legend across the Continent. The Welsh, we may suppose, were more at home with these Celts than with their Norman masters, and over the generations doubtless much Breton blood came back to Wales through the seed of the soldiery.

The link was to be maintained, too, long after Norman kings gave way to English. Trade between Brittany and the southern Welsh ports was always brisk; Breton fishermen worked the Welsh fishing grounds, Breton onion men toured the Welsh market towns on their bicycles; Welsh exiles, like Henry Tudor's Uncle Jasper, took refuge in Brittany; the Revd T. Price of Cwmdu, Powys, produced his Breton Bible. Today a host of students, folk singers, littérateurs and patriots travel to and from between the festivals, demonstrations, libraries and language schools of the two countries. They are like sufferers seeking mutual therapy: citizens of minority cultures, both threatened always by the presence of a metropolitan neighbour, linked somewhere in the folk memory by the knowledge of common origins, and happy to puzzle together, as through those spindly family letters you find in chests in attics, through their bewilderingly related orthographies.

If that plaque on the wall at Rhos confidently announces Prince Madog's place of embarkation, at Mobile, Alabama, a sign erected in 1953 by the Daughters of the American Revolution commemorates his place of arrival with even more assurance. 'In Memory of Prince Madoc', it says, 'who landed on the shores of Mobile Bay in 1170 and left behind, with the Indians, the Welsh language.' We may take this too as figurative: for whether Madog really landed there or not, whether any Indians really did learn to mutate their consonants, certainly travellers from Wales have left an ineffaceable mark upon the map and character of the USA.

'Is this California?' asked the infant Bob Owen Croesor when, in the early 1900s, he was first taken from his high farmstead home to the neighbouring village of Carreg in Gwynedd. He assumed California was somewhere around, having heard of so many people going there, and when he went to school in the village he found there not a single child without a relative in the United States. At the same time in South Wales, from where thousands of men had taken their families to work in the burgeoning coalfields of Pennsylvania, the names of Scranton and Wilkes-Barre were almost as familiar as those of Bargoed or Pontarddulais, and a familiar imprecation was 'Oh to hell with you, go to Philadelphia and feed the canaries!' The American connection was close and living, and in many American towns *eisteddfodau* were regularly held, Welsh chapels thrived, and Welsh newspapers were published.

This was only the culmination of a long association, even if you don't count Madog and the Mandans. Welshmen had been prominent in the creation of the Great Republic. At home the Welsh literati were passionate supporters of the American Revolution, which they saw as a blow for their own radical values, and indeed American independence has been described (by the historian Gwyn A. Williams) as the first modern Welsh political cause, the first to excite the interests and arguments of all educated Welshmen. In the uprising of the thirteen colonies people like Iolo Morgannwg and Dr Price Llantrisant saw the beginning of a new social order, akin in their minds to the Welsh system of society they had long idealized in their imaginations, and offering Wales too hope for a different future.

And in the field, Welshmen were no less fervent. Among the generals of the Revolutionary Army, fourteen were Welshmen: of the fifty-six men who signed the Declaration of Independence, eighteen were of Welsh descent. Robert Morris of Montgomery stock was the financier of the revolution, Dr Richard Price, the man mourned by the French Republic's assembly, drew up the American Republic's first budget. When once it was established successive waves of Welsh people emigrated to the new society, escaping enclosures, high rents, tithes, religious prejudice and Englishmen, and sometimes hoping to create a sort of Welsh National Home on the other side.

Much of Pennsylvania was settled in the first place by Welsh Quakers, who stamped it with their own sober character and gave it their own melodious names, Bryn Mawr, Narberth, Bala-Cynwyd. Whole families of Baptists went from Swansea, Glamorgan, to Swanzey, Connecticut. In Tennessee, in the 1850s, the Revd Samuel Roberts of Llanbrynmair in Gwynedd, known in the Welsh literary memory as 'S.R.' the radical publicist, established a disastrously unsuccessful Utopia on land unfortunately bought from people with dubious title to it: in New Cambria, western Pennsylvania, intended to be 'the home of a free and enlightened people when the Old Cambria is neglected and despised', the whole structure of Welsh Nonconformist life was reconstructed slate for slate. The Welsh Americans were nothing if not idealist: in the Civil War they stood almost as one man with the North, and this is the message that a visiting Welsh minister, Morgan Rees, ventured to offer to 'Mad Anthony' Wayne's armies, fighting the Indians in 1794:

'Tis to be lamented that the Frontiers of America have been peopled in many places by men of bad morals. It will therefore be necessary to have such communications with the different tribes as to convince them of the good will of Americans in general. Some Americans might have their residence in the Indian towns, and the Indians, in like manner, reside in some of the principal towns on the frontiers, so that Americans and Indians might become one people.

'Mad Anthony''s response is not recorded.

Thomas Jefferson liked to claim that his father was born within sight of Snowdon, and in return the memorial hall at Llanfair Ceiriog, which we visited in an earlier chapter, has erected a commemorative plaque: it was unveiled by a representative of the State Department in 1933, and says simply: 'To the Memory of a Great Welshman, Thomas Jefferson'. A more suggestive reminder of the old relationship, though, is the farmhouse called Penbanc, near Llanboidy in Dyfed. This is one of your proper Welsh farms—reached up a long, long drive off a country lane, embedded in a scoop among its own fields, guarded by cheerful barking dogs, snug and simple in the old Welsh way. An open fire burns in its parlour. Ornaments are ranked about. The lady of the house and her daughter, as likely as not, are jam-making or chopping marrow in the kitchen, and even as you stand on the doorstep the farmer arrives all smiles and muddy boots from the yard. This was once the home of the Adams family, whose scion Henry Adams emigrated to America from England in about 1636. His great-grandson was the second President of the United States, his great-great-grandson was the sixth President; but at Penbanc, having more important things to think of, they know nothing about it.

From many of the ports of Wales, throughout the nineteenth century, emigrants sailed to America, travelling often in groups of families, and seen off sometimes with a farewell sermon on the beach. All over Wales posters advertised forthcoming sailings of the *Albion* from Caernarfon, the Fine Fast-Sailing *Triton* from Aberteifi, or the ships of the South Wales Atlantic Steamship Company ('Mattresses Provided Free'); later there were repeated attempts to maintain a liner service, the apogee of the trade occurring when one day in 1909 the citizens of Abergwaun woke up to find lying in their harbour the magnificent four-funnelled *Mauretania*, sailing for New York next day. She never returned to Abergwaun, however, the Atlantic trade petered out, and the saga of the Welsh hegira to America was soon all but forgotten. Yet it was different from most great emigrations; for one thing most of its travellers were going reluctantly, and for another they travelled in a spirit all their own, nearer in kind to the original traffic of the Puritans, three centuries before, than the vast contemporary movement of Germans, Italians, Scandinavians and Englishmen to the New World.

When the *Albion* sailed as promised from Caernarfon in 1818, with a Cardigan master (Captain Llewelyn Davies) and an all-Welsh crew, the complement of passengers, mostly from Llŷn, soon organized shipboard life on strictest chapel lines. They elected for themselves a committee of elders, a *seiat* so to speak, and they determined that swearing and blasphemy should be punished by a half ration of water and the wearing of a badge, that proven liars should be obliged to clean the privy for three days, and that chamber-pots should be emptied overboard before people were up and about ('Penalty, to be the last to be served with food'). They cleaned the ship by rote. They inspected the children regularly for cleanliness. And they talked, and talked, and talked, about Wales.

'Oh!' confided Mr Peter Lewis in his diary, translated 140 years later by Dr Ll. Wyn Griffith, 'Oh, our old country and its inhabitants. Many were our troubles and griefs in it; but now farewell: good fortune to its peoples and a blessing on their endeavours, peace within its walls and prosperity in its mansions.' On 24 May, three days out of Caernarfon, some of the crew said they could still see Wales. On 26 May a man went up to the captain, who was taking sights, and sadly asked him 'Can you see Llanuwchllyn with that glass?' On 13 June, when they saw their first icebergs, they spent a long time discussing what they looked like. 'At last we decided that one was like Moel y Gath in Merioneth, the other like the head by Garn where Gabriel Davies grazes his sheep.'

But when, half-way over, the *Albion* passed a ship bound for Britain, and Captain Davies asked if anyone would like to join her, nobody wanted to: and by the time they sailed into Amboy, New Jersey, and the

336

committee had seen that everybody was washed and properly dressed for the arrival, they were properly gratified when the American customs men said they were just the sort of immigrants America needed —'Welsh, Scots and Germans were the best'.

And what became of them? We shall never know. They were doubtless assimilated in the end, for once they had got over their homesickness, abandoned their language, and perhaps blurred the edges of their idealism, Welsh immigrants generally became altogether American. They were seldom so assiduous as the Scots or the Irish in cherishing their ethnic image, and the several Welsh colonies soon faded into the American background, leaving only exotic place-names behind—Bala, Kansas, or Gwalia Teg, Nebraska. Many eminent Americans, all the same, have liked to talk of their Welsh origins. D. W. Griffiths the film director wildly boasted of his descent from 'Griffydd King of Wales'. Frank Lloyd Wright claimed Iolo Morgannwg's bardic symbol as his own family crest. Governors, senators, generals, bankers, actors, writers, musicians, all look back, if only from a comfortable distance, from Pentagon or Capitol Hill, from Hollywood or Wall Street, to the distant hills and swart terrace towns that fostered them far away, in those 8,000 square bumpy miles that hardly one of their fellow-countrymen in a thousand could place upon the *Reader's Digest Atlas*.

Now and then the tide has gone the other way, and Americans have come to Wales. In the 1780s the privateer John Paul Jones, 'Father of the US Navy', repeatedly turned up along these shores. He bombarded Abergwaun once, sailing away with 500 guineas ransom money, he often watered his frigate *Ranger* at Caldy Island, and in a famous anecdote he once went ashore anonymously at Tenby—dressed all in black, the legends say, with a riding whip in his hand. The *Ranger* carried a Welsh quartermaster, and Jones was much admired by South Wales seamen, who used to sing a song about him:

> An American frigate, a ship of great fame,
> Mounting guns forty-four, from New York she came,
> For to cruise in the Channel of old England of great fame,
> With a noted commander, Paul Jones was his name . . .

American warships were in Wales waters again in 1916, when the

Atlantic Fleet had a base at Caergybi, in the Second World War thousands upon thousands of American servicemen passed through Wales on their way to the Normandy invasion, and today there is a very secret American tracking station at Brawdy in Dyfed, by whose domes and electronic riggings the prowling submarines of the Atlantic bottom are located.

American scholars are always to be found in the libraries of Wales, collating versions of medieval *cywyddau*, or dissecting the internal scansions of *Under Milk Wood*. Now and then Americans have settled in Wales: Quaker whalers at Milford, factory managers in the industrial south, even miners in Rhondda—285 of them in 1911. In 1925 William Randolph Hearst the newspaper magnate bought the Norman castle of St Donat's, on the Glamorgan coast, added to it parts of a fourteenth-century English priory, spent unimaginable sums on its reconstruction and intermittently lived in it as a magnate should, surrounded by lackeys and film stars.

And here is a last sad Welsh-American memento. Among the bleak but exciting mountains called the Arennigs, in southern Gwynedd, whose high plateaux and sudden humps are set in a huge expanse of marsh and moorland, one ridge is recognizably the greatest—Arennig Fawr, Great Arennig, whose summit is often hidden in mist, but looks terribly remote even on the finest day. Through binoculars, when the weather is clear enough, you may see a small protrusion at the top, like a holy place, or the grave of a Montenegrin prince. It is a memorial erected in 1945 to eight young Americans who died, in these waste highlands so far from home, a particularly lonely and unnecessary death. On the night of 4 August 1943, their Flying Fortress flew into the mountain a few feet below the summit and exploded, killing all its crew—whose captain was Lieut. James Platt of Boise, Idaho, and each of whose members, by symbolic chance, came from a different State of the Union. The remains of their aircraft were gathered into a bowl of stones, and a slate stone was placed there, 2,000 feet up, to record their names. Near the foot of the mountain lives the man who carried the slab to the summit, strapped to his back, and from his living-room window he can see the pile of stones up there, when the clouds clear.

Many another foreign people has left its traces, solid or intangible, upon the soil of Wales.

For centuries for instance the Vikings, *Y Cenhedloedd Duon*, the Black Nations, raided and intermittently settled on these coasts, sacking Tyddewi four times in a row, trading wines, hides, butter and cloth for slaves, horses, honey and malt, leaving a trace of their language in place-names like Swansea, Bardsey, Flat Holm and Great Orme, and in one solitary Runic inscription, far inland at Defynwy in Powys. The different-sized stones, one small, one big, that sometimes crown the gateposts of Dyfed farms are thought by some archaeologists to be memories of Viking stockades, which were decorated with the heads of male and female captives. The strain of red-haired and freckle-faced Welshmen in the north is said to be a legacy of Viking lust.

The first Welsh Spaniards, fable fondly says, were shipwrecked survivors of the Armada settled in Gwynedd, the engaging evidence being that farm dogs up there are often called Perro, which means 'dog' in Spanish; and the first of the famous Thomas bonesetters of Môn valley was a shipwrecked Spaniard. In South Wales the connection is less fragile, for there have been close links with Spain ever since the steel industry, running out of its own iron ore, took to importing it from the Basque country. Besides, in the nineteenth and early twentieth centuries whole families of Spanish ironworkers and miners settled in South Wales. At Merthyr a street was built especially to house Spanish immigrants, called King Alphonso Street: at Aber-craf in the Tawe valley a quarter of the town was nicknamed Spanish Row. The effects of this influx were unexpected. The inhabitants of King Alphonso Street turned out to be fervent anti-monarchists, the householders of Spanish Row set racy precedents by drinking wine on Sundays and playing accordions in the streets, and the militantly syndicalist Spanish workmen gave Welsh trade unionists all sorts of new ideas. The Spaniards were excellent Rugby players, and they became very popular: many Welshmen learnt Spanish from them, and in the pits one often heard shouts in purest Galician echoing through the galleries—*caballista*, the miner would call to the pony-man, *uno caballo!*

Welsh Italians have also been influential. The fathers of them all were the Bracchi brothers, who came from the Po Valley in 1890 to open a café in the South Wales coalfield, and have left behind them there a thriving progeny of Italian café proprietors, ice-cream sellers, grocers and video-tape renters, almost all claiming descent, if not to the same family, at least to the same part of Italy. To this day they and their shops are known generically as 'Bracchis', and it is they who have given the coalfield much of its legendary fizz—not to mention its physiognomies, for half the young men you see down there have a distinctly Mediterranean look, if not in the bone structure, at least in the eye and the strut.

In the eighteenth and nineteenth centuries many Scots came to Wales, mostly as agents of English supremacy—as gamekeepers to great landlords, as colliery agents and overseers, and sometimes as soldiers for the repression of unrest. In the First World War hundreds of Belgian refugees came, and have left memorials of their craftsmanship in many a church fitting and village hall, while in the aftermath of the Second World War some of the sad flotsam of Europe found its landfall on this unlikely beach—Polish exiles, like the sad little community which was to live ever after in its shanty-barracks in Llŷn, or the German prisoners who, when all was over, married Welsh girls and stayed in Wales, sometimes bringing to tea-table or tavern corner tales as strange as anything in the Mabinogion of their far origins in Prussia or Pomerania, and their bitter wanderings across the battle-fronts.

And in the Great Coal Rush the whole world came—Americans, Germans, Italians, Frenchmen, Spaniards and many others hoping to better themselves in the mines, West Indians, Greeks, Italians, Arabs, Indians and Scandinavians to find berths on the colliers. In Cardiff, their metropolis, the descendants of these adventurers linger. The Greek Orthodox Church still functions there, presided over generally by a Cypriot priest, there is a handsome new mosque paid for mostly by the Libyans, happily incongruous in a concrete waste of council estates the little Islamic Centre raises its wonky turrets into the sky, and from clubs and pubs across the city comes the exhilarating beat of reggae.

In the valley of the upper Tawe, north of Castell Nedd, stands the extremely grand mansion called Craig-y-Nos, Rock of the Night. It is a hospital now, but has not lost all its opulence. Its gardens are spacious still, its forecourt speaks of footmen and plumed carriage horses, and high on the hill above still stand the remains of its private station, marked Craig-y-Nos in Great Western Railway lettering.

This was the home, in the heady days of *fin de siècle*, of the most highly paid of all opera singers, the Italian–Spanish Queen of Song,

Adelina Patti. For twenty years she queened it in that improbable court, and she made it all her own. She built her own theatre there, with a drop-curtain showing her as Semiramide driving a chariot! She built a clock tower on top, and a Winter Garden, and a suite of rooms especially for the entertainment of Edward VII! She mimed a silent *La Traviata* to celebrate the opening of the shooting season! She sang the Welsh national anthem at the Brecon Eisteddfod of 1889! She came home there, in terrific style, by special train from her Command Performances and World Tours! She lived there, having outlasted her first husband, a French marquis, with her second, a French tenor, and her third, a Swedish baron! And though she died (in 1919) far away in Paris, it is almost impossible to go to Craig-y-Nos even now without sensing her ample, lovable and preposterous presence.

She is not the only foreign musician to have left a memory in Wales. Handel, it is said, got the idea for the 'Hallelujah Chorus' during a visit to one of Daniel Rowland's prayer-meetings, to which he was taken by the strongly Methodist Countess of Huntingdon. Mendelssohn came to Wales in 1829: it did not greatly stir him, as Scotland stirred him, but still while staying at the house of a mine manager at Coed Du, near Rhyd-y-mwyn in Clwyd, listening to the interminable trickle of the Alyn river outside his window, mingled perhaps with the drip of a true Welsh drizzle, he was polite enough to offer his host a composition, *The Rivulet*, Opus 16 No. 4, allegedly inspired by the experience.

And Richard Wagner, legend says, came in a state of high exaltation, looking for the earliest roots of *Parsifal* in this most ancient sanctuary of knights and enchanted castles. He is supposed to have stayed for a time at Nanteos, whose squire of the day was George Powell the poet, and there to have held in his very hands—*Oh! Wunder!*—like Roberts the harper before him, that old black fragment of the Holy Grail, the very talisman or reliquary of Wagnerianism. What ecstasy! What orchestration! *Oh! Heilig hehrstes Wunder!*

Welsh people of many kinds, down the years, have established foreign settlements of their own—exiled Catholics plotting their plots and preparing their grammars in Italy—engineers in the iron-mines of Spain or the copper-mines of Chile—managers from Cardiff, running John Cory's eighty steam coal bunkers around the world—South Wales seamen, so familiar in Latin America, and for so long, that there used to be a Swansea Cemetery in Cuba—John Hughes of Merthyr, building the first steel mills in Tsarist Russia, and founding the town of Hughesovka (Yuzovka to the Russians), which still shelters, though later renamed Stalino, and later still Donetsk, many comrades of Welsh descent.

But of all the footholds the Welsh have established in foreign parts, the most remarkable is certainly the colony of Y Wladfa, The Colony, established in 1865 in the largely unexplored Patagonian territory of Argentina. This set out from the start to be entirely Welsh, in language, culture, religion and loyalty. Though Patagonia was Argentinian territory, it had not been settled—it was almost the last temperate region, in fact, to be colonized by Europeans. Only a small number of Indians lived there, and the Welsh proposed to establish an autonomous colony, under the suzerainty of the Argentine Government at Buenos Aires. The Argentinians welcomed the idea of having the country developed for them (though for a time they suspected a British plot behind the venture), and so in 1865 the first 153 settlers set sail from Liverpool aboard the ship *Mimosa*, 447 tons.

The vicarious Moses of this exodus (for he did not go himself) was an independent minister, Michael D. Jones of Y Bala, who had emigrated to the United States, but had come to realize that a second-generation Welsh-American there was, to most purposes, no longer a Welshman at all. Jones wanted there to be a Welsh Israel somewhere, in which the settlers could live for ever after in an ambience of unsullied Welshness, all on their own. A Nova Cambria had already failed in Brazil, but then it was based upon material aspirations. Y Wladfa would be different. Religion (strictly chapel) and Language (absolutely Welsh) were to be its governing factors. It would be a Promised Land for a strictly Chosen People: and the Mosaic precedent was reverently recognized, for the very first sermon preached in Patagonia had as its text the story of the Israelites in the wilderness.

Y Wladfa was a wilderness too, much wilder than had been thought, and though there were three ministers to guide them through it in spiritual terms, the original pioneers included only two farmers. The valley of the Chubut, where they first settled, was terribly dry sometimes, fearfully flooded at others, and the early years were plagued by many and varied hazards—the usual Welsh quarrels, of course, but also the unforeseen hostility of Indians (who killed three Welshmen in the pampas), the irritating interference of Argentinians (who wanted to draft the young men into their army), the unexpected arrival of 'Butch' Cassidy and the Sundance Kid (who murdered Michael D. Jones's own son), and the intractable nature of the terrain ('the Devil made Patagonia', one settler said, 'and he made it as like his own special home as two pies'). Sometimes the colonists thought of giving up and going away to the Transvaal, where the Afrikaners had recently undertaken a very similar Great Trek, and for just the same reasons. Some did give up and go home.

Most of them persevered, though, and little by little they succeeded. Having laboriously irrigated the Chubut valley, and made it golden with wheat, they explored deep into the Andes, and started a second settlement, for sheep-rearing this time, in a place of majestic beauty they called Cwm Hyfryd, Lovely Valley. For a time they really did have their New Wales, self-governing in most essentials, where life was ruled absolutely by Welsh traditions. Everybody over the age of 18, men and women, had equal political rights—Hywel Dda made modern. The economy was managed by a co-operative society, shipping its own products in its own ships—authentic Robert Owen. Friendly relations were established with the Indians, in the egalitarian spirit of Iolo or the Revd Morgan Rees. The Sabbath was as scrupulously observed as if Daniel Rowlands or Howel Harris had been there in person. Names like Dyffryn Williams (Williams's Valley) or Hirlan Uffernol (Hellish Long Bank) appeared on the large-scale maps of Argentina, and by the 1920s visitors were surprised to come across a breed of wiry pampas horsemen, half-Spanish in style and appearance, who habitually spoke Welsh and who maintained, in their isolated farms and tin-roofed hamlets, all the social forms of Powys or Gwynedd.

The Welsh Patagonians never got very rich, but they were able to keep their culture almost complete, down to a daily Welsh newspaper, at least until the Second World War. It is still alive. Patagonians are always among the overseas visitors at the National Eisteddfod, competitors from Wales win prizes in Patagonian *eisteddfodau*, and sometimes Welsh people go on package tours to inspect their one and only overseas colony. Bruce Chatwin the English novelist, visiting the Welsh settlements at Christmas 1974, found their Welshness hearty still, enjoyed Mrs Ivor Davies's tea, and reported that 'the Welshmen cheered up all who saw their bright and weather-beaten faces'. Nevertheless year by year Y Wladfa becomes a little less Welsh, and a little more Argentinian: Spanish gradually replaces Welsh as the natural language of the children; the legacies of Hywel, Owen, old Iolo and the champions of the Revival become ever more remote; and when, in 1982, thirty-six Welsh soldiers were killed in the sinking of a British ship in the Falkland Islands war against Argentina, it was reported in tragic irony that the pilot who fired the fatal missile was a Welshman from Patagonia.

In the 1980s there was a man living near Pontypridd who liked to say that his great-uncle had been Prime Minister of Australia, while his niece was married to the President of Egypt. Such has been the travelling opportunism of the Welsh, and they have turned up all over the world, in the past as in the present, in distant parts and unlikely situations, and often unmistakable.

You could always tell the Welshmen on the medieval pilgrim road to Santiago, because they took their harps with them. You could possibly guess the origins of John Evans, the missionary inventor of the Cree alphabet in nineteenth-century Canada, by his fatal fondness for squaws, or of John Davies, who first translated Christian hymns into the Tahitian tongue, by the fact that the hymns all happened to be Welsh. Who but a Welshman would have pointed out, as did Sir Thomas Herbert (in *Some Yeares Travels into divers parts of Asia and Afrique*, 1638), that the isle of Chumro, north of Madagascar, was obviously of Welsh origin? Who would have named a place New South Wales, but Captain Thomas Jones of Llanddewi Skirrid, Gwent? What Governor of the Western Pacific but Sir Hugh Wyn-Thomas would have proved himself such an accomplished performer upon the Tongan nose-flute?

There have been Welshmen on nearly all the great British voyages of discovery, Cabot to Captain Scott. It was Thomas Jones whose seventeenth-century voyages to the Arctic provided much of the local colour for Coleridge's Ancient Mariner, while David Samivell, poet and physician, whose bardic name was Dafydd Ddu Meddyg, Black David the Doctor, was Captain Cook's medical officer, and saw him die on the beach in Hawaii. The Welsh have been indefatigable missionaries too. A plaque on the old village smithy at Ffaldybrenin, Dyfed, remembers Timothy Richards, died 1915, who went from that small place to take the Christian faith to China, and was awarded the

Order of the Double Dragon. Half a century later Winnie Davies of Llandudno carried the word to Central Africa: and there in the Congo, after three years of slavery to a local rebel leader, General Ngalo, in 1968 she was murdered.

Generally speaking the Welsh have reached out eagerly to other peoples, other customs. Trevor Fishlock, *The Times* correspondent in Wales in the 1970s, called xenophobia 'a rare strain in Wales'. After the Napoleonic wars repatriated Hessian prisoners sent a message to the people of Llanfyllin, where Augeraud found his bride, to say that 'the kindness and the favour shown to them by the esteemed inhabitants of the town will ever remain in their thankful remembrance': the hundreds of German prisoners who decided not to go home after the Second World War have long been assimilated, and have often prospered exceedingly. Cardiff, the home of the first big black community in Europe—more than 4,000 people between the world wars —experienced a nasty race riot in 1919, when a black man was killed and several were injured, and before the First World War, during a time of particular social tension, there were anti-Jewish riots in the Gwent industrial valleys. For the most part nowadays, though, the foreign immigrants of Wales, be they Pakistanis, Chinese, Poles or Jamaicans, do not often complain of prejudice.

Perhaps, in this as in much else, the curiosity of the Welsh redeems them. The first black man ever seen in Cricieth, in the north-west, was taken there in the 1740s as a child-servant. He spoke no proper language, contemporary chroniclers assure us, 'only dog-like howls and screams', but he grew up a local celebrity, adored by all the local girls, with a Welsh wife and seven Afro-Welsh children. (He became a stern chapel-goer, too, and on his death-bed in 1791 declared that what he regretted most in life was having played, during his irreligious youth, the violin on Sundays.)

Nevertheless the Welsh are not, as a people, natural cosmopolitans. On the contrary, they are a people of intense collective instinct, agonizingly prone to homesickness. 'There's nowhere I like so much as Wales', Captain Davies rather discouragingly told his passengers on board the *Albion*, and many a Welsh emigrant has come home again to die, or at least to publish his memoirs. Among those who stick it out abroad life is shot through often by an insatiable pining for the particular sounds, colours, feelings and suggestions of the Welsh landscape. There is a programme on BBC Cymru, the Welsh-language radio service, in which Welsh exiles across the world are engaged in telephone conversation: and touching it is to hear how moved they often are to speak the old language once again, however rusty it has become, groping sometimes to remember the right adjective, master a half-lost construction, while the Italian traffic rumbles by outside, or the bleepings of American police cars interrupt the flow.

The Welsh have seldom looked to the world outside simply in rejection of their own country, however miserable its climate, narrowing its demands or limited its opportunities. By the standards of most European countries their proportion of emigrants is small: in the nineteenth century, the century of the great migrations, the proportion was four times bigger in England, seven times bigger in Scotland, and twenty-six times bigger among the unhappy Irish. When the Welsh have had to go, they have gone to escape political, or economic, or religious, or social circumstance: and that generally means in effect, though they do not always see it so, that they have gone to escape the intrusion into their lives, in one way or another, of their one stupendous neighbour, England, Lloegr in Welsh—that mightiest of all cuckoos in the nests of history.

10. The Neighbour

Owain Glyndŵr must have known, when he contemplated the state of affairs at the start of the fifteenth century, that whatever he did, Wales was trapped. The most exhilarating victory of Welsh arms, the boldest demonstration of Welsh sovereignty, would never have kept the English out for long: geography, history, economics, demography, all conspired to place Wales in a position of perpetual inferiority. Nevertheless Owain became, in his own time and ever after, the chief champion of the Welsh cause against the English. Did his followers really understand that cause? Did they realize the true relationship between these disparate forces? Perhaps not—perhaps they thought of it as a war between equals. But they were to be disabused in the end, and Wales still lives, in all its aspects, essentially in reaction to England—not always in opposition, not always in harmony, but always in response to that tremendous presence in the east, the Welshman's only neighbour.

A ᴌᴌ down the eastern perimeter of Clwyd, Powys and Gwent red
dragon signs on main roads announce to travellers from England
that they are entering Wales: and all down that countryside too,
from Point of Ayr, Y Parlwr Du, on Liverpool Bay in the north, to
Chepstow at the mouth of the Wye in the south, the undulating bumps
and ditches of Offa's Dyke mark the frontier agreed between the
medieval leaders of the Welsh and the Anglo-Saxon kings of Mercia.
Four hundred years after the Act of Union, there is no mistaking that
this is a demarcation between nations, and there are places here and
there where it even feels like a frontier between States.

One of these is the village of Llanymynech, in Powys, which stands
with its back to a Welsh limestone ridge, riddled with old mines and
quarries, and its front to the flatlands of English Shropshire.
Llanymynech possesses the true essence of frontierness, as Domodos-
sola does, or Brownsville, Texas. It consists of a few houses, a couple of
pubs, a scatter of shops and petrol stations, and it looks for all the world
as though around the corner there will be a red and white pole to mark
the frontier crossing, a customs house with stern warnings in the
window, and policemen in their respective uniforms, holding perhaps
their respective automatic rifles, beneath their separate flags. Where do
we change our money? you may wonder. Is there a duty-free shop
somewhere? Might they not confiscate that manuscript about dissident
activity in the polytechnics?

As it happens the sensation is almost comically apt, for not only does
Offa's Dyke run a few hundred yards east of Llanymynech, but the
present administrative border between Powys and Shropshire, and so
between England and Wales, runs slap down the middle of the street,
through the churchyard (behind the second tree from the wall) and
over the bridge at the bend in the road beyond the petrol station. There
are people buried in that churchyard with their heads in Wales, their
feet in England, and the landlord of the White Swan Inn actually pays
both Welsh and English taxes, besides having a marker in the middle of
his long bar announcing where the frontier crosses it.

Although the Welsh language survives fitfully, if at all, in these
English borderlands, the sense of transition is still strong in such a

place: and this is not surprising, for the frontier between England and Wales is one of the oldest in Europe, older by far than the lines which so fatefully divide France from Germany, Spain from Portugal, or the Swedes from the Norwegians. At least since the eighth century England has ended at Llanymynech, Wales has begun; and long before that too travellers in this dangerous country must have been all too well aware of a difference in kind, between the plainsmen to the east of the village, and the hill-men to the west.

> Taffy was a Welshman, Taffy was a thief,
> Taffy came to my house and stole a leg of beef.
> I went to Taffy's house, and found him in bed,
> I took a big cudgel and hit him on the head.

The vicious old rhyme, metamorphosed into a nursery jingle, recalls the days when the frontier between Wales and England was as lawless as anything in the American West. Offa's Dyke may have been constructed by consent between Celt and Saxon, but it became in later years a perilous no man's land between Welsh and English. No love was ever lost along this line. The Welsh thought the English 'had made an enemy of God himself' (1165), the English thought the Welsh (1282) 'that repulsive people—why have they not been annihilated from the earth?' When a fourteenth-century Mayor of Chester was kidnapped by the Welsh they took him to Mold and gave him a pie to eat, but when he cut it open he found only a rope inside, and with that rope they hanged him. Raids and counter-raids, burnings and reprisals were incessant, and if Welsh raiders crossed the frontier to rustle a herd of cattle ('steal a leg of beef'), an English posse was legally entitled to chase them in hot pursuit and burn their houses down (find them in bed, that is, and hit them on the head).

You can still sometimes sense the resentments of this long and venomous conflict. Even now along the border there are people vehemently to disclaim all trace of Welshness, or rather less frequently of Englishness, for no better reason than historical memory. The old antipathy has left behind it some psychological confusion of the spirit, hanging upon the atmosphere like a storm that does not clear, but keeps rumbling and spitting around the hills.

Nowhere can you feel this ancient *malaise* more naggingly than in the Black Mountains, where the Welsh counties of Gwent and Powys meet the English county of Hereford, and where even in modern times certain tracts of country have been tossed back and forth repeatedly between Wales and England. It is magnificent country, but baleful. Some ten miles long by eight miles wide, rising to nearly 2,700 feet, the Black Mountains consist of three roughly parallel ridges, moorlands covered with bracken, heather and bilberry, grazed by mountain sheep, wandered over by pony-trekkers, exercised on by soldiers with blackened faces and crossed by the high tracks of the drovers. Of the three deep valleys that are sunk in this compact sandstone massif, inhabited by perhaps 500 souls in all, two are dead ends, and though many tourists penetrate the hills nowadays, the Black Mountains remain hauntingly wild and empty.

This was always uneasy territory—the most lawless in Great Britain, it was said as late as the 1800s. Here the Welsh guerrillas hid themselves away from the Normans in the lusher lands below, here Richard de Clare was murdered in the hanging beech woods of Grwyne Fawr, and the old resentments of the place were never quite dispersed. The local Welsh, wrote an Anglo-Norman chronicler of Llanthony Priory in the thirteenth century, were savages and vagabonds, without religion, and when the English writer Walter Savage Landor bought the same priory in 1808, intending to settle in the mountains, he was soon driven out by the distinctly unwelcoming natives in a welter of lawsuit and recrimination—'I hate and detest the very features of the country', he wrote before he left, 'I can never be happy here, or comfortable, or at peace'. English settlers still sometimes find the inbred peculiarity of the valleys hard to manage. It is a queer part of the world, and queer dark things happen there, from incest to inexplicable suicide, from sheep-rustling and bomb-laying to whispers of witchcraft. Drifting through the 80 square miles of the Black Mountains you may feel the anxiety of the frontier festering still, its causes long since forgotten, like the indeterminate unhappiness of a house that has known bad times.

All down the medieval frontier, and at its extremities, the English built cities and castle towns. Liverpool, Chester, Shrewsbury, Ludlow, Hereford, Bristol, look on the map like so many guard-towers watching the Welsh approaches, and they have always been inextricably concerned with the affairs of Wales: actively, by dominating its economy and powerfully influencing its social progress, passively, as targets of Welsh attack and destinations of Welsh emigration.

Liverpool for instance (Lerpwl to the Welsh) has a claim to be the real capital of North Wales, though it stands some twenty miles from the frontier, and it has long regarded Clwyd and Gwynedd as part of its own hinterland. Along the coast of Ynys Môn stand the remains of the ten semaphore stations by which, in the nineteenth century, the port of Liverpool was warned of a ship's impending arrival out of the Irish Sea (in a test in 1830 a message was sent from Liverpool to Caergybi and back again, 140 miles in all, in 23 seconds): and the Liverpool pilots still work out of comfortable quarters at Porth Linas, on the north coast of Môn, commuting there by train and taxi from Merseyside, and taken out to the incoming ships in a spanking cutter which is the best-known boat on the North Wales coast.

The nearest thing to a North Wales daily newspaper is the *Liverpool Daily Post*, the nearest international airport is Liverpool's Speke, and when they go on a shopping spree Welshwomen from Aberdaron to Y Bala like to make a day of it in Liverpool. Many thousands of Welsh people have settled in the city for good, too, as businessmen, as teachers, as ministers and especially as sailors—they used to call the Liverpool-based Blue Funnel Line 'the Welsh Navy'. Much of the money for the College by the Sea came from the Liverpool Welsh; the community has produced many Welsh scholars, several poets and Saunders Lewis, the most passionate of all twentieth-century Welsh patriots.

At the other end is the port of Bristol, Bryste, for centuries the true metropolis of South Wales—the Welsh Emporium, as it was called in 1833, whose trading ships hawked their cargoes of hardware and groceries all around the little Welsh ports, whose every merchantman had Welshmen in its crew, whose policemen and garrison troops were called in to put down Welsh unrest, and whose pubs still include the Llandoger Trow, on the quay called the Welsh Back, near the old Welsh Market House.

Until the coal boom much of South Wales lived by feeding and supplying Bristol. We read in 1567 of the ship *Le Turtaile de Milford* sailing from Milford to Bristol with sheep skins, lamb pelts, herrings and salmon: later the range was widened to include vegetables, gulls' eggs, rabbits and wood faggots for the heating of bakers' ovens. In Gwent some families made a living collecting snails for Bristolians, who were popularly supposed to live on them (though actually the chief customers were blowers in the Bristol glass factories, who ate them as a prophylactic against tuberculosis).

The towns in between, Chester (Caerllion Fawr), Shrewsbury (Amwythig), Ludlow (Llwydlo), Hereford (Henffordd), the fine English country towns of the border, were linked to Wales in another way, for they were the front-line fortresses. From the walls of Chester, from the towers of Shrewsbury, from the castle at Ludlow and the Wye bridge at Hereford, you can see the Welsh hills beckoning, forbidding or challenging, as the mood takes you, and the civic annals of them all are full of skirmishings, burnings, threats and revenges of the frontier. From these powerful bases the potentates of the Marches, terrible earls like Hugh of Avranches, formidable bishops like Odo of Hereford, sent out their punitive missions and expeditions of conquest: at Ludlow the Tudors set up the Council of Wales and the Marches which was for several generations the real governing power of Wales, and the comfortably half-timbered inns and houses of the place, watched over so snugly by church and castle, still make it, for Welshmen travelling out of their bare moorland country, an epitome of English advantage.

All these were profoundly, deliberately English places, for all their Welsh connections. They were statements of supremacy. Even now a feast day at Hereford Cathedral, with the Bishop magnificent in his cope and mitre, the canons stately all around him, the vergers wearing their medal ribbons from the Second World War, the puck-faced choristers and the rubicund Herefordian gentlemen of the choir— even now, when the organ thunders out some mighty anthem of Anglicanism, a ceremony in Hereford Cathedral can seem a theatrical affirmation of English sovereignty.

Yet here and there, all the same, that frontier has never quite coalesced. Owain Glyndŵr refused to recognize it, planning to incorporate Chester, Shrewsbury, Ludlow and Hereford into Wales, and Welshness still spills over into the territories on the other side of the Dyke. All those towns are full of Welsh people, the most popular of Welsh-language magazines, *Y Cymro*, is published in Oswestry, Shropshire, and the country called in Welsh Erging, in English Archenfield, remains a true hybrid to this day. It is a fertile triangle of southern Herefordshire, and in it the Welsh kept their autonomy long after the frontier had been established. Somehow they contrived to sustain their own laws, language and social systems under English rule, but they paid a price for the privilege: the priests of the three Archenfield churches, Domesday Book tells us, were obliged to act as messengers for the English king, when he had instructions to convey to the Welsh across the border: and as for the young men of Archenfield, 'when the army goes forth against the enemy, these same men, according to custom, make the Vanguard, and on the return, the Rearguard'.

How resiliently Erging survived you may see by the place-names of the region now, ranging in their Welshness from the uncompromising Bagwyllydiart to accommodations like Dewchurch, Dewi's Church, and by family names which are still absolutely Welsh, like Cadwallader, or Welsh in disguise—Beddoes, which is Meredith really, or Lello, which is Llywelyn. Far more than many parts of Wales proper, Archenfield retains a feel of ancient Celticness, and among all the constructions of the frontier, among all the castles and cathedrals the English built to stress their commanding presence, the most compelling is the famous little church of St David at Kilpeck, whose foundation long preceded their coming, and whose fabric still reminds us of what was there before. All the intricacy, mystery and humour of the Celtic imagination informs this little building: grotesque small figures, of forest or stream, surround its porch and ornament its eaves; its narrow nave is dark, austere and suggestive; its numen is sly; it is like a little cell of *Cymreictod*, Welshness, left behind like a Celtic recusant on the wrong side of the line.

Gleaming of brass, swathed in white steam, the special trains swept through the English railway towns, in the years before the Second World War, carrying their armies of South Walians up to London for the annual Rugby match against England at Twickenham. In those days Welshmen, even English-speaking Welshmen, not only looked and sounded different from Englishmen, but dressed differently too, and to watchers on the station platforms there was no mistaking the Welsh Rugby specials as they rushed past. Cloth-capped and silk-scarved, with dark suits of baggy cut, the Welshmen crowded the corridors like people from another continent, pinch-faced rather, sharp-eyed, talking hard and sometimes singing as they swept through Chippenham, Swindon and Didcot Junction. Everybody knew who they were, for they had been coming that way, by one means or another, to sell their cattle, to find jobs, to watch their boys win at Twickenham, for at least 500 years.

Many a Welsh Pony or Drover's Inn, across the breadth of southern England, testifies to the immemorial passing of the Welsh; at Stockbridge in Hampshire, in the heart of English England, an old printed sign on a house still proclaims *Gwely da, pridd da, cwrw da*—'Good Bed, Good Pasture, Good Beer'; and Paddington Station, where those Rugby specials ended their journey, still often seems, with the Welsh names and voices echoing beneath its great glass roof, like an enclave of Wales in the English capital. If Lloegr has always pressed upon the Welsh, it has always pulled them too. It stands there inescapably, at the back of every Welsh mind, affecting every Welsh action public or private.

Ever since the departure of the Romans, Welsh men of ambition have found it necessary to ingratiate themselves with their overbearing neighbours: even Hywel Dda was virtually a client king of the Kings of Wessex, even the Llywelyns were ready to pay tribute to the English Crown, and Edward I and his successors never found it difficult to recruit Welsh stewards and commanders for their conquered territories. The princes of Powys not infrequently allied themselves with the English against their fellow Welsh; the Tudors took with them to London, or so it seemed to Londoners, half the gentlemen of Wales. Many Welshmen have migrated to England as the place of last resort—desperate miners out of work, gone to the factories of Slough or Cowley, or the poor Welsh women who used to earn a living weeding London's parks and gardens. Many more have found it a place of blessed escape, from the confines of too Welsh a Welshness, or an avenue beckoning them to power—a glittering alternative. Lloyd George realized that the way to real fame lay in England rather than in Wales when, preaching Welsh separatism to a political meeting at Newport in 1895, he found himself howled down by his audience of merchants and businessmen—'we've had enough', cried Alderman Robert Bird, 'of all this Welsh business!' The politician's horizons shifted from that day, and when he had achieved the supreme power he craved for, his bookplate used to show a winding river running away out of the Welsh hills to the Palace of Westminster, the whole bathed in a refulgent sunrise, decorated with daffodils but lettered in English.

Whatever its appeal, the proximity of England has distorted the

Welsh view of Welshness, and permanently disturbs the national equanimity. When in the Mabinogion Brân's warriors returned with his head from Ireland, they stayed in a sea-shore palace in Dyfed in which, they had been told, all worries would be expunged from their minds, provided only that they did not open a particular door. They lived there in perfect harmony for eighty years, the Assembly of the Wondrous Head, until one day they opened that door and had their first view in the direction of England. And when they looked they remembered all their sadness, and all their anxieties, 'and from that moment they could not rest, save that they set out . . . towards London'.

The list of Welsh people who have made good in England is endless: statesmen, actors, writers, bishops, lawyers by the thousand, press lords, courtesans, Beau Nash, booksellers, scholars, Ivor Novello, John Williams the great Jacobean jeweller, John Nash the great Regency architect, footballers, musicians, Ivor Roberts-Jones the sculptor, who made the statue of Winston Churchill in Parliament Square, television producers so numerous that to judge by the names on the credits practically the whole industry is in Welsh hands, heads of Oxford colleges ('We won't have Evans at any price', it was said during an election for the Mastership of Pembroke College in 1864, 'and as for Price, O 'eavens'), Oliver Cromwell's great-grandfather (né Williams), Margaret Thatcher's paternal forebears (nés Roberts), Lloyd George of course, innumerable trade union leaders, several Lord Mayors of London, a Historiographer Royal and three Speakers of the House of Commons (one of whom, Sir John Trevor, introduced the system of calling upon members by name to speak in debates—his squint was so terrible that when he indicated a speaker simply by gesture, as had been the custom hitherto, nobody was sure whom he meant). Welshmen have filled the offices of Prime Minister, Foreign Secretary, Home Secretary, Chancellor of the Exchequer, and many have become British Ambassadors—the first *Cymro Cymraeg* to represent Her Britannic Majesty abroad was T. Ifor Rees, who went from Rhyd-y-Pennau, an almost unnoticeable hamlet in Dyfed, to head the mission to La Paz in 1944. Hundreds have become judges: the savage judge who sent the Tolpuddle Martyrs into exile in 1834 was a Welshman, John Williams, and so was Edmund Davies, who sentenced the Great Train Robbers in 1964, and so was Judge Jeffreys of the 1685 Bloody Assizes, described in the British *Dictionary of National Biography* as the worst criminal judge who ever disgraced the English bench.

London has had its Welsh enclaves and societies since the time of the Tudors. In the nineteenth century there were at least nine London pubs where you could regularly hear *canu penillion*, and several others catered especially for Welshmen—sea-captains for instance frequented the Seven Stars at London Bridge, while literary men favoured the Bull in Walbrook, or the King's Head in Ludgate Street. There are still Welshy pubs in London, and Welsh private hotels, especially around Paddington and Bloomsbury, and there are Welsh churches and chapels, and a Welsh school, and the inevitable Rugby club.

Sometimes they have been there so long that their links with Wales itself have become tenuous. As long ago as 1606 John Owen the Welsh epigrammatist, himself educated at Winchester and Oxford, and resident at Warwick, laughed at somebody who claimed to be 'one of the *London* Davieses'—dear me, nothing to do with *Wales*! But they have not always abandoned their homeland, and actually there have been times when London was truly the cultural capital of Wales—the Welsh antiquarian revival of the eighteenth and early nineteenth centuries was chiefly cherished by the many societies of London exiles, the Cymreigyddion, the Gwyneddigion, the Gomerian, the Ofyddion, the Canorion, the Ceredigion, or the still-flourishing Cymmrodorion. No, by and large the London Welsh are as devoted to Wales as anyone, except that, in the wisdom of their worldliness, they prefer to live well away from the place.

In the days of the British Empire the lure of England was more compulsive still, for then it offered Welshmen opportunities over half the world. The very name of the Empire was first put on paper, it is said, by John Dee, Queen Elizabeth's Welsh savant, and the first of organized Welsh emigrations (*pace* Prince Madog) was to one of the oldest of British colonies, Newfoundland, where in 1617 the settlement of Cambria was incompetently established: it occupied the extreme eastern corner of the island, around Cape Race, and gave itself all the proper place-names, Brecon, Cardigan, Pembroke, Cardiff, Vaughan's Cove, before withering away after a few years in ineptitude and homesickness.

In later years no possession of the Empire was without its Welshmen, and there were big communities in places like Toronto, Durban, Sydney and Auckland, sticking together with St David's Societies and *eisteddfodau* until, after a generation or two, most of their members were absorbed into colonial Britishness. There were Welsh nabobs in India, and several Welshmen made great fortunes in the West Indies: in Jamaica many descendants of their slave-families still keep their names, Evans, Williams or Griffiths, while retaining too, it seems to some ears, faint Carib echoes of a Welsh accent. Several Welshmen became colonial governors, like Sir Hugh of the Tongan nose-flute, and there was at least one Welsh colonial Prime Minister —the flamboyant William Morris Hughes of Australia, who became the most vividly assertive of imperialists, and travelled so far from his paternal terrace house in Glamorgan as to cry of the British Empire as a whole, after the First World War, 'What other worlds have we to conquer? We are like so many Alexanders!'

Often they took with them skills that were desperately needed in the colonies: sheep-farmers to Australia, miners to the Transvaal, tunnellers to the Indian railways, quarrymen almost everywhere—in the 1900s a quarryman earning about £1.50 a month in North Wales could make £1 a day in Australia. Often they went, though, as they went to the United States, only *faute de mieux*. An emigrant from Gwynedd, travelling by train to join his ship at Tilbury in the 1920s, found himself in the company of a Welsh poet, D. R. Griffith. When the two parted company, the poet slipped a piece of paper into the young man's hand, and this is what he found upon it:

> *Wrth hwylio dros y cefnfor*
> *I wlad Awstralia bell,*
> *Yn nyddiau eich ieuenctid*
> *I chwilio am amser gwell,*
> *Na fo i chwi anghofio*
> *Hen Gymru fach ein gwlad,*
> *Lle siglwyd crud eich mebyd*
> *Dan ofal mam a thad.*

> As you sail over the ocean
> To the far country of Australia,
> In the days of your youth
> In search of a better time,

The Neighbour

Let you not forget
Little old Wales our country,
Where the cradle of your childhood was rocked
Under the care of Mam and Tad.

For the Welsh were not natural imperialists. They had no conquering instinct—on the contrary, they were often instinctively at one with the conquered, and they did not take naturally, as the Scots did, to the ruling of the world (it used to be said that the Welsh-like babu-English of the Indians had its roots in the well-known propensity of Welsh soldiers for mixing with the natives). Among all the famous epitaphs of the imperial era, only one refers to a Welshman, and that (at Jamalpur in India) in a not very commanding context: HERE LIES GWILYM ROBERTS, WHO DIED FROM THE EFFECTS OF AN ENCOUNTER WITH A TIGER, A.D. 1864. Of course there were enthusiastically imperialist Welshmen among the thousands who stormed across the world in those heady years of dominance, who flaunted the far-flung authority of the British Crown or forcibly introduced the natives to the wonders of a regulated currency and the Gatling gun. More often than not, though, the best-known of the Welsh empire-builders were notable more for their empathy than their hubris.

The most famous of them all indeed was perhaps the least imperial—William Jones the orientalist and law-maker, who though thoroughly Anglicized by Harrow and Oxford, sprang from a farming family of Ynys Môn, and was introduced once to George IV as a Welshman who knew every language but his own (he spoke forty-one). Jones went out to India, as a High Court judge, chiefly as a means of pursuing his oriental studies, and threw himself absolutely into Indian affairs—not Anglo-Indian affairs, like nearly all his colleagues, but the cultures, the laws, the pastimes, the botany, the zoology, the history and the religions of India itself. He was the first European to master Sanskrit, and it was he who began the first codification of the Hindu and Muslim laws in India—a task worthy of Hywel Dda, in which indeed he was helped by a host of indigenous Blegywryds. Through it all Jones was terribly affected by the climate. He built himself a kind of bunker, in the outskirts of Calcutta, in which he buried himself against the sun's heat: but the sun beat him anyway, and he died there in 1794, aged 48.

The English *Dictionary of National Biography* says of Jones that 'he felt none of the contempt which his English contemporaries showed to the natives of India'. On the contrary, he struck up deep friendships with many of them, and was regarded by Indians themselves as one of the greatest oriental scholars of the time. There is a memorial to him in Calcutta Cathedral, and it shows him sitting among his law-books, high-browed and attentive, while around him his Indian colleagues, in loincloths and turbans, help him to puzzle out an obscurity of the Islamic penal code, or an anomaly perhaps in the Sanskrit law of inheritance—a Welshman without Welsh, never to set eyes on his own country again, but radiating still, a sentimental patriot might suppose, some old goodness of Cymru.

In 1882 Major Baldwin Evans of Rhuddlan in Clwyd found himself gaoler to the Egyptian nationalist Arabi Pasha, captured by the British after his insurrection at Alexandria. When Arabi was transferred to exile in Ceylon he wrote a letter to the Welshman, and this is what it said:

> In the name of God, the Merciful and the
> Compassionate, my good and Honourable Friend, Mr Evans:
>
> I beg to offer you my devotion for the great zeal and trouble you have taken on our behalf during the examination of our case, and also for your frequent visits to us in our prison cell. I pray God to reward you for your great kindness to us in our hours of grief and darkness, and we beg of you to accept our most grateful thanks. I have done this in my own hand to be a remembrance and a lasting sign of the great esteem and friendship I have for you.
>
> AHMED ARABI, THE EGYPTIAN

The lampoonist and tavern-keeper John Jones—Jac Glan-y-gors, or Jack Bogside—gave literary form in the 1800s to a figure well known, and well loathed, among the prouder kind of Welsh. His character Dic Siôn Dafydd went into the folklore immediately as the generic Welsh sycophant, aping all the ways of his English master, despising his own. He is of course a familiar figure of every subject society, the collaborator, the man who believes he can better himself by adjusting to his rulers' preferences, and in Wales he has been prominent since the days of the Romans: in the porch of Caerwent church there is a monument to a Roman praetor erected with fulsome expressions of indebtedness by the council of the conquered Silurians. Gruffydd Roberts, exiled in Milan in 1567, wrote of his own kin that 'as soon as they see the river Severn, or the bell-towers of Shrewsbury, and hear an English-man say "Good Morrow", they start to lose their Welsh from their memory . . .'.

There were always Welshmen ready to copy the manners of the Normans and the English, and when the gentry deserted Welshness for Englishness many a social climber went with them. 'They glory in wearing the badge of their vassalage', wrote Ieuan Brydydd Hir, 'by adopting the language of their conquerors, which is a mark of the most despicable meanness of spirit.' It was not only Englishmen, in the nineteenth century, who believed the Welsh language to be the curse of Wales: many Welsh people thought so just as vehemently, and did their best to discourage their children from using it. The example of so many successful Welshmen, from Anglican parsons dining with their squires to the editors of the toadying *Western Mail* in Cardiff, seemed to show that to be as English as possible was the surest way to get on in the world, and there were Welshmen even in Wales who, like those London Davieses, tried to forget that they were really Welsh at all.

Dic Siôn Dafydd is still alive—alive and flourishing. Powerful segments of the bourgeoisie prefer not to be thought of as Welsh —well, not *too* Welsh, enough to be interesting to visitors perhaps, enough to make faintly ethnic jokes at cocktail parties, but never enough to damage a political prospect or threaten a business deal. In rural Wales there are still bucolics ready to tip a cap to an English lord. In small-town Wales many a shopkeeper prefers not to endanger his profits by putting up a sign in Welsh. Some people say that the Welsh industrial working class as a whole, by offering its loyalties to English political parties, English trade unions and English popular culture, has done to Wales in this century what the absconding Welsh gentry did in the time of the Tudors.

Times change, though, and to be Welsh is less unfashionable than it used to be, to be English less sure a promise of success. 'I'm as Welsh as the next man', declares the stockbroker once more, adjusting his tie pugnaciously, and now he may even go so far as to confide in you his paternal antecedents among the farming community of Ceredigion (though perhaps not yet, not so early in the evening anyway, among the Swansea dockers). The remaining gentry are prouder than ever of their immemorial pedigrees, while their children, as likely as not, have changed their names by deed poll from Mary Price to Mair ap Rhys, will speak English only under police duress, and play Welsh rock records day and night in attic rooms decorated all over with patriotic posters. As for those deracinated workers of the industrial valleys, all too often they seem to look back with a sad wistfulness to their Welshier origins, and wish they had not lost the language of their forebears —'I'm not saying I miss it, mind, I'm not saying that, there's not much call for it in Abertillery, but still . . . it's a pity, isn't it?'

For even Dic Siôn Dafydd, one suspects, was a good Welshman at heart—or would like to have been: and many a Welshman fated to be his progeny feels a melancholy in his condition, as he peers puzzled and affronted at the locked splendours of his heritage, or hears, if only in translation, the judgement of Siôn Mowddwy (*fl. c.*1600):

> *Och ŵr, Cymro ni cherais*
> *O le a sut êl y Sais.*

> Ugh, man, a Welshman I never did like,
> Who becomes, wherever, however, an Englishman . . .

One sunny day in 1966 a remarkable sight was to be seen among the fields of Ynys Môn, beside the Caergybi road. Like a swarm of gleaming, buzzing, chafing insects an entire British Army division had suddenly debouched over the meadows, and wherever you looked there were tents going up, and rows of camouflaged trucks, and armoured cars, and helicopters on transporters, and dispatch riders skidding about in the fresh mud, and military policemen in blanco'd white, and groups of officers studying maps, and cooks stirring pots at field kitchens. Engines roared, radios chattered. It seemed to have nothing whatever to do with Wales, so green and silent all around: and nor did it, for the British were simply on their way once more, along the road Telford had built for them 150 years before, to impose London's imperial authority upon the warring factions of Ireland over the water.

Nothing illustrates better the place of Wales in the English scheme of things than its situation astride the routes to Ireland. In some ways Wales is nothing more to England than a country in between. It was from Wales that the Normans invaded Ireland in the first place, and most of the main roads and railways were built to take the English more quickly to their Irish possessions—Telford's road in fact, built specifically as a result of the Act of Union between England and Ireland in

1800, was the very first publicly constructed road in Wales. Countless Britons see the Welsh countryside, even now, only from the windows of their cars and trains on the way to the Irish ferry ports—'it looked nice enough', they say, 'bit melancholy perhaps, but I didn't really notice'. The fastest coach services in Wales were always those to the ferry ports, and the only express trains ever to enter North Wales are the Irish boat trains, which stop very reluctantly, if at all, at the Welsh towns along the way. Across the body of this country the troops have always gone, as they did in 1966, to keep the Irish quiet: and when, after the Easter Rising in Dublin in 1916, the British deported a number of the rebels (those they did not shoot) it was in Wales that they were imprisoned—in R. J. Lloyd Price's disused whisky factory, as it happens, at Frongoch near Y Bala.

But if the Welsh have been so embroiled, willy-nilly, in England's long Irish preoccupation, this is only a paradigm of their inescapable participation in everything London decrees, organizes, endures or, to a rather lesser extent, achieves. Vastly different though their history is from that of the English, looking at the world as they often have from totally different points of view, still their affairs are governed inescapably from London. They are in thrall. Where the English go, there go the Welsh. The enemies of England are *ipso facto* the enemies of Wales. If there is an economic slump in Birmingham, there is a slump much worse in Rhondda. If there is trouble in Ulster, clear the Caergybi road.

One gets a queer feeling walking through the churchyard of Aberhafesb in Powys, a place as far as you could hope to find from the guns and trumpets: for beside the path there lies upon a gravestone, exactly modelled in marble, the sword, belt and plumed busby of an officer in the 8th (King's Royal Irish) Hussars—Charles Hilton Woosnam the rector's son actually, who just had time to celebrate his coming of age before dying in the King of England's service in 1910.

But then many, many thousands of Welshmen, from scores of Aberhafesbs, have died at one time or another in that service. For 800 years England's wars have been Wales's wars, however remote their causes from the needs or aspirations of the Welsh people. A third of the English army at Crécy was really Welsh, and many historians think the bowmen of Gwent and Glamorgan won the fight. The English Wars of the Roses, the English Civil Wars, all embroiled Wales deeply. The

epic little battle of Rorke's Drift was fought by the South Wales
Borderers. In the First World War 280,000 Welshmen joined the
armed forces, a higher proportion of Welshmen than of Englishmen,
and 35,000 died—all over Wales you may still see the sculpted figures
of their memorials, with heads bowed sometimes, with rifles reversed,
still mourning the slaughtered Pughes, Owens, Joneses and Morrises,
lost at Mons, or Gallipoli, or Gaza, or At Sea, gassed or drowned or
burnt alive, listed regiment by regiment, or rank by rank, on the marble
plinths below. In the Second World War the centres of Cardiff and
Swansea were devastated by bombs, 730 people were killed, and the
blaze of the bombed oil tanks at Pembroke Dock, which burnt for three
weeks, cast its lurid and gloomy glare over half Dyfed: the Germans,
reporting in triumph the success of such raids on Wales, called them,
reasonably enough, raids on England.

At least during the years of British world power the Welsh were
conditioned to think of war in terms of British glory, and to claim their
share of it with pride. Lord Tredegar, who took part in the tragic and
asinine charge of the Light Brigade at Sevastopol, was regarded ever
after as a Welsh national hero, and sits sculpted on his charger outside
the National Museum; the oyster-men of Mumbles renamed their
varieties of oysters proudly after the victories of the Zulu War; in the
Boer War the children of Rosemarket, Dyfed, paraded around the
village with flags flying, singing 'Rule, Britannia', the boys carrying
sticks to make do for guns; it was a Welshman, Ivor Novello, who wrote
one of the theme songs of the First World War, 'Keep the Home Fires
Burning'. In 1914 the Welsh went to war persuaded that they would be
fighting for the future of small nations like their own—'the little five-
foot-five nations', Lloyd George called them—but they were soon
caught up in the jingo brutalism of it all. 'Is Christ a God of War?' asked
one patriotic preacher. 'Jesus Christ came as the Field Marshal of the
armies of Israel; and the character of Jesus Christ has not changed even
today!'

Strategically Wales has generally been an anxiety to England—the
long coastline looks open to flank attack, and especially if Ireland fell to
an enemy, Wales would be the next step towards a conquest of
England. In the nineteenth century Lord Palmerston, fortifying the
kingdom against the French, thought it necessary to turn Milford
Haven into one of the most strongly defended places in the British
Isles: though most of its great muzzle-loaders are gone now, and its

strongpoints are turned into hotels and oil company depots, still all the glower of a fortress greets you as you enter the great harbour, the ramparts and the island block-houses strewn around, the suggestion of hidden telescopes monitoring your progress. A century later, when the British faced invasion by the Germans, Wales was fortified in a different way, and on many a beach and narrow pass you may still see tank traps disguised as old stone walls, or pill-boxes sunk in the ground like rocky outcrops.

On the other hand Wales has also seemed to the English an inner fastness. Wales is the place to send prisoners to, well away from the centres of power: in both world wars hundreds of thousands of prisoners were kept in Welsh camps, and it was in a mental hospital at Abergavenny that Rudolph Hess, Hitler's deputy, was confined after his flight to Scotland in 1941 (he was allowed a weekly walk in the Welsh countryside, and loved to climb up Pen-y-Fâl, the shapely hill that overlooks the town). Wales is a place to keep things safe in: in 1940 the treasures of the National Gallery were hidden in an air-conditioned cave near Blaenau Ffestiniog. Wales is a place for arsenals: Pembroke Dock was for a time the foremost naval shipyard of the world, while the ordnance factory established at Bridgend in 1939 became during the Second World War the biggest of all British munitions factories, with 35,000 women working in it. Wales is a place of raw materials: in the First World War Welsh steam coal was the *sine qua non* of victory, and every night in 1918 some 250 trains left the coalfield for Scotland with fuel for the Grand Fleet at Scapa Flow. And above all perhaps Wales is a place for a last stand, the ultimate bunker, if all comes to the worst, of Britishness in Britain—Fortress Wales, in fact: somewhere in these mountains, if ever England had fallen to Nazi Germany, in an ironic reversal of old roles the British resistance would have established its headquarters.

Wales is still a British military base today, where arms are stored, troops are trained, tactics are perfected for use against the enemies of the British kingdom. The secret squads of the Special Air Service rehearse their skills in the southern mountains. Fighter aircraft flash breakneck through the narrow valleys of mid-Wales. There are experimental missile stations on the coast, and vast areas of the moorland called Epynt, in Powys, are permanently appropriated by the military, so that travellers up there often see the long brown line of infantrymen labouring through the bracken, or hear the thunder of artillery. At Castlemartin in Dyfed there is a tank gunnery range, used by both the British and the West German armies: if you stand by the control tower there on a wet day, when the flatlands in front are all mud and slush, the dim shapes of the tanks, pitching and heaving along their tracks, look like so many rats crawling over the countryside.

Such sadnesses, such squalors, such wasted loyalties! Near Devauden, in Gwent, there stands on an isolated hump the tiny church of the Holy Cross at Kilgwrrwg, where the hermit Gwrrwg established his cell in the days of the Celtic faith. It is the most tranquil place in the world. A circular churchyard surrounds the building, there is an ancient crooked cross among the trees, a wooden boot-remover stands in the porch, for it can be a muddy clamber up there, and through the roof the ivy creeps. The church is lit only by candles, from a candelabra in the chancel, and it stands in absolute silence, far from all traffic in a bowl of the low Gwent hills, looking westward to the distant outlines of the Black Mountains, Pen-y-Fâl and Holy Skirrid.

Among the few dead in the churchyard lies Richard Morgan of that parish, Able Seaman, Royal Navy, who died at sea on the destroyer *Garland* (940 tons) on 11 November 1918. His body was brought sadly home to this quiet corner of the Wales that nurtured him: of all the million British servicemen who lost their lives in the Great War to end all wars, he was the last to go.

Such is the fate of history. The old Welsh poets understood it all too well—*Poni welwch-chwi'r sŷr wedi'r syrthiaw?*—'Do you not see the stars fallen?'—and in both world wars there were poets of Welsh blood to mourn it on all humanity's behalf: Wilfred Owen, David Jones, Edward Thomas in the first war, in the second Alun Lewis of Aberdare, who from his hospital bed in Poona looked homeward with the eyes of every soldier, in every army

> And like to swan or moon the whole of Wales
> Glided within the parish of my care . . .

If it strikes especially bitterly in Wales, that cannot be helped. The events which have bound the infinitesimal nation of Wales to the world power of England have denied the Welsh any real independence of action for several centuries. Politically, in a unified British State, the interests of 2.75 million Welsh people are bound to be subsidiary to the interests of 46 million English: during the past century the Conservative Party has never held much more than a third of the Welsh parliamentary seats, yet for most of that time Conservative governments have ruled Britain, and so have ruled the Welsh. Economically Wales is considered ancillary to England: pits are closed, mills are started, according to the needs of the British State, and if in good times English migrants flood into Wales for jobs, in bad times Welshmen are expected to look for work somewhere else. Historically Wales is doomed to be a satellite of England simply because it is there, disregarded or even disliked by the vast majority of the English people, misunderstood by nearly all of them, but still never to be let loose, ever again, to pursue its own policies like another bloody Ireland.

Lately British governments have paid lip service to the idea of Welsh nationhood, by setting up a Welsh Office, for instance, whose head is always a member of the Cabinet, and by making concessions on the use of the Welsh language, so that a Welsh citizen can now get a bilingual driving licence, or even dispute his tax demand in his own language. But the relationship does not really change, and is given ceremonial ratification nowadays by the investiture of the heir to the English throne as Prince of Wales, a custom instituted in its present pomp by that most ambivalent of Welsh patriots, David Lloyd George. The inescapable Goscombe John designed the regalia when in 1911 the future King Edward VIII was invested at Caernarfon at Lloyd George's instigation (the prince himself thought the occasion rather ridiculous), and the excessive enthusiasm of local landowners can be gauged by a plaque still standing on a wall near the castle, recording the generosity of the quarry-owner Sir Charles Assheton-Smith, Baronet, in demolishing three perfectly good Georgian houses, at a time of terrible poverty among his work force in the slate towns, 'in order that some thousands of his countrymen might witness the investiture of the Prince of Wales'.

Loyalties seemed just as fervent when the ceremony was performed again in 1969, and Charles Edward David was invested as the twenty-first titular Prince of Wales since the death of Llywelyn ap Gruffudd, *Ein Llyw Olaf*. Caernarfon Castle was brilliant with flags, canopies and specially designed chairs, the whole ensemble being supervised by the prince's uncle the Earl of Snowdon, né Armstrong-Jones and descended from sea-captains down Cricieth way. The harbour was alive with yachts, motor boats and the minesweeper *Cardiff*. Castle Square seethed with sightseers from all over the world, and through it coach-loads of dignitaries passed importantly by to deposit their passengers at the King's Gate. All the grandest of the Anglo-Welsh were there in full fig, Lords Lieutenant and High Sheriffs, judges and clerics and the last of the great territorial magnates, and all the poshest of the Welsh Welsh too. Bands played, guns fired, and the Queen of England presented her son to the Welsh people through the high archway of the Queen's Gate, opposite the blank space left to this day by the demolition of Assheton-Smith's houses—she in a yellow pearl-embroidered hat, he in a brand-new coronet.

The crowds cheered, and went home clutching their souvenir mugs. The dignitaries dispersed, taking with them their specially designed chairs. The Vice-President of the United States, packing away his Welsh origins (he was Hubert Humphreys), flew back to Washington, where Welshness does not win many votes. The Queen, the prince, their aides, ladies-in-waiting, bodyguards, policemen, secretaries, valets, chauffeurs, maids and clanking cavalrymen returned over Offa's Dyke to the imperial capital in London. And on the very same day, in Cardiff, six men were sentenced to imprisonment for their membership of the Free Wales Army, a quasi-military organization dedicated to achieving the independence of Wales by force. 'I sought to serve Wales', said Dennis Coslet, miner, 29, speaking in Welsh. 'I will not forget Wales in my lonely cell.'

Actually the Prince Charles who was presented to the people, or more pertinently to the television cameras, that day, was the Welshiest Prince of Wales for ages, in that he was the first to make an attempt to learn the Welsh language. Royal apologists make the most of the infinitely tenuous blood link between the House of Windsor and the House of Tudor, and even with Glyndŵr and the Llywelyns. In fact the maddest Nazi geneticist, viewing the pedigree of the Queen of England, would hardly oblige her to stitch a red dragon to her hacking-jacket, or tattoo her with a leek. There is nothing remotely Welsh about the British royal family, and there is no pretending either that the kings and queens of England have often been fond of Wales. They have never maintained houses in the country, they have never succumbed to the spell of its culture, as they have so enthusiastically adopted the kilt, sporran and porridge of the Scots, and they have generally seemed reluctant to visit the place. Nevertheless just as the Welsh have been obliged to pay duty to the kings and queens, with varying degrees of spontaneity, so most of the kings and queens have found it necessary, before or after their accession to the throne, gingerly to make some contact with the Welsh. In 1850 Edward Parry wrote a book about their visits to the country starting with Julius Caesar and ending with Queen Victoria. Here is a more selective register:

- William I went to Tyddewi in 1081, risking the journey across a violently hostile Wales with an escort of only a few knights: he was ostensibly on pilgrimage to the shrine, but was more probably making a strategic reconnaissance.

- William II led two ignominiously unsuccessful invasions of Wales.

- Henry I had a son by the incorrigible Nest.

- Henry II, about to step upon a slab bridge at Tyddewi, was screeched at by a woman that it was the Stone of Speech, *Llech Lafar*, and that it had prophesied his killing by a man with a red hand if he dared to cross it: he crossed it anyway, and died in his bed in France.

- John arrested the Bishop of Shrewsbury at the altar of Bangor Cathedral, releasing him against a ransom of 200 hawks.

- Henry III ran away in his night-shirt from Grosmont Castle when Llywelyn Fawr attacked it, and complained that Painscastle in Powys was the worst place for wolves in his entire kingdom.

- Edward I, while at Rhuddlan Castle in 1281, ordered the payment of £1. 0s. 0d. 'to a certain female Spy, to purchase her a house, as a gift'.

- Edward II was born at Caernarfon, and was immediately presented to the assembled Welsh chieftains, so legend says, as a native-born Prince of Wales who spoke not a word of English.

- Richard II, surrendering at Flint to the future Henry IV, was deserted even by his greyhound Mathe, who fawned upon his enemy like a Ci Siôn Dafydd.

- Henry IV, fighting Glyndŵr, stabled his horses at the high altar of Ystrad Fflur.

- Henry V was born at Monmouth—'All the water in Wye', said Fluellen, 'cannot wash your majesty's Welsh plood out of your pody, I can tell you that.'

- Edward V, aged 12, was campaigning in Wales when he heard he was king: three months later he was dead with his little brother in the Tower.

- Henry VII, surprised by pursuers at dinner with the Mostyns at Mostyn Hall in Clwyd, hid in a closet: the place laid for him at table was explained away as an old family custom, in case an unexpected guest arrived, and an extra cover was habitually laid at the Mostyn dinner-table until the Second World War.

- Queen Elizabeth I is reputed to have had a baby at Plas Eglwyseg near Llangollen: she was known to the Welsh as *sidanen*, 'silky one'.

- Charles I, staying at Aberhonddu after the Battle of Naseby in 1645, wrote to his son the 15-year-old Prince of Wales warning him to 'prepare for the worst': but it was three years before the king was beheaded.

- Charles II had a mistress from Dyfed, Lucy Walter 'the Rhosmarket siren', who was mother to the Duke of Monmouth: on the run after the battle of Worcester he travelled as Mr William Jones.

- James II the Roman Catholic made the pilgrimage to Holywell to pray for a son: two years later his prayer was answered, and the consequent threat of a Catholic succession put paid to the House of Stuart.

- George III wore Bala stockings for his rheumatism.

- George IV, stuck at Caergybi by adverse winds in 1821, abandoned the royal yacht and became the first king to board a steamship.

- William IV crossed the border once, in 1806, when he was staying in Shropshire: a tree was planted to mark the event, and Sir Richard Puleston, Bt., who had ushered him into Wales, was in consequence allowed to bear, as a crest of honourable augmentation, an oak tree, pendant therefrom an escutcheon charged with three ostrich feathers within a coronet.

⮞ Victoria was brought into the world by David Davies from Dyfed, and declined to sleep in the slate bed especially made for her at Penrhyn Castle.

⮞ Edward VII was brought into the world by John Williams from Dyfed, and during a visit to Y Bala was presented with a gigantic commemorative flask of R. J. Lloyd Price's Welsh whisky.

⮞ George V, in Caernarfon for the investiture of his son the Prince of Wales, thought 'the dear boy did it all remarkably well and looked so nice': during the coal strike of 1910, when troops were sent to Tonypandy, he repeatedly enquired after the health of the pit-ponies.

⮞ Edward VIII, visiting the depressed areas of South Wales in 1936, told the miners: 'Something must be done. You may be sure that all I can do for you I will.' Three weeks later he abdicated, and never set foot in Wales again for the rest of his life.

⮞ George VI, dressed as an admiral, went to Cardiff to encourage its people at the height of the German air raids in 1941.

⮞ Elizabeth II, dressed as a Druid, was made a member of the Gorsedd of Bards of the Isle of Britain—*y Gwir yn erbyn y byd!*—under the bardic name of Elisabeth o Windsor.

Five of the royal yachts were built at Pembroke Dock—the last was the lovely *Victoria and Albert*, 1899. At Portskewett, Porth Sgiwed in Gwent, at the Welsh end of the Severn railway tunnel, there used to be a Royal Siding, now unused and overgrown, into which royal trains were shunted to give their occupants a last quiet night's sleep before proceeding into Wales. In the church of Penmynydd in Ynys Môn there is an alabaster tomb of two members of the Tudor family: it is worn smooth by the fingers of supplicants who wrongly supposed it to be the tomb of Henry VII himself, and thus possessed of some Royal Virtue.

In 1905 Wales was visited by members of that archetypally English enterprise, Scott's last expedition to the Antarctic. Before leaving for the south their ship the *Terra Nova* put into Cardiff to fuel, full bunkers having been offered as a gift by the coal-owners of South Wales, and the Welsh greeted her with enthusiasm. The grimy port was hung with flags, receptions of many kinds were arranged, endless crowds made their way through Butetown to see the little vessel at the quay, and the Mayor and Corporation, in the full glory of their chains and ermined robes, went on board to wish the crew good luck. The Englishmen of the *Terra Nova*, though, were not so taken with Cardiff as Cardiff was with them. Edward Wilson thought the affectionate hooting of ships' horns, sirens, guns and bells no more than 'a perfectly hideous din', while Titus Oates wrote in his diary of their proud aldermanic visitors: 'The Mayor and his crowd came on board and I never saw such a mob—they are Labour Socialists. The only gentleman I have seen come aboard is the telephone operator.'

The English indeed have seldom disguised their distaste for things Welsh. Until very recently the very word 'Welsh' was a pejorative in their language. A Welsh mile was always interminable, a Welsh cricket was a louse, a Welsh pearl was a fake, a Welsh law brief was exceptionally obscure, a Welshman's hug was the itch, a Welshman's fiddle was the itch too, Welsh parsley was the hangman's rope, Welsh rabbit was toasted cheese, when you said someone was making a Welshman's hose of something you meant he was twisting it, and if you accused him of Welshing you were accusing him of failing to pay a bet.

Some of this prejudice is doubtless as old as England itself, and dates from the time when the Saxons were battling so fiercely against the obstreperous and peculiar tribesmen of the Welsh hills. The long battles of the Norman invasions cannot have helped either, fought as they were by hapless English levies in the rain. When Llywelyn Olaf visited London with some of his nobles in 1277 they found themselves jostled by crowds wherever they went, 'staring at them as if they had been monsters, and laughing at their uncouth garb and appearance'. In the fourteenth century there were anti-Welsh riots at Oxford, and a mob stormed the streets howling 'War, war, war, slay, slay, slay the Welsh dogs and their whelps', and obliging Welsh scholars to piss on the town gates and then kiss the spot. In the sixteenth century John Skelton told, in his *Merry Tales*, how God tired of all the Welshmen who had gone to Heaven, and who troubled everyone else with their 'craking and babbling': St Peter, he said, went out of Heaven's gates 'and cried with a loud voice; Cause Bobe; that is much as to say, roasted cheese, which thing the Welshmen hearing, ranne out of Heaven at a great pace. And when St Peter saw them all out, he suddenly went into Heaven and locked the door and so sparred all the Welsh-men out.'

The flood of Welshmen who followed the Tudors to London incited, as immigrants to London are inclined to, some distinctly racialist reactions. On St David's Day they used to bake ginger-bread Welshmen, skewered: Pepys records, 1 March 1666, an effigy of a man 'dressed like a Welshman' hanging by the neck from a pole. Sir Thomas Overbury, in his *Characters*, expressed what was probably a common enough English view of the generic Welshman:

He hath the abilities of the mind in *potentia*, and *actu* nothing but boldnesse . . . Above all men he loves an herald, and speakes pedigrees naturally. He accounts none well descended, that call him not cousin; and preferres Owen Glendower before any of the nine worthies. The first note of his familiarity is the confession of his valour . . . To conclude, he is precious in his own conceit, and upon S. Davies day without comparison.

Often enough fear or distrust has been at the bottom of these emotions. The long Welsh resistance cost thousands of English lives, and perhaps there was a residual superstitious thought that the Welsh, the last of the original Britons, might one day come back to England and claim their own. 'As to how things are in the land of Wales', reported an official from North Wales in 1296, 'we still cannot be any too sure . . . As you well know, Welshmen are Welshmen . . .' 'Beware of Wales', warned *The Libelle of English Policye* in the fifteenth century, 'Christ Jesus must us keep, That it makes not our child's child to weep.' More often, though, the bigotry has been based upon sheer ignorance. The English have always been astoundingly ignorant about Wales— even now, cultivated people living within a few miles of Offa's Dyke know nothing whatever about its history or its culture, and don't much want to either. Over the centuries this blank incomprehension has often expressed itself in contempt and contumely, and helped to keep the old relationship sufficiently sour.

One could make an anthology of English Cymruphobia or con-descension. Defoe on Welsh towns: 'The most to be said of this town [Aberhonddu] is what indeed I have said of many places in Wales, viz, that it is very antient.' Dr Johnson on Welsh rivers: 'Let us jump over it [a stream in Clwyd] directly, and show them how an *Englishman* should

treat a *Welsh* river.' Matthew Arnold on the Welsh language: 'The
sooner the Welsh language disappears the better—the better for
England, the better for Wales.' Evelyn Waugh on Welsh manners:
'Everyone in Wales has black spittle and whenever he meets you he says
borra-da and spits.' Thackeray on Welsh hospitality: 'If ever you go to
Dolgelley, don't stay at the Lion Hotel, For there's nothing to put in
your belly, And the waiter don't answer the bell.' Celia Fiennes, 1698,
on Welsh people: 'Barefoote and bare leg'd a nasty sort of people.'
Archbishop Thomas Herring, 1740, on the Welsh landscape: 'Like the
rubbish of creation.' A quarry manager, 1900, on Welsh workmen: 'So
ignorant and childish that there is no coping with them.' Archbishop
Cosmo Lang, 1910, on Welsh *hwyl*: 'That mysterious possession
affecting the Celtic temperament which makes the speaker say he
knows not what, and excite the audience they know not why.' A
seventeenth-century MP on Welsh country folk: 'Devil worshippers,
living like thieves and robbers in their mountains, the most base,
peasantly, perfidious people in the World.' The London *Daily
Telegraph*, 1860s, on Welsh geography: 'A small country, unfavourably
situated . . . with an indifferent soil and inhabited by an unenterprising
people.' A Royalist officer, 1640s, on the prospect of a posting to
Wales: 'If your Highness shall be pleased to command me to the Turk,
or Jew, or Gentile, I will go on my bare feet to serve you, but from the
Welsh, good Lord, deliver us.' An English visitor on Welsh patriotism,
1860: 'It appears to me that the Welsh people think that Wales was
made for the Welsh alone.' Louis Heren, journalist, 1982, on the state
of the Union: 'We are stuck with Wales.' Herbert Asquith, soon to be
Prime Minister of Great Britain, on the possibility of visiting the
western part of the kingdom: 'I would sooner go to hell.'

Most of all it has been that 'craking and babbling' of the Welsh
language that has made English hackles rise. The Blue Books of
Treason, as we know, declared it the cause and front of every kind of
moral turpitude, but most Englishmen seem to have disliked it for less
specific reasons. Perhaps it is the sheer foreignness of the tongue that
so unnerves and therefore irritates them, and brings out some self-
defensive scorn—the very idea that after all these centuries a tongue so
utterly unrelated to their own should survive within the confines of
their kingdom! Also Welsh possesses the menace of a secret language,
making them feel they are being talked about behind their backs, or
plotted against. They realized very early the power of Welsh poetry,

which is why they repeatedly tried to degrade the status of Welsh professional bards: in 1402 they enacted a law to banish 'many diseases and mishaps which have happened before this time in the land of Wales by many wasters, rhymers, minstrels and other vagabonds', and in the sixteenth century they declared peripatetic poets and musicians to be vagrants legally whippable, stockable or deprivable of their ears.

And they always laughed at the language. 'The native jibberish is usually prattled throughout the whole of Taphydom', wrote an Englishman genially enough in the seventeenth century, and few of his compatriots ever have learnt to take it more seriously. Comical distortions and misunderstandings have resulted. Abaty Cwm Hir, which means the Abbey of the Long Valley, used to be Englishized as Come Here Abbey. The mountain called Moel y Golfa, the Bare Hill of the Place of the Pass, comes out still as Molly Golfa. The Normans made a brave enough try at transliterating the name of Llanidloes, as Thlanydleys, and Leyland's sixteenth-century version of Eifionydd, Hiujonith, at least has charm. Llandarcy, however, the name the Anglo-Persian Oil Company gave to its new refinery at Swansea in 1922, does not refer as one might suppose to some otherwise forgotten St Tarsi: it honours the company's founder, William Knox D'Arcy, and recognizes only the sacred nature of the catalytic cracking process.

Unless you count the Channel Islands, whose sovereignty the Normans brought to England with them, Wales is the oldest of the English colonies—and may well turn out to be the last. In some ways its condition is a classic illustration of imperialism, in which the entire destiny of a small country is engorged by that of a larger, economy, culture, politics and all. One often detects in the attitudes of the Welsh towards the English the postures that Indians used to adopt towards their masters of the British Raj, and one sees in the attitudes of the English towards the Welsh nearly all those mixed motives, from the benevolent to the venal, which once impelled them towards the dominion of the world.

Here as in the Empire at large, in modern times English domination has seldom been brutal, but often enough the troops have been sent in to quell a disturbance, and then the scene is pure imperialism: the cowering indigenes pressed against their walls, the cavalry clattering, lances gleaming, moustaches waxed, up the streets of Wrexham, Tonypandy, or Llanidloes—a troop of dragoons arriving at Merthyr in 1800 showed the natives what to expect of their swordsmanship by slicing the crown off a man's hat and cutting a dog in two outside the Star Inn. In 1856 a former Indian Army officer, applying for the post of Chief Constable of Caernarfonshire, suggested that he would be particularly suitable for the job 'as in India he had served against the Hill Tribes on the Western Frontier'. The Chief Constable of Glamorgan in 1910 had learnt his trade in the Egyptian gendarmerie—'with a dervish yell and batons drawn', it was said of his constables at one affray among the miners, 'they dashed out . . . and cut a way clean through the densely packed mob'. The garrison towns of Wales have played a role exactly like the cantonments of British India—Aberhonddu for instance, whose barracks stand beside a tree-lined boulevard with flags flying and sentries at the gate, was garrisoned specifically to ensure military control over the tumultuous communities of the coal valleys to the south, just as Secunderabad, say, kept its eye on the dissidents of Hyderabad.

Textbook imperialism too has been the English exploitation of Welsh resources. In the fifteenth century Adam of Usk thought Wales to be worth £60,000 a year to England: by the nineteenth century its value was incalculable. Cocoa from Ghana—opium from India—gold from South Africa—coal and iron from Wales: such were patterns of the imperial economy, when the whole Empire was no more than Greater England. No matter that Wales, like India the opium-source, played an active as well as a passive role in the imperial process: essentially it remained a provider of raw materials, with the result that its own economy has always been unbalanced—always extracting or processing, seldom actually creating. Scores of English capitalists made their vast fortunes out of Wales, just as they might have made them out of Canada or Australia. When they were ennobled for their success, as a Lord Roberts might choose Kandahar for his title, so they requisitioned names from this nearer colony: and just as imperialists elsewhere are remembered in Cox's Bazar or Jacobabad, so Wales was bequeathed its Butetowns and Beauforts.

The twentieth-century poet 'Gwenallt', David Gwenallt Jones of Pontardawe in Glamorgan, saw the awful march of the Forestry Commission's conifers as cultural imperialism of the most sinister kind, systematically eroding Welsh rural society:

Fforest lle bu ffermydd . . .
Ac yn y tywyllwch yn ei chanol hi
Y mae ffau'r Minotawros Seisnig . . .

Forest where there used to be farms . . .
And in the darkness in the middle of it
Is the den of the English Minotaur . . .

Certainly those gloomy woodlands, spreading everywhere over the bare hills, fundamentally change the feel of Wales, and other English exploitations, too, have been astonishingly insensitive to Welshness. In the 1950s the Corporation of Liverpool, in England, decided that the valley of the small river Tryweryn, running down to the Dee near Y Bala, would make a convenient reservoir for the supply of free water to Merseyside. The fact that the hamlet of Capel Celyn stood in the middle of the site did not deter them: nor did the fact that it was one of the very Welshest parts of all Wales. Their brochure describing the project did not mention that it was in Wales at all, and the name of not a single Welshman appeared upon it: the water engineer was from Liverpool, the consulting engineers were from London, the landscape consultant was Frederick Gibberd, CBE, the contractors were from Wolverhampton and the Fishery Adviser from Aberdeen. The Welsh local authorities found themselves powerless to oppose the scheme, and Welsh patriots were infuriated by it—nearly thirty years later the slogan *Cofiwch Dryweryn*, 'Remember Tryweryn', is still to be seen in fading white paint on rocks and stone walls here and there: but it made no difference anyway, and as in bitter confirmation of an old fairy-tale, all that is to be seen of Capel Celyn today is the shining blue surface of the lake (and a memorial building which Mr Gibberd designed to house the tombstones from the chapel yard).

Sometimes the imperial allegories are harsher still. There is a little lake in Dyfed, Llyn Eiddwen, which standing lonely in the low hills above the sea, used to be the site of a famous annual prayer meeting. Hundreds of people went there, parked their wagons around the lake like so many Boer-trekkers in the veld, sang their old Welsh hymns, sighed and shouted to their charismatic preachers. Go there now, and you will find it dominated by campers of a different kind—a shambled community of English caravan people, with old buses and rusty cars, with beards and dogs and raggety clothes, settled there apparently permanently upon that once holy shore. No language but English is

heard at Llyn Eiddwen today: and every now and then, with a violent
screech, a rumble and a flash of red, a fighter aircraft of the Royal Air
Force hurls itself towards the lake, which is used as a practice target,
when the weather is favourable, several times a day.

Generally, though, the colonial presence has been more subtly,
insidiously or unconsciously inserted. Gradually, gradually, Englishness has seeped into even the remotest parts of Wales, and streng-
thened the ascendancy of the one culture over the other simply by
being there. Year by year the corner shops, so long in the hands of
Morgans or Pughes, are taken over by Smiths or Brackenburys, as the
trading posts of the Englishmen captured the business of Cree or Zulu
in other territories far away. Thousands of English people have retired
to the former seaports of the Welsh coast, now transformed into
holiday resorts: speaking not a word of Welsh, generally learning not a
word either, indifferent to the history of Wales, impervious to its
culture, doing all they can to make their new home as much as possible
like their old one, just as they would in the plains and jungles of
Empire.

On a hill outside Monmouth, the Kymin, the imperial metaphor is
made complete with an example of that ultimate expression of English
dominance, the hill-station. Up there above the Wye all is just like
Ootacamund. Delectably encouched in their gardens the little villas lie,
trellised, rose-embowered, with lazy fat Labradors lying on their
verandahs, reached by nooky lanes and given authentic Ooty names
—Cedars, Rosedale, Lilac Cottage or Mountain Home. Far, far away
is the jabber of the natives!

But *chwarae teg*, fair play, there have been countless Englishmen and
women devoted to Wales, as there were countless devoted to India, and
many more are fascinated rather than frightened by the fact of its
foreignness bang next door. Wales was an obvious choice of residence
for the Lady of Palmyra, the marvellously unconventional Lady Hester
Stanhope, who lived in a cottage near Aberhonddu before going off to
marry her Bedouin chief. It provided a happy home for the Ladies of
Llangollen, Eleanor Butler and Sarah Ponsonby, 'the most celebrated
virgins in Europe', who closeted in their half-timbered house 'like two
little old gentlemen' were visited by all the swells who passed by on
their way to Ireland, and by every touring notable. John Bright loved

Llandudno so much that he went there every summer for twenty-five years: his five-year-old son, taken for a walk through St Tudno's churchyard in 1864, suddenly said 'Oh Mama, when I am dead I want to be buried here'—a week later he died of scarlet fever, and there in the yard he lies.

Shelley lived for a time in the Elan Valley, near Rhayader, and for a time near Porthmadog, running away from there after an alleged attack on his life by an unsympathetic shepherd. His friend Edward Trelawney brought both wife and mistress to his house near Usk (but Mrs T., we are told, 'was so manifestly superior to her rival in mind and person that she had the suffrage of all classes . . .'). Swinburne used to like pub-crawling in Aberystwyth with his friend George Powell of Nanteos, and Tennyson is said to have been inspired to write 'Crossing the Bar' by watching the tide at Abermo. George Fox the evangelist had a vision on the top of Cadair Idris: Charles Darwin was excited by that mountain too—'Old Cader is a grand fellow!': so was Thomas Love Peacock—'On the top of Cadair Idris, I felt how happy a man might be with a little money, and a sane intellect, and reflected with astonishment and pity on the madness of the multitude.'

Gladstone, who married a Welsh wife, worked so enthusiastically for Welshness that for years half the farmhouses of Wales contained a picture of him, along with William Williams Pantycelyn and Bishop Morgan the translator of the Bible: on the southern flank of Yr Wyddfa an inscribed rock marks the spot where in 1892 the Grand Old Man, aged 82, addressed a huge crowd on the subject of 'Justice for Wales', and joined in the hymn-singing afterwards. The man who finally broke the political hegemony of the Watkin Wynns in Clwyd was an Englishman, Stuart Rendel, who won a famous election there in 1880: Eton, Oxford, Anglican and an arms manufacturer by trade, he so identified himself with Welsh causes that he became known as 'The Member for Wales', and in 1897 he gave to the nation the land, in Aberystwyth, for its National Library.

Ben Jonson studied the Welsh language. Graham Sutherland lived and painted for years at Picton Castle in Dyfed, the home still of the Philippses who had supported Griffith Jones and his Locomotive Schools so long before. Mountain-climbers of every kind, from stately Victorian pioneers to earthy virtuosi of the 1980s, have frequented Eryri: when John Hunt, who led the first ascent of Everest, was made a peer in 1966, he chose to call himself Lord Hunt of Llanfair Waterdine. In the churchyard at Oystermouth was buried, at the height of the evangelical movement, that champion of purity in thought and speech, Thomas Bowdler. It was Thomas De Quincey the opium-eater who wrote that a world-weary man who sought the peace of a monastery without its gloomy captivity could not do better than wander around the inns of North Wales—'sleeping, for instance, and breakfasting in Carnarvon; then, by an easy nine-mile walk, going forwards to dinner at Bangor, thence to Aber—nine miles; or to Llanberris; and so on for ever . . .'.

And of all the Englishmen who have concerned themselves with Wales, few have treated the matter with more delicacy and subtlety of instinct than the greatest of them all, William Shakespeare. It has been argued (of course) that Shakespeare was a Welshman himself, so well did he know the foibles of the people, and there are several places in Wales which he is claimed to have visited. More probably he drew his knowledge from the Welsh drovers he must have seen all his life passing through Stratford-upon-Avon, and from the all too assertive Welsh colony which then swarmed in full coxcombry through Tudor London.

We see many types of Welsh person, scrupulously drawn, in the pages of Shakespeare's plays. We see the Welsh gentleman, proud but touchy, gifted but in English eyes risible, in the person of Owain Glyndŵr himself:

GLENDOWER. I can call spirits from the vasty deep.
HOTSPUR. Why, so can I, or so can any man;
  But will they come when you do call for them?

GLENDOWER.   . . . At my birth
  The frame and huge foundation of the earth
  Shaked like a coward.
HOTSPUR. Why, so it would have done at the same season if your mother's cat
  had but kitten'd.

We see the Welsh captain *in genere* in the person of Fluellen, pedantic about the arts of war, vain, quick to quarrel, preposterously patriotic in his Welshness, yet with it all a skilful soldier, and stout of heart —'Though it appear a little out of fashion, There is much care and valour in this Welshman . . .' The archetypal Welsh lady is Lady Mortimer, Glyndŵr's daughter, so soft-hearted, so inarticulate in English, so sweet-voiced to the lute (LADY PERCY. Lie still, ye thief, and hear the lady sing in Welsh. HOTSPUR. I had rather hear Lady, my brach, howl in Irish). The essential Welsh buffoons tumble in farce and misunderstanding among the oaks in *The Merry Wives of Windsor*. Shakespeare nearly always got them right: not just for English audiences, who could find in these characters their prejudices entertainingly confirmed, but also for Welshmen, who must have recognized the truths behind the caricatures (and not least perhaps for Queen Elizabeth and her powerful Welsh courtiers, John Dee, Robert Cecil, who would hardly have wanted the land of the Tudors lampooned . . .).

Platoons of Welsh scholars have devoted themselves to the Welshness of Shakespeare. The bank where the wild thyme grew has been confidently located near Aberhonddu. Prospero is said to be a portrait of John Dee. Fluellen (a corruption of Llywelyn) is thought to have been modelled upon the character of Dafydd Gam, that one-eyed stalwart who tried to murder Owain Glyndŵr, and who was himself killed on the field of Agincourt. Sharp-eyed scholars have discovered at least one line of authentic *cynghanedd*—'My conceal'd lady to our cancell'd love' (*Romeo and Juliet*, Act III, Scene 3).

In 1911 there arrived at Chepstow a well-heeled and resolute American physician, Dr Orville Ward Owen of Detroit, who believed on indistinct evidence that the original manuscripts of Shakespeare's plays (actually by Bacon, he thought) were deposited in sixty-six iron chests in the bed of the river Wye, where it passed by the town below the castle. He spent many thousands of pounds building a coffer-dam to explore the site: but all he found in the mud was the substructure of a hitherto unsuspected Roman bridge, and he was not much interested in that.

The effect of these attitudes and acquaintances, over a thousand years and more, has been to leave the neighbours in an uneasy equilibrium. It is almost a miracle, given the odds, that Wales survives as a recognizable entity at all, still a different place, still cherishing a separate culture, still speaking Welsh, just across that open frontier. Of course it is an uneven balance. The English by and large know little, and care less, about the Welsh, but the Welsh are all too knowledgeable about the English, and most of them would probably admit that if they have to live within the shadow of a mighty Power, better the English Power than most. At least it is an adversary worth the fighting! The most furious Welsh separatists admit to the majesty of the English tradition, the arcane splendour of Parliament, even at a pinch the style of British arms: the sternest of Welsh republicans is prepared to concede a vulgar fascination to the monarchy. If Welshmen despise many of the English people who come to live in Wales, many more are welcomed with respect and affection.

But uneven, of course. History and geography have seen to that, and have made of the Welsh one of Europe's most absolute minorities. They do not form a detached fragment of a wider whole, like the German-speakers of Poland or Czechoslovakia, or the Austrians of the Italian Tyrol, or the Swedish minority in Finland, or even the Scots-Irish in Ulster. The Welsh are on their own. Nobody else speaks their language or shares their history. There is no Greater Wales to which they can look as irredentists, or whose spokesmen can back their cause at the United Nations. Only a few peculiarly lonely communities, the Basques or the Armenians perhaps, share something of the Welsh condition, and even they may find it difficult to grasp: the truth is that the Welsh are engaged in a perpetual protest often without knowing it, a protest less in the intent than in the instinct—a protest with which many of them vehemently disagree, in fact, against a force which does not always understand what the protest is about.

For at heart British governments of any political persuasion regard Wales simply as a region of the United Kingdom, like the North-West, or East Anglia. Its culture is an irrelevance in the world of the twentieth century, and since it has inexplicably survived the worst that force and legislation could do to stamp it out, is best left to be killed by a moderate degree of kindness. Why, they say, have not scores of Welshmen themselves pursued these policies, as members of British governments down the years? Is not the majority of the Welsh populace quite content with the way things are? Look what happened in 1979, when they held a referendum about Welsh autonomy—five to one against the idea!

Yet oppression it is, by the nature of things, just as the referendum offered only such a pale inkling of self-government that almost nobody really believed in it. The Welsh relationship with England, 2.75 million beside 46 million, 8,000 square miles beside 50,000, half a million speakers of the Welsh language against the hundreds of millions of English-speakers across the whole world—the colossal imbalance so affects the Welsh sense of identity that the protest has long been dispersed, like a mist, through the whole landscape of Welsh life, revealing itself in sudden flares of half-realized resentment, and in a profound sense of mingled sadness and frustration: the neuroses of a family that no longer quite knows itself, its personality having been so long rebuffed, denigrated, overawed or patronized by the heedless grandeur of the people next door.

11. The Resistance

What did Owain Glyndŵr want, as his guerrillas stormed about the hills at his command, and the Welsh students hastened home from Oxford to join them? A Welsh Nation-State, we hear him shout, sovereign among sovereignties, sustaining its own culture under the authority of its own 'mighty and magnificent prince'! And what did his simpler supporters want, as they followed him so loyally towards the inevitable tragedy? They wanted to live, no doubt, in a country they could call their own, they hoped for better things in a time and a place of poverty. But really perhaps, prince and people alike, they were all fighting for something not so easy to articulate—a return to that half-imaginary Golden Age, that lost age of dignity, which survived deep within the Welsh consciousness. They could never achieve it, and perhaps they knew that. Their brief years of triumph represented a climax in the history of Wales, but changed nothing in the end: for the Welsh always were, and perhaps always will be, in a condition of resistance against the present, yearning sometimes for a more magnificent past, sometimes for a future more rewarding. It is the nature of the people: very likely the genius too.

I N a somewhat grimy park beside the dual highway in Pontypridd, along the road from William Edwards's famous bridge, two men stand in bronze statuary, sculpted by—who else?—Goscombe John RA. They are Evan James, died 1878, and his son James, died 1902, and they are the author and the composer respectively of the Welsh national anthem, *Mae Hen Wlad fy Nhadau*, 'Land of my Fathers'. The father was a weaver, the son a publican, and just as they are unlikely progenitors of a patriotic hymn, being about as far removed as anyone could be from Elgar or Rouget de Lisle, so the hymn itself is rare among national anthems in being entirely without arrogance. It does not wish Wales to be mightier yet, or want its enemies confounded: it records only a determination that Welshness, especially Welshness embodied in the Welsh language, shall somehow survive—not conquer anyone else, not distribute its own splendours across the nations, but simply *parhau*, remain in being. *O! bydded yr hen iaith barhau!*—'Oh, may the old language survive!' The Messrs James do not look fiery men at all, and the anthem too, which can bring a ready tear to the eyes of most Welsh patriots, is more an expression of commiseration than of majesty.

This is the style of Wales. Its foreign wars have been entirely defensive—since the emergence of Wales as a nation, in the eighth century perhaps, its only aggressive actions have been sporadic raids over Offa's Dyke, 'to steal a leg of beef'; although for centuries Welshmen thought they had a right of sovereignty over the whole of the Isle of Britain, the only serious design upon English territory was Owain Glyndŵr's. The Welsh have seldom suffered from national ambition, only national grievance. In ancient times it expressed itself in ambush and guerrilla skirmish against the Normans and English in Wales: more recently it has been channelled into a national mood of unappeasable radicalism, vented in spasmodic outbursts of anger generation after generation down the years.

Each of these cries of frustration has been in some sense a call to preserve a Welsh consciousness, whether it be a manner of life, or a mode of faith, or a political entity, or just a sense of place and self-respect. There can be few dissident movements anywhere in the world so old as the long resistance which is, *mutatis mutandis*, the one constant purpose of Wales. Lousy Corporations, Despot Dukes, Kings, Regents, Haughty Aristocrats, Exploiters, Traitors, Capitalists and Fascist Pigs of every kind have found themselves assaulted by Welsh radicals, with bludgeon as with broadsheet: dimly amid the smoke of battle the Welsh Identity, like some veiled idol, grimly and sometimes mockingly surveys the still undecided campaign.

Welsh radicalism first found its modern voice, first flexed its muscles, in a ruthless clash of ideologies in the 1830s. The best way to get the feel of this conflict is to drive across the bleak and tremendous moorland country, the Blaenau or Valley Heads, that separates the Gwent and Glamorgan coal valleys from the pastoral country of mid-Wales, rising to some 1,300 feet above the deep clefts of Ebbw, Sirhowy, Rhymni and Rhondda on one side, the gentle Usk on the other. This is country unlike any other in Wales, partly because of its terrain, partly because of its fateful associations, and coming to it is like entering some high forcing chamber of history. Up your road goes, up the steep limestone ridge, pocked with caves and old workings and the remains of tramways, until crossing the ridge of the escarpment you find the harsh expanse of the Blaenau stretching there before you. Across it runs the cruel Heads of the Vallies highway, car, trucks and motor-bikes crawling through the wind, and there are huddled clumps of houses around, and mounds that are the remains of long-abandoned workings, and half-obliterated tips. It is colourless but compelling —the air rasping, the moorland glowering, and on the south side of the road the industrial valleys suddenly plunging away with their mines and chapels and railway tracks jam-packed and canyon-like towards the sea.

From this stern belvedere, in the 1830s, the ironworkers and colliers of the Blaenau looked down to Merthyr, Tredegar and Nant-y-glo, and saw the Baileys, the Crawshays and their kind accumulating wealth almost unimaginable in their mansions and mock castles. Everything was new down there then, and raw, and abrasive, and forceful. Only a few years before those valleys had been pure farmland and sheep-run, and the workers had nearly all been imported. Many of them came from impoverished rural communities elsewhere in Wales; they knew nothing about the industrial life, had never heard of a trade union, and had probably worked for nobody but Owen Jones Tŷ-mawr, who was their second cousin on their mother's side and a fellow member of Bethesda Calvinist.

They already made, nevertheless, a tough and distinctive community: old-school rural Welsh, God-fearing and sometimes bookish, leavened by rougher incomers, footloose Englishmen from the Midlands or the West Country, or Irishmen living in coveys of their own with their fierce wives and raggety children. Except for the Irish perhaps, these people cherished very early a strong sense of social grievance. Conditions in the ironworks and coal-mines were fearful. Women in filthy rags pulled appalling loads along tramways, children hardly more than infants worked underground, or did hideously dangerous tasks in iron-foundries. 'I have been below [in Plymouth Mines, Merthyr] six or eight months', said Susan Reece, aged 6, in 1849, 'and I don't like it much. I come here at six in the morning and leave at six at night.' 'I work here [at Penydarren] cleaning the iron ore', said Margaret Morgan, aged 80. 'We start at eight o'clock and finish at six o'clock.' 'I have been a hammer-man for two years', said Evan Hopkins, aged 11. 'I work from six in the morning until six at night. The work is very hard and makes me sweat sadly.' 'I work for twelve hours a day and I stand all the time except when I eat my food', said Morgan Jenkins, aged 6. 'I have not been burned yet.'

The rule of the ironmasters was absolute. They controlled everything. They owned the housing, they offered the only jobs, they ran the infamous Truck Shops in which their employees were obliged to do virtually all their shopping, often at extortionate rates: the very last of these still stands at Rhymni, now used partly as a recreation club, and its solid buildings beside the railway line speak powerfully still of the days when it had its own grocery, ironmongery, furniture and drapery departments, its own butchers and bakers, its own farm, brewery, slaughterhouse, stables and railway siding, the whole dominating the domestic life of the entire community, and providing unfailing profits for the Rhymney Iron Company (head office, London). Even at their most paternal, the ironmasters were like the great plantation owners of the slave colonies. Up the road from Rhymni stands Trefnewydd, Newtown or Butetown, which was built in the 1800s, on enlightened classical lines, to be a model settlement for the ironworkers, but which looks in fact remarkably like a punishment barracks; while the monumental stables erected by the Guests at Dowlais, with a school above them for the education of infant dependants, pointedly if unintentionally suggested that in the order of the iron industry horses and humans were of equal social status.

The capital of these miseries was Merthyr Tydfil on the river Taf Fawr, dominated by its several enormous ironworks. Just recognizable, embedded in the mass of this ferociously growing town, were the houses and values of the country settlement that had been there in the previous century—still called, if only figuratively, 'the village'. For the rest, Merthyr was all iron, all furnaces, slums and chimneys, 30,000 people without a public sewer, its river banks one long line of rubbish, its streets obstructed with heaps of ordure and rotting garbage, the whole overlooked, as in a fairy-tale, by the great mansions of the capitalists beyond the smoke. Carlyle thought this one of the squalidist and ugliest places on earth, but in the very year of his visit to the town *Black's Picturesque Guide to Wales* was able to draw its readers' attention to 'the following mansions in the vicinity': Cyfarthfa Castle (William Crawshay, Esq.), Dowlais House (Sir Ivor Bertie Guest, Bt.), Aberammon (Crawshay Bailey, Esq.), Plymouth House (Anthony Hill, Esq.)—ironmasters' houses every one of them, and almost obscenely opulent.

The masters knew very well that trouble was bound to come. Far from being cowed or sullen, the work force was immensely lively. Sick and hungry the people may often have been, but they lived their lives to the hilt, throwing themselves into activities of every kind, from drink to athletics, from cock-fighting to Unitarianism, with a terrific gusto. The population was young, energetic, unruly and high-spirited—Lord Melbourne, surveying it with distaste from London, called Merthyr 'the worst and most formidable district in the kingdom'—and it was full of clever craftsmen and sharp intellects. When trouble did come, said a report to the Government at Westminster, 'the causes of the Ebullition were neither momentary nor specific, but rather the effect of a high state of excitement for a long period'.

'There go the Devils', a woman screamed one day in 1831, as the Crawshay family passed by on their way to church. The early decades of the nineteenth century, when so much of Europe stirred towards revolution, were frightening years for the magnates of the valleys. At Nant-y-glo the Baileys built their fortress towers, and garrisoned them with Workmen Volunteers. At Hirwaun Francis Crawshay built a three-storey watchtower on the mountain above the ironworks, and armed it with brass cannon—allegedly just a folly, but 'that's where their spies were', local people tell you to this day, pointing to its grey ruins, 'keeping an eye on the workers'. Cyfarthfa Castle was not entirely ornamental, either: it stood watchfully amidst its park, surrounded by a wide field of fire, slitted for muskets and moated, on the town side, by its ornamental lake.

The strangest militants to protest against the injustices of this Iron Age were a group of terrorists who called themselves, nobody knows why, the Scotch Cattle. They operated in 'herds' of ten or a dozen men, each under its own *Tarw*, Bull, and for fifteen years, in the 1820s and 1830s, they constituted a secret guild in the country east of Merthyr, 'The Black Domain'. They organized strikes, they terrorized blacklegs, profiteers, unfair employers and grasping contractors, and they forced the work-people into their first experience of collective action. Their style was brutal. 'Damn you', said one of their threatening letters to company officials, 'you damned set of toads that you are!' 'O Lord look on thy situation', uncooperative miners were told, 'for you shall be in hell before Monday morning.' 'We are determined to draw the hearts out of all the men named above', a proclamation warned strikebreakers, 'and fix two of the hearts upon the horns of the Bull . . . So we testify with our blood.' Nevertheless they seem to have had most of the people with them, and they were never betrayed to the authorities. 'Scotch Law', the protection of a comrade against Authority at all costs, whatever the circumstances, became part of the social code of the industrial valleys, and remains powerful to this day: when in 1983 a man at Abercwmboi, Glamorgan, helped the police to send three burglars to jail, the whole village ostracized him.

Gunshots, the blast of horns, drum-beats somewhere—these were the signs that the Cattle were holding one of their meetings on the mountain. Often just the distant sound of them was enough to frighten a grasping shopkeeper into lower prices, or send a blackleg scurrying home from the works. If not, terrible things ensued. Commandos with blackened faces, disguised in masks or skins, might call at your house at midnight, blowing horns, rattling chains, lowing and growling, to smash your windows, destroy your furniture, set fire to your curtains and leave their red mark upon the door. Rapacious merchants found their stores sacked and their ledgers thrown into the street, disobliging companies had their wagons burnt and their canal barges sunk. 'The wayfaring traveller', said the highly respectable *Merthyr Guardian*, 'passes the scene of outrages often bordering on murder, in silence and fear . . . all that he sees is a living proof, that from Dowlais to Abergavenny, TO HIM THERE IS NO LAW.' The Scotch Cattle stormed on until 1835, when Edward Morgan, miner, 32, was hanged in Monmouth gaol for his part in an affray—martyrdom to his comrades, object lesson to Authority.

But by then anyway the primitive protest of the Bull and his herds had been overtaken by a more sophisticated demonstration of the people's anger, the Merthyr Rising of 1831. This was very nearly revolution—rumour said it was part of a much wider insurrectionary plot, and it was claimed that a wandering corps of pedlars was co-ordinating a rising with secret messages, like the strange sellers of *chupattis* who heralded the Indian Mutiny. Certainly it was during the Merthyr Rising, at Hirwaun, that the red flag of revolution was first flown in Britain—stained with calf's blood, they said, and raised above the mob together with a loaf of bread on a stick.

The affair was sparked crudely enough by a cut in wages at the Cyfarthfa works, but social reform was what the rioters demanded. The planning, such as it was, took place chiefly in the pubs of Merthyr, in those days the chief repositories of Welsh political awareness, and if it began rationally enough, it ended in chaos, thousands of armed workers roaming the town and the countryside around, with guerrilla forces setting up road-blocks, destroying Truck Shops, taking violent vengeance on managers and harsh agents, and threatening to throw the whole area town and Blaenau into armed revolution.

It was put down, of course. The troops came in and did that, killing several rioters in a fracas outside the Castle Hotel. The huge crowds sullenly dispersed, taking their dead with them: all over the Blaenau, we are told, mourning widows buried their corpses surreptitiously in the night, to avoid official reprisals. Eighteen ring-leaders were arrested. Most of them were sentenced to transportation, but one of them, Richard Lewis, called Dic Penderyn after his home at Aberafan, was hanged at Cardiff in August 1831. He protested his innocence to the end, and innocent he seems to have been; and so as the Welsh resistance gained an ambivalent new ethic, 'Scotch Law', in the Black Domain to the east, in Merthyr Tydfil it found an equivocal martyr, whose name was to go into the folklore with the Llywelyns and the Owains, and who is intimately remembered by Welsh people still.

Ask almost anyone in the streets of Aberafan, which adjoins the steel town of Port Talbot in Glamorgan, and you will be directed to Dic's grave in the churchyard of St Mary's, at the western end of the town. He was buried there, where he had a parochial right to be buried, only after repeated refusals by Anglican clergymen nearer Cardiff to allow his interment in their graveyards. So on the back of a wagon his corpse had lurched village by village through the Vale of Glamorgan to the town where he was born. He was already a popular hero, and huge crowds stood in the street, all around the churchyard wall, silently listening to the funeral service. Behind the church the hills arose; before it, in those days, there was nothing much but the sea.

Dic's grave is jammed tightly between others, as though for reassurance, and his immediate neighbours include a piquant pair. Next to him is a proper Establishment figure, a Portreeve of Aberafan no less, who must now and then turn down there, one feels, to find himself beside so famous a felon. But next to *him* there lies the carter who conveyed poor Dic's body so sadly through the Vale to Aberafan. He asked then that when his own time came he should be buried somewhere near: and when it came, he was.

A digression now on egalitarianism—far far up the valley of the Nantcol, in the fierce Ardudwy mountains of southern Gwynedd —beyond the last tourist café of the coast, the last bed-and-breakfast notice, the last trekking stable—past Salem Chapel where the devil lurked in the old lady's cloak—over the river, and over again—far up there to the glacial plateau at the top, barren and boggy, where there stands the fine old farm called Maes-y-Garnedd. From this almost inconceivably remote place, in the roadless seventeenth century, came John Jones the regicide, one of Cromwell's most resilient lieutenants, who signed King Charles I's death-warrant, and later had his own signed in return—such can be the fury of the Welsh radical conviction, which can link such secret corners of a small secluded country with the great moral conflicts of the world!

'Open your eyes!' cried Morgan Rees that fiery Welsh-American moralist, addressing his countrymen still at home. 'Why are your tyrants great? Because you kneel down and cringe to them. Rise up! You are their equals!' It is true that there is an element of cringe and self-abasement to Welsh attitudes, partly tactical and opportunist, but partly bred into the people by so many centuries of alien brainwash. But to balance it there has always been a robustly democratic streak, which has led men like Colonel Jones ('whose insolence towards the neighbouring gentry', wrote Thomas Pennant a century after his death, 'is still spoken of, to this day, with much warmth') into sometimes quixotic, sometimes noble crusades towards the levelling of things.

During every great battle for human equality, Welsh voices have been raised boldly and sometimes vociferously in the egalitarian cause—in the English Civil War, in the American War of Independence, in the French Revolution, in the American Civil War, in the Boer War, in the Soviet Revolution, in the civil rights campaigns of our own time—and proud though they have been of their own pedigrees, and devoted to their own princes, to many Welshmen the paraphernalia of aristocracy have always been repellent and absurd. 'No Nobleman resides within ten miles', bragged an advertisement for a house in early nineteenth-century Powys, 'nor any Busy Sporting Esquires.'

The English monarchy itself, diligently though it might press its Tudorian or Glyndŵrian connections, has not been immune. The Welshman William Parry plotted to kill Queen Elizabeth I in 1584, and was hanged for his failure, while 'If a tyrant King I meet', claimed the incorrigibly republican Iolo, 'Clench fist and knock him down!' When Queen Victoria died in 1901 the only hunt in her kingdom to continue its meets during the period of mourning was the Tivyside Hunt in Dyfed, provoking a bitter poetic complaint, signed by 'A Loyal and Disgusted Sportsman', in the *Cardigan and Tivyside Advertiser*.

> Then hasten, old comrades, away
> Our mourning we'll put off today.
> We'll think of our Queen, and all she has been,
> Later on, but just now we can't stay.

In the great depression of the 1930s South Wales miners used to chant:

> We'll make Queen Mary do the washing for the boys,
> When the Red Revolution comes,
> We'll put the Prince of Wales on the Means Test!

Today there are still often young Welsh people to demonstrate against the royal family, when its members come to Wales—it is one of the very few places in all their possessions where they can never be sure of their reception: and when in 1981 the Prince of Wales was married at

Westminster at colossal expense, with matchless display and to almost universal gush, the only letter of criticism in *The Times* of London ('vulgar ostentation') came from an address in Gwynedd.

But then just as a royal wedding is meant, we are told, to be a glorious epitome of all our weddings, so Welsh republicanism, confined as it has been to an articulate minority, has only been an expression of profounder resentments. The Welsh are conscious always of being a lesser, poorer people, and this has made their patriots more sensitive than most to the patronizing or its concomitant the servile. It is not so much the monarchy that sticks in those Welsh gullets, more the sycophancy attending it, with all its social and national implications, and the struggle against lick-spit in all its aspects is a running theme of Welsh radicalism: not the kings but the courtiers have been the most detested, not the squires but the agents, not the bosses but the scabs and blacklegs—in short the *bradwyr*, the traitors who will let down their families, their *bro*, their class or their country for the favours of the mighty, and so break the ranks of self-respect.

Our next skirmish of the resistance was in the green countryside, and we will choose a lonely spot to imagine its partisans in action, on the mountain road which leads westward out of Rhayader in Powys, winding over the foothills of Pumlumon to Pontarfynach and Aberystwyth on the coast. Some eight miles from the town this highway passes through a twisting defile of bitter isolation. The hills there are entirely treeless, and the river Ystwyth flows with a cold grey sheen along a shaly bed. There is no sign of human life: only the sheep nibbling the sedgy turf, and the high hovering birds.

At this place in the early nineteenth century there stood a toll-house, one of hundreds throughout Wales: and here on 9 October 1843 the Green Revolution in Wales, the rural side of the resistance, reached one of its theatrical climaxes. After dark that night there came storming along the road from Rhayader a grotesque troop of horsemen, carrying flares, cudgels and guns. Their faces were blackened with soot, and they were dressed in rough women's clothes—skirts flapping over their breeches, shawls flying, here and there a ribboned bonnet. They were the Maids of Rebecca, sworn to destroy all toll-houses, and variously thought to have taken their name from 'Big Rebecca' of Llangolman in Dyfed, who lent her clothes to one of the burlier original riders, or from

Genesis 24: 60—'and they blessed Rebekah, and said unto her, "Thou art our sister, be thou the mother of thousands of millions, and let thy seed possess the gate of those which hate them" '. They rode through the night in silence, but when they reached the toll-house, with wild cries of 'Becca! Becca!', with gun-shots and skidding hoofs, they threw their flares on to its thatched roof, and in a moment it was all ablaze. An elderly woman was the toll-house keeper, and when she came hurrying out somebody fired a gun in her face, injuring both her eyes: and so the whole bizarre squadron went galloping off again through the darkness, out of the glare of the burning building, away over the empty ridge.

Rebecca was only the most flamboyant expression of the discontent which had seized the poor country people of Wales in the aftermath of the Napoleonic Wars. One great rural grievance was the proliferation of enclosures, by which more and more of the common land of Wales was legally fenced off by landowners and denied to its peasantry, but there were countless others—tithes, cripplingly high rents, evictions, the price of food, the alien Englishness of landlords, magistrates, parsons and gamekeepers, all compounded by the demands of a rising population and the general hardship of the times.

Violence resulted. There were riots over enclosures. There were riots over the price of bread—Welsh country people lived largely on bread, and some families spent almost all their income on it. Farmers, corn-merchants, shopkeepers, bakers, packhorse men, the crews of trading schooners, gamekeepers, bailiffs, agents, all at one time or another were attacked by furious mobs. Squatters clung pathetically to the concept of the *tŷ unnos*—the right supposedly decreed by Hwyel Dda to claim your own plot of common land, if you could build a house on it within twenty-four hours. In Dyfed a vicious running war—*Rhyfel y Sais bach*, 'the War of the little Englishman'—was fought for several years against Mr Augustus Brackenbury from Lincolnshire, who rashly built himself a house on land recently enclosed, and found it repeatedly burnt down. Time and again troops were brought into Wales to deal with disturbances. 'For you my heart bleeds!' declared Mr Justice Harding, sentencing three men to death at Cardiff Assizes for rioting over high food prices, but he added: 'Nothing is more unjust, than to be inflamed against a *market*, because the general price of it is dear . . . A *market* is governed by such principles of mutual convenience between the buyer and the seller, that it cannot be fairly accused of artifice, or oppression.'

Poor people in Wales did not see it in those terms, and Rebecca unforgettably dramatized all their discontents. The idea of toll roads, by which landowners improved and maintained public highways in return for toll fees, was not in itself a bad one, and certainly improved the Welsh highway system, but it was open to countless abuses. Conscientious landlords might see it all as public service, less scrupulous people leased their toll-rights to professional toll-farmers far away, and merely maintained the roads that gave access to their mansions. Sometimes a traveller had to pay three or four different tolls in the course of a single journey: market towns were often ringed with toll gates—Rhayader had six, one at each entrance. The tolls were a cruel burden on farmers, especially in parts where lime had constantly to be brought by cart for the fertilizing of poor land: they were an everyday, inescapable metaphor for the condition of their lives.

Rebecca then blazed into action to right an almost universal grievance. The movement was half-obscured in mystery, like the Scotch Cattle of the industrial valleys, and was as much symbolic as specific. Its guiding genius, if it had one, is often thought to have been a Dyfed lawyer, Hugh Williams, who was certainly concerned with far more than mere toll-house dues, but with the whole structure of society in Wales. Its fighting commanders were pointedly Welsh in language and style, and had the more or less open support of many ministers, lawyers and magistrates—people of the educated Welsh middle classes, groping their way towards the inheritance of national leadership from the landed gentry.

Many more brutal men joined Rebecca, though, riff-raff, thugs and vagabonds followed along, and it could be sinister and ruthless. Over many parts of central and southern Wales the posses rode, night after night between 1839 and 1843, setting toll-houses afire, horsewhipping keepers, sometimes widening their targets to include a river weir, the outbuildings of a grasping farmer, or a particularly heartless workhouse. It did not pay to oppose Rebecca. Several people were murdered, at least one was blinded, many barns were burnt to the ground. Blood-curdling letters were sent to landlords and Anglican clergymen ('Ministers of the National Whore'). People who gave evidence against rioters were intimidated or beaten up—that old lady on the Rhayader road, though she had time to recognize her assailants before the gun went off, refused ever to identify them. A hostile attorney in Dyfed, James Thomas, known locally as Jimmy Genteel, was trussed up and placed in an animal pound, to be released next morning when he paid the statutory fourpence for the redemption of stray beasts. In 1843 the Chief Constable of Glamorgan, tipped off by an informer, went to the smallholding of Cwm Cile Fach, near Llangyfelach, to arrest two alleged Rebeccaites. The father of the house attacked him with a stick, the mother hit him with an iron bar, one of the sons hit him with a hammer, another attacked him with a hatchet, and Miss Margaret Morgan first threw a saucepan of boiling water at him, and then cut his head open with a reaping hook.

Rebecca was skilfully and subtly organized, all the same, and to this day nobody knows all the secrets of the conspiracy. A reporter of *The Times* partly penetrated the organization, and has left us a description of one of its meetings, at Cwm Ifor near Llandeilo in Dyfed. The members met at night in the graveyard of a Baptist chapel, and talked for several hours crammed tightly into the little schoolroom above the chapel stable. The proceedings were in Welsh, were minuted as held in 'the first year of Rebecca's exploits', and began with a rehearsal of some improving aphorisms—the price of liberty was vigilance, an army of principles was superior to an army of soldiers. Then they got down to specifics. Grievances were listed—tithes, church rates, high rents, tolls. Rules were agreed to: traitors were to be reported to 'The Lady', all females except the generic Rebecca herself were to be forbidden the secrets of the movement. It was resolved that no Englishman should be allowed to remain as a landlord's steward in Wales, and that farmers should be urged not to get into debt. The meeting broke up at midnight, the conspirators dispersed among the tombs, and the reporter went home unexpectedly sympathetic to Rebecca's purposes.

In time Rebecca became far more than a mere destroyer of toll-booths, but a general redresser of popular wrongs, and even a guardian of popular morals. Reluctant fathers were confronted with their illegitimate children, or obliged to marry betrayed mothers. Wife-beaters were admonished. The vicar of Bangor, in Gwynedd, was forcibly reconciled with his estranged wife. A rich spinster of Castell Emlyn Newydd was made to hand over £1 to a farm boy who, having high-spiritedly kissed her on the cheek for a bet at a wedding party, had been fined that amount for common assault. The vicar of Penbryn in Dyfed was ordered to return to its Nonconformist owner a family Bible seized in lieu of tithes, on pain of arson in his vicarage and mutilation of his self. For a few months Rebecca truly was the voice of poor rural

Wales, and some of its leaders—Shoni Sgubor Fawr (John Big Barn), Dai'r Cantwr (Dai the Singer), Jac Tŷ-isha (John Hughes)—were to become popular heroes in the mould of Dic Penderyn: the first a well-known barefoot boxer, the second a poet and preacher, the third a farmer's son so bucolic that he had never set eyes on a railway train.

Rebecca subsided, gradually, in sporadic rick-burnings and riotings, and mass public meetings. Shoni, Dai and Jac were all apprehended and transported to Australia, none of them ever to return. Their sufferings were not, however, pointless. Rebecca was one undoubted success of the Welsh resistance. Though thousands of troops were used to suppress the insurrection, though its leaders were savagely punished, in 1844 an Act of Parliament did what Rebecca demanded, reforming the whole system of toll roads and eventually abolishing them. Gradually too, in the course of the nineteenth century, the other peasant grievances were alleviated, and Rebecca was to be remembered not so much for its savageries as for its rough justice, even for its innocence and naïvety. Lady Charlotte Guest, translator of the Mabinogion, spoke for the people when she mourned in her diary the fate of poor Jac Tŷ-isha, shipped away from Wales for ever in the very first steamship he had ever seen—'free child of the mountain, with all his faults and all his grievances and all his romance!'

Perhaps not thousands of millions, but at least some of Rebecca's seed honour her still in Wales. One of the very last toll roads in the country was the embankment over the Glaslyn estuary at Porthmadog. In 1980 the right to its fees was acquired from an Irish peer by a charitable association of local citizens, and with a long historical memory; and in gratitude perhaps to Dic, Shoni, Jac and all the other mingled rogues and heroes who rode for The Lady, they named themselves the Rebecca Trust (though long before that actually, if you were of the *bro*, or looked Welsh enough, the employees of the toll-gate forbore to collect your cash . . .).

Now we stand outside a respectable hotel in the middle of Newport, Gwent—the Westgate Hotel, two stars in the Automobile Association handbook, in which Rotary holds its luncheon meetings, and office anniversaries are celebrated. It was here in 1839 that Welsh radicalism confronted the soldiers of Queen Victoria in an all too brief pitched battle. Times had changed since Merthyr. By now the valleys were ringed with military bases, at Aberhonddu, Abergavenny, Cardiff, Merthyr: on the other hand the Welsh industrial radicals were now part of a massive movement, Chartism, that had fired working people all over Britain, demanding specific parliamentary reforms like universal suffrage and voting by ballot. Welsh Chartism had begun among the wool-workers of mid-Wales, Llanidloes having been entirely taken over by activists for a few days earlier in the year. It reached its fateful climax in the south, though, and nowhere in Britain did the movement assume so nearly revolutionary a form. We can follow its one great action, the march on Newport in 1839, as one would follow a military campaign: it had its generals, its divisions, its order of advance, and finally, forlornly, its short exchange of fire with the forces of the British status quo, poking their muskets from the windows of the Westgate Hotel.

The cast of this sad, spectacular but farcical drama was arresting. Hugh Williams, who had hovered so tantalizingly on the fringes of Rebecca, lurked around this movement too. So did the inescapable Dr Price of Llantrisant, who used to attend Chartist demonstrations in a cart drawn by goats. Then there was Zephania Williams, free-thinking landlord of the Royal Oak, Blaena, who had on his walls a picture of the Crucifixion cryptically subscribed 'This is the man who stole the ass', and there was William Jones of Pontypool, watchmaker and quondam actor, and there were hordes of picturesque supernumeraries, Jack the Fifer and David the Tinker and Israel Firman the herbalist or sorcerer, whom we have already met. The chief defender of law and order was Thomas Phillips, Mayor of Newport, who claimed maternal descent from Dafydd Gam of Agincourt, but who was the son of a labourer on the Ebbw Vale cinder tips, and was to become famous later for his passionate refutation of the Blue Books of Treason. The general of the Chartist army was John Frost, Justice of the Peace, property owner, a former Mayor of Newport himself, but so radical of spirit and impetuous of personality that when Lord John Russell, Secretary of State, once threatened to remove his name from the register of magistrates, Frost replied: 'Whether your Lordship will retain my name, or cause it to be erased, is to me a matter of perfect indifference, for I set no value on an office dependent for its continuance, not according to the mode in which its duties are performed, but on the will of a Secretary of State.'

Some Chartists called themselves Moral Men, and were against all violence, but in Gwent the pace was set by Physical Force adherents. Their armouries were in the high moorland of the Blaenau, where in limestone caverns on the bluffs, Eglwys Faen the Church of Stone, Agen Allwedd the Fissure of the Key, they stored their weapons and made their ammunition from stolen gunpowder. Their meeting-places were the pubs, the Bush at Newport, the Coach and Horses at Blackwood, Coed-duon, the Bristol Beerhouse at Pontypool, the Red Lion at Tredegar. The immediate cause of their march on Newport was the imprisonment in Monmouth of one of the most famous of the English Chartists, Henry Vincent, 'the Demosthenes of Chartism', together with several of his associates, and from the start they planned it as a neo-military operation.

Their force of several thousand men of Gwent, mostly miners and ironworkers, some genuinely inspired by the cause of political reform, some bullied into joining, some tagging along for the excitement and the loot, was to advance southwards to Newport in three columns: one in the west, commanded by Frost himself, one in the centre commanded by Zephania Williams, one in the east under William Jones the watchmaker. They would join forces at the Welsh Oak inn, Cefn, on the outskirts of Newport, march into town in the small hours, demolish the bridge over the Usk behind them, overpower the garrison and take over the place, sending a detachment to Monmouth to release the Demosthenes of Chartism. What would have happened after that, nobody seems to have considered, but some of the simpler campaigners assumed they would then march on London.

They were grouped in ramshackle military formations. Frost was their Conventional-General—commander-in-chief, that is—and below him there were Senior Officers in command of brigades, Junior Officers with battalions of fifty men each, and Deacons with platoons of ten men each. The army was armed with guns, swords, pikes, billhooks and bludgeons. Its password was 'Beanswell', the name of a Gwent hamlet—the cry 'Beans' to be answered by 'Well'—and the men were assembled with extraordinary secrecy from all over the Gwent and east Glamorgan valleys, some marching many miles through the night to join their musters. George Shell, aged 19, found time to write to his parents from Pontypool on the night of 4 November 1839, and this is what he said:

Dear parents,—I hope this will find you well, as I am myself at present. I shall this night be engaged in a struggle for freedom, and should it please God to spare my life, I shall see you soon; but if not, grieve not for me. I shall fall in a noble cause. My tools are at Mr Cecil's and likewise my clothes.

Yours truly, George Shell.

All the memorials of this doomed enterprise may still be seen. The caverns are still there of course, high on the escarpment of the Blaenau. Most of the pubs thrive. And though the Westgate Hotel at Newport has been rebuilt since then, still the bullet-holes in its inner porch are there to remind us that in the square outside its doors the Battle of Newport took place on 5 November 1839 and the Chartists of the Valleys were sent reeling home in ignominy.

For it all went wrong. The raggle-taggle columns, streaming down the valleys in terrible weather through the night of 4 November, got steadily drunker, slower, more confused and less disciplined as they advanced. Frost's column, and Zephania Williams's, reached the Welsh Oak more or less to schedule, but William Jones's men, the eastern column, started hours late, boozed and squabbled all the way, and failed to keep the rendezvous. Frost decided to proceed anyway, and on the morning of the 5th led an advance guard of several hundred men into Newport. The town was shuttered, the streets were deserted, and they marched without opposition to the Westgate, where Sir Thomas the Mayor was installed with a force of thirty soldiers of the 29th Regiment, and a number of special constables. The Chartists crowded into the square outside the hotel: the Mayor appeared cautiously, first on a balcony, then at the door; suddenly a shot was fired, and the battle began. Some of the Chartists broke down the door of the hotel with hatchets, and there was hand-to-hand fighting inside. Others shot their muskets through the windows. The soldiers fired at random into the crowd blundering about outside. In less than fifteen minutes it was all over, and the Chartists were dispersed in panic, slipping away up the side-streets of the town, or streaming back towards their own valleys. They left behind them the authentic debris of a battlefield: nine dead bodies including George Shell's, weapons, blood, broken glass all over the street and an acrid cloud of cordite in the air. The dead lay out there all day, and soldiers with muskets prevented anyone approaching them.

The Anglo-Welsh Establishment took a terrible revenge. Horrifying sentences were handed down when the judges arrived at Monmouth

Assizes, attended by trumpeters and javelin men, to enforce the law of treason: eight men were condemned, as the law decreed, to be drawn on a hurdle to a place of execution, to be hanged until they were dead, to have their heads severed from their bodies, and to have their bodies quartered for the disposal of Her Majesty the Queen of England. In the end all were reprieved, but without being allowed so much as a last meeting with their families, were instead shipped off to Australia for life. Quite right too, thought Macaulay the historian, who was of the opinion that universal suffrage was incompatible with civilization: they were 'great criminals . . . who would, if their attempt had not been stopped at the outset, have caused such a destruction of life and property as had not been known in England for ages'.

Again, the people did not think so—1,400,000 signatures were appended to petitions asking for their pardon. Most of them died in Australia nevertheless, but the most famous of them all, the clever and idealistic John Frost, was pardoned at last in his seventy-first year, and came home in triumph to Newport, where the horses were removed from the shafts of his flower-decked carriage, and faithful old comrades pulled it through the town instead. He lived to be 93, and if he was a 'great criminal' in life, has become a hero in death even among the South Wales Establishment. A square in Newport is named for him, and a museum, and high in the Blaenau, above the village of Beaufort, there is a cave marked on the map as John Frost's Cave, where in the prime of his life, they say, the Conventional-General planned his one campaign.

It is not easy to find, among the myriad outcrops and declivities of Mynydd Llangynidr, but two cairns on the ridge act as markers to it, as they did no doubt in the time of the conspiracy, and pilgrims down the generations, together with panting groups of schoolchildren on local history projects, have left a hazy track to its entrance. Ponies with long shaggy manes, almost down to their feet, roam the heather up there; the view is marvellous, northward to the high peaks of Bannau Brycheiniog, southward over Ebbw and Abertillery, Pontypool and Newport to the sea; the silence of the Blaenau is broken only by the distant rumble of the traffic on the Heads of the Vallies road, or the blast of racing engines, perhaps, from the rough quarry track below, where the descendants of the Welsh Chartists love to skid their Hondas and Suzukis.

*

Not far away the town of Tredegar, in the Sirhowy valley of western Gwent, has played a specialized part in the long resistance.

High above it a little clump of toppled tombs and coffin-shaped bumps in the ground is to be found on the edge of the moors near the public cemetery, surrounded by the remains of an iron fence. It is a sad and rather eerie place, the wide moorland all around being broken here and there by the flat silhouettes of mine-tips, like ziggurats, or the mesetas of the Indian country, and all its epitaphs, some in Welsh, some in English, record a single date of death, 1849. Its graves feel deliberately shunned or exiled out there, enclosed within their iron barrier, and this is not just fancy: for they are the graves of cholera victims, who died in one of the squalid epidemics that swept these valleys in the nineteenth century, and whose very corpses were considered contagious.

Several such cemeteries are hidden away in the coal valleys, and the fire of Welsh resentment has been stoked by fearful memories of disease and ill health. Tuberculosis raged among the cramped industrial terraces, typhoid was endemic, and the bronchial diseases of the miner's and quarrymen's life were generally summed up, as they still are, in the single helpless epithet 'The Cough'. In 1914, when 348 sputum specimens were taken at random from public footpaths in Swansea, 198 were found to contain tuberculosis bacilli; in 1918 infant mortality in the coalfields was 116 per thousand. Standards of hygiene were grim—thousands of people in the Welsh quarry towns never had a bath in their whole lives—and notions of first aid were primitive: cobwebs were used to stop bleeding, bacon fat and tea-leaves were applied to burns, dust in an eye was removed by a comrade's lick. In Rhondda in the 1930s few people over 40 still had their own teeth, and indeed a common twenty-first birthday present was to have them all extracted.

It was in Tredegar that the workers first did something to fight these miseries. There in the 1890s they established a Workmen's Medical Aid Society, employing its own doctors: members paid threepence in the pound of their wages in return for free medical attention, dentistry, spectacles, drugs, midwifery, even artificial limbs. It was a famous success. By the 1920s its two large surgeries, still standing, were as grand as municipal buildings, or even cinemas, and its doctors included the novelist A. J. Cronin, who wrote about it in *The Citadel*, and whose house is still shown to visitors, up the hill across from the lower surgery. Almost every family in town subscribed to the society, and if you met a man with a glass eye he was sure to have got it free, 'on issue', as the rules said, 'of a doctor's note'.

And from the Workmen's Medical Aid Society of Tredegar, Gwent, still greater things ensued. In 1923 Aneurin Bevan, of Charles Street, Tredegar, was elected to the Hospital Committee, which worked in tandem with the Society: thirty-two years later, as Minister of Health in London, he was to launch the British National Health Service, the first truly all-embracing public health scheme, and a model for the whole world. It is too much to claim that the one scheme was modelled on the other, as Tredegar people sometimes like to think, but who can doubt that Bevan, as he prepared his mightiest of all Medical Aid Societies, thought now and then of the surgeries in the valley long before? The miseries of The Cough and the TB were part of his own experience: more than that, it was his own grandfather who had, almost a century before, erected those iron railings around the cholera cemetery on the hill.

Up in the north the men of the slate quarries rebelled at last against the supremacy of the omnipotent quarry-owners, half-industrialists, half country gentlemen, who held their entire society within their grip, and whose profits during the nineteenth century had been described (by the *Mining Journal* itself) as 'almost fabulous'. By the end of the century the quarrymen had their own union, the North Wales Quarrymen's Union: and in the year 1900, at Lord Penrhyn's Bethesda quarries, they went on strike for fairer conditions. It was to be the longest industrial dispute in British history.

Its undertones of nationalism were unmistakable. Only Englishmen, Scotsmen or very Anglicized Welshmen could hope to get a managerial job in the quarries, but Welsh-speaking Welshmen, *Cymry Cymraeg*, were still the only people who had mastered the highest skills of the industry, the grading and judging of stones, the subtle splitting of them. Yet Lord Penrhyn utterly refused to recognize their union, refused even to meet its representatives: and when the men went on strike, he simply closed the quarries down. They were closed for three years, until the quarrymen abjectly surrendered, and the industry never recovered from the dispute, struggling into the new century a surly shadow of its old confident self.

It was a miserable affair, growing ever more bitter as the months passed, as Lord Penrhyn never flinched, as the workers' resolution weakened, and the first blacklegs (*cynffonwyr*, tail-waggers, fawners, as they called them up there) began to creep back to work. Harsh sanctions were imposed by the union upon these backsliders. Their names were published in newspapers, they were driven out of chapels, they were stoned by infuriated women, they were refused service in shops and beer in bars, they had rats thrown into their front doors. *Nid oes bradwr yn y tŷ hwn*, announced placards in windows—'There is no traitor in this house'. 'No man who betrays his fellow-workers', said a letter in *Yr Herald Cymraeg*, 'can belong at all to Christ's religion.' The *cynffonnwyr*, driven from the Nonconformist chapels, went to the Anglican churches instead: Welsh people, *proper* Welsh people, stayed on strike.

They were humiliatingly defeated in the end—so humiliatingly that when at last they gave in, Lord Penrhyn having proved as absolutely impervious to arbitration as he was to the strike itself, several hundred men found themselves on a management black list, and were refused work anyway. The bitterness was never absolved; the very name of Penrhyn became a Welsh anathema, and seventy-five years later people in Bethesda still remembered who had been loyal to the people's cause, and who had been *bradwyr*.

Yet it was a victory too, for it gave the people of the quarry towns a new sense of communal power, in a religion sloughed in neo-feudalism. For a few years Bethesda became a household name all over Britain, and families whose circumstances had hardly changed in a century found all of a sudden that they were in the vanguard of social progress. If capitalists everywhere admired Lord Penrhyn's 'plucky stand against trade union blackmail', working-class people everywhere subscribed to Bethesda relief funds, or flocked to the concerts given by the three Bethesda choirs which toured all Britain raising funds.

Besides, the castellated presence of Penrhyn had already played a symbolical role in a wider struggle of the time. As the quarrymen fought for their rights as craftsmen, so the people of the country around, like people all over rural Wales, had been fighting for their emancipation as citizens, and stirring against all the territorial magnates who ruled their lives so absolutely. *Trech gwlad nag arglwydd* was the cry—'the land is mightier than the lord': and in 1890 David Lloyd George, standing as a radical Liberal for the Caernarfon

Boroughs in his first parliamentary election, found himself opposing Hugh Ellis-Nanney, who was not only the squire of Lloyd George's own village, Llanystumdwy, but had also been Agent to Lord Penrhyn of Penrhyn Castle and the Bethesda quarries.

It was like a Morality. Ellis-Nanney lived in Plas Gwynfryn, a huge mock-Gothic mansion which he had recently built on a hill above the village, surrounded by a glorious park: Lloyd George had grown up in a small terrace house in the village street, almost opposite the Feathers Inn. It was street against park, Welsh-speaking Baptist cobbler's ward against English-speaking Anglican agent of Mammon—Us against Them with a vengeance. Lloyd George himself embellished the images in a famous speech. 'I see that one qualification Mr Nanney possesses', he cried, 'is that he is a man of wealth, and that the grand disqualification in my case is that I am possessed of none . . . the Tories have not yet realized that the day of the cottage-bred man has at last dawned!'

He was right. Not only did the cottage-bred man win that particular contest, but all over Wales the people succeeded to political power. The squirearchy was swept from its seats of authority, and the county councils were dominated by men of the middle classes, farmers, doctors, shopkeepers, ministers, small businessmen. First as a stronghold of Liberalism, then of Labour, the country has been left of centre ever since, and since Lloyd George's day all its authentic heroes, every one, have been bold and often militant radicals—if not cottage men exactly, certainly not men of the Plas. It is apt that Ellis-Nanney's great house of Gwynfryn, having been in its time a nunnery, an old people's home and an unsuccessful hotel, is now only a burnt-out ruin on its commanding hilltop site: while the cobbler's cottage in the village below has a commemorative slab upon it, and is portrayed on picture postcards.

As the nineteenth century turned into the twentieth, and the half-rural South Wales of the Black Cattle and the Chartists became the vast industrial region of our own day, the Welsh resistance there assumed the form that the whole world came to recognize: the struggle of the coal-miners for dignity and sufficiency, with its strikes and its lock-outs, its grand but pitiful images of hunger, anger, fellowship and despair. The Welsh coal industry reached its climax just before the

First World War. By then the iron industry had almost disappeared, because the ore reserves were used up, and the steel industry was confined to two or three towns, but King Coal was supreme. From east to west of the coalfield a quarter of a million men produced, in 1913, 56.8 million tons of coal, two-thirds of it going overseas. The masterful old pioneers of the industry, good or bad, were mostly in their graves by then, and huge financial combines owned most of the mines, with their headquarters generally in London. The profits were vast. The future must have seemed limitless.

Peace of a kind had reigned in the coalfield since the tragedy of the Chartists. Strikes and disturbances were scattered, sporadic and generally ineffective, and when the South Wales Miners' Federation, 'The Fed', was formed in 1898 its tactics were generally mild. Its leader for years was a miner of literary leanings, William Abraham, known always by his bardic name Mabon, and he believed that the interests of coal-owners and coal-miners were fundamentally the same. He achieved what he could by conciliatory means, notably a sliding scale of wages, by which wages depended upon the current price of coal, and an annual miners' holiday which is still known as Mabon's Day. Many of the evils of the valleys were abolished—the truck system, the employment of women and children underground —and wages were generally high by most standards, which is why there was never a shortage of labour, immigrants continuing to pour into the valleys well into the twentieth century. By and large the values of the chapels still prevailed, the Welsh language and its culture robustly survived, and Mabon (presently to evolve into the Right Honourable William Abraham, LL D, MP, and to be accused of an unseemly materialism) stood there in his respectable beard and gold watch-chain as a guarantor of moderation.

Yet the whole vast construction was to collapse almost as quickly, and almost as violently, as it had erupted in the first place. The industry itself, which seemed so indestructible, was really about to start upon its catastrophic decline. As ships turned to oil fuel Welsh steam coal lost its magnificent monopoly, and from the end of the First World War until our own time the coal industry has been in unrelieved decline. Nothing could stop the rot. After the Second World War all but the smallest mines were nationalized, but it made no difference: by 1984 the 485 collieries of 1913 had dwindled to 29 big pits and 80 minute private mines, and the work force of a quarter of a million men had shrunk to some 23,000. From the steam coal valleys of the east to the anthracite districts of the west the whole great coalfield, once a wonder of the world, sank into apparently permanent doldrums. In 1935, when 200,000 Welsh miners were unemployed, Thomas Jones suggested that the whole area should be officially declared a Grand National Ruin: by 1984, when unemployment was nearly as bad, at least one pit really had been turned into a museum, and the coalfield swarmed with industrial archaeologists.

As to the miners, those 'slaves of the lamp', no wonder it was among them that the Welsh protest was fiercest, the radicalism most generally extreme. All down the years we see the valleys in a state of mixed despondency and defiance, now it seems all spiritless in defeat, now furiously up in arms again. Mabon's methods were soon discarded, as the union leaders learnt their power, and the clash between the new school of miners' leader on the one side, the coal-owners and Authority on the other, repeatedly came very close to revolution. What scenes, what signs! We see 20,000 men singing their hymns, shouting their slogans at the Rocking Stone. We see a trumpeter going through the streets of Tonypandy to call the men on strike. We read of lock-outs and police informers and movements of troops, of women hurling themselves upon the ranks of policemen as their husbands are carted off to jail. 'Shut your mouth', a man hisses allegorically at a constable, so the evidence shows, 'or if you want trouble you can have it, so —— off!'

We hear the faint strains of *Cwm Rhondda* emerging from the depths of Dare Colliery, where the men spent more than two weeks in a 'stay-down strike'—fed with shoe-box hampers sent down by their wives, opening each day with prayers, greeted when they came to the surface at last by the colliery male voice choir with 'Praise God from whom all Blessings Flow', as the great crowd stood, so a reporter wrote, every head bared, 'silently in an attitude of reverence'. We see rioting crowds of Tonypandy squeezed between the massed ranks of policemen from London and the fixed bayonets of the infantry sent there by the Home Secretary, Winston Churchill, in an act which was to earn him the undying resentment, to this very day, of people in South Wales. We see great processions of protest against the degrading means test, respectable in their best Sunday clothes, gloves and high heels, laughing and singing twelve abreast through the streets of Rhondda.

To many Welsh people in those cruel times Communism offered an answer, and they saw their own struggle for fairness as a microcosm of a much greater campaign. When the Spanish Civil War broke out 174 Welshmen went off to fight in the Republican cause, 122 of them miners—the largest regional group in the International Brigade. Welsh sea-captains, long familiar with the iron-ore route to Bilbao, repeatedly defied the Nationalist blockade to take food to beleaguered Basque republicans, and two of them, Captains 'Potato' Jones and 'Ham-and-Eggs' Jones, have gone into the folklore. Asked why he was going to Spain, one volunteer replied pithily 'The Powell Duffryn Coal Company is Fascism!', and at home whole Welsh communities really did feel, as they faced the great coal combines, that they were standing up to just the same enemies as their men with the Brigade in Spain.

Lenin himself, looking at South Wales in 1921, wondered if he was seeing 'the beginning of the real proletarian movement in Great Britain in the Communist sense . . . the beginning of a new era'. Five years later the police superintendent of Monmouth, hearing a crowd of miners singing 'The Red Flag' outside the Assize Court, remarked ominously 'We've got a cage in Monmouth for birds who sing that song'. Certainly there were moments when it seemed that South Wales might decide upon the Communist solution to its problems. There were Communist Mayors, Communist councillors, and busy Communist Party branches, manned often enough by men and women long respected in chapel, school and Workmen's Institute. 'Marxism for us', wrote Gwenallt the poet, 'was a real gospel; a religion, a social religion, and we were ready to live for it, to sacrifice ourselves for it, yes, and to die for it.'

Maerdy in particular, high up there at its bleak valley-head, became a Communist town, known to Fleet Street as Little Moscow, and to Welsh conservatives as a very omen of revolution—ruled, as the *Western Mail* put it in 1926, by 'a Red Reign of Terror'. Up there nearly everything was organized by the Party: concerts and communal kitchens, hunger marches, delegations to confront the bosses or defy the police. Young Pioneers marched in demonstrations alongside Boy Scouts, and Comrade Wharton, aged 13, was a member of a children's delegation to the Soviet Union. Soviet delegates came to Maerdy, too, and the town talisman was a gold and red banner presented to it by the working women of Krasnaya Presnya, Moscow, which was kept reverently in the Workmen's Institute, and draped over coffins at Communist funerals. The red flag, which had first been seen in these islands up the road at Hirwaun a century before, flew defiantly in the Rhondda in the 1930s.

The revolution never quite came. The Workers' Freedom Groups never took to arms, all the fiery graduates of the National Labour College in London preferred in the end to rely upon the ballot-box. Nevertheless this grim period of defiance, distress and near-starvation, leavened by a defiant exuberance of comradeship, remains in most people's minds the epitome of the Welsh resistance. It was not overtly nationalist—after 1945 'The Fed' became part of the British National Union of Mineworkers, and when the Prince of Wales, the future Edward VIII, visited the valleys in 1936, he was received with trust and affection. When the miners marched on London in those years, it was not to blow up Parliament, only to petition it. Nevertheless all the protests, all the strikes, all the violence did assume specifically Welsh forms, and spoke, if not always in the Welsh language, at least in a strong Welsh accent. In the eyes of the world at large, and especially of the English, probably nothing in the history of Wales has been more characteristically Welsh, more immediately Welsh of style and meaning, than the long rebellion of the South Wales miners against the injustices of the twentieth century.

The fire has faded from the valleys now. The unemployed of a later depression seem numbed by the long misery of the decline. There was still a Communist Mayor of Rhondda in the 1980s, and the party is still alive in Maerdy, but if there is a revolutionary movement it is lying very low. The past often seems more alive than the present in Aberdare or Ebbw, and the harsh memories of the struggle are softened by nostalgia. Remember when they complained to Arthur Horner about the food on the hunger march? 'Who says the cook's a bastard?' says Horner to the crowd, 'Who says the bastard's a cook?' somebody shouts back—oh! we had some comical fellows then. Remember when Dai Jones, who couldn't abide foul language, let loose on the pit-manager?—'Holy Father', he says, 'close thine sacred ears for five minutes while I tell this ignorant bugger what I think of him, in his own language!' Remember the collections for Spain, when the Civil War was on?—God man, there wasn't anybody in the village, not a living soul, didn't give something. Remember old Jack Russia, swaggering about Senghennydd there in his Spanish beret, and how Mam put on her hat with the feathers for the Means Test March, it makes you laugh now, and bloody Churchill sending the soldiers in, and the

Carnival Jazz Band up at Ystrad, the Ystrad Spuds we used to call them?

And remember Nye Bevan? Of all the characters to emerge from this great sad struggle, Aneurin Bevan of Tredegar was the most compelling and the most majestic. A figure of aristocratic confidence and style, he was a miner's son, a miner himself in his youth, and Labour Member for Ebbw Vale for nearly thirty years. To Englishmen he was in many ways everything they most detested about the Welsh—his high insistent voice infuriated them, his lordly style bewildered them, his loyalty to Britain seemed to them dubious—was it not Bevan that Churchill himself, in the middle of the Second World War, called 'a squalid nuisance'? To the Welsh of the valleys he seemed a prince. His authority was unchallengeable, and long after his death his constituency at Ebbw Vale remained the safest Labour seat in all Britain.

There was something elemental to this grand (and merry) figure. His first major speech in Parliament, in 1929, was described by one newspaper as being 'like some great disturbance of nature'. More than anyone he seemed able to give the grievances of the coalfield a universal meaning, and though he was not every Welshman's Welshman (he cared little for the Welsh language or its culture) still his memorial on a hill above Ebbw Vale can properly stand in memorial to all the champions of the coalfield struggle. It was originally to consist of three great granite boulders, representing the three branches of his constituency, Ebbw Vale, Tredegar, Sirhowy, to which he spoke from that high meeting-place on the Blaenau. A fourth and greater boulder was added, though, to symbolize the fact that he spoke also to the world.

'Kindly disposed by nature', the Scottish Socialist Keir Hardie wrote of the Welsh in 1898, 'genial in their relationships one to the other, loving justice and hating oppression, they can easily be roused to battle for the right.' Easily roused to battle for anything, more cynical observers might suppose, surveying the nature of Welsh history, and remembering its frequently martial bias, but in fact a recurring strain in the defence of the Welsh identity has been pacifist. From the Quaker ironmasters of early nineteenth-century Castell Nedd, who declined to make arms, to the thousands of conscientious objectors who have refused to use them, there have always been Welsh people, more than in most countries, ready to denounce the use of force. One of the favourite archetypes of chapel Wales was Henry Richard, 'The Apostle of Peace', secretary of the Peace Society and an early advocate of a League of Nations, whose statue still stands in the square in his home town of Tregaron, and whose name is still remembered, if nowhere else, in schoolroom books of Great Welshmen. When, in 1983, the people of Pen-y-groes in Gwynedd were asked their opinion about the basing of nuclear missiles in Britain, 86 per cent were against the policy, 6 per cent for.

In both world wars there were many eminent Welshmen to stand against the tide of patriotic belligerence: T. Gwynn Jones, one of the literary giants of his day ('a pacifist', as he described himself, 'with the emphasis on the fist'), Thomas Rees, one of the leading theologians (whose irrepressibly anti-war opinions made him virulent enemies in all Christian denominations), Thomas Parry-Williams, one of the most admired of twentieth-century poets, Iorwerth Peate, one of the most gifted of folklorists, George Thomas who was later Speaker of the House of Commons and later still Lord Tonypandy, Gwynfor Evans who was to be the first Welsh nationalist Member of Parliament. In 1939 Plaid Cymru, the Welsh political party, dismissed Hitler's war entirely as 'a clash of rival imperialisms, from which Wales, like the other small nations of Europe, has nothing to gain but everything to lose' (though the authorities of the State never did quite decide whether an objection to war on nationalist grounds was sufficiently conscientious . . .).

Brave, provocative, sometimes pig-headed views! And in our own time it was a group of women from Wales who, marching across England to the American nuclear missile base at Greenham Common in Berkshire, set up an encampment there which was to become one of the most famous of all peace demonstrations, emulated and wondered at, abused and denigrated all over the world, as month after month they and their thousands of successors blockaded the airfield—becoming, with the barbed wire always to be seen behind them, the police always pushing them into vans, the armed soldiers in their camouflage suits always eyeing them over their automatic rifles, and the terrible half-focused shapes of the base behind them, symbolic figures, whether you loved or loathed them, of humanity's fears and angers.

*

By now, in the last quarter of the twentieth century, the Welsh resistance is back where it started, and its chief activists are not labour leaders or social reformers, who have mostly come to compromise, but nationalists. Patriotism was of course the oldest element of the struggle, reaching far back to Welsh battles against the Saxons, or even against the Romans before them, and the old saws and traditions of Welsh independence had never been altogether forgotten—the Old Man of Pencader's brave words to Henry II, which we heard for ourselves so long ago in Chapter Two, or the gnomic saying, attributed to Taliesin himself, which promised that whatever happened to the rest of Britain, Wild Wales would always be Welsh. In the late nineteenth century indeed Welsh nationalism enjoyed an astonishing resurgence —there was a short-lived nationalist party, *Cymru Fydd*, 'Wales Will Be', which Lloyd George for a time supported, and Home Rule seemed within reach for Wales as it was for Ireland.

But the Great War stifled it. Welsh patriotism was subsumed into British, Welsh labour movements became part of greater British organizations, the Labour Party, which replaced the Liberal Party as the overwhelming political force of Wales, was London-based and thoroughly British. The vast majority of the Welsh people were reconciled to sharing the fate of the United Kingdom, its humiliations if necessary but preferably its triumphs. The University of Wales worked almost entirely in English (even until the 1920s its department of Welsh Studies!) and the Welsh seemed destined, in the post-war world, to obey their most obvious destiny, abandon the struggle at last, and slide gradually into Britishness. 'Home Rule is sometimes spoken of', wrote W. Watkin Davies in his book *Wales* (1925), 'but it is generally by the theorists and doctrinaire pedants . . . The discordant cry of the extreme nationalist is occasionally heard, with its glorification of all that is vulgar and unworthy of preservation in the Welsh tradition. But this wins little sympathy.'

Into this historical hiatus, in 1936, three respectable Welsh intellectuals threw a blazing brand. The British Government had decided to establish a new bombing-school for the Royal Air Force. Several English sites had been considered and spared—Holy Island in Northumberland after a protest in *The Times*, Abbotsbury in Dorset because of its breeding swans—so the Air Ministry decided instead upon Llŷn, a region almost poignantly rich in Welsh memory, entirely Welsh-speaking, proud of the poets, priests, seamen and shipbuilders it had contributed to the history of the nation. The people of Llŷn were horrified, protests poured into London from all parts of Wales, but the Government refused to meet a delegation to discuss the issue, and the Royal Air Force went ahead. The focal point of the range was to be Pen-y-berth, one of the most storied of the Llŷn homesteads, claiming connections with Owain Glyndŵr himself: by September 1936 this ancient place had been demolished, and the first buildings of the school had been erected.

Just a week after the destruction of Pen-y-berth three men set fire to the new buildings. They were an unlikely trio of saboteurs. Saunders Lewis we have already met, scholar, poet, playwright, a Catholic convert of passionate views and European loyalties. D. J. Williams was a former miner, a schoolmaster, a writer of short stories, whose round spectacles and Pickwickian eyes made him seem innocence incarnate. And the Revd Lewis Valentine was a Baptist Minister who looked jolly, kind and altogether Christian. Together, at dead of night, these improbable terrorists crept through the perimeter fence of the range, threw petrol over an empty hut, and despite the irritating dampness of D.J.'s matches, set fire to it. It burnt in no time, but hardly had its flames died away than the Revd Mr. Valentine, Mr. D. J. Williams and Saunders Lewis the playwright were standing before the desk at Pwllheli police station, explaining to a bemused duty officer what they had done (and discussing while they awaited their removal to the cells, so legend says, the sonnets of Robert Williams Parry).

And what they had done was this: they had expressed the Welsh sense of grievance, the old resistance, in a frankly nationalistic way —not as an aspect of social reform, but in the older way, for the sake of Wales and Welshness, *er mwyn Cymru*. They were charged in Caernarfon with arson, but the Welsh jury failing to agree, their case was transferred to the Old Bailey in London, where twelve men true, good and English soon saw that they were sentenced to nine months in Wormwood Scrubs. Even Lloyd George was infuriated—'this is the first Government that has tried Wales at the Old Bailey . . .'.

The effect upon young Welshmen was electric—'it is difficult now', wrote the critic R. M. Jones thirty years later, 'to imagine what a thrilling impact this happening had'—and since the Second World War the endemic and almost organic sense of Welsh protest has coalesced above all around the nationalist idea. It has its ups and downs still—sometimes plunged in self-pitying despair, sometimes cock-ahoop after an election victory—but as 'D.J.' himself once remarked to Dafydd Iwan, touching him on the arm as a later batch of patriots went down to the cells, 'Don't worry, Dafi *bach*, though we lose today, there's always tomorrow.'

This, the oldest and the newest of the Welsh resistance movements, takes many forms. It is fought constitutionally, in elections by Plaid Cymru, the Party of Wales, or illegally in acts of violence by shadowy subversives, the Free Wales Army, the Welsh Socialist Republicans ... It can be sober, literary, godly, supported by bishops, or it can be darkly conspiratorial. Its champions have ranged from the saintly Gwynfor Evans, an Oxford-educated market gardener with a passion for Welsh literature and cricket, to the strangely charismatic John Jenkins, a former army sergeant, a mystic, a firebrand, who spent ten years in prison for his attempt to blow up a dam in 1970—'I thank a kindly fate', he wrote then, 'for my great good fortune in being born a Welshman in this day and age, and for having been given the opportunity to serve the cause of my dear country and beloved people.' Its purposes vary too, some of its activists being concerned only for the cultural independence of Wales, some combining patriotism with Marxism, some willing to settle for autonomy within a federal Britain, others wanting a break from England as complete as Ireland's.

Nationalism is inescapable in Wales today. At one extreme it manifests itself in a proliferation of Welsh language classes, a flowering of Welsh poetry, a flood of Welsh publications and the couple of Plaid Cymru MPs who habitually represent Gwynedd, that heartland of the Welsh resistance, in Parliament at Westminster. At another it is surrounded by all the symptoms of subversion and surveillance—the bomb in the recruiting office, the unexplained fires, the howl of the police sirens and the midnight knock on the cottage door, the tapped telephone, the whisper of the Special Branch. Very few people have been injured in this struggle—it was Saunders Lewis who said that Welshmen should shed no blood but their own in the struggle for their country—but it toys with violence all the same, and often comes close to tragedy. If it seems variously baffling, irritating, ominous and ludicrous to the English, it disturbs many of the Welsh too, and the issue of the language in particular, the very core of the Welsh identity, ironically divides the people.

For every Welsh person who speaks Cymraeg today, four do not, and this gives rise to complexes of many kinds—fear, suspicion, resentment, impatience, even a brand of snobbery. Welsh-speakers tend, often despite themselves, to look down upon the rest as Welshmen *manqués*: those who speak only English sometimes despise, or pretend to, those who cling to so archaic and parochial a vernacular. Innumerable miseries attend the fight to preserve the language against the colossal onslaughts of English, pouring over Offa's Dyke each day in a torrent of print, speech and television—young men and women go to gaol for defacing signs or occupying offices—parents club together to prevent the Anglicization, or alternatively the Cymricization, of schools —parliamentary motions are debated—furious letters are sent to editors—grants are given, withheld or considered—societies spring up, flourish or decay—controversies rage about jobs going to, or denied, Welsh-speakers, or non-Welsh speakers, or well-qualified applicants from Wolverhampton, or members of Cymdeithas yr Iaith Cymraeg, the Welsh Language Society—hotels decline to take cheques made out in Welsh, bookshops refuse to take cheques made out in English—half the motorists of Wales cheer, and half of them groan, to find the Welsh name of a place displayed above the English version, or Criccieth spelt with two *c*'s, the English way, instead of only one.

It is hard for citizens of ampler and more fortunate countries to realize how addictive is the nationalist passion among the minority of Welsh people who are subject to it. It is like a love affair, patriotism of a degree and intensity experienced by English people, say, only at times of extreme national danger. Your active Welsh patriot, one who consciously works for the Welshness of Wales, lives and dreams his country and his culture. It is his hobby, his profession, his ecstasy. Every aspect of life is affected by his obsession, every event is measured by its significance to Wales, every public figure by his attitude to Wales, every work of art by its Welshness, every rise in the price of gold, or drop in the inflation rate, or arms agreement, or trade dispute, is judged by its effect upon *Cymru* and *Cymreictod*.

The more elementary of the patriots think only of Wales itself, and spend their lives in a state of rankle, forever spitting at the Sais. The more sophisticated yearn to see Wales part of a far greater whole, of Europe, of Christianity, of Civilization—Welsh patriotism, Saunders Lewis once wrote, should live not in a materialistic spirit of narrow nationalism, but *mewn ysbryd hael ac o gariad at wareiddiad a thraddodiad a phethau gorau dynoliaeth*—'in a generous spirit of love for civilization and tradition and the best things of mankind'. But generous or narrow, placid or fierce, often at odds in the incurable Welsh way, the patriots at least have this in common: a truly fatal enthralment. We will end this story of the underground, then, with two very different actions of the contemporary Maquis.

For the first we will pay a visit to the home of Gwynfor Evans in the foothills of Mynydd Du in Dyfed, above the market town of Llangadog. It is a modern house, built by Gwynfor's architect brother-in-law, but it is profoundly impregnated with the quality of Welshness. There are Welsh books everywhere, Welsh pictures, Dafydd Iwan on the record-player, and when the family is assembled there, Rhiannon, Alcwyn, Dafydd, Meleri, Guto, Meinir, Branwen, Rhys and their various spouses too, life is lived with the particular mixture of tang and orthodoxy, hierarchy tempered with humour, that is the best Welsh domestic style—straight talk on serious subjects, plenty of laughter and perhaps a tingle of gossip, good simple food (sans wine, alas for the likes of us) and grace before dinner. Visitors are frequent, and sometimes a whole coach-load of Welsh people arrives, members of a chapel outing perhaps, or ladies of Merched y Wawr, 'Daughters of the Dawn', who file through Gwynfor's drawing-room with excited respect, as though he is their prince or president.

At Talar Wen, in 1981, Gwynfor Evans announced that unless the British Government, having reneged on an earlier promise, allowed Wales a Welsh television channel of its own, he would starve himself to death. Few Welsh people doubted that he meant it. He had long maintained that the survival of the Welsh language, and so in his view of Welshness itself, largely depended upon the influence of television, so immense was its effect upon the minds and aspirations of the young. Until then Welsh-language programmes had been scattered piecemeal among the three existing TV channels, generally at unrewarding times: Gwynfor (as all Wales called him) believed they should be con-centrated in a single channel offering the Cymry Cymraeg a complete modern television station. He was, he said, perfectly willing to die in so patently just a purpose.

Here was a Welsh situation *par excellence*—a Celtic one even, for the ancient tribal leaders had always been ready to sacrifice themselves for a cause. Was he really serious, they wondered in London? Could Government take a chance? What would happen if he died? Welsh people of many unexpected kinds united behind Gwynfor Evans,

British politicians and journalists of all parties called him a charlatan or a poseur—there were repeated questions in the House of Commons, constant demonstrations in Wales, slogans were scrawled on bridges and walls from one end of the country to the other—*Aberth Gwynfor*, 'Gwynfor's Sacrifice'!—and through it all, away down there at Talar Wen, besieged by reporters, crowded about by well-wishers, Gwynfor Evans maintained an air of gentle bemusement, perhaps a little tinged with irony. He was undoubtedly ready to die. He *expected* to die indeed, faced as he was by the most intransigent British administration for many years, and he had a last family photograph taken, Rhiannon, Dafydd, Branwen and all the others proudly around him on the lawn. He knew that nothing could do more for the Welsh nationalist cause than his death in such circumstances! But Margaret Thatcher's Tory government, already cruelly embroiled in Ireland, had no stomach for a Welsh martyrdom, sensed the angry strength of Welsh feeling, and authorized *Sianel Pedwar Cymru*, Channel Four Wales, 'Ess Pedwar Eck' as they phoneticize it in Wales—the first such service in any of the minority languages of Europe, offering the whole range of the TV genre, comic cartoons to drama to quiz games to documentaries, and most telling of all, in a way, programmes from the continent of Europe dubbed directly, Czech, French or German, into Welsh. *Aberth Gwynfor* joined *Cofiwch Dryweryn* in the inexpungible repertoire of Welsh graffiti, still to be seen on rocks and bridges across the land.

It was an ideal victory of Welshness—peaceful, popular, frank and innocent. Love of country takes many forms, though, and our second action, only a distant glimpse of an action this time, is of a more disquieting kind, more atavistic, taking us back more directly to the oldest resentments of the Welsh. There! Over there!—the thin spiral of smoke, hazy in the morning, which seen on mountainside or sea-shore strand casts a peculiar *frisson*, part law-abiding shock, part shamefaced admiration, over many a gentle Welsh patriot: the smoke which shows that the holiday cottage or weekend home of yet another English family has been put to the torch by the young Welsh activists —the guerrillas still at large, for good or evil. better or worse, after a thousand years of the resistance.

But at its best the radical instinct of the Welsh runs deeper than nationalism or economics, and is concerned in all its manifestations with the human condition itself. It is a profound if intermittent feeling for dignity, embedded in the nature of the Welsh tradition—dignity in private life, dignity in nationhood. If it has often expressed itself in violence, just as often it has shown itself in the great pacifist movements of Wales. It has generally set itself against Powers and Potentates, against the pretensions of authority, against snobbery, against arrogance. In its long fight against inequities of so many kinds it has given this country a noble theme, even fulfilment of a sort: even, all in all, some touch of epic.

Epilogue

DAFYDD AP THOMAS from Glamorgan, walking over London Bridge, was accosted by a sage with a strong Welsh accent, asking him where he had cut his fine hazel staff. From the hill above the farm at home, Dafydd said. 'Take me there at once', cried the seer, '*brysiwch*, hurry, I will show you wonders!' So they travelled back along the drovers' route to South Wales, and went to the hillside where the hazel trees grew, and there the wise man disclosed a hidden entrance in the ground, and in they crept, and in a great underground chamber they found a prince and all his warriors, sleeping all in armour beside their weapons. Disturbed by their approach, the prince stirred, sprang to his feet with sword in hand and cried 'Does Wales need us? Has the day come?' 'Not yet', replied the sage, 'Sleep on, sleep on': and so the two of them tiptoed away again along the tunnel to the secret door, and the prince returned to his rest.

It may have been Arthur himself down there, it may have been Owain Lawgoch, but it may well have been Owain Glyndŵr. His cause faltered as the years passed, the English armies reconquering, *bro* by *bro*, the country of the Welsh. Fainthearts changed sides, Sycharth was burnt to the ground. Harlech fell to the English in 1409, and with it Owain lost not only the symbol of his sovereignty but also his beloved wife, two daughters and three grandchildren, all carried away to London. By 1414 he was a fugitive, and by 1417 he had disappeared for ever. 'Very many say that he died', records the earliest Welsh annal of these events, 'the seers maintain that he did not.' Only the folklore variously records his fate. It tells us that in the last months of his life the old hero met the abbot of Glyn-y-groes, Valle Crucis in Clwyd, alone on a morning walk. 'You are up too early, Abbot', chaffed Glyndŵr, but the priest replied gnomically. 'No, sire,' he said, '*it is you who are about too soon . . .*'

A turn of the page, and he was gone. Some tales have him dying in a last desperate skirmish in the woods of Dinmore, on the Herefordshire border. Others say he died at Monnington Straddel, in the nearby

Golden Valley, where his daughter Alice lived with her English husband John Scudamore. Others again tell of his last days in the round tower of Kentchurch Court, in the parish of that mysterious Siôn Cent who has himself sometimes been identified in the folk-memory as the hero's *alter ego*. As for the English chroniclers of the time, they unanimously pictured him dying miserably on the run, 'in desert places and solitary caves—a finall reward mete and prepared by God's providence'.

Wales is littered still with his mementoes. Wherever you go, he seems to have been. Here he held court, there he hid in a high cave, this mansion he burnt to the ground, this one he visited incognito ('and when the stranger was gone, came a messenger to the house, and he said to the servants, "Tell your master it was The Lord Owain who betook of his hospitality last night . . ." '). High in the foothills of Pumlumon are the twin quartz boulders, *Cerrig Cyfamod*, the Covenant Stones, which commemorate his rout of the Flemings in 1400. On a steep hillside at Pilleth in Powys four tall redwoods, in a stone enclosure, mark the burial-place of the dead after his victory of Bryn Glas in 1402. At Caerfyrddin he consulted Hopkin ap Thomas ab Einion the magician, at Corwen the slash of his dagger shows on the church porch, outside the castle of Usk several hundred of his men were publicly executed in 1405. Tourists crowd through his supposed Parliament House at Machynlleth; motorists on Telford's road to Caergybi wonder at the great old tump beside the A40 at Glyndyfrdwy, and stopping to enquire at the petrol station, are told it is Glyndŵr's Mound. Inns, cafés, streets, housing estates, footpaths are named for the hero, and a few visitors find their way to Sycharth (on Sir Watkin's land, as it happens), to wander meditative above the moat, and imagine Owain's happy household there:

> *Na gwall, na newyn, na gwarth,*
> *Na syched fyth yn Sycharth . . .*
>
> No want, no hunger, no shame
> No one is ever thirsty at Sycharth . . .

Owain, the country's hero, left his country ravaged by his passing. Everywhere towns were ruined, castles destroyed, houses burnt, fields desolated, livestock dead or driven away. Trade and commerce was crippled, and a great depression hung over the land. For generations some parts of Wales remained depopulated: it took decades, centuries perhaps, to repair the damage of the great adventure. The English, while offering Glyndŵr himself a pardon, which he scorned even to decline, clamped their authority upon the Welsh more harshly than ever—'*Beware of Wales, that it make not our child's child to weep!*' Desolate and disillusioned, haunted by the outlawed remnants of its own armies, Wales lay in a condition of abject defeat from which it has never quite recovered.

Yet never did Welsh patriots doubt that in Owain Glyndŵr they had possessed a true champion, a leader worthy of their loyalty, or that their disastrous insurrection had been a moment of triumph. Even in his last fated wanderings, the prince was never betrayed. Even in his death he was not abandoned, but was simply transmuted there and then into myth. The poets sang no elegies for him, as they had mourned the passing of Llywelyn Olaf, for they did not admit his going. He had simply joined the pantheon of the Golden Age, the trustees of that other state of being for which the Welsh imagination has so often yearned. He sleeps in his cavern still, awaiting the call: one day perhaps a sage will lead us there.

In the mean time Wales restlessly endures its destiny. There are many thousands of Welsh people who have long abandoned the struggle for the Welsh identity, and submitted to geopolitics. But there are many now, as there have always been, whose lives are guided still by the very same passions that fired Owain and his *Plant* nearly six centuries ago—the passions of a powerless people, in a small country, trying to honour their deepest instincts.

It is not easy to be Welsh. Old torments attend the condition, like curses from a Celtic fairy-tale. There is the Torment of the Confused Identity—when is a Welshman not a Welshman, are some more Welsh than others? There is the Torment of the Torn Tongue—the anxieties of a society ripped apart by love, scorn, longing or rejection of its native language and culture. There is the Torment of the Two Peoples—the ambivalence of the Anglo-Welsh relationship, bitter-sweet, love-hate, never altogether frank. And behind these conscious *malaises* there is the more elemental *Angst*, only half-realized in Wales, which oppresses all such minority peoples, Jews in their dispersal, blacks of the New World, exiled Palestinians, lonely Afrikaners—the yearning, profound and ineradicable, for their own inviolable place in the world.

Yet Welshness is not a debilitating condition, not for the patriot. On the contrary, it often makes the blood race and the adrenalin run. The happy ending was never the Celtic preference anyway, and being Welsh is, at the least, extremely interesting. Living in such a country, supporting such a grand, unselfish and utterly harmless cause, following in such footsteps—it can be the fire of life, to those who see it so! The torments of Wales may be enervating collectively, but they can stimulate the individual marvellously. They hold one always on the brink, arguing and wondering, and they lead the mind towards braver purposes still, towards an understanding of the poetry and the spirituality of all things.

Besides, dear God, the compensations! I am half Welsh, half English, and like Giraldus before me I am proud of the best in both races: but it is the Welsh in me, my sense of timeless kinship with this most fascinating corner of Europe, that has brought me chief delight. It has made me rich in the most opulent kind, for everything I have described in this book belongs to me, as it belongs to all the Welsh who recognize it—every dapple of those clouds, every lichened boulder, every spin of the pit-wheel or plume of cooler, every Kazoo blast or limpid alliteration of *cynghanedd*! 'Small enough to feel itself a tribe or even a family'—even now Wales is not so sophisticated, or so dehumanized, as to be beyond the affections of personal possession.

Nor so big, end to end, that one cannot be familiar with it all. I know of nothing more exhilarating than to travel through this marvellous park in the spirit of membership—tea with Mrs Jones Pentwyn perhaps, or sherry with the Prices of Rhiwlas—thumbs-up to the pickets huddled over their brazier outside the striking steel-mill, wave of the free hand from Owen the butcher at his chopping-block as you pass down Stryd Fawr—call on Gwynfor, perhaps, to discuss a point of history, or Twm for the loan of a book at the College by the Sea—blow me, if we don't run into W.P. after the game, Emyr too, look, by the bus-stop!—and so home in the end, as the sun goes down, to the smell of the wood fire sparking up, and the pant and flip-flop of the cows coming up the lane, and Geraint on the tractor behind grinning at you through your kitchen window all rosy cheeks and ginger eyebrows beneath his battered hat . . .

And not just Wales today, either, but all of the once-and-future kingdom glides within the parish of my care. Not an episode I have described in these pages but I have felt some part of me tugged into participation, on one side or the other, whether it be at the soup-kitchens of Maerdy or beneath the castle walls of Harlech. I am all Wales in one! The peasants are me, the miners, Rebecca's horsemen are me, Pantycelyn and Anne Griffiths, the princes and their ladies, the bards, the priests—I am Owain himself, and the divine Dafydd, and Nest, and Hywel Dda, and before them too I inhabited the ancient mysteries of stone and seer—myth-maker, shape-changer, there go I! The thrill of the indestructible language echoes within me, in the voices of its poets speaking down the ages, and time and again, when I walk in the woods or on the high bare mountains, I know myself at one, ecstatically, with the winds and the wild creatures.

Such can be the fulfilment of feeling Welsh in Wales, but I do not claim it as peculiar to ourselves. The country I have celebrated in this book is not just a country on the map, or even in the mind: it is a country of the heart, and all of us have some small country there.

TREFAN MORYS, 1984

Further Reading

FOR a small country Wales has been very thoroughly written about. The fifty-odd titles I list here, all in English and mostly contemporary, would seem to me to make a well-balanced small library, within its monolingual limits, for the enthusiastic general reader.

Reference

The University of Wales's great dictionary of the Welsh language, modelled upon the *Oxford English Dictionary*, is only half-way through the alphabet so far, but the one-volume *Y Geiriadur Mawr* (Swansea, 1971) is big enough for most people. The University's bilingual National Atlas is unfinished too. A useful large-scale physical atlas is *Hamlyn's Leisure Atlas of Wales* (London, 1981), which unlike the Ordnance Survey maps gives both Welsh and English place-names. The Society of Cymmrodorion's *Dictionary of Welsh Biography* (London, 1959) lists Welsh worthies down to 1940.

General History

The standard history will certainly be the six-volumed *Oxford History of Wales*, but so far only one volume has appeared: Kenneth O. Morgan's *Rebirth of a Nation: Wales 1880–1980*. In the mean time there are *Wales Through the Ages*, edited by A. J. Roderick (Llandybie, 1959), David Williams's *History of Modern Wales* (London, 1977), and Gwynfor Evans's passionate *Land of my Fathers* (Swansea, 1974), together with *An Historical Atlas of Wales*, by William Rees (London, 1959).

General Studies

Gwyn Williams's *The Land Remembers* (London, 1977) is rather like my own book, only shorter and better. Dai Smith's *Wales! Wales?* (London, 1984) looks at Wales from the viewpoint of the industrial valleys. Emyr Humphreys' *The Taliesin Tradition* (London, 1983) explores the Welsh identity through the medium of the poetic tradition. Trevor Fishlock's *Wales and the Welsh* (London, 1972) is the best reportage on modern Wales.

Particular History

On Celtic Wales: *Britain and the Western Seaways*, by E. G. Bowen (London, 1972) and *The Celtic Church in Wales*, by Siân Victory (London, 1977). On the Normans: *The Norman Conquerors*, by David Walker (Swansea, 1977). On Owain Glyndŵr: *Owen Glendower*, by J. E. Lloyd (Oxford, 1931). On the social disturbances of the nineteenth century: *Before Rebecca*, by David J. V. Jones (London, 1973), *The Rebecca Riots*, by David Williams (Cardiff, 1955), *The Merthyr Rising*, by Gwyn A. Williams (London, 1978), *John Frost*, by David Williams (Cardiff, 1939), *The North Wales Quarrymen, 1874–1922*, by R. Merfyn Jones (Cardiff, 1981). On the South Wales coal industry: *South Wales Miners, 1898–1914*, by R. Page Arnot (London, 1967), *The Fed*, by Hywel Francis and David Smith (London, 1980), and *Cardiff and the Marquesses of Bute*, by John Davies (Cardiff, 1981). On the Patagonian adventure: *The Desert and the Dream*, by Glyn Williams (Cardiff, 1975). On the Methodist Revival: *Religion and Society in the Nineteenth Century*, by E. T. Davies (Llandybie, 1981).

Art and Architecture

Art in Wales, edited by Eric Rowan (Cardiff, 1978), is an illustrated history covering the years from 2000 BC to AD 1850. The best general survey of architecture is *The Historic Architecture of Wales*, by John B. Hilling (Cardiff, 1976). *Powys*, by Richard Haslam (London, 1979) is the first of a projected series on the buildings of Wales, begun under the advisory editorship of Nikolaus Pevsner. A seminal work was Iorwerth Peate's *The Welsh House* (Liverpool, 1946): Peter Smith's *Houses of the Welsh Countryside* (London, 1975) is a lavish successor. On urbanism in Wales there are *The Towns of Wales*, by Harold Carter (Cardiff, 1966) and *The Towns of Medieval Wales*, by Ian Soulsby (Chichester, 1983). *Castles in Wales*, published jointly by the Automobile Association and the Welsh Tourist Board in 1982, is better than it sounds.

Further Reading

Literature

Three collections of Welsh writing translated into, or composed in, English: *The Penguin Book of Welsh Verse*, translated by Anthony Conran (London, 1967), *The Oxford Book of Welsh Verse in English*, chosen by Gwyn Jones (Oxford, 1977), and *The Penguin Book of Welsh Short Stories*, edited by Alun Richards (London, 1976). *The Mabinogion* is properly marvellous in the translation by Gwyn Jones and Thomas Jones (London, 1963). The standard literary history is Thomas Parry's *History of Welsh Literature*, translated by H. I. Bell (Oxford, 1955), but a useful brief introduction is *Highlights in Welsh Literature* by R. M. Jones, Prince Charles's tutor on the subject (Swansea, 1969). *Profiles* (Llandysul, 1980), by the English-language writer Glyn Jones and the Welsh-language writer John Rowlands, is a critical account of modern Welsh authors working in both languages. The University of Wales publishes a valuable series of monographs called *Writers of Wales*.

Folklore

The most beguiling collection of folk stories is *The Welsh Fairy Book*, by W. Jenkyn Thomas, first published in 1907 but reissued in Cardiff, 1979. The most entertaining folklore book is T. Gwynne Jones's *Welsh Folk-Lore and Folk-Custom*, first published in 1930, but reissued in Cambridge, 1979.

Maritime

Two excellent studies of local maritime matters are *Porthmadog Ships*, by Emrys Hughes and Aled Eames (Caernarfon. 1975) and *Maritime Heritage*, by J. Geraint Jenkins (Llandysul, 1982), which is about the ships and seamen of southern Ceredigion. A more general view is given by *Cymru a'r Môr, Maritime Wales*, a bilingual series published by the Gwynedd Archives Service, Caernarfon.

Travel

The classic descriptive works are Giraldus Cambrensis' *Itinerary of Archbishop Baldwin Through Wales* and *Description of Wales*, both written in Latin in the twelfth century but available in translations made by Sir Richard Colt Hoare in 1806; *Tours in Wales*, by Thomas Pennant, first published *in toto* in 1781; and *Wild Wales*, by George Borrow, first published in 1862, still in print but always more popular with English people than with Welsh. From a multitude of guidebooks I recommend especially the two-volumed *Companion Guide* by Peter Howell and Elizabeth Beazley (*North Wales*, London, 1975, *South Wales*, London, 1977), and *The Shell Guide to Wales* (London, 1969), with a gazetteer by Alun Llewellyn and a splendid historical introduction by Wynford Vaughan Thomas.

The translation of *The Mabinogion* by Gwyn Jones and Thomas Jones, from which there is an extract on page 85, was published by Dent, London, in 1948. Alan Llwyd's *englyn Cymru*, on page 154, was published by Christopher Davis, Swansea, in 1978. The lines by R. S. Thomas on page 141 were published by Rupert Hart-Davis in *Poetry for Supper*, 1958. A fuller account of the voyages of the *Albion*, extracted by the late Dr Ll. Wyn Griffith from a nineteenth-century pamphlet, appeared in *Cymru a'r Mor*, No. 5 (Caernarfon, 1980). I have been unable to trace the relatives of Mr William Jackson, author of the poem on page 270, which appeared in the booklet *Stone and Steam in the Black Mountains*, by the Revd D. A. Tipper (Littleborough, Lancashire, 1975), but hope they will be pleased to find him quoted here.

Index of Names

The Welsh letters ch, ff, ll, and rh are indexed separately (after c, f, l, and r respectively)

Abaty Cwm Hir, 95, 113, 121, 375
Aberaeron, 308–9
Aberafan, 392–3
Aberconway, 69
Abercwmboi, 391
Abercynon, 269, 313
Aberdare, (Aberdâr), 89, 116, 313, 366
Aberdaron, 42, 97, 352
Aberdaugleddyf, 262
Aberdyfi (Aberdovey), 285, 293
Aberedw, 177
Aberfan, coal-tip disaster, 278–9
Abergavenny (Y Fenni), 40, 108, 255–6, 301;
 recusants, 101–2; mental hospital, 365
Abergwaun (Fishguard), 269, 336, 337;
 French landing in 1797, 187, 329–31
Aberhafesb, 363
Aberhonddu (Brecon), 208, 209, 373, 376,
 381, 400
Abermo (Barmouth), 83–4, 147, 258, 379
Aberpandy, 283
Aberriw (Berriew), 218
Abertawe, *see* Swansea
Aberteifi (Cardigan), 257; castle, 302
Abertillery, 313, 362, 403
Aberystwyth, 28, 40, 146, 172, 294, 379, 395;
 castle, 69, 137, 301; National Library, 209,
 379; University College, 242; resort, 284–5
Abraham, William ('Mabon'), 138, 408, 409
Abse, Dannie, 326
Abse, Leo, 326
Adam of Usk, 376
Adams family, and US Presidency, 335
Ambleston (Treamlod), 235
Amlwch, 109, 145, 194, 261, 265–6
Angle, 225, 234
Anglesey, *see* Môn
Anglesey, seventh Marquis of, 234
Arabi Pasha, 360
Archenfield (Erging), Herefordshire, 353–4
Arennig Fawr, memorial to US airmen, 338
Armstrong, Fergus, 148
Arnodin, Ferdinand, 306
Arnold, John, 101–2
Arnold, Matthew, 239, 374

Arthur, King, 3, 59, 421, 423; Round Table,
 56, 96, 217, 333
Arthur's Stone, Gower, 78
Arthur, Prince, s. of Henry VII, 71
Asquith, Herbert, 374
Assheton-Smith, Sir Charles, 367
Assheton-Smith, George, 232–3
Assheton-Smith, T. millionaire, 186
Augeraud, Lt., French prisoner, 331–2

Bae Colwyn (Colwyn Bay), 286
Bailey, Joseph and Crawshay, 280–1, 388–90
Baker-Gabb, Richard, 229
Bala Cynwydd, 334
Bala Lake (Llyn Tegid), 18, 21, 42
Baldwin de Boller, 63
Bangor, 97, 107, 173, 207, 380, 398
Bardsey (Ynys Enlli), 83, 96–7, 319, 339
Barmouth (Abermo), 83–4, 147, 258, 379
Barry (Barri), 196–7, 261, 272, 323
Basaleg, 25
Beaufort, 403
Beaumaris (Biwmares), 69, 300
Beddgelert, 29; Gelert's grave, 34
Bede, Venerable, 93
Belloc, Hilaire, 12
Berriew (Aberriw), 218
Bethesda, 266, 279–80; Methodist meetings,
 116; revivalism, 119–20; and Port Penrhyn,
 280; 1900 strike, 405–6
Bethlehem, Dyfed, 327
Bevan, Aneurin, 405, 412
Birkenhead, Lancashire, National Eisteddfod,
 161
Biwmares (Beaumaris), 69, 300
Black Mountain (Mynydd Du), Dyfed, 49, 305
Black Mountains (Mynydd Du), Powys/
 Gwent, 32, 98, 106, 295; massacre of Nor-
 mans at Crug Dial, 65–6, 351; spring of
 Partrisio, 89–90; railway, 229, 270; charac-
 ter, 350–1
Blackwood (Coed-duon), Chartist pub, 401
Blaen-Cwm, 277
Blaena, 400
Blaenafon, 145, 256, 282

Index

Blaenau, the, Heads of the Vallies road, 388, 403; mining community, 388–9; Merthyr Rising, 392–3; Chartist armouries, 401, 403
Blaenau Ffestiniog, 267, 365
Blegywryd ap Einon, 223, 225, 359
Blorenge, 31
Bold, Revd Hugh, 108
Bontddu, 264
Borrow, George, 228, 264, 275, 296
Bottom Hundred (Cantref Gwaelod), 24–5
Bowdler, Thomas, 380
Bowen, Revd Euros, 132
Boyce, Max, 128, 245–6
Brackenbury, Augustus, 396
Brân the Blessed (Bendigeidfran), 41, 68, 128–9, 206, 321, 323, 356
Branwen, 41
Brawdy, Dyfed, US tracking station, 338
Brecon (Aberhonddu), 208, 209, 373, 376, 381, 400
Bridgend, Glamorgan (Pen-y-Bont), 283, 330, 365
Bright, John, 378–9
Bristol, 257, 351–3; castle, 68
British Broadcasting Corporation, 156; and Welsh abroad, 345–6
Bro Morgannwg (Vale of Glamorgan), 281
Broad Haven, Dyfed, 82
Brunel, Isambard K., 262
Brut y Tywysogyon (Chronicle of the Princes), 59–60, 95, 324
Brute dynasty, lapidarists, 135
Brychan Brycheiniog, 321
Bryn Derfel, 96
Bryn Glas, 422
Brynbuga, *see* Usk
Buckley, Sir Edmund, 233
Builth (Llanfair-ym-Muallt), 67–8, 252
Burges, William, 301
Bute family, 196, 226, 275
Butetown, 376, 389

Cadair Idris, 106, 283, 379
Caerdydd, *see* Cardiff
Caerffili (Caerphilly), 62, 66, 300
Caerfyrddin (Carmarthen), 54, 55, 82, 108, 194, 218, 422
Caergybi (Holyhead), 148, 261, 268, 269, 285, 307, 352; non-stop dancing competition, 176–7; Telford's highway, 304, 422; Holy Mountain prospect, 319; US base, 337–8
Caerleon (Caerllion), 54, 56–7; Christian martyrs (Julian and Aaron), 90
Caernarfon, 54–7, 66, 69–70, 150, 165, 283, 286, 300, 307, 335–6, 367–8, 380; Welshness of, 165; seamen of, 258
Caerphilly (Caerffili), 62, 66, 300
Caerwent, 54, 56, 360

Caerwys Eisteddfod, 219
Caio, 57
Caldy Island (Ynys Byr), 22, 102, 337
Cantref Gwaelod (Bottom Hundred), 24–5
Capel Celyn, 377
Caradog (Caractacus), 54, 138, 139
Cardiff (Caerdydd), 53, 54, 103, 146, 178, 209, 258, 261–3, 312–13, 340; and international Rugby match, 176, 180–1; industrial boom, 195, 275; Bute dynasty ownership, 226, 275–6, 312; railway services, 270, 275, 312; Tiger Bay, 275, 313; castle, 301, 312; Irish quarters, 322; Greek Orthodox Church, 340; black community, 345; wartime bombing, 364, 371; visited by *Terra Nova*, 372
Cardigan (Aberteifi), 257; castle, 302
Carlyle, Thomas, 274, 390
Carmarthen (Caerfyrddin), 54, 55, 82, 108, 194, 218, 422
Carnhuanawg (Thomas Price), 106
Carreg Cennen castle, 300
Cas-gwent, *see* Chepstow
Casgob, 80
Casnewydd, *see* Newport, Gwent
Castell y Bere, 301
Castell Cerinion, 144
Castell Coch, 301
Castell Dinas, 301
Castell Emlyn Newydd (Newcastle Emlyn), 229, 398
Castell Nedd (Neath), 275, 340, 412
Castell-paen (Painscastle), 63, 81, 369
Castlemartin, Dyfed, 366
Catrin o Ferain (Katheryn of Berain), 185, 295
Cawdor, Lord, 233, 330, 331
Cecil, Robert, 381
Cefn Brith, 109
Cefn Mabli, 229
Cefnamlwch, 175
Cegidfa (Guilsfield), 26
Cemaes, 64, 105
Chantrey, Francis, 235
Charles I, 370, 393
Charles II, King, 109; Dyfed mistress, 370
Charles, Thomas, 111
Chatwin, Bruce, 343
Chepstow (Cas-gwent), 56, 218, 296, 349; elver traps, 255; castle, 300
Chester, 330, 350–1, 353; legionary headquarters, 54; earldom, 62
Chirk Castle, legendary wolf, 27–8; ironwork gates, 134
Chronicle of the Princes (*Brut y Tywysogyon*), 59–60, 95, 324
Chubut valley, Patagonia, 342–3
Churchill, Sir Winston, 409, 411, 412
Cilmeri, 67–8, 95
Cilycwm, 200, 251

432

Index

Cistercians, 94–6
Cleddau estuaries, 258, 324
Clochfaen, Llangurig, 106
Clough, Sir Richard, 295–7
Clynnog, Morris, 99
Clynnog, 222
Clyro, 106–7; Maes-yr-Onnen chapel, 297
Coed-y-Brenin forest, 264
Coed-duon (Blackwood), 401
Cohen, Rabbi Kenneth, 326
Coleridge, Samuel T., 344
Colwyn Bay (Bae Colwyn), 286
Conwy, 69, 307; mussel gatherers, 255
Constantine, Roman Emperor, 69–70
Cordell, Alexander, 140
Cornewall-Lewis, Sir George, 230, 310
Cornwall, 53, 158; and Celtic community, 317
Cors Fochno, 19; Great Toad of, 28, 269
Cors Goch (Tregaron Bog), 19, 42, 95, 216
Corwen, 86, 422
Cory, John, 341
Coslet, Dennis, 368
Cothi valley, 83
Council of Wales and the Marches, 194, 353
Cowbridge (Pontfaen), 17
Craig Aderyn, 41, 329
Craig-y-Nos, 340–1
Craigcefnparc, 150–1
'Cranogwen' (Sarah Jane Rees), 186–7
Crawshay, De Barri, 282
Crawshay, Mrs, of Dan-y-Parc, 281
Crawshay, Robert T., 281
Crawshay, William, 273, 274, 280, 390
Cricieth, 149, 285, 345; castle, 300
Crickhowell, 281; bridge, 305
Croesor, 241
Cromwell, Oliver, 109, 356, 393
Cronin, A. J., 404–5
Crug Dial (Cairn of Revenge), 65–6
Crumlin viaduct, 304
Cunedda, 91
Cwm, Jesuit college, Herefordshire, 100–2
Cwm Cywarch, 236, 240, 244
Cwm-yr-Eglwys, 23
Cwm Hyfryd, Patagonia, 343
Cwm Ifor, Llandeilo, 398
Cwmdu, 106, 333
Cwmystwyth, 231
Cwrt y Cadno, Llanpumsaint, 83
Cydweli (Kidwelly), 185, 300
Cyfarthfa Castle, 273, 280, 390–1
Cymdeithas yr Iaith Cymraeg (Welsh Language Society), 156, 202
Cynal Fawr, Huw Lloyd's Pulpit, 84
Cynfelin (Cunobelinus; Cymbeline), 24, 25
Cywarch river, 236

Chwilog, 149, 222

Dafydd ap Gruffydd, 68
Dafydd ap Gwilym, 122–3, 171–2, 201; and Cistercians, 95; use of birds, 140; and Llanbadarn Fawr, 294
'Dafydd Ddu Meddyg' (David Samivel), 344
Dafydd Gam, 208, 381
Dafydd Llwyd, 187
'Dai'r Cantwr' (Dai the Singer), 399
D'Arcy, William Knox, 375
Darwin, Charles, 379
Davies, David, capitalist, 195–8
Davies, David, doctor, 371
Davies, Edmund, judge, 356
Davies, Elizabeth, nurse, 187
Davies, Revd Henry, 149
Davies, John, hymnist, 344
Davies, Capt. Llewelyn, 336, 345
Davies, W. H., poet, 142
Davies, W. Watkin, author, 414
Davies, Winnie, missionary, 345
Davies brothers, ironworkers, 134
Dawkins (later Pennant), George, quarry-master, 279
de Clare, Lord Richard, 65–6, 270, 351
De Quincey, Thomas, 380
de Wallingford, Brian, 65–6
Dee, John, 150, 357
Defoe, Daniel, 19, 20, 27, 100, 373
Defynwy, 339
Denbigh (Dinbych), 143, 295; mental hospital, 119; birthplace of Stanley, 144; castle, 301
Derfel, holy man, 96, 97
Derry Ormond, Dyfed, 230
Devanna (Tŷ Faenor), Powys, 113–14
Devauden, Richard Morgan memorial, 366
Devil's Bridge (Pont ar Fynach), 12, 231, 303
'Dewi Honddu' (Joseph Leycester Lyne), 121–2
Dewi Sant (St David), 77–8, 91–2, 94, 96, 102, 121, 138, 176
Dewisland (Pebidiog), 77, 322
'Dic Penderyn' (Richard Lewis), 292–3
Dinas Brân, 301
Dinas Emrys, 29
Dinas Mawddwy, 199, 233
Dinbych, see Denbigh
Dinbych-y-pysgod (Tenby), 144, 325, 329
Dinefwr Castle, 36, 301
Dolforwyn, 67, 302
Dolgellau, 53, 165, 264, 283, 374
Dolwar Fach, Powys, 131
Dolwyddelan, 301, 321
Donne, John, 130
Dowlais, 274
Drayton, Michael, 127
Driscoll, Jim, boxer, 177
Dwygyfylchi, 24

Index

Ebbw Fach mansion, 280; viaduct, 304
Ebbw Vale (Glynebwy), 256, 272, 388, 403, 412
'Eben Fardd' (Ebeneser Thomas), 222
Edward I, King, conquest of Wales, 67–9; castles, 69, 206, 306; bastide towns, 306–7; at Rhuddlan castle, 369
Edward II, King, 69, 369
Edward V, King, Welsh campaign, 370
Edward VII, King, at Y Bala, 371
Edward VIII, King, 367, 371
Edward the Black Prince, 181–2
Edwards, John Owen, dog-breeder, 145
Edwards, O. M., educationalist, 240
Edwards, Thomas ('Twm o'r Nant'), 142–3
Edwards, Revd William, bridge-builder, 303, 387
Eglwys Fair Glantaf, 270
Eglwys Wen (Whitchurch), 120
Eglwysilan, 330
Eifionydd, 208, 220, 222
Eisteddfod Genedlaethol (National Eisteddfod of Wales), 52–3, 154–8, 171, 184, 209, 371
Elan valley, 379
Elias, John, 111, 122
Elizabeth I, Queen, 254, 370; plot to kill, 394
Elizabeth II, Queen, 368, 371, 381
Elizabeth, Queen of Rumania, 310
Elizabeth, Queen Mother, 242
Ellis, Robert, 243
Ellis-Nanney, Hugh, 407
Enlli, Ynys (Bardsey), 83, 96–7, 319
Epnt, 365–6
Erddig, 230, 234
Erging (Archenfield), Herefordshire, 353–4
Eryri mountains, 18, 21, 51, 56, 66, 185, 268; goats, 40; plants, 42; castles, 69, 307
Evans, Maj. Baldwin, 360
Evans, Caradoc, writer, 143
Evans, Christmas, Baptist, 11, 122
Evans, Ellis ('Hedd Wyn'), 161
Evans, Evan, poet, 105, 361
Evans, Gwilym, and Welsh Remedy, 148
Evans, Gwynfor, politician, 416, 418–19
Evans, John, missionary, 344
Evans, John, of Patagonia, 31
Evans, John, of Waunfawr, explorer, 320, 321
Evans, Nicholas, painter, 116
Evans, Ruth, 131–2
Evans, Theophilus, priest and writer, 105, 283
Ewloe castle, 301

Faenor (Vaynor), 281
Fan, nr Llanidloes, 265
Farr, Tommy, boxer, 178
Fiennes, Celia, 100, 374
Firman, Israel, 326–7, 400

Fishguard (Abergwaun), 269, 336, 337; French landing in 1797, 187, 329–31
Fishlock, Trevor, 345
Flat Holm Island, 22–3, 146, 339
Flemings, 324–5
Flemingston, 169
Flint (Y Fflint), 69, 307, 369
Fox, George, 109, 379
Francis, Revd James, 108
Free Wales Army, 368, 416
Frongoch, 231
Frost, John, 400, 401, 402, 403; Cave, 403
Fuller, Thomas, 216, 254

Ffaldybrenin, 344–5
Ffestiniog, 84, 121, 259, 266

Garlick, Raymond, 103
Garndolbenmaen, 154
Gelli-groes, 326
Geoffrey of Monmouth, 83, 333
George II, King, 231
George III, King, 370
George IV, King, 370
George V, King, 371
George VI, King, 35, 37
Gerald de Windsor, 185
Gerallt Gymro, see Giraldus Cambrensis
Gibberd, Frederick, 377
Gibbs, John, 310
Gilbert, Alfred, 195
Gilbert de Clare, 62
Gilchrist, Percy Carlyle, 145
Gilpin, William, 296
Giraldus Cambrensis (Gerallt Gymro, Gerald the Welshman), descent, 65, 160, 424; on Welsh choral singing, 137; on the Welsh, 165, 166–7
Gladstone, William Ewart, 379
Glamorganshire Canal, 258
Glyn-y-groes (Valle Crucis), 421
Glynceiriog, Memorial Institute, 243–4
Glyndyfrdwy, Owain's mound, 422
Glynebwy, see Ebbw Vale
Gogerddan, 229
Goldcliffe, flood in 1606, 24
Gower Peninsula (Gŵyr), 23, 324, 325
Grassholm Island, 41
Graves, Robert, 183; englyn, 153
Great Orme peninsula, 309, 339
Greenham Common, Berkshire, 413
Griffith, D. R., poet, 358–9
Griffith, 'Madam' Sidney, 174–5
Griffith, Wyn, writer, 183
Griffiths, Anne, hymnist, 131–2, 425
Griffiths, D. W., film director, 337
Griffiths, Owen, cancer-curing formula, 148
Grigg, John, 167
Grosmont (Y Grysmwnt), 83

Gruffydd ab yr Ynad Coch (Gruffydd Son of the Red Judge), 68, 130
Gruffydd ap Rhys, 72
Guest, Lady Charlotte, 399
Guilsfield (Cegidfa), 26
Guto'r Glyn, 30
'Gwenallt' (David Gwenallt Jones), 376, 410
Gwenllion, 185
Gwrtheyrn (Vortigern), 29
Gwrych, castle, 301
Gwydion, 36-7
Gwynne, Revd Alban, of Aberaeron, 308-9
Gwynne, Revd Ellis, 111
Gwynne, Sackville, patron of harpists, 230
Gŵyr (Gower Peninsula), 23, 325
Gypsies, 326-9

Hafod Uchtryd, 231-2, 234, 296
Hall, C. H., 24
Hamilton, Sir William, 262-3
Hanbury-Williams, Ferdinand Capel, 229
Handel, G. F., 341
Hanmer, John, 207
Hardie, Kier, 412
Harding, Mr Justice, 396
Harlech, 19, 25, 69, 206, 300, 425
Harrieses, dynasty of magicians, 83
Harris, Howel, 173-6, 216, 343
Haverfordwest (Hwlffordd), 34, 296, 326
Hearst, William Randolph, 338
'Hedd Wyn' (Ellis Evans), 161
Hendy Gwyn (Whitland), 94, 223, 252
Hengwrt, Vaughan family of, 230
Henry I, King, 185, 369
Henry II, King, 41, 71, 369, 414
Henry III, King, 67, 68, 369
Henry IV, King, 369, 370
Henry V, King, 370
Henry VII, King, 185, 187, 333, 370; Welsh origins, 70-1, 227, 230; Dyfed landing, 331
Henry VIII, King, 71, 99, 224
Herbert, Gen. Sir Otway, 87
Herbert, Sir Thomas, traveller, 344
Hereford, 62, 107, 351, 353
Heren, Louis, 374
Herkomer, Herbert, 155, 157
Herring, Archbishop Thomas, 374
Hess, Rudolph, 365
Hill, Anthony, 390
Hill, Thomas, 282
Hinde, Revd J. Y. W., 106
Hirwaun, 390-1, 392, 411
Hoadly, Benjamin, Bishop of Bangor, 107
Hoddinott, Alan, 138
Holyhead, *see* Caergybi
Holywell (Treffynnon), 88, 99-100, 370
Honddu valley, 92, 121-2
Hodd, Archibald, 282
Hopkin ap Thomas ab Einion, 422

Hopkins, Gerard Manley, poet, 152, 193
Hopkins, Thomas, ironmaster, 282
Horner, Arthur, 411
Howell, Revd George, 119
Howell, Col. John, 230
Hughes, John, and Russian steelworks, 342
Hughes, John ('Jac Tŷ-isha'), Rebecca leader, 399
Hughes, John Ceiriog, poet, 15-16, 243
Hughes, Richard, author, 145-6
Hunt, Lord, of Llanfair Waterdine, 379-80
Huntingdon, Countess of, 341
Hwlffordd (Haverfordwest), 34, 296, 326
Hywel Dda, 'the Good', 60, 184, 245, 396; and Welsh laws, 223, 224; client-King, 355
Hywel y Fwyall (Hywel the Axe), 181-2
Hywel ap Gruffydd, 181
Hywel Sele, 80, 208

Ieuan Wyn, 172
Ifor ap Llywelyn ('Ifor Hael'), 192
Ilston, Gŵyr, 113
Inglis-Jones family, of Derry Ormond, 230, 233
Iorwerth ap Owain of Caerleon, 66, 90
Isio, 89-90, 98, 270
Iwan, Dafydd, 202-3, 225, 416, 418

Jackson, William, 270
James I, King, 219
James II, King, pilgrimage to Holywell, 370
James, Evan, poet, 387
James, James, composer, 387
James of Saint-Georges, architect, 69-70
Jarman, Geraint, 138
Jean d'Espagne, 206
Jefferson, Thomas, 335
Jehovah's Witnesses, 122
Jelf, Revd W. E., 105-6
Jenkins, Dafydd, legal historian, 224
Jenkins, John, nationalist, 416
John, King, 369
John, Augustus, artist, 133, 329
John, Goscombe, sculptor, 133, 138, 367, 387
John, Gwen, artist, 133
John Big Barn ('Shoni Sgubor Fawr'), 399
John Paul II, Pope, 103
Johnes, John, 228
Johnes, Marianne, 232, 235
Johnes, Thomas, 231-2, 234, 296
Johnson, Samuel, 66, 105, 173, 295, 373-4
Jones, Bobi, poet, 132
Jones, Dafydd, hymn-writer, 251
Jones, David, poet, 366
Jones, David Gwenallt ('Gwenallt'), poet, 376, 410
Jones, Revd Edmund, 111
Jones, Elis Gwyn, artist, 222
Jones, Emrys, anthropologist, 216

Jones, Evan, healer, 148
Jones, Revd Griffith, 237, 379
Jones, Griffiths Rhys, choir leader, 138
Jones, Gwyn, scholar, 85
Jones, Col. H., soldier, 183
Jones, Capt. 'Ham and Eggs', seaman, 410
Jones, Inigo, architect, 303
Jones, Col. Jenkin, Puritan, 109
Jones, Revd John, 108
Jones, John ('Jac Glan-y-gors'), lampoonist, 360-2
Jones, John, collier, 273
Jones, John, regicide, 393
Jones, John Paul, American seaman, 337
Jones, Mary, and the Bible, 111, 113
Jones, Michael D., and Y Wladfa, 342, 343
Jones, Owen, designer, 134
Jones, Capt. 'Potato', seaman, 410
Jones, R. M., scholar, 425
Jones, Revd Richard, 118
Jones, Richard Robert ('Dic Aberdaron'), 188-90
Jones, Fr. Robert, Jesuit, 101
Jones, Sir Robert, surgeon, 148
Jones, T. Gwynn, author, 413
Jones, Thomas, Arctic voyages, 344
Jones, Thomas, civil servant, 241, 244
Jones, Thomas ('Twm Siôn Cati'), 200
Jones, Thomas, scholar, 85
Jones, Capt. Thomas, seaman, 344
Jones, Walter, soldier, 183-4
Jones, William, Chartist, 400, 401, 402
Jones, William, scholar, 359-60
Jonson, Ben, 379

Katheryn of Berain (Catrin o Ferain), 185, 295
Kemeys-Tyntes family, 229
Kenfyg, 23
Kennard, T. W., 304
Keynes, John Maynard, 169
Kidwelly (Cydweli), 185, 300
Kilgwrrwg, 366
Kilpeck, Herefordshire, 354
Kilvert, Revd Francis, 106-7, 302
Kitchener, Lord, 183
Knighton (Trefyclawdd), 112
Koppel, Heinz, 326
Kymin, the, Monmouth, 378

Landor, Walter Savage, 312, 351
Landsker, the, 324-5
Lang, Archbishop Cosmo, 374
Laugharne, 202
Lavedan, P., 308
Lavernock Point (Trwyn Larnog), 146
Lawrence, T. E., 144
Leland, John, 18, 24, 42, 375
Lenin, Vladimir, 410
Lewis, Alun, poet, 366

Lewis, David, martyr, 101-2
Lewis, Owen, Bishop, 99
Lewis, Peter, emigrant, 336
Lewis, Richard ('Dic Penderyn'), 292-3
Lewis, Samuel, topographer, 284
Lewis, Saunders, author, 132, 233-4, 352, 415-18
Lewis-Lloyd, Emmeline, 188
Liverpool, 257, 285, 330, 342, 351-2, 377
London, 356-7, 373, 380
Ludlow, 351, 353
Lyne, Joseph Leycester, ('Dewi Honddu'), 121-2

Llanaber, 105
Llanandras (Presteigne), 63, 199-200
Llanawden, 86
Llanbadarn Fawr, Dyfed, 172, 294
Llanbadarn Fawr, Powys, 86
Llanbadarn Fynydd, holy well, 88
Llanbedr, Gwynedd, 76
Llanbedr Painscastle, 106
Llanberis, 88, 380
Llanboldy, 335
Llanbrynmair, 334
Llandaff, 107
Llandanwg, 97
Llandderfel, 96
Llanddewi Brefi, 92
Llanddewi Skirrid, 344
Llanddona, clan of witches, 322
Llanddowror, 237
Llandeilo, 98, 218, 398
Llandeilo Graban, 29, 301
Llandetty, 109
Llandinam, 195, 197
Llandovery (Llanymddyfri), 39, 131
Llandrindod, 270, 283-4, 329
Llandrwg, sea-shore church, 23
Llandudno, 40, 100, 285, 309-10, 378-9
Llandudoch (St Dogmael), 321
Llandysul, 111, 179
Llaneilian, 108
Llaneleu, 295
Llanelian-yn-Rhos, malevolent well of Elian, 89
Llanelidan, 144
Llanelli, Glamorgan, 272
Llanelli, Gwent, 26
Llanelwy (St Asaph), 189
Llanfachreth, and Vaughans of Nannau, 222
Llanfair-ar-y-Bryn, 230
Llanfair Discoed, 177
Llanfairfechan, 80
Llanfair-ym-Muallt (Builth), 67-8
Llanfair-yng-Nghornwy, 105
Llanferries, Clwyd, 285
Llanfihangel Crucornau, 99, 101-2, 229

Llanfihangel-y-Pennant, 113
Llanfihangel Tal-y-Llyn, 108
Llanfihangel-y-Traethau, 121
Llanfyllin, 331–2, 345
Llangadog, 418
Llangamarch Wells, 284
Llangattock, 119, 281
Llangefni, 172
Llangeitho, 111; postmistress, 188
Llangelynnin, 293; commemorative stone, 327
Llangenni, 134–5
Llangesty, Powys, and Raikes family, 234
Llangollen, 254, 301, 370; international Eisteddfod, 154; canal-aqueduct, 304; Ladies of, 378
Llangorse Lake (Llyn Syfaddan), 19, 20, 71
Llangrannog, 186
Llangurig, 106, 148
Llangyfelach, 398
Llangynidr, bridge, 305
Llangynllo, 108
Llanidan, 86–7
Llanidloes, 40, 254, 263, 269; lead-industry, 264, 265; Chartist wool-workers, 400
Llanilltyd Fawr (Llantwit Major), 91, 322
Llanishen, Royal Ordnance factory, 144
Llanllyfni, 16
Llanon, 81
Llanover, Lady ('Gwenynen Gwent'), 186, 193
Llanpumsaint, 83, 91
Llanrhaeadr-ym-Mochnant, 37,104
Llanrothall, Herefordshire, 100–1
Llanrwst, 16, 225; bridge, 303
Llansantffraid, 131
Llanthony, 92, 121, 351
Llantrisant, 190, 400; Royal Mint, 283
Llantwit Major (Llanilltyd Fawr), 91, 322
Llanuwchllyn, 18, 116, 336
Llanvaches, 109
Llanwrtyd, 283–4
Llanwynno, 33, 178
Llanbydder, horse-fair, 32, 329
Llanychaiarn, 28
Llanymddyfri (Llandovery), 39, 131
Llanymynech, 265, 349–50
Llanystumdwy, 167, 237, 332, 407
Llewellin, John and Martha, farmers, 235
Llewellyn, Richard, author, 140
Llewelyn, Harry, show-jumper, 31
Lloyd, Henry, soldier, 182
Lloyd, Hubert, landowner, 232
Lloyd, Hugh, physician, 148
Lloyd, Professor J. E., 4
Lloyd, Revd Rhys Jones, 108
Lloyd, Richard, of Dyfed, 291
Lloyd, Richard, uncle of Lloyd George, 167
Lloyd, Thomas, landowner, 172

Lloyd George, David, 39, 167–9, 183, 237, 367, 414, 415; and Baptist chapel memorial, 113; and Llanfrothen Church case, 118; and Church disestablishment, 119, 120; and Balfour Declaration, 237; and England, 353; and First World War, 364; MP for Caernarfon Boroughs, 406–7
Lloyd Wright, Frank, 291, 315, 337
Llwyd, Alan, 153–4
Llwyd, Huw, 84, 141
Llwyn Madoc, 'the Milk Stone', 84
Llwyn Madog, Powys, 188
Llwyn-y-pia, 282
Llŷn, 146, 148, 165, 188, 271, 297, 319; folk story, 6, 414–15; characteristics, 21, 22, 100; bombing-range, 414–15
Llyn y Cau, 28
Llyn Cowlyd, 19–20
Llyn Eiddwen, 377–8
Llyn y Fan Fach, legend of, 49–50, 146
Llyn Glaslyn, 17, 19, 28
Llyn Idwal, 20
Llyn Morys, 218
Llyn Padarn, 185
Llyn Syfaddan (Llangorse Lake), 19, 20, 71, 206
Llyn Tegid (Bala Lake), 18, 21, 42
Llyn Terfyn, 18
Llywarch Hen, 129
Llywelyn Goch ap Meurig Hen, 141
Llywelyn ap Gruffyd ('The Last'), 67–8, 95, 130, 182, 302, 372
Llywelyn ap Iorwerth ('The Great'), 67, 113, 369

'Mabon' (William Abraham), 138, 408, 409
Machynlleth, 197, 207, 208–12, 422
Macsen Wledig (Magnus Maximus), 57, 69
Madocks, William, 307–8
Madog ap Owain Gwynedd, 319–21, 333
Maenclocheg, 108
Maenorbŷr (Manorbier), 63, 65, 301
Maentwrog, 86
Maerdy, 276–7, 410–11, 425
Maes-y-Garnedd, farmhouse, 393
Maes-yr-Onnen, chapel, 297
Manorbier (Maenorbŷr), 63, 65, 301
Marconi, Guglielmo, 146
Margam, 58–9, 225
Margaret Ferch Evans, 185–6
Mari Evan ('Mari y Fantell Wen'), 121
Mathias, Roland, poet, 132
Mathias, William, composer, 138
Matthews, Grendell, 150–1
Mawddach estuary, 106, 264
Melbourne, Lord, 390
Melchior family, 97–8
Melus the Physician, 146
Menai Bridge, graveyard, 134

Menai Strait, 66, 86, 187, 229, 234; Roman crossing, 51; bridges, 304–5
Mendelssohn, F. B., 341
Merlin (Myrddin Emrys), 29, 82–3, 96
Merthyr Mawr, 23
Merthyr Tydfil (Merthyr Tudful), 145, 326. 376, 388, 390; industry, 258, 272–4, 388
Middleton, 172
Milford (Milffwrd), Dyfed, 269; fishing port, 257, 262–3; oil industry, 263; US whalers, 338; shipping, 352–3; fortification, 364
Mold (Yr Wyddgrug), 220, 269, 350
Môn (Anglesey), 22, 66, 229, 265, 307, 359; resistance to Rome, 50; Druids of, 50–1, 171; copper industry, 145; bone-setters, 148; oyster-fleets, 257; semaphore, 352
Mond, Sir Alfred, 326
Monmouth (Trefynwy), 102, 303, 370, 392, 410; Norman castles, 62; Geoffrey's Window, 83; recusant meetings, 101; Cap, 254; river port, 258; Breton stronghold, 332; Assizes, 402–3
Monnington Straddel, Herefordshire, 421–2
Montgomery (Trefaldwyn), 63–4, 199
Morgan, Edward, hanged in 1835, 392
Morgan, Guto ('Guto Nyth Brân'), athlete, 178
Morgan, Henry, buccaneer, 199; capture of Panama, 188, 218
Morgan, Kenneth O., 168–9
Morgan, Margaret, Rebeccaite, 398
Morgan, Mary, child murderer, 199–200
Morgan, Thomas, soldier, 182–3
Morgan, William Bishop, 104, 379
Morgan family, of Tredegar, 226
'Morgannwg, Iolo' (Edward Williams), and National Eisteddfod, 154–5, 157; character, 169–70, 394; and Welsh-Madan colony, 320; and American Independence, 334
Morlais castle, 301
Mormons, 122
Morris, holders of the name, 217–18
Morris, Robert, financier, 334
Morris, Valentine, landowner, 296
Morriston (Treforys), 218, 272; Tabernacle, 114, 299
Mortimer, Edmund, 207, 208
Morus, Huw, poet, 219, 243
Mostyn family, 234, 370; and Llandudno, 309
Mostyn, Hon. E. M. L., 309
Mumbles, the, headland, 301, 311; oyster-fleets, 257, 364
Myddfai, Doctors of, 146–7
Mynydd Du (Black Mountain), Dyfed, 49, 305
Mynydd Du, Powys/Gwent, *see* Black Mountains
Mynydd Newydd, coal-pit, 116

Mynydd Preseli (Preseli mountains), 266; Rosebush resort, 285–6
Myrddin Emrys (Merlin), 29, 82–3, 96

Nanhoreb, 298
Nant-y-Glo, 280, 388, 390
Nant-y-Moch, 37
Nant-y-Moel, 116, 137
Nantclwyd Hall, 144
Nanteos, 230, 379; and the Holy Grail, 233, 341
Nantlle, 186, 266
Narberth, 334
Nasareth, Gwynedd, 327
Nash, Beau, 356
Nash, John, 296, 308, 356
National Eisteddfod, *see* Eisteddfod Genedlaethol
Neale, J. M., 275
Neath (Castell Nedd), 275, 340, 412
Nefyn, 173, 257–8
Nelson, Horatio, Lord, 25, 262–3
Nest, 185
Nevern, 26
New Quay, 269
New Radnor, 310–11
Newborough, 69
Newborough family, 229, 234
Newcastle Emlyn (Castell Emlyn Newydd), 229, 398
Newport (Casnewydd), Gwent, 56, 108, 178, 262, 283, 355; church of Sts Julian and Aaron, 71; Transporter Bridge, 305–6; and Chartists, 399–401
Newton, Robert, 199
Newtown (Trenewydd), 145, 195, 329, 389
Neyland, 262
Nicholas, Jemima, cobbler, 187
Nicholas, Peter, sculptor, 192
Novello, Ivor, 356, 364

Offa, King of the Mercians, 62
Offa's Dyke, 60, 71, 205, 208, 349–53, 368, 387
Ogmore (Ogwr), 303
Ogwen, Dyffryn, 135
Ogwr, *see* Ogmore
Old Cwmbran, 221
Old Radnor, 86
Oswestry, Shropshire, 353
Overbury, Sir Thomas, 373
Owain ap Cadwgan, 185
Owain Glyndŵr (Owen Glendower), *passim*; nature of rebellion, 4–5; its climax, 205–8; its end, 421–3
Owain, Gwynedd, 65
Owain Lawgoch ('Red Hand'), 182, 206, 207, 331
Owen, Bob, scholar, 241–2, 333

Index

Owen, Daniel, author, 143
Owen, Ellis, poet, 190
Owen, George, historian, 22, 23, 322
Owen, Goronwy, poet, 105, 243
Owen, John, epigrammatist, 357
Owen, Johnny, boxer, 178
Owen, Judge Lewis, 199
Owen, Robert, social reformer, 145, 343
Owen, Wilfred, poet, 366
Owen Glendower, see Owain Glyndŵr
Oxford University, 104, 144, 237, 356
Oystermouth (Ystumllwynarth), 146, 380;
    castle, 301

Padley, Mrs Silvanus, 237
Painscastle (Castell-paen), 63, 369; Roman
    pavement, 81
Paisley, Revd Ian, 323
Pale, Quaker chapel, 270
Palmerston, Lord, fortification of Wales,
    364-5
Pantasaph (Pantasa) friary, 103
'Pantycelyn' (Revd William Williams), 111,
    174, 425
Pantycelyn farm, 131
Parc-y-Meirch, 30
Parr, Thomas, 172
Parry, Edward, and royal visits to Wales, 369
Parry, Robert Williams, poet, 415
Parry, Dr Thomas, and Oxford Book of Welsh
    Verse, 171
Parry, William, plot to kill Elizabeth I, 394
Parry-Williams, Thomas, poet, 413
Partrishow (Patrisio), 86
Parys mountain, 265-6
Patagonia, Y Wladfa, 342-3
Patti, Adelina, 340-1
Peacock, Thomas, L., 379
Peate, Iorwerth, 413
Pebidiog (Dewisland), 77, 322
Peibo, 82
Pelagius, 93, 144
Pembroke (Penfro), 330, 331; Norman castle,
    62, 66, 300; Dock, 261, 365; wartime bom-
    bing, 364; building of royal yachts, 371
Pen-y-berth, RAF bombing site, 415
Pen-y-Bont, Glamorgan (Bridgend), 270,
    283, 330, 365
Pen-y-Fâl, 365
Pen-y-groes, 413
Penarth, 227, 261, 331; naked bathing, 172
Penbanc, Llanboidy, farmhouse, 335
Penbryn, 398
Pencader, the 'Old Man', 206, 414
Penclawdd: ponies, 31-2; cockles, 311
Penfro, see Pembroke
Penhow, 61; castle, 301
Peniarth, Wynne family of, 230, 231
Penmachno, 104, 236

Penmaendewi (St David's Head), 22
Penmaenmawr, 249
Pennant, Richard, quarry-owner, 279, 280
Pennant, Thomas, writer, 66, 186, 300, 394
Penrhyn, Lord, 405-6, 407
Penrhyn Castle, 279-80, 301, 371, 407
Penrhyndeudraeth, 145, 285
Penrhys, holy well, 88-9
Penry, John, 109
Pentre Ifan, cromlech, 79
Pentrefelin, 149
Pepys, Samuel, 373
Perry, Grace, 187-8
Phaer, Dr Thomas, 325
Philipps family of Picton, Dyfed, 226, 234, 379
Philipps, Sir John, landowner, 230
Phillips, Peter, magician, 84
Phillips, Thomas, and Newport riot, 400
Pilleth, Battle of, 187, 422
Piozzi, Mrs, 295
Pistyll, 97
Pistyll Rhaeadr, 19
Plaid Cymru (Party of Wales), 413, 416
Plas Eglwyseg, Llangollen, 370
Pont ar Fynach (Devil's Bridge), 12, 231, 303
Pont-y-Cysyllt, aqueduct, 304
Pontardawe, 376
Pontfaen (Cowbridge), 17
Pontrhydfendigaid, 95
Pontypool, 400, 401, 403
Pontypridd, 191, 303-4, 387
Port Penrhyn, 280
Port Talbot, steelworks, 218, 262, 311, 393
Porth Dinllaen, 307, 308
Porth-Gain, 222, 258
Porth Linas, pilot quarters, 352
Porthmadog, 118, 218, 268, 271, 307, 319,
    379; slate ships, 258-60
Portmeirion, 217, 296-7
Powell, George, aesthete, 230, 341, 379
Powell, Revd William, 108-9
Powis castle, 301
Preseli mountains (Mynydd Preseli), 79, 266;
    Rosebush resort, 285-6
Prestatyn, 286
Presteigne (Llanandras), 63
Price, Cadwaladr, embezzler, 231
Price, Revd John ('The Solitary'), 106
Price, R. J. Lloyd, 231-4, 363, 371
Price, Revd Rice, 107
Price, Richard, political scientist, 330
Price, Richard Watkin, landowner, 231
Price, Revd Thomas (Carnhuanawg), 106,
    333
Price, Sir Uvedale, cult of the Picturesque,
    296
Price, Dr William, physician, 190-2, 204, 400
Prichard, Revd Rees, 39
Pritchard, Capt. Griffith, 261

Index

Pryce, Sir John, landowner, 218
Pryce-Jones, Sir Pryce, first mail-order business, 145, 195
Prys, Thomas, poet, 140
Pryse, Pryse, landowner, 229
Prytherch, Robert Rees, 149–50
Puleston, Sir Richard, 370–1
Pumsaint, 228, 264
Pwllheli, 244, 271, 286, 326

Quaker's Yard, 145

Raglan (Rhaglan), 100, 145, 269, 300–1
Ramsey Island (Ynys Dewi), 41, 42, 272
Recorde, Robert, 144
Rees, Revd Morgan, 335, 343, 393
Rees, Sarah Jane ('Cranogwen'), 186–7
Rees, T. Ifor, diplomatist, 356
Rees, Thomas, theologian, 413
Rendel, Stuart, 379
Richard II, King, 369
Richard, Henry, 413
Richards, Timothy, 344–5
Rivals, the (Yr Eifl), mountain, 47
Robert of Rhuddlan, 64
Roberts, Albert, harpist, 329
Roberts, Bartholomew, pirate, 199
Roberts, Gruffydd, priest, 99–100, 360–1
Roberts, Gwilym, epitaph, 359
Roberts, John, harpist, 98, 136–7, 328–9
Roberts, Kate, novelist, 143
Roberts, Lloyd, harpist, 328–9
Roberts, Robert, refused Anglican burial, 118–19, 120
Roberts, Revd Samuel, of Llanbrynmair, 334
Roberts, William, poet, 235
Roberts-Jones, Ivor, sculptor, 356
Robertson, Henry, 270
Roger de Montgomery, 63
Rosemarket, 364
Rowlands, Daniel, 111–12, 340, 343
Royal Welch Fusiliers, 39, 183
Royal Welsh Agricultural Show, 252
Russell, Bertrand, 3rd Earl Russell, 145
Ruthin, 296
Rhigyfarch, 129
Rhiwlas, Gwynedd, 230, 234
Rhodri Mawr, 60
Rhondda valleys, 88–9, 196, 218, 304; mining, 272, 388, 404; US miners, 338; stay-down strike, 409; Communism, 411
Rhos-goch, 81
Rhos-on-Sea, 319, 333
Rhoslan, 82
Rhosneigr, 285
Rhuddlan, 360; Statute of, 69
Rhulen, 90, 98
Rhyd-y-mwyn, 341
Rhyd-y-Pennau, 356

Rhymni (Rhymney), 241, 388–9
Rhys, Sir John, scholar, 236–7
Rhys ap Dinefwr, 65, 147
Rhys ap Tudor, 65, 218

St Augustine, 92–3, 105
St Beuno, 42, 60, 88, 91, 97
St Cadoc, 91
St David (Dewi Sant), 77–8, 90–2, 94, 96, 102, 121, 138, 176
St David's Head (Penmaendewi), 22
St Derbyn, church dedications, 91
St Edern, churchyard, 147
St Ellyw, church of, Llanelieu, 295
St Francis Xavier, college, 101
St Govan, cliff-face hermitage, 91
St Illtyd, 91, 99; priory church, 102–3
St Melangell, 42
St Non, 92
St Padarn, 91; monastery, 294
St Patrick, 322–3
St Samson of Dol, 322
St Tanwg, Llandanwg, chapel of rest, 97
St Teilo, 91; sacred relic, 97–8; holy well, 99
St Ursula, 91
St Winifred, Holywell, 88, 99–100, 326
Salusbury, Sir John, 64–5
Samivel, David ('Dafydd Ddu Meddyg'), 344
Sarn Badric, 25
Sarn Gynfelin, 25
Sarnau (Causeways), 24–5
Sarnau Elen (Sarn y Lleng), 55–7
Savin, Thomas, 285
Scott, Sir Walter, and Telford's aqueduct, 304
Scudamore, Alice, 422
Scudamore, John, 422
Segontium, Roman military station, 56, 70
Seiont, river, 66
Senghennydd, pit explosion of 1913, 277–8
Shakespeare, William: Fluellen, 181, 370, 381; and the Welsh, 380–1
Shelley, Percy Bysshe, 379
'Shoni Sgubor Fawr' (John Big Barn), 399
Shrewsbury, 62, 68, 270, 351, 353
Silurians, 57
Siôn Cent, 83, 98,422
Siôn Dafydd, 369
Siôn Mowddwy, 362
Siôn Wyn of Chwilog, 222
Sirhowy valley, 388, 404, 412
Skelton, John, 372–3
Skirrid, The (Ysgyryd Fawr), 98–102
Skomer island, 42
Smart, Christopher, 141
Snowdon (Yr Wyddfa), 11–12, 39–40, 269, 270, 379
Snowdon, Earl of, 367–8
Soar-y-Mynydd, chapel, 298
Solva, 257–8

Index

Somerset family of Raglan, 100, 101, 226
Somerset, Edward, Marquis of Worcester, 145
Stanhope, Lady Hester, 378
Stanley, Sir Henry Morton, 144, 199
Stephens, Thomas, 237
Strata Florida, *see* Ystrad Fflur
Strata Marcella (Ystrad Marchell), 100
Strube, cartoonist, 168
Sutherland, Graham, 379
Swansea (Abertawe), 146, 201, 262, 270, 283, 311, 326, 404; phosphate schooners, 258; pilot boats, 258; seafront railway, 269; nickel works, 272; transformed by heavy industries, 274–5; motoring documents, 283; University College, 311; and Port Talbot, 311; German bombing, 311, 364; emigrants to America, 334
Swansea Bay, 311
Swinburne, Algernon Charles, 379
Sycharth, 9, 422
Sykes, Wirt, 127–8

Tacitus, 51, 54
Taff Vale Railway Co., 116
Talar Wen, Dyfed, 418–19
Talgarth, 173–6, 301
Taliesin, 129, 206, 291, 414
Tate, General William, 329–31
Telford, Thomas, 362, 422; highway and canal, 304; Pont-y-Cysyllt aqueduct, 304; Britannia Tubular Bridge, 304, 305
'Telynor Cymru' (John Roberts), 98, 136–7, 328–9
Tenby (Dinbych-y-pysgod), 144, 325, 329
Tennyson, Alfred, Lord, 379
Thackeray, William Makepeace, 374
Thatcher, Margaret, 356
Theroux, Paul, 297
Thomas dynasty, bone-setters, 148, 339
Thomas, Clara, 84
Thomas, Dylan, 132, 141, 201–2, 311
Thomas, Ebeneser ('Eben Fardd'), poet, 222
Thomas, Edward, poet, 17–18, 366
Thomas, Evan, poet, 39
Thomas, Fred, boxer, 177–8
Thomas, George, Speaker of the House of Commons, 413
Thomas, James ('Jimmy Genteel'), 397–8
Thomas, R. S., poet, 132
Thomas, Sidney Gilchrist, scientist, 145
Thomas, Thomas, boxer, 177
Thrale, Henry, 39–40
Times, The, London, and Rebecca, 398
Tinkinswood, cromlech, 78
Tintern, 87
Tintern Abbey, 121, 144, 226, 296
Tongwynlais, 301
Tonpentre, 148

Tonypandy, 89, 272, 276, 282, 371, 409
Traherne, Thomas, 130–1
Trallwng (Welshpool), 86, 276
Trawsfyndd, 55, 84, 161
Treamlod (Ambleston), 235
Tredegar, Lord, 364
Tredegar, Gwent, 226, 273, 388; Chartist pub, 401; cholera epidemic of 1849, 404, 405; Bevan and, 412
Trefaldwyn (Montgomery), 63–4, 199
Treffynnon (Holywell), 88, 99–100, 370
Treforys (Morriston), 114, 218, 272, 114, 299
Trefriw, 284
Trefyclawdd (Knighton), 112
Trefynwy, *see* Monmouth
Tregaron, 38, 215, 332, 413; bog, 19, 42, 95, 216; woollen industry, 254
Treherbert, 277
Trelawney, Edward, 379
Trelleck (Trelech), 79, 145
Trelystan, 36
Tremadog, 144, 261, 308
Tremeirchion, 295
Trenewydd (Newtown), 145, 195, 329, 389
Treorchy, 272, 276, 313
Tre'r Ceiri (Town of Giants), 47, 48, 52
Trevithick, Richard, 145, 269
Trwyn Larnog (Lavernock Point), 146
Tryweryn, river, and Merseyside water, 377
Tudur Aled, poet, 30, 33
Twll y Filiast (Greyhound's Kennel), 33
'Twm Siôn Cati' (Thomas Jones), 200
Tyddewi (St David's), 92, 96, 171, 207, 339, 369
Tywyn, 158, 293; cricket team, 178

University of Wales, 242–3, 414
Usk, Adam of, 158
Usk (Brynbuga), Powys, 379, 422; church organ, 28; grave of martyr Lewis, 102; church inscriptions, 158, 183–4; bridges, 305

Valentine, Revd Lewis, 415
Valle Crucis (Glyn-y-groes), 421
Vaughan, H. M., author, 193, 230
Vaughan, Henry, poet, 131
Vaughan, William, of Llangyndeyrn, Dyfed, 71
Vaynol, 36, 232–3
Vaynor (Faenor), 281
Victoria, Queen, 145, 328, 329, 371, 394
Vincent, Henry, 401
Vortigern (Gwrtheyrn), 29
Vosper, Sydney Curnaw, 87

Waddington, Benjamin (Lord Llanover), 186
Wagner, Richard, 341
Walter, Lucy, 370
Ward, Frank, 18

441

Watkins, Vernon, 132
Watson, Richard, Bishop of Llandaff, 107
Waugh, Evelyn, 374
Wedlock, Harry, 277–8
Welsh Language Society (Cymdeithas yr Iaith Cymraeg), 417
Welsh National Library, Aberystwyth, 243
Welsh National Museum, Cardiff, 243, 249
Welsh National Opera, Cardiff, 137, 312
Welshpool (Trallwng), 86, 276
Wesley, John, 110
Whitchurch (Eglwys Wen), chapel, 120
Whitebrook, 105
Whitland (Hendy Gwyn), 94, 223, 252
Wilde, Jimmy, boxer, 178
William I, King, 65, 369
William II, King, 369
William, IV, King, 370
William ap Hywel ap Torwerth, 172
William de Breos, 'The Ogre', 64
Williams, D. J., writer, 415
Williams, David, political scientist, 330
Williams, David, shipbuilder, 260, 261
Williams, Edward, stonemason, *see* 'Iolo Morgannwg'
Williams, G. J., scholar, 171
Williams, Grace, composer, 138
Williams, Gwyn, scholar, 44
Williams, Gwyn A., historian, 334
Williams, Hugh, lawyer, 397, 400
Williams, Sir Ifor, educationalist, 240
Williams, J. P. R., Rugby player, 149, 181
Williams, John, archbishop, 250
Williams, John, jeweller, 356
Williams, John, judge, 356
Williams, Revd John, of Môn, 105
Williams, Sir John, physician, 147, 371
Williams, John Lloyd, of Benares, 146
Williams, Thomas, industrialist, 195
Williams, Waldo, poet, 132, 159
Williams, William, MP, 237–8
Williams, Revd William ('Pantycelyn'), 111, 174, 425
Williams, Revd William, of Llanfyllin, 331–2
Williams, Sir William, Speaker of the House of Commons, 356

Williams, Zephenia, Chartist, 400, 401, 402
Williams-Ellis, Sir Clough, 120, 217, 296–7
Williams-Wynne family, , 193, 227, 234
Wilson, Richard, 133
Windsor family, and Penarth, 227–8
Wingfield, Maj. Walter, 144
Wittgenstein, Ludwig, 193
Woosnam, Charles Hilton, 363
Workmen's Medical Aid Society, Tredegar, 404, 405
Wrexham (Wrecsam), 269
Wyn-Thomas, Sir Hugh, 344
Wynne-Ellis, 105
Wynnes of Peniarth, 230–1

Y Bala, 18, 42, 165, 215, 342, 352, 371, 377
Y Cymro, magazine, 353
Y Fenni, *see* Abergavenny
Y Fflint (Flint), 69, 307, 369
Y Grysmwnt (Grosmont), 83
Y Rhyl, 286
Y Wladfa, Patagonia, 342–3
Ynys Byr (Caldy Island), 22, 102, 337
Ynys Dewi (Ramsey Island), 41, 42, 272,
Ynys Enlli (Bardsey), 83, 96–7, 319, 339
Ynys Môn, 229, 265, 307, 359; Druids and, 171; coastal semaphore stations, 352
Yorke family of Erddig, 230, 234
Young, Arthur, 37
Young, Gruffydd, archdeacon, 207–8
Yr Eifl, the Rivals, mountain, 47
Yr Iforiaid, the Ivorites, 192
Yr Wyddfa (Snowdon), 11–12, 39–40, 269, 270, 379
Yr Wyddgrug (Mold), 220, 269, 350
Ysbyty Cynfyn, 86
Ysgyryd Fawr (The Skirrid), 98–102
Ystrad Fflur (Strata Florida), Cistercian monastery, 95, 203, 303, graves of chieftains, 95; chancel ruin, 95–6; Holy Grail, 98
Ystrad Marchell (Strata Marcella), 100
Ystrad Mynach, 272
Ystradfellte, 48, 56
Ystradgynlais, 216, 219
Ystumllwynarth (Oystermouth), 146, 380; castle, 301